Ken
Northern
Olympics,
the FBI to   e ultim...
and hand-d   .rea Richard Jewell's clearance letter.

Journalist **Kevin Salwen** was a long-time *Wall
Street Journal* reporter and editor who ran the paper's
south-eastern section during the Olympic Games. He
is the co-author (with his daughter, Hannah) of *The
Power of Half: One Family's Decision to Stop Taking
and Start Giving Back.*

Kent Alexander was the U.S. Attorney for the
Northern District of Georgia at the time of the 1996
Olympics. He spent hundreds of hours working with
Jewell to find the bomber, and later unanimously true
story of the beleaguered Richard Jewell—Atlanta 1996.

THE SUSPECT

AN OLYMPIC BOMBING,
THE FBI, THE MEDIA,
AND RICHARD JEWELL,
THE MAN CAUGHT IN THE MIDDLE

KENT ALEXANDER & KEVIN SALWEN

HODDER

First published in Great Britain in 2020 by Hodder & Stoughton
An Hachette UK company

1

Copyright © Kent Alexander and Kevin Salwen 2019

The right of Kent Alexander and Kevin Salwen to be identified as
the Author of the Work has been asserted by them in accordance
with the Copyright, Designs and Patents Act 1988.

Photographs: Insert, pages 1, 2 (middle, bottom), 3 (bottom), 10 (middle),
12 (bottom), 13 (bottom), 16: Courtesy of Dana Jewell. 2 (top): Courtesy
of Nadya Light. 3 (top), 6 (top), 7, 10 (bottom, left), 12 (top left): From
the personal files of Don Johnson, courtesy of the Johnson family. 4–5:
Courtesy of Lewis Scruggs, from the family scrapbook. 6 (bottom):
Courtesy of Don Johnson II. 8 (top): Courtesy of the Atlanta History
Center. 8 (bottom): Courtesy of Kent Alexander. 9, 10 (top; bottom, right),
11 (bottom), 15 (bottom): Courtesy of the FBI. 11 (top): Photo by Kevin
Salwen, courtesy of the FBI. 13 (top), 14: Reprinted with permission of
the *Atlanta Journal-Constitution*. 15 (top right): Courtesy of Lin Wood.

A CIP catalogue record for this title is available from the British Library

Paperback ISBN 9781529365870
eBook ISBN 9781529365887

Printed and bound in Great Britain by Clays Ltd, Elcograf S.p.A.

Hodder & Stoughton policy is to use papers that are natural, renewable
and recyclable products and made from wood grown in sustainable
forests. The logging and manufacturing processes are expected to
conform to the environmental regulations of the country of origin.

Hodder & Stoughton Ltd
Carmelite House
50 Victoria Embankment
London EC4Y 0DZ

www.hodder.co.uk

For Diane and Joan,
and for unsung heroes everywhere

CONTENTS

Late Friday afternoon, Richard Jewell tousled his Doberman Lacy's short brown fur, clicked the TV remote, and hoisted himself off the couch. His standard twelve-hour graveyard shift lay ahead—"1800–0600," as he'd scribbled in police-speak on his calendar. Jewell swung into the tidy peach-and-white wallpapered kitchen of his mom's apartment he temporarily called home. He grabbed a pair of apples from the table and dropped the fruit into his backpack for a future snack. Then he tucked in his white polo shirt, branded on the left chest with a red Olympic flame, snapped on his fanny pack, and slipped out the door of Apartment F-3.

There could hardly have been a more mundane start to the demarcation line of a man's life.

As Jewell was bouncing along in the MARTA subway car, his thoughts turned to how little time he had left in his current work. Since losing two straight law enforcement jobs, his hunt for permanent employment had been frustrating. No police forces were hiring until after the Olympics, and in nine days the Games would be over and he'd be unemployed again. He had work to do.

Hopping off the train, Jewell descended International Boulevard, the lime-green lanyard that held his credentials swinging across his ample belly. Downtown Atlanta, traditionally a ghost town after work hours, had become home to the newly constructed Centennial Olympic Park. The twenty-one-acre city of pavilions, stages, and exhibits was now the heartbeat of the world's largest sporting event, the 1996 Olympic Games. Here in the crowded park, the blue and gold of Sweden mixed with the red and white of Canada, the black, yellow, and red of Germany. Thais mingled joyfully with Tanzanians, Americans, and Brazilians. Entering the park, Jewell could smell the chlorinated water cascading from the fountains shaped to form the Olympic rings. He loved hearing the squeals of the children as the water shot skyward. The park was a party for all ages.

Impatient to start his shift, Jewell marched across the park's pathways constructed of more than two hundred fifty thousand commemorative bricks. Atlantans had purchased the etched pavers for $35 apiece as their way of supporting the host city—and crafting personal messages. By now, Jewell had read hundreds of the two-liners: "A smile worth 1000 words—CES," "Loving memory, Lt. Bob Connors," "In love and laughter, Terri ❤ Geoff," even "Elvis Presley 1935–1977."

Jewell arrived nearly half an hour early at his post, the five-story light and sound tower for the park's main concert stage below. White canvas draped over the steel frame; a sloped roof allowed the summer rains to easily slip off onto the month-old sod below. Jewell approached the day-shift guard, Mark Tillman, and offered to take over before six o'clock. When Tillman accepted, Jewell reminded him, "Hey, I'm cutting you out. Make sure you're here early." By six A.M., Jewell knew, he'd be ready to leave.

Although he was primarily assigned to guard the entrance, Jewell viewed his role as protector of the entire perimeter and interior. So, as Tillman walked away, Jewell carefully circled the tower built for AT&T and NBC, even looking under the three dark-green benches facing the main stage for anything amiss. All clear. Then Jewell climbed the interior stairs of the temporary structure, surveying the five floors to make sure each person had the appropriate blue wristband. He greeted the staffers by name. The process took less than fifteen minutes. It was business as usual, and for Jewell that was just fine.

Good security, Jewell believed, required two elements. The first was attentiveness. One of his favorite games was to close his eyes and try to precisely recall the nearby scene—the color and make of parked cars, signs on the pavilions, the straw panama hat of the Olympic volunteer standing a dozen feet away. The second attribute was unpredictability. Each night, Jewell patrolled at odd intervals. Ten P.M. outside the tower; 10:30 inside. Maybe both again at 11:15, then again at 11:45. Stay sporadic. Don't set patterns.

For the next several hours, Jewell made his checks, taking in the music and the sights. Occasionally, his thoughts drifted to the security risks at hand. In the past three years the world had witnessed a deadly procession of attacks: the World Trade Center truck bomb, two sarin gas attacks in Japan, and the hideous murder of 168 adults and children at an Oklahoma City federal building. Just two days before the Opening Ceremony in Atlanta, TWA Flight 800 had exploded mysteriously off the coast of Long Island, killing all 230 on board. Law enforcement officers in the park were telling Jewell they thought the downing was an act of terror.

Jewell harbored quiet doubts whether his provincial law enforcement experiences in rural Habersham County had prepared him for what might befall the 1996 Games. "Me and you are just pretty much good old boys from North Georgia," he confided to a police friend. "Hell, what the fuck is terrorism up there to us? Somebody writing on the street signs. Or knocking down mailboxes with a baseball bat, or threatening to kill the neighbor's cat."

At 11 P.M., the R&B band Jack Mack and the Heart Attack took the stage to start their set. Fifty thousand people now jammed the park, with a quarter of them crowded in the expanse between the tower and the main stage. In the middle walked Alice Hawthorne, wearing festive red lipstick, a white Albany State T-shirt, and matching white Keds. She strolled side by side with her daughter Fallon. The night was the perfect birthday gift for the fourteen-year-old, well worth the three-hour drive from South Georgia.

At 12:30 A.M., as Jewell stood guard, he noticed seven young men who had walked over from the nearby Speedo tent. The group, who the FBI would later call the "Speedo Boys," clustered near two of the front green benches. Jewell watched them pull twelve-ounce Budweisers from a green pack. They grabbed the cans, poked holes, and then pulled the tabs to "shot-gun" the beers in unison. *Frat boys*, Jewell thought in disdain. He'd seen plenty of that nonsense in his campus cop job at Piedmont College.

Jewell took note of a second green pack under the far left bench occupied by two of the Speedos, but never saw them touch it. Probably just more beer, he decided. These guys could be at it all night. Annoyed, Jewell returned to his post by the entrance on the other side of the tower.

Twenty minutes later, Jewell circled back. The rowdy young men had now littered the ground with over a dozen of their empties. Enough, Jewell fumed. He flagged down Georgia Bureau of Investigation (GBI) Agent Tom Davis, the assistant commander of park security.

Davis embodied Jewell's professional dream. Five-foot-eleven and a former college athlete, the agent had a still-muscular physique covered with law enforcement trappings—a state-issued black mesh police vest, badge, phone, walkie-talkie, and 9mm Smith & Wesson. Davis listened carefully as Jewell shouted over the music; the agent agreed to handle the Speedo Boy problem. But moments after Davis left, several of the beer guzzlers breezed past Jewell and began disappearing into the crowd. *Damn*, Jewell thought. He sprinted after Davis to inform him of their movement.

As Jewell and Davis spoke, the chubby guard looked at the vacated benches. Wait. Something was wrong. There, beneath the shadow-cloaked seat, lay a large olive-green backpack. *Damn drunks*, Jewell thought. "Hey, Tom," he yelled over the music. "They left one of their bags right under that bench." Pointing, he hollered, "How do you want to handle this situation?"

What "situation"? Davis wondered to himself. The Olympics had been a week of abandoned bags, drunk partiers, and forgetful tourists. *Ain't nothing to this*, he thought. *We're probably going to have another bag where we're going to blow up somebody's Mickey Mouse stuffed toy.* Davis shrugged. They walked up to within a yard of the bag to look for a tag. But they saw none and began hunting for the pack's owner.

Jewell pointed out two Speedo Boys still in sight, and Davis hustled after them. "Did y'all leave a bag up here?" he shouted. "Not ours," came the reply. *No big deal*, Davis thought. He returned to Jewell and asked the guard to help find the owner. They split up, Jewell to the west side of the tower, Davis to the east. "Excuse me, ma'am, did you leave a bag?" "Sir, is that yours?" No one claimed the pack.

They met back at the front of the tower, again a few feet from the pack. Over the blaring music, a distressed Jewell grabbed Davis's arms. Jewell's "seventh sense," as he would later describe it, told him something was wrong. He pressed Davis again: "What do you want to do about this situation?" The GBI man continued to believe that Jewell was overreacting, maybe a little overzealous. Just the week before, the security guard had insisted that the tower's aluminum siding needed shoring up and that a small opening surrounding the sound and light cabling be sealed.

Still, with no one claiming the bag, Davis decided to follow the next step in protocol, the same as officers across the city had done more than a hundred times in the eight days since the Opening Ceremony. Davis radioed the Centennial Park command center, a "27." Suspicious package report. It was 12:57 A.M.

ACROSS THE PARK, FBI bomb technician Bill Forsyth picked up Davis's call. He gathered his ATF counterpart, Steve Zellers. The pair, designated Assessment Team 33, began weaving through the crowd. Meanwhile, Jewell climbed the tower steps to deliver a "pre-warning." "It's a suspicious package," he told people on all five levels. "If I come back in here and tell you to get out there will be no questions, there will be no hesitation. Drop what you're doing, and get the fuck out."

Jewell made a mental note of who was on each floor, totaling the head count at eleven. He left the tower to help Davis discreetly back people away from the bag.

The two men began to create a small perimeter roughly fifteen feet from the pack. Other law enforcement officers arrived to help. As they buffered the crowd, Jewell spotted the bomb techs, both wearing white shirts, emerge from the mass of revelers, hurried but far from panicked. Davis pointed the techs to the pack. It was 1:05 A.M.

Standing less than ten feet from the bench, Jewell watched Forsyth and Zellers study the package. Forsyth dropped to his knees for a better look. Penlight in hand, he crawled on his stomach toward the pack. His training was clear: Do not touch the bag. The flap or buckles could be booby-trapped. But sometimes bomb techs go with their gut. Forsyth broke protocol and peered inside. In the flashlight beam, there was no missing the danger. Wiring. Pipes. End caps. Timing device. Forsyth froze for a second, then jumped back. He froze again, waiting for an explosion.

Jewell stared as the tech cautiously crawled away "just as slow as fucking molasses in wintertime," the guard later would say. When one of the agents switched off his radio, Jewell gulped. The guard knew from the Bomb Response course he had taken four years earlier that radio waves could trigger a device. The ATF agent, Zellers, urgently asked Davis for his flip phone, then sprinted away from the tower toward Techwood Drive. "God," Jewell gasped, "he don't even fucking want to use a cell phone around it." It was 1:08 A.M.

Zellers frantically dialed the Bomb Management Center at Dobbins Air Force Base. His call registered as "BMC #104," the 104th full-fledged bomb threat since the start of the Olympics. The center quickly dispatched its Render Safe team armed with equipment to disarm the device. Dobbins was a twenty-minute drive from the park. It was 1:10 A.M.

Jewell's worst suspicions confirmed, he sprinted back into the tower. "Get out. Get out now!" he yelled on each level. On the fifth floor, two of the spotlight operators dawdled, pausing to shut down the equipment. "Fuck that," Jewell barked, grabbing both men and shoving them down the stairs.

Certain the tower was clear, Jewell was the last to leave. Jack Mack and the Heart Attack played their song "I Walked Alone." It was 1:15 A.M.

By now, over a dozen uniformed officers formed a human shield and, for the next several minutes, expanded the perimeter that Davis and Jewell had begun. They'd already pushed back two hundred people spread across the lawn immediately in front of the device. Thousands more stood between there and the stage. Managing the crowd wasn't easy. Many were "drunker than skunks, smoking dope," one agent later explained. Others, including Alice Hawthorne and her daughter Fallon, were paying more attention to the music than the officers. It was 1:19 A.M.

Park Commander Tommy "Foots" Tomlinson arrived. Davis briefed the supervisor in staccato police-speak: probable improvised explosive device; Dobbins notified; bomb team in route, expected arrival 01:30.

The officers continued to push the crowd away from the package. A mob of dancing, singing, intoxicated people partied between the tower and stage. The Hawthornes had called it a night and were walking toward the exit, twenty feet from where Tomlinson and Davis were meeting. They paused for a final photo.

Tomlinson surveyed the scene and weighed a full evacuation. He feared a stampede. It was 1:20 A.M.

Time had run out.

PART 1

STRIVING

CHAPTER 1

On an early spring day in 1987, Billy Payne perched on the chestnut brown tufted-leather couch in Atlanta Mayor Andrew Young's well-appointed office. For the past year or so, the graying thirty-nine-year-old real estate lawyer had overseen an ambitious $2.5 million capital campaign for a new sanctuary at his suburban Dunwoody church. Payne proved to be a tireless fundraiser, energized by the art of the ask, and racked up win after win until reaching the lofty goal. Then came the day when the minister blessed the sanctuary and asked Billy to speak. On the pulpit, the sense of goodness hit him "like a sledgehammer." He had brought people together to create something so much bigger than any of them.

Driving home that Sunday from the church, Payne told his wife, Martha, how he wanted to replicate the emotion with an even bigger idea. But what? Payne rose at four the next morning and began scribbling on a yellow legal pad. One idea jumped out: Billy Payne wanted to bring the Olympic Games to Atlanta.

The audacious dream would have been an incredible long shot for someone with broad international connections. That certainly wasn't Payne, a suburbanite who had never travelled outside the country. Two decades earlier, Payne had snared All Conference honors as a defensive end for the University of Georgia Bulldogs. But in the decades since, the lawyer with the unstylish glasses wouldn't have made a single roster of Atlanta power players.

Payne had one attribute, though, that was hard to miss upon meeting him: Beneath the everyman veneer lay an intensity that bordered on manic. Payne's golf games had become legendary among friends. He hit first off the tee, regardless of who had the honors, and was too impatient to play more than two hours, often walking off the course after thirteen or fourteen holes. Everyone knew that was just Billy. His spitfire attitude, he believed, came from an unquenched desire to please his father, who was also his best friend. After youth sports events, Billy would ask, "Are you proud of me?" Porter Payne's reply was always swift and direct: "Doesn't matter, Billy. The only thing that matters is, did you do your best?" Years later, Billy would say, "Never once in those hundreds or thousands of conversations with my dad could I ever respond that, yes, I had done my best." That intensity, coupled with bad genes, triggered Billy Payne's first heart attack. He had a triple bypass at age thirty-four, just after his father died of heart failure at fifty-three.

Payne now sat face-to-face across the coffee table with the mayor. Looking far younger than his fifty-five years, Young, a civil rights icon, *was* an elite Atlanta power broker. His path had begun in the ministry in the late 1950s, and he grew close to Martin Luther King Jr. They marched across the Edmund Pettus Bridge in Selma, Alabama together, stood unbowed against police and military in Birmingham, and fought segregation at the "swim-in" at St. Augustine, Florida. Young was also with King when he was murdered in Memphis in April 1968. In the decades that followed King's death, Young went on to become a U.S. congressman and the first African American to be a United Nations ambassador. Since 1982, he had served as Atlanta mayor.

Payne knew his time with Young was short, and he enthusiastically launched into a rehearsed minute-and-a-half speech, an urgent bull rush on what the Centennial Olympic Games could mean to Atlanta. Putting the city on the international business map. Bringing millions of visitors to town. Shining a world spotlight on the post–civil rights era South. Surely that last point would resonate with Young. But the mayor's face was a mask of impassivity.

Payne was certain he was failing to win over the mayor. *That wasn't very good*, he thought. *I'd better go another direction.* Desperately stretching his pitch, Payne started improvising. He badly needed Young and the city as an ally. Still nothing. Finally, Payne offered a final tack, noting how the Olympics could affect the children of Atlanta. How meaningful and motivational could the Games be for them? Wouldn't the great athletes inspire kids to their own excellence?

Finally sensing a reaction, Payne paused. Young lifted his head slowly, then stared into the lawyer's eyes. Only then did Payne begin to realize how badly he had been misreading Young's silence.

In a slight Cajun drawl, Young began to describe the moment he fell in love with the Olympic Games. The year was 1936, and Andy Young was the four-year-old son of a New Orleans dentist. Through the open windows of the family's home on hot summer nights, Andy could hear the proclamations of "Heil Hitler" and the singing of "Deutschland über alles" from a local Nazi party headquarters only fifty yards away. When he asked his father to explain, Dr. Young chaperoned his little boy to the movies. Their focus was the newsreel, not the film, a Movietone newscaster narrating Jesse Owens's feats at the Berlin Olympics. Four times Owens stood atop the winner's podium, proudly displaying gold medals in the 100-meter and 200-meter sprints, the long jump, and the 4x100 relay. Afterward, as the father and son headed home, Dr. Young shared a lesson of ability triumphing over hatred. "Nazism and white supremacy is a sickness," he told his son. But "you can't help them unless you try to understand them."

Payne listened intently as the mayor completed his recollection. Instinctively, he knew there was no need to sell the Olympics any further.

In fact, Young already had pivoted to a completely different line of thinking—of feeling, actually—about Billy Payne. The reverend-turned-mayor's mind turned to his old friend, Martin Luther King. For years, Young recalled, the civil rights leader had believed he would die early for The Movement. That fear of leaving the earth prematurely fueled an urgency to act boldly. Listening to this man before him now, with a heart condition and a vision borne in a house of God, Young saw in Payne a similar "looking-death-in-the-face" character trait. For Young, it was a providential moment. The mayor was all in.

BACK IN HIS OFFICE, Billy Payne cobbled together the Atlanta Nine, an ad hoc group of highly successful businesspeople and socialites, or as Young later quipped, "Ex-jocks in midlife crisis and exiles from the Junior League." Payne soon quit his law practice and took out a $1.5 million personal loan to fund the start of this dream.

The group could hardly have had a more quixotic task. After all, few could view Atlanta as anything but an utter long shot. Athens was already a clear favorite for the 1996 Games, still nine years in the future.

The Olympic Games had been created in Greece in the eighth century

BCE as a religious event to honor the god Zeus. Footraces, discus throws, boxing, wrestling, and the pentathlon would be added over the following centuries. Every four years, a time period called an Olympiad, wars would pause as athletic competitions blossomed in a spirit of pagan piety. But in the fourth century CE, the Games were relegated to history, victim to a push for Christian purity across the Roman State.

Then in 1896, a French aristocrat with a passion for Greek philosophy, Baron Pierre de Coubertin, led an effort to relaunch the Olympic Games in Athens, Greece. Athletes from fourteen countries were sponsored by their schools or sports clubs; no one would march behind a national flag until 1908. De Coubertin retained as much of the ancient Olympic flavor as possible for the all-male Games, handing winners olive branches and silver medals embossed with the head of Zeus. Runners-up took copper; gold would not emerge until eight years later. In all, athletes in that first Modern Olympic Games competed in forty-three events, with crowds in the tens of thousands cheering on the newly added sports of fencing, cycling, and tennis.

Not a single Olympics had been held in Greece since then. But by 1987 word was spreading that Athens had become enamored of hosting the centennial of the Modern Games. The chance that any competitor might beat out the Greeks was deemed so remote that an Indianapolis executive, armed with $50 million of philanthropic funds to bring sports events to his city, refused to even consider a bid. "The '96 Olympics will be in Athens. Anyone who spends a nickel trying to get the '96 Games is wasting his money," he told the *Atlanta Constitution*.

Even a pair of dreamers like Payne and Young couldn't ignore Atlanta's shortcomings. In sports, its pro teams ranged from second rate to awful, triggering *Sports Illustrated* to dub Atlanta "Loserville, U.S.A." Despite individual stars like Hank Aaron and Pistol Pete Maravich, not a single Braves, Falcons, or Hawks team ever had carried a championship trophy down Peachtree Street. The city's few high-end restaurants mostly were in strip malls; another was housed in a La Quinta Inn. The subway was so limited its map was shaped like a stick figure.

All those weaknesses were trivial compared with the troubles in Atlanta's tired and failing downtown. Crime was rampant, with the murder rate consistently among the nation's worst. White flight and congested roadways had taken their toll. Despite strong growth in suburban areas, the city's core was shrinking and left Atlanta as the hole in a doughnut, with a population of just 450,000 in a metro area of more than four million.

But Payne and Young had a far more buoyant view of Atlanta, and they would draw often on its history while selling the city as host for the Centennial Games. Originally called Terminus for the train lines that ended there, the city grew into a crucial rail depot for the American South during the Civil War. After General William Tecumseh Sherman torched much of the city to the ground in 1864, Atlanta became central to the South's post–Civil War rebuilding effort. In December 1886, a full century before Billy Payne's Olympics epiphany, the *Atlanta Constitution*'s progressive editor, Henry W. Grady, stood before the vaunted New England Society of New York to sell what he called the "New South"—a place he proclaimed newly rooted in industry, not the ignoble prejudice of the plantation system. Gazing into an audience that included Sherman himself, Grady offered a description of Atlanta that would resonate for decades: "I want to say to General Sherman—who is considered an able man in our hearts, though some people think he is a kind of careless man about fire—that from the ashes he left us in 1864 we have raised a brave and beautiful city."

Grady's phrase was clearly aspirational. Atlanta had by no means yet arrived, but boosterism had long been at the city's core. "Atlanta's business is self-promotion. We have always sold first, then kept the promises afterward," local advertising executive Joel Babbit once told the *New York Times*. But in the coming century, Atlanta would distinguish itself as the cradle of the civil rights movement, sidestepping much of the rioting that plagued other American cities. Its business leaders, never missing a branding opportunity, christened Atlanta "the city too busy to hate."

Young and Payne knew they could market the city with interracial bonhomie. They could also highlight Atlanta's recent string of wins. Hartsfield airport was challenging Chicago's O'Hare for the nation's busiest. The Democratic National Convention was coming in 1988. Global brands dotted the city's tree-filled landscape: Coca-Cola, UPS, Delta Air Lines, Georgia-Pacific. A seven-year-old television network called CNN was garnering Atlanta outsized international attention, as the station beamed its innovative 24/7 news programming around the world.

By the time the Atlanta team submitted their official bid to the United States Olympic Committee in September 1987, Payne was confident their sales pitch was packed with enough positives to win. The USOC examined all fourteen bidding cities based on existing athletic facilities, hotel availability, quality of airport and driving access, and more. Within a few months, the committee had narrowed the choice to Atlanta and Minneapolis-St. Paul. In May 1988, Payne and Young—who had completed his second term as mayor and had become a full-time co-leader of the bid committee—received the news they had been hoping for: The U.S. Olympic Committee named Atlanta as the American choice to compete for the 1996 Games.

THE ATLANTA TEAM WOULD have two years to convince the eighty-five members of the International Olympic Committee (IOC) that their city was a better choice to host the Centennial Games than the other five competing finalists. The winner would need forty-three votes.

Payne and Young approached the sales process in diverging but connected ways. Payne's strategy might have been called the High School Class President Plan: He theorized that humans, regardless of social class or status, overwhelmingly voted for candidates they liked personally, especially in secret ballots as used in the IOC's selection process. Electors who weren't accountable to anyone would more likely vote for their friends at the end of the day. In fact, that concept was so elementary to Payne, he found himself befuddled why other cities let those he labeled "junior-level bureaucrats" with little in common with the voting members lead their bidding processes.

As a result, Payne's instruction to his team began with a simple "We want to make every one of 'em our friend." Atlanta Nine member Charlie Shaffer, a senior partner at the elite law firm of King & Spalding, had captained legendary North Carolina coach Dean Smith's first UNC basketball team. He was assigned to meet with IOC former athletes. Payne paired affluent socialites Ginger Watkins and Linda Stephenson with especially well-heeled voters, adding instructions for one important meeting: "Wear the biggest diamond in your collection."

At any event attended by an IOC voter, Payne extended his arm for a warm handshake and offered a smiling "Hi, I'm Billy" or "How y'all doin'?" The rest of the Atlanta Nine followed suit. In time, they began hearing "How y'all doin'?" coming back to them in heavy Chinese, Spanish, and French accents.

VOLUNTEERS METICULOUSLY CRAFTED DOSSIERS on each of the eighty-five voters, their likes and dislikes, family members, favorite cocktails. A Russian delegate had a taste for the Tennessee whiskey he mistakenly called "John Daniels." A Swiss IOC member wrote fiction in English and longed to get his novel published. The Panamanian loved tailored suits. The Austrian favored horses. Central and South American voters admired Roberto Goizueta, the charismatic Cuban-born CEO of hometown Coca-Cola. Atlanta organizers arranged for personal meetings, where Goizueta—who technically wasn't supporting any country's bid—charmed them in Spanish. Delegates were wooed one by one and in groups. For the 1988 Seoul Olympics, the Atlanta organizers sent a heart-melting children's chorus. When delegations visited Atlanta, they were offered meals and accommodations not at the usual sterile luxury hotels but instead in elegant homes that echoed the fabled Tara from *Gone with the Wind*.

While Payne pushed the friendship strategy, Young, ever the politician, examined the IOC roster though a different prism. His calculations started with vested interest. The Dutch had bankrolled more than $1.5 billion in Atlanta, including two Ritz-Carlton hotels; the Japanese had invested heavily too. They each had built-in financial reasons to support Atlanta. Young's primary weapon, though, came from his years as United Nations ambassador during the Carter administration. Scanning the list of IOC voters, he immediately recognized Africa as the most promising bloc of votes, with nineteen committee members representing the continent. Young was close with Nigeria's president and had supported the independence drives of Namibia and Zambia. There were natural Atlanta ties too. The Kenyan IOC representative was a Coca-Cola bottler.

When courting IOC voters, Young relied heavily on a pitch focused on Atlanta's civil-rights history. The city was the birthplace of Martin Luther King, a point emotionally on display during specially arranged tours of the King Center led by the icon's widow, Coretta. When Africans mentioned the American South's shameful history of slavery, Young would parry: "You can blame the white people for buying us, but dammit, you all sold us."

Chuckling, he urged that a vote for Atlanta would reflect support for a city where everyone—even descendants of former slaves—were doing well.

Payne and Young knew the Olympic bidding process had a well-earned reputation for graft and payoffs, and they strived to steer clear. Occasionally, though, the Atlanta team skirted rules by offering gifts of nominal value in what they considered a spirit of friendship. They provided a purebred Georgia bulldog puppy to a Mexican IOC voter, but gifts were never central to the Atlanta team's grand design.

Instead, in the final few months, Payne and Young leaned heavily on a stealth strategy: They urged IOC voters to view Atlanta as their default option. The Olympics host-city selection process, they knew, would be formal and rapid-fire. All IOC delegates would gather in a single room. A secret ballot would be held, after which the city with the lowest score would be eliminated. The next round would occur immediately afterward, without additional discussion, and again the lowest vote getter would be knocked out. The process would continue until the fifth ballot when a winner was selected in head-to-head competition. Once the voting started, Young noted, it would be the purest voting system he had ever heard of, with no room for lobbying, horse-trading, or corruption. At every opportunity, the Atlanta committee would offer this message: We understand if you favor another city, maybe out of alliance or allegiance. No hard feelings. But if that city is eliminated, please make us your No. 2. That meant shifting their votes to Atlanta once their favorite had been beaten. Or, as Payne viewed it, their second-best friend.

ATHENS REMAINED THE CLEAR sentimental favorite as the September 1990 vote approached, but the European candidate wasn't alone. Melbourne, Australia, packaged its proposal smartly, using a compelling theme of "Time for Another Continent" to play to the IOC's desire for broader international appeal. Toronto had strong credentials too, carrying with it the United Nations' designation as the most multicultural city on earth.

On September 18, decision day finally arrived. The Atlanta team assembled at the New Takanawa Hotel in Tokyo was absolutely unable to discern what announcement awaited. That morning, Young had gathered sixty members of the American contingent near a tranquil pond outside the hotel, cautioning that the vote could go the wrong way. "Just the fact that we got here makes us a winner," he offered, the way a Little League dad might say, "You played your hardest." Payne was having none of it. He expected to win.

Just before sunrise at Underground Atlanta, a rundown shopping and entertainment district in Atlanta's core, thousands gathered in front of a live TV feed from Tokyo. Atlantans, once blasé about the bid, had sprung to life. This previously far-fetched idea now seemed possible. On the ABC affiliate, a correspondent breathlessly proclaimed the impending decision as "the most important in the history of this city since General Sherman marched through here." Down the street, the *Atlanta Journal-Constitution* (*AJC*) had put together several banner headlines for its front page. One version lamented the city's loss to Athens or Toronto; the other celebrated Atlanta's victory. An editor stood poised to call the production room with instructions of which to run.

Inside the delegates' room in Tokyo, the voting began. Ballots One and Two offered little surprise. Two long shots—Manchester, England, and Belgrade, Yugoslavia—were knocked out. Athens was in the lead. IOC officials tracked the vote by hand on committee notepads embossed with the Olympic rings. Round Three brought an end to Melbourne's another-continent idea. Three cities remained, each with a path to the Games. Athens and Atlanta suddenly were tied for the lead at twenty-six apiece, with Toronto close behind. Two voting rounds would follow. Would the "make us your second choice" push by Payne and Young pay off?

Round Four eliminated Toronto. Athens had gained four votes and stood at thirty. But Atlanta had climbed into the lead with thirty-four. Now, with only two cities left for the final round, would Toronto's backers switch to Athens, the historic favorite, or Atlanta, the striving town with big ambitions?

Within minutes, the delegates completed their voting. Soon after, back in the Takanawa Ballroom, IOC President Juan Antonio Samaranch stepped to the podium in a navy suit, pale blue shirt, and royal blue tie. White Olympic flags bracketed the stage, which featured a state-of-the-art sixteen-panel video screen. A silent chorus of eighty-five members of the IOC, all formally dressed for the occasion, stood behind him. In halting English, the Spaniard expressed the "gratitude of the Olympic movement to the six candidate cities, their countries and their people, for their great interest in our Centennial Games." More than five hundred people waited expectantly in the ballroom.

For Payne, Young, and the Atlanta team, the tension was crushing. For a split second, Payne's exhaustion caught up with him. He had traveled to more than one hundred countries in three and a half years since the first meeting in Young's office. *Just get it over with. Announce any city*, he thought. *Please, please, just let me sleep.*

Samaranch worked his way methodically toward the announcement of the host of the Games of the 26th Olympiad. Then, for eighteen torturous seconds, Samaranch shuffled papers at the podium as IOC members shifted their weight behind him. Finally, he arrived at the only sentence that mattered.

"The International Olympic Committee has awarded the 1996 Olympic Games to the city of . . . " He paused a final beat for effect. ". . . Atlanta."

Andy Young wept at the announcement; Payne and the rest of the Atlanta team leapt, fists pumping. Hugs, screams, then more hugs. Thirteen time zones and nearly seven thousand miles away, fireworks erupted in the morning sky above Underground Atlanta. In the joyous mob, strangers high-fived.

This crazy long shot had actually come through.

WITHIN AN HOUR THE *AJC* Extra edition was rolling off the press in Atlanta, snapped up by joyous sports fans eager for more news and a keepsake. In reality, readers would later learn, the final vote had not been close, 51–35, with Samaranch casting his ceremonial vote once the winner was clear. Young and Payne's plan had worked, with Atlanta picking up three-quarters of Toronto's votes. The Atlanta team had made fifty-one of 'em their friends.

The *AJC*'s first-run banner headline would be reprinted on T-shirts and posters for years: IT'S ATLANTA! Just below, in a smaller font, the paper ran a less heralded and unintentionally foreboding subhead: CITY EXPLODES IN THRILL OF VICTORY.

CHAPTER 2

Richard Jewell was born Richard Allensworth White on December 17, 1962, in Danville, Virginia. His mother, Bobi, having struggled through three miscarriages, was ecstatic. She and her husband, Bob White, named their son after legendary race car driver Richard Petty.

Bobi was a feisty, churchgoing 5'2" spitfire with unflinching moral rectitude that she coupled with a salty tongue. Her portly husband, who played Santa at Christmas, was a faithful Christian too, or so she thought: A half-dozen years into their marriage, Bobi discovered what she called his "roving eye," and divorced him for cheating. Bob White continually fell behind in child support, leaving Bobi and three-year-old Richard to live frugally on her salary as an office clerk at an insurance agency. A year later, Bobi met John Jewell, a trim, handsome Vietnam Army vet who stood over a foot taller than she was. Jewell also shared Bobi's Christian faith, beautifully singing solos in the choir. They dated for a year, often with the cherubic Richard tagging along, then married.

The newlyweds and Richard moved to Atlanta in 1969 and settled into a rhythm. Monday through Friday were workdays, with Richard going to school then day care. On nights and weekends, John was master of the kitchen and played the piano after dinner. Bobi baked, gardened, and did the laundry and ironing.

They also put down roots in the Brookhaven Baptist Church, where Richard fancied himself an usher-in-training. At nine, he raced through the aisles before Sunday services, handing out programs to congregants whose well-being he viewed as his personal responsibility. Richard was the kind of youngster who adults adored but other kids thought overeager, even bratty in the words of one peer. But Richard paid little heed to their annoyance. He was naturally drawn to helping others.

John Jewell legally adopted Richard and became the boy's "Pop." The youngster delighted in telling people his new last name, "J-E-W-E-L-L—like a piece of jewelry, but just with two 'l's.'" Richard and his pop grew close. They fished, watched movies, and occasionally golfed together at John's favorite public course. At times, his dad could be a bit distant, but young boys rarely notice. Bobi was the tough-love parent, insisting that Richard politely thank adults and address them as "Ma'am" or "Sir." For minor transgressions, she would sternly yell "RICHARD!" More serious breaches would provoke Bobi to pull out John's belt for a spanking. Despite her often-overbearing parenting, Richard always felt his mother's love. Their home was filled with pets, the number swelling at one point to five dogs and two cats. Bobi also made sure the family indulged Richard's passion for the Atlanta Braves. Mostly, they watched their "Bravos" on Ted Turner's Superstation, but sometimes splurged on tickets to cheer on the team in person.

Richard's parents signed him up for the Royal Ambassadors program through church, known colloquially as "Boy Scouts for Baptists." But he much preferred playing basketball on Brookhaven Baptist's indoor court. He had a solid outside shot, though like most of the squad he relied mostly on hustle and determination. As one teammate joked, they were "short and white."

Senior year of high school ushered in major changes for the Jewell family.

In January 1982, John Jewell relocated to Albany, Georgia, for a new position as marketing director at the Duggan Insurance Agency. Bobi stayed behind as Richard worked toward graduation. John commuted to Atlanta on weekends, then would drive the 180 miles back to South Georgia with carloads of china, crystal, and other breakables for the new house he and Bobi had bought. Richard went to a school college fair and took a shine to the auto-body curriculum at South Georgia Technical and Vocational School. Few would have considered him particularly adept with his hands—his big-boned stockiness presenting a natural barrier—but he loved cars and could see himself in that line of work.

That June, on the Thursday of graduation, Richard took a final walk through Towers High School's tiled halls, glancing at the maroon and gold banners declaring "Good Luck Seniors" and "Go Titans." He had made some friends, but never fully engaged. His yearbook, *The Olympiad*, included just a single reference to Richard: the requisite senior photo on a checkerboard page of girls in V-neck drapes and boys in royal blue tuxedo jackets, ruffled shirts, and oversized velvet bowties. Richard had neatly combed his auburn page-boy bangs straight down to the edge of his eyebrows, or as some classmates hard-heartedly called them, his "unibrow." Only two people had signed Richard's senior yearbook, one good-naturedly referring to him as "Round head." Richard was ready to move on.

On a blazing hot Friday in June following Richard's graduation, the Jewells pulled away from their Atlanta home for the last time.

John moved Richard into his South Georgia Tech dorm room. Forty miles away, he and Bobi settled into their new home in Albany, an attractive brick ranch with white shutters and a small trellised front porch. Each morning after breakfast, John donned a jacket and tie. After he drove off, Bobi let out the two dogs, checked the cats' litter box, straightened up around the house, and left for her new job in the billing department of a furniture store. In the evenings, John took a seat at the maple upright piano in the living room. He would pull out stacks of sheet music and artfully play church hymns when happy, classical pieces when he was a little down.

It quickly became their routine. Until it wasn't.

Early in the second week at the new house, Bobi pulled her yellow Chevy Chevette into the driveway after work, parking by John's blue Pontiac wagon. Climbing their home's side steps, she entered through the kitchen, and the dogs rushed to greet her. Oddly, there was no aroma of dinner cooking, John's usual role. Bobi called out, "John?" Silence. She called his name again, more loudly, her high-pitched voice echoing down the hallway. Puzzled, Bobi made her way through the house. She looked in their bedroom, then Richard's, then the guest bedroom. All empty. In the living room, her eyes settled on a six-inch stack of sheet music on the bench. Had John been home playing all day? Something was wrong.

Bobi reached the kitchen, where she spotted her husband's black leather attaché case on the white Formica counter. A white envelope rested on top, a lone word, "Bobi," penned in John's hand. She lifted the envelope and apprehensively opened it. Inside was a single folded sheet from a yellow legal pad, with text she would recall nearly verbatim for years.

My dearest Bobi,

I have been a failure all my life. Getting a job with Duggan I thought I would be able to conquer the world. When I married you, you were my strength, and thought I could find it. I'm a failure. I'm leaving. Your life and Richard's will be much better without me in it. In my way, I will always love you.

John

Numb, Bobi's mind turned to the stack of music in the living room. What had he been playing? She rushed to the bench, her heart pounding as she sifted through sheet after sheet. Bach, Beethoven. All classical. The music of his dark moods.

Bobi called John's boss, Leonard Duggan. Did he know where John was? No, but he'd be right over. Duggan's arrival only deepened her spiral. "Bobi, didn't John tell you?" Duggan said. "I'm sorry, but I had to let him go two weeks ago."

The next day, Bobi drove to South Georgia Tech, where she delivered the sad news directly to Richard: John had left. Richard was confused. "Left what?" Bobi handed him the letter, and her son sat down to read. A long minute passed. Looking up, incredulous, he declared, "Mama, this isn't right. I can't believe Pop would do that." Bobi stared her stricken son in the eye, saying simply, "I'm going to have to take you out of school for a while." She needed him to work.

John Jewell did not call the next day or the one after. Law enforcement put out an APB for him, but the man had simply disappeared. Richard would never return to college, and he and Bobi would never see John Jewell again.

MEMBERS OF THE BROOKHAVEN Baptist Church showed up like it was Easter Sunday to help Bobi and Richard resettle into Atlanta. The Monaco Station apartment complex was a half-dozen bland red-brick buildings clumped around an asphalt lot. Out front on Buford Highway, six lanes of traffic zipped along a jumble of strip centers, gas stations, and fast-food restaurants.

Six weeks had passed since John Jewell's disappearance. The Brookhaven Baptists had taken up a collection to pay for the moving truck back from Albany, and were now bearing fried chicken, potato salad, chips, Cokes, water. Richard's former basketball teammates lugged the family's furniture up two flights of slatted concrete steps to Apartment F-3. The boys wedged all they could into the modest two-bedroom apartment. Bobi already had lightened their load considerably, having discarded or sold virtually all of John's possessions, including the upright piano.

Bobi spent no time coddling Richard in their shrunken family's new reality. She handed him the keys to John's car and instructed him to land a job fast. Richard found work at an auto-repair shop up the road and began to pitch in on the rent. He learned that even small luxuries like the occasional chocolate-glazed Krispy Kreme doughnut or Dairy Queen hot fudge sundae were now on his own dime.

Tensions ran high in the cramped household. She was fastidious, he was a slob, and together they resembled a humorless version of the '70s sitcom *The Odd Couple*. Richard would later complain to friends that Bobi was on him all the time, her grievances ranging from his messy room to his staying out later than expected. But nothing set Bobi off like her son's irresponsible driving. Within three months of returning from South Georgia, Richard got his first speeding ticket. He was hit with two more citations in the next eight months. Furious that her insurance premiums would rise and further strain their shoestring budget, she snapped that this "crap" was unacceptable. Now nearly twenty years old, Richard painfully learned that she had kept at least one of John's personal belongings: his belt. Richard longed to move out.

Within a few months, he found work with higher pay. The U.S. Small Business Administration hired him in Atlanta as a supply clerk in the department that aided disaster-ravaged areas. On his first day at the Richard B. Russell Federal Office Building in downtown Atlanta, Jewell headed off to get his government ID. He opted not to smile, his pale blue eyes fixed seriously on the camera. He knew this job could change the trajectory of his life, and he planned to make the most of it.

At the SBA, Jewell proved to have such an uncanny clairvoyance for co-workers' needs that colleagues nicknamed him Radar, after the character from *M*A*S*H*. He always strove to exceed expectations. During a 1984 flood in eastern Kentucky, Jewell drove a supply truck to the area himself, maneuvering around the rising waters to reach a critical destination where a thousand people had been evacuated. When he saw how short-staffed the field office was, he volunteered to work extra days on the victim-relief effort. Upon his return to Atlanta, Jewell received a glowing letter of commendation.

Jewell's SBA stint allowed him to develop two of the deepest, most meaningful friendships he had ever experienced.

The first began in 1985. During another devastating flood, Jewell was manning the phones in Atlanta and speaking regularly with a West Virginia contractor named Dave Dutchess, who was setting up field operations. The pair developed a foxhole friendship and cemented their relationship soon after when Dutchess stayed with the Jewells on a work trip to Atlanta. Dutchess was an unlikely kindred spirit. A decade older than Jewell, the long-haired, bearded mountain man was a skilled outdoorsman who several years later would win two international bowhunting championships. The exotic new friend, with eyes even bluer than Jewell's, seductively spoke of days hunting and fishing on a secluded twenty-acre spread he rented in rural Lost Creek, West Virginia. A mesmerized Jewell couldn't help but contrast that life with his own stifled existence in his mother's apartment.

Jewell offered to drive Dutchess the 550 miles home through the Blue Ridge Mountains. As they approached Lost Creek, the roadsides teemed with deer. He inhaled the crisp, pure mountain air as if he were an inmate just released from prison.

Jewell came to eagerly anticipate his drives to West Virginia. There, Dutchess taught his suburbanite friend the rural life. They shot guns, muzzleloaders, bows—and Jewell was a natural. Standing under a tall cedar tree in Dutchess's backyard, he fired a 30–30 lever action Winchester rifle for the first time and nailed a bull's-eye twenty-five yards away. Dutchess just had to marvel, *He outshot me, that little fucker*. They hunted deer in the dawn hours, stationing themselves in full camo at separate stands. During their long waits for prey, they whispered to one another over walkie-talkies. "Dave, can you hear me?" Jewell drawled. "Yeah, I can hear you," came the reply over crackling airwaves. A few moments later, Dutchess summoned, "Richard, can you hear me?" Jewell chuckled and responded, "Yeah, I can hear you." The exchanges broke the chill and silence of the mornings, even as their laughter warned away the deer.

Back in the house, Dutchess and Jewell talked well into the night, eating venison, pizza, and the Snickers bars that Jewell had toted north from Atlanta in his duffel. They confided about sensitive subjects, Jewell describing the heartbreak of his pop's abrupt departure and the oppressiveness of living with a loving but taskmaster mom. Over time, Jewell began to speak of his dream career: Having honed his skills in handling weapons and experienced the satisfaction of helping disaster victims in need, Jewell wanted to be a cop.

One frigid winter day, after several Lost Creek visits, the two camouflage-clad men stepped out of a stove-piped warming shack perched on a bluff. The West Virginian approached Jewell and slid his straight blade knife, a Buck 119 Special, from its sheath.

"Because we're brothers, let's become blood brothers," Dutchess proposed. Jewell tensed. Since childhood, he had harbored an outsized, almost paralyzing fear of needles. But Dutchess pushed, urging Jewell to seal their friendship with their blood. "I'll go first."

Dutchess jabbed the edge of the blade into the meaty portion of his left palm, just below the thumb. The red trickle turned Jewell's stomach. Now it was his turn. Fear rising, Jewell nervously grumbled, "I don't know about this." But he slowly unsheathed his own identical knife, swallowed hard, and ever-so-tentatively pressed the blade's tip to his flesh. Nothing. Jewell then jabbed lightly again and again. Finally, a single drop emerged. "Well, alright," Dutchess exclaimed. They gripped their left hands together in a soul shake, their blood mingling and lives intertwined. They would call each other "brother" from that day forward.

Jewell's second meaningful friendship from his SBA years could not have been more different.

G. Watson Bryant Jr., an irreverent and wise-cracking SBA lawyer in his mid-thirties, had an office down the hall from Jewell. An adopted son of the South, Bryant hailed from a well-off New York family that had sent him to St. Christopher's boarding school in Richmond, Virginia, and then to Vanderbilt University. Bryant partied through college but later settled down enough to earn a law degree from the University of South Carolina. At the SBA, the brawny attorney with thinning sandy blond hair was an unusual match for a staid government office, or any organization for that matter. A committed libertarian with a deep-seated distrust for authority, he utterly lacked a filter between his hyperdrive brain and profanity-happy mouth.

Bryant and Jewell shared a love for the arcade video games *Galaxian* and *Xevious*, which they played on lunch breaks at the nearby CNN Center. Bryant took a shine to "Radar" and tried to mentor him, especially on financial responsibility. Jewell was generous to a fault. Despite his meager salary, he would surprise Bryant by delivering a diet Coke and chocolate bar one day, then offering to pay for Chick-fil-A the next. Knowing that the lawyer shared his passion for the Braves, Jewell bought him a pricey team cap. Bryant appreciated the gestures but chided the clerk, "Richard, if you had two dollars, you'd spend five."

Jewell left the SBA in 1987 after four years, a casualty of the Reagan administration's smaller-government limit on renewals of temporary contracts. By that time, he already had laid the groundwork for breaking into law enforcement, moonlighting in store security at Richway, a retailer that would later become Target. In street clothes, Jewell spied on potential shoplifters, surreptitiously working his way through the aisles to improve his sight lines in a retail version of deer stalking. Under store policy, no suspect could be charged until leaving the premises with unpurchased merchandise. So, Jewell, alongside store security chief and friend, Rob Russell, would rush outside ahead of the suspected thief, crouch in bushes adjoining the parking lot, and prepare to pounce. Time and again, they took down the thieves.

Jewell moved on to join a private detective agency working for Radio Shack, then became a guard at the downtown Marriott hotel. He saw the positions as part of a strategy to burnish his security résumé.

In 1989, at the age of twenty-six, Jewell finally left Bobi's apartment, arranging to live rent-free at Post Place Apartments just up the road in exchange for serving as a courtesy officer. His housing settled, Jewell wanted more time to apply for law enforcement positions, and to get in shape. At 5'8" and more than 215 pounds, he could meet few police-force physical standards. So, he quit the hotel and found an assistant manager position at a TCBY yogurt shop. Even there, Jewell was strategic, encouraging DeKalb police to swing by for free sundaes. While they ate, he quizzed them about job openings.

At the TCBY store, Jewell flirted with an attractive and friendly young woman who said she was employed at a local MCI call center. He asked her out, but she declined, explaining she was already dating someone. They could be "friends." But Jewell was determined to reach her outside the yogurt shop to deepen their relationship. So, he repeatedly dialed the toll-free number at MCI's 400-operator phone bank until she answered. The young woman began to join him to watch movies in his apartment as long as the connection remained platonic. Jewell still hoped for more, occasionally leaving roses and notes on her car at work.

One night in December 1989, she agreed to join Jewell at Bobi's for dinner to celebrate his twenty-seventh birthday. After he picked her up, Jewell confided to her that his mother thought they were dating. He hoped she didn't mind. Inside the apartment, Jewell tried to show Bobi how close they were by putting his arm around her and trying to hold her hand. It was all finally too much. She ended the friendship and changed her phone number.

All the while, Jewell remained close with his Richway buddy Rob Russell, a glib giant of a man with a hefty double chin and thick-lensed glasses. Educated at a local college and trained as a classical pianist, Russell was the same age as Jewell. Early in their friendship at Richway, Russell realized what a good voice Jewell had, including a flair for mimicking singing styles from Chuck Berry to Van Halen. Russell had formed a band called The Pump, and when they needed a new lead singer, he tapped Jewell. In performances on local college campuses, Jewell thrived at center stage. "This next song's by Lynyrd Skynyrd, and we've only heard two or three garage bands attempt to do it," he told an audience. The Pump then launched into the classic Southern rock anthem "Free Bird."

Russell shared Jewell's desire to break into law enforcement. That meant slimming down considerably. In the afternoons, the two men walked laps at a local high school track. At night, they played basketball. Russell dropped seventy pounds during that stretch. Jewell, a voracious eater of all the wrong foods, wasn't nearly as successful.

Beyond losing weight, Jewell also knew he needed to clean up his driving record to launch his new career. Aside from the three incidents in those first few months after returning to Atlanta, he had been nailed four more times in the used Camaro he'd purchased—twice for speeding, once for driving with a suspended license, and another for a fender bender while following too close. Other mishaps, like shearing off his fog lights on his way to visit Dave Dutchess at Lost Creek, went unreported. Russell landed a law enforcement job first, in East Point, a rough Atlanta suburb with serious crime issues. Jewell, meanwhile, unsuccessfully applied to other local forces—Smyrna, DeKalb County, and the Atlanta Police Department (APD).

Those rejections didn't weaken his resolve. He lapped up police information wherever he could find it. In March 1989, Fox launched a new TV show called *Cops*, featuring unscripted *cinema verité* scenes of police followed by camera crews. Jewell was spellbound, recording the episodes in VHS and binge-watching long before the practice became common. As each episode began, he sang along with the intro music. *Bad boys, bad boys, whatcha gonna do, whatcha gonna do when they come for you?* Then, as the actual police work unfolded, Jewell would hit pause and summon his roommate, Todd Welsh, a fellow courtesy officer and a DeKalb County cop. Jewell would replay the scene, then critique the police response and ask Welsh what he would do in a similar situation. The roommate found Jewell overly enthusiastic; he would have appreciated if his sloppy co-worker spent more time picking up after himself than watching police shows.

In early 1990, Russell caught wind of a job opening at the Sheriff's Department in Habersham County, a largely rural area about eighty miles northeast of Atlanta. He asked an acquaintance at the department if they could use his buddy, Richard, drilling down on whether they hired "big boys." When word came back that the department already had some 300-pounders, Jewell needed no prodding.

On February 8, 1990, Jewell dressed early for his start as a Habersham County deputy sheriff. Like all deputies, he wore a uniform of a tan shirt with brown epaulets, a space on the right breast for a nameplate, and a gold-star badge on the left. Still living in Atlanta, Jewell was so excited that he raced to see Russell to show off his uniform before making the drive north. They agreed: Jewell looked good.

Like most new hires, Jewell began on the lowest rung of jailer, with starting pay a paltry $11,873 a year. The jail, housed on the third floor of the county courthouse, was a fetid and smoky lock-up that reeked of cigarettes, booze, and body odor. Air circulated poorly within the tan and white cinder-block walls. One previous deputy had considered the place so foul that he trained on the job for three hours, went outside to get a Coke, and never returned. Another who would come and go said, "I wouldn't walk my dog through that jail."

None of that mattered to Jewell. At twenty-seven, he was in law enforcement.

Jewell completed the two-week state course required for his jailer's certification, then ambitiously added any other class he could. He breathlessly awaited the moment that the sheriff let him enroll in the six-week Georgia peace officer training. Once Jewell earned that credential, he would be authorized to make arrests, serve warrants, and work accidents, all in his own police cruiser. Until that time, Jewell used his off hours to ride shotgun in the cars of higher-ranking deputies.

Three months into the job, Jewell's heavy-handedness almost derailed him. On May 26, 1990, the department's phone rang very early in the morning. A DeKalb County officer was on the line. Does Richard Jewell work in Habersham? Yes. What does he do? He's a jailer. Is he a certified peace officer? Well, not yet. That's all the caller needed to hear. The DeKalb police drove to Jewell's apartment, handcuffed him, and locked him up for impersonating an officer.

The next day Jewell was released on a signature bond, and the sheriff wanted to know what the hell had happened. Jewell scrambled to explain and then filed a written report. He had been working as a part-time courtesy officer at the Post Place apartment complex in Atlanta. At one A.M. on Saturday, he saw a couple in the outdoor hot tub with a twelve-pack of beer. He wrote: "The female had on only a t shirt and the male only a pair of boxer shorts, which were around his knees."

Jewell approached the couple, wearing a store-bought Georgia sheriff's cap and carrying a gun he would keep holstered. The pair claimed to be visiting friends. But when Jewell asked for a unit number, the man offered "1210." There was no such number in the complex. Jewell asked them to leave.

The male trespasser lunged at him, but Jewell sidestepped. Jewell put the man in a full nelson, pinning him on the hood of a car, then wrestled him to the ground. When the DeKalb police arrived, Jewell described the incident.

He added that he was a deputy with the Habersham County Sheriff's Office moonlighting as a courtesy officer. The cops took the man away.

Jewell told his Habersham bosses he was shocked when the police returned to lock him up the next night. But as they both knew, Jewell was not yet a certified peace officer. He lacked arrest authority.

Seventy-two residents of Post Place signed a petition on Jewell's behalf, hoping the charges of impersonating a public officer would be dismissed. The judge allowed Jewell to plead to a misdemeanor of disorderly conduct, no fine, and twelve months' probation. He also granted Jewell first offender status, which meant his criminal record would be expunged following probation. Finally, in a routine condition of such cases, the judge ordered Jewell to be evaluated to see if counseling was necessary. The judge wished him luck. When Jewell later went to his psychological evaluation, it took only fifteen or twenty minutes. "There's nothing to this," the counselor told Jewell. "Don't worry about it."

The sheriff ultimately decided not to discipline Jewell, who resumed his overnight shift at the Habersham jail. After persevering for more than another year, Jewell was promoted to dispatcher, allowing him to leave the foul lockup behind. Then in December 1991, Jewell got the call he so desperately wanted: The sheriff was assigning him his own police cruiser.

The journey had been far from a straight path. But road deputy Richard Jewell finally held the keys to his future.

CHAPTER 3

The 1996 Games were shaping up to be the largest peacetime event in world history. Billy Payne already knew that the Summer Olympics ran roughly four times the size of the Winter Games—far more athletes, visitors, and venues. But even by that measure, Atlanta was expected to be supersized.

A key reason was the lessening of geopolitical conflict. In 1980, only eighty nations had participated in the Moscow Olympics after President Jimmy Carter led a Western boycott over the Soviet Union's invasion of Afghanistan. Four years later, the Soviets countered, downsizing the Los Angeles '84 Olympics by holding back their Eastern bloc satellite republics. Then world events took a turn. A year before Atlanta won the Games, the Berlin Wall fell. Over the next half-decade, global leaders looked for ways to engage internationally and found the 1996 Olympics right in the sweet spot. A total of 197 nations would bring 10,700 athletes. Some two million visitors would pour into the city. Twice as many tickets would be sold in Atlanta as in Los Angeles '84 and Barcelona '92 combined. And 15,000 journalists would be on hand to chronicle it all.

Payne recognized that the task facing him was staggering. He already had bucked Olympic tradition by becoming the first leader of a bid to then manage the Games as CEO. But the reality of what needed to be accomplished now hit hard. The world would be arriving in a few short years, and construction emerged as his biggest challenge. A dozen new sports venues needed to be built, including the Olympic Stadium. Nearly fifty other venues would require retrofitting or improvement. Each project demanded financing, zoning, architectural work, permitting, hiring, and logistics. The list felt endless. Payne needed a strong second in command.

In March 1991, Payne found his chief operating officer in A.D. Frazier, a brash chain-smoking lawyer-turned-banking executive. Frazier had demonstrated his organizing acumen in 1977 when at age thirty-two he planned Jimmy Carter's presidential inauguration. Now forty-six and partial to rimless round eyeglasses, Frazier was ready for a new challenge. From the start, Frazier focused on delivering the Games on-budget and on-time. The price tag had been set at a whopping $1.6 billion, including hiring nearly five thousand employees and supporting an additional fifty-five thousand volunteers.

Frazier studied two models for host cities. The first was Montreal '76. Government run and funded, that Olympics had been a fiscal disaster, saddling the city with debt of more than $1 billion. A decade later, when Payne first visited Andy Young, the mayor spoke of Montreal still being $700 million underwater. Montreal's experience so spooked future potential hosts that Los Angeles had been the only city in the world to bid for the Games held eight years later. In contrast, Los Angeles relied primarily on private funding, existing facilities, and nongovernment management. The results were starkly different. By the time CEO Peter Ueberroth closed the books, the event had netted a $215 million *surplus*, which the LA organizing committee used to support youth sports across the United States. Ueberroth's memoir, *Made in America*, became a must-read for Frazier and his team at the Atlanta Games.

Venue planning remained among the most important issues for the Atlanta organizers, known as ACOG, the Atlanta Committee for the Olympic Games. They were determined to create first-class facilities without saddling communities with white elephants after the Games, so they sought clever ways to repurpose several destinations. The largest venue, the $235 million track-and-field stadium, was slated to become the Braves' new home when the Olympics left town. But the 85,000-seat behemoth that would host the Opening Ceremony, as well as track and field stars Carl Lewis and Michael Johnson, was hardly configured for baseball. So, architects designed the structure with a bulging southwest corner. After the Games, half of the stadium would be lopped off and the rest reconfigured to create a major league ballpark akin to Baltimore's Camden Yards.

Meanwhile, new open-air swimming and diving pools would be built at Georgia Tech, at the top end of downtown, and would later be enclosed to become the school's natatorium. The built-from-scratch horse park in Conyers and the tennis center in Stone Mountain would require far less transformation, just some downsizing for exurban city use. Other construction projects, like the velodrome for cycling, would simply be torn down.

CHAPTER 3

IN NOVEMBER 1992, FBI Special Agent Dave Maples stood amid three cubicles on the tenth floor of ACOG's headquarters in the Inforum, a sparkling three-year-old glass building adjacent to blocks of rundown low-rises and deserted asphalt lots. A U.S. Naval Academy grad, Maples had joined the FBI in 1971. Thirteen years later, the lanky and laconic Tennesseean became the agency's Olympics expert, first in Los Angeles '84, then Calgary and Seoul '88, and most recently Albertville and Barcelona '92. He had just returned from living in Spain for three years and working closely with top Olympics security officials there in planning for the recently-ended Summer Games.

He surveyed the team. Maples found himself particularly intrigued by Richard "Stock" Coleman, a Georgia State Patrol commander and former chief bodyguard for then-Governor Jimmy Carter. Coleman and an Atlanta Police lieutenant comprised the sum total of the Olympics security team at that moment, each only on part-time loan to the Games. The third cubicle had been reserved for the FBI.

Maples thought the clean-cut Coleman seemed pleasant enough. He had a solid pedigree, including a Marine Corps background and coursework at the Bureau's National Academy in Quantico. But Coleman, whose brother chaired the Georgia General Assembly's powerful Appropriations Committee, had a curious approach to Olympics security planning. Coleman believed that worrywarts overstated the time and effort required to protect visitors. His strategy would be far simpler, he explained to Maples and others; he would just wait until about six months before the Games, then instruct police chiefs: "All right, this is your responsibility; this is your venue. I want you to make it safe like you would a sporting event. . . . Now run that son of a bitch and call me when you get a problem."

Maples listened, stunned.

Even as he let Coleman expound, Maples knew the man had no idea what was coming. Any host city had the usual array of theft, prostitution, robberies, murders. Atlanta had seen its crime rate worsen so badly that by the early 1990s one local journalist suggested that the informal motto should be changed to "a city too busy to reload." Most of those day-to-day crime matters would remain the responsibility of local and state police when the Olympics came to town.

But the reach of the Games transformed every host city into a magnet

33

for the truly dangerous, especially those seeking an Olympic-size mega-phone from the media. Bomb scares had numbered over one hundred at every Summer Olympics since 1984. Nearly all were empty threats, but each required investigation. In one case at the Los Angeles Games, an LAPD officer discovered an unexploded device under a Turkish team bus. Investigators soon determined that the police officer had secretly planted a fake bomb himself so that he could "find" it and be declared a hero. Far more troubling was the ominous expansion of domestic militias at home. Although those groups hadn't yet struck at a major U.S. sporting event, the FBI knew their threat was growing.

Law enforcement couldn't ignore the stepped-up threat of international terrorism. Communiques from intelligence officers were filled with cautions about the Irish Republican Army, Hamas, and the Tamil rebels in Sri Lanka, who had distinguished themselves by not only inventing the suicide belt but assassinating two heads of state as well. Those groups and others remained an ocean away from Atlanta in 1992. Of course, Maples was keenly aware of one international event that surely even Coleman could grasp: Munich.

In 1972, German officials, eager to dispel the memories of Adolf Hit-ler's propaganda-infused 1936 Berlin Olympics, had touted Munich '72 as "The Cheerful Games." Those words took a ghastly twist when Palestinian commandos stormed the Olympic Village dormitories of Israeli athletes and coaches. A gruesome eighteen-hour standoff unfolded in front of a shocked world TV audience. Finally, machine-gun fire and a grenade-triggered explosion brought the crisis to a head. Jim McKay of ABC Sports delivered the news at 3:24 A.M. Munich time: "Our worst fears have been realized tonight. . . . There were eleven hostages. Two were killed in their rooms, yesterday morning. Nine were killed at the airport, tonight. They're all gone." A West German policeman and five of the terrorists lay dead as well.

In Atlanta, "Munich" would become shorthand for protecting the '96 Games, especially the new dorms at the Olympic Village on Georgia Tech's campus. But Maples's worries ran far beyond those walls: Law enforcement personnel needed to secure sixty athletic venues spanning 247 miles of Geor-gia from the Savannah sailing course on the Atlantic coast to the Columbus softball complex on the Alabama line. Traffic had to move, airspace called for safekeeping, heads of state required protection.

In prior Olympics outside the United States, other host countries had simply called in their armies. In Seoul '88, after a threat of an attack on the marathon, South Korean officials stationed the military every ten yards for the entire race route. But the United States had to work under *posse comitatus*, an 1878 Act of Congress that barred the use of federal troops to enforce domestic laws and make arrests. In Atlanta, state and local law enforcement, combined with private security, would primarily have to comprise the thirty thousand security personnel ACOG committed to have in place. That wouldn't be easy. Metro Atlanta only had a pool of 2,500 sworn officers, roughly one-sixth of the number in metro Los Angeles in 1984.

None of that phased Coleman, the state's putative security leader. After all, he told Maples, Atlanta had successfully hosted the 1988 Democratic National Convention without a hitch. The state would be fine. "There's no great mystique to it," he argued. "You fill up a stadium and you empty a stadium; you fill a park and you empty a park. . . . What it comes down to is that guy on the corner waving his damn arms and blowing the whistle."

Coleman was ultimately demoted to planning and overseeing the cross-country Olympic Torch Relay. The assignment would keep him out of Georgia for long stretches.

IN LATE FEBRUARY 1993, a Pakistani foreign national named Ramzi Yousef drove a rented yellow Ford Econoline van from New Jersey into Lower Manhattan. The back of the vehicle was loaded with a 1,200-pound homemade bomb. Yousef parked in a garage beneath New York City's iconic World Trade Center, then lit four twenty-foot-long fuses before leaping into a waiting car and speeding away. Twelve minutes later, the massive bomb exploded. The device fell short of Yousef's goal to bring down the towers, but six people died and more than a thousand others were injured. In what years later would become known as "World Trade Center I," workers and visitors were trapped in forty-five elevators. Evacuation of the fifty thousand employees from the Twin Towers took over four hours. Repairs would cost an estimated $250 million. Later, when agents arrested Yousef and his associates, law enforcement realized just how much worse the nightmare could have become. The terrorists had also been plotting to blow up the George Washington Bridge, the United Nations, and other New York landmarks.

With the Olympics just three years off, international terrorism had arrived on the American mainland.

OLYMPICS SECURITY PLANNING LURCHED forward. Officials already had decided that ACOG would be responsible for securing the venue entrances and interiors. Frazier hired former Dallas Police Chief Bill Rathburn as ACOG's head of security. Prior to his stint in Dallas, Rathburn had been No. 2 at the Los Angeles Police Department and that force's point man at the LA Olympics. Meanwhile, state and local officials would protect the perimeters of the venues. The FBI would handle intelligence gathering and would spearhead any "critical incident" during the Games. But for the Bureau, one disastrously mishandled event remained a bitter fog around the planning.

Two days after the World Trade Center bombing, the U.S. Bureau of Alcohol, Tobacco, and Firearms prepared to execute a search warrant at the seventy-acre Waco, Texas, compound of the Branch Davidian cult. The group's self-proclaimed messiah, David Koresh, espoused doomsday prophecies and declared that all women having sex with him became his disciples. Among his many "wives," some were as young as twelve. Although the sect was armed with hundreds of assault weapons and grenades, the ATF decided to storm the compound and alerted the media in advance. The operation went horrifically wrong, as four government officers and six Branch Davidians died in a gunfight. President Bill Clinton then ordered the FBI to assume responsibility, and the Davidians and law enforcement began a tense fifty-one-day standoff.

Ultimately, the FBI attempted to breach the compound walls with tanks and tear gas to flush out Koresh and his followers. The FBI's results were even more disastrous than the ATF's. First came an armed battle. Then fire engulfed the compound, inflamed by tear gas launched by the Bureau's forces. By the end, seventy-six Branch Davidians lay dead, including twenty-five children. The national media, camped out since the original ATF assault, covered it all.

Waco instantly became a battle cry for militia groups throughout rural America, who centered on the FBI's heavy use of firepower. Anti-government radicals vowed to avenge April 19, 1993, the day of the final siege.

ACOG SECURITY CHIEF RATHBURN urged that all major security decisions fall to a team comprised of only the most vital Olympic law enforcement agencies.

Even though ACOG was a private, nongovernment organization without actual law enforcement power, he envisioned himself as an ex-officio member. The Secret Seven was born. The FBI represented the Feds while the State Patrol and Georgia Bureau of Investigation handled the state's duties. Four local forces rounded out the group, with the Atlanta Police Department as the largest. Rathburn at first hosted the Secret Seven with ACOG-funded breakfasts at the downtown Ritz-Carlton. But soon, the group's law enforcement members began to suspect that Rathburn's bosses at ACOG were primarily interested in unloading private security duties onto government-funded law enforcement. They began meeting without him.

The FBI's new special agent in charge (SAC) in Atlanta, David "Woody" Johnson, took over as Secret Seven host in March 1995. Assigned to lead the office through the 1996 Olympics, the former commander of the FBI's elite Hostage Rescue Team could easily have been mistaken for the brother of Paul Newman. Beyond his wavy silver hair and hazel eyes, Johnson and the actor shared an unspoken self-assuredness with no trace of diffidence or smugness. He was renowned within the Bureau for a daring mission in international waters that resulted in the first arrest of a suspected terrorist overseas. Among the Secret Seven, as at the FBI, Johnson was deeply respected.

The six men and Atlanta Police Chief Beverly Harvard gathered in the FBI's fourth-floor executive conference room. The twenty-foot polished-wood table was scattered with background documents and venue maps. Framed photos of President Clinton and Attorney General Janet Reno looked on, as did one of FBI Director Louis Freeh, who was known as Louie throughout the Bureau. The small group quickly began to bond, forming an intra-agency camaraderie so missing at Waco. A few others joined, including the local ATF head. The name never changed, though the group was no longer secret nor seven.

Issue by issue, the Secret Seven debated and resolved a list of security questions, easing but never fully quelling their worries about domestic or international terrorist attacks. One particularly vexing matter was how to assemble the promised force of thirty thousand personnel. A major piece of that answer, they recognized but never came to trust, would have to be private security guards. Richard Jewell would later be part of that force.

AMONG THE SECRET SEVEN's biggest worries was Centennial Olympic Park.

Back in the summer of 1992, Billy Payne had fallen in love with a gathering place at the Barcelona Olympics. Las Ramblas, a tree-lined stretch of pedestrian streets, and two plazas had emerged as the nightly party spots where international visitors mingled with locals and athletes, no ticket required. That sense of togetherness perfectly captured the emotion that had ignited Payne's passion for bringing the Olympics to Atlanta. For more than a year afterward, Payne stewed over Atlanta's lack of a similar space. Piedmont Park was too far from the sports venues to be a magnet. The streets inside the Olympic ring couldn't easily be closed off from traffic. The downtown Woodruff Park was a postage stamp.

At his Inforum office, Payne had a balcony that he used whenever he needed to vent his frustration or temper, which had become infamous. At least once a day, he would open the glass door, stomp outside, and privately let off steam. Often, he watched drug deals ten floors below on seedy Techwood Drive. One day in the fall of 1993, out on his balcony venting again, Payne saw with fresh eyes the acre upon acre of dilapidated buildings, homeless encampments, and soup kitchens. "Well, there's our gathering place," he exclaimed.

Within days, Payne told Bert Roughton, the lead Olympics reporter at the *Atlanta Journal-Constitution*, that he dreamed of "a grand plaza, a huge open space" for people to congregate. Payne's idea was so vague, the reporter told readers, that he had no idea on cost, financing, or even what it might look like. Then Roughton quoted Payne's startling timetable: "I figure we have about six months' time to pull it off." The schedule sounded ludicrous to Roughton. For past projects, Atlanta had shown almost no ability to move at any pace but slowly, and a project of this magnitude would require not only significant land accumulation but also tens of millions of dollars in funding. In his piece, Roughton deadpanned that the plans seemed "a bit ambitious." When he expressed that view to Payne, the Olympics' chief dreamer smiled, "But so was winning the Games."

Discounting the idea, *AJC* editors slipped Roughton's article onto page six of the local section. They should have known better. Five and a half weeks later, Payne unveiled a breathtaking plan to create the largest in-town public space built in a major American city in a quarter century. "What I think we need is a magnificent gathering place so our visitors can mix with Southerners and experience firsthand the friendliness of the American South," Payne gushed, naming the project Centennial Olympic Park. "This could be the permanent legacy we have been looking for." This time, the *AJC* started its coverage on the front page.

Within months, corporate and philanthropic funders had pledged enough money for the state to acquire twenty-one acres of squalid downtown blocks. Some property owners sold, others donated their sites, and the state used eminent domain to capture a few. Centennial Park was becoming a reality.

Law enforcement initially loved the idea. The FBI's Maples, for one, had worried about hundreds of thousands of visitors milling about on urban streets before and after events. Peachtree Street's narrow sidewalks weren't Las Ramblas, and vehicle traffic made for a dangerous element. But as plans developed, the Secret Seven grew concerned. The park quickly evolved beyond open green spaces to plans for entertainment stages, playful fountains, corporate pavilions, and food tents. In short, Centennial Olympic Park was emerging as one of the largest attractions of the Olympics.

Some on the Secret Seven began to consider the park as a "hard target" for attack. In their view, it would be the second-highest profile risk, next to the heavily fortified Olympic Village. Several members pressed for the park to be declared an official venue, with ACOG providing magnetometers and full interior security. Bill Rathburn shared many of the group's concerns. He pushed for basics of solid law enforcement and crowd control—a fence around the park, narrowed entrances, and restricted admission.

AJC reporter Melissa Turner soon broke the news that the park would now be enclosed and that other security measures were coming as well. "The 21-acre park, originally promised as the grand gathering place for the Olympics, will turn away visitors once it is filled," she wrote. "And that's likely to happen most nights during the Games." Moreover, a hierarchy would be established for park entry, reported Turner, citing Rathburn in her sourcing. With hundreds of thousands of visitors downtown on any given day, ACOG needed to set priority for who would fill the park, which could accommodate around fifty thousand people. Sponsors and their guests would receive premium treatment. Then came Rathburn's most controversial line. He told Turner, "This will not be a public park."

Suddenly, critics positioned the new comments as a class matter, even one of race, in which the affluent could gain access to the park and the less well-heeled would be excluded. Payne was furious. In the next day's *AJC*, he backpedaled from his own security chief. No one, Payne told Turner, will be getting preferential treatment for entry to the park. Not a soul.

The Secret Seven and other law enforcement officials finally concluded that the state-owned park would need to be protected through a detailed, if hodgepodge, security plan. State, local, and federal agencies would send nearly four hundred personnel. Cameras would be installed around the perimeter, as would a fence with wide open entrance points. Corporate sponsors like AT&T, Budweiser, Coca-Cola, and Swatch would provide a smattering of private security guards. Unlike the athletic venues, there would be no magnetometers or bag checks.

Centennial Olympic Park would remain Billy Payne's "people's park," open to all.

CHAPTER 4

Kathy Scruggs joined the *Atlanta Journal-Constitution* in December 1986 with dreams of becoming a star police reporter. She longed to mimic the career of Edna Buchanan, the hard-boiled *Miami Herald* cop reporter who churned out a breathtaking 230 gory, shocking, and, at times, empathetic articles a year. Just months after Scruggs arrived at the *AJC*, Buchanan won the Pulitzer Prize for General News Reporting. The police beat *and* journalism's highest award offered an intoxicating aspiration for Scruggs.

Born in 1958 in Athens, Georgia, just two miles from the UGA stadium where Billy Payne played football, Kathleen Scruggs was raised in affluence. She grew up essentially as an only child, having a distant relationship with her decade-older brother, Lewis. Kathy idolized her father, Lewis Scruggs Sr., viewing him as the embodiment of movie star Cary Grant, suave and charming. Bubber, as he was known, had built a thriving insurance agency, and he drove one of the town's few Cadillacs, sometimes loading up his family for vacations to their second home on Florida's Gulf Coast. He doted on his only daughter, a strikingly beautiful blonde and blue-eyed girl, getting Kathy a thoroughbred named Foolish Pleasure in sixth grade and sending her to newly opened private Athens Academy.

Kathy's mother, Nancy, kept the family's home and passed on to her daughter a lifelong distaste for cooking. Nancy routinely pulled salmon croquettes and chicken pot pies from the freezer to warm in the oven for dinner. When the family built a new house, Nancy asked the architect if she could construct it with no kitchen, just a microwave and a refrigerator. The architect gently mentioned the issue of resale and she moved off the idea.

Despite Kathy's loving relationship with her parents, they could be demanding. At six, when she still had baby fat, Bubber and Nancy began to insist that she weigh in each morning and report the results. Humiliated, Kathy cleverly figured out a distraction, rising early and preparing her parents' breakfast. In the bustle of the morning, they soon forgot about the scale.

That ingenuity would become a lifelong trait. During a high school summer break, Bubber hired Kathy to take photos of houses underwritten by his company. She roped in her cousin and closest relative, Bentley. The work itself wasn't challenging, but some of the residences were in Athens's less-affluent communities. One afternoon, the girls pulled up in an old white van outside a ramshackle home. They stepped onto the sidewalk to take pictures. Suddenly, a woman bolted out of the front door with a shotgun, aimed directly at the girls. The homeowner wanted answers fast.

Kathy quickly lowered her camera, perkily announcing, "Congratulations, your house has been nominated for yard of the month!" Within minutes, the homeowner had gathered her family in the yard for a group portrait. Kathy snapped photo after photo, making sure to include the house in the background for the underwriting staff. Then she and Bentley hopped back in the van, turned the corner, and burst into laughter.

Kathy regularly attended the Beech Haven Baptist Church her parents helped found, but never completely warmed to the authority of religion. She did, though, learn early about the power of her looks. With an alluringly raspy voice and long blonde curls, she could tell that men were attracted to her. She posed coquettishly for photos, filling the family scrapbook with images that radiated sexuality. She began dating older men, sneaking cigarettes, and experimenting liberally with alcohol and pot. Her literary tastes gravitated toward the edgy, reading and rereading Hunter S. Thompson's drug-laced *Fear and Loathing in Las Vegas*. During high school, Bentley thought her wild cousin was running so fast that she stopped spending time with her for several years.

Scruggs chose Queens College, a small women's school in Charlotte, North Carolina, where she joined the paper and then signed on to the Sigma Upsilon writing society. After junior year, she interned at the *Charlotte Observer*, a plum local summer job. On campus, she continued to develop her sense of personal daring. Although she joined Phi Mu sorority, Scruggs cast her eye beyond boys at intercollegiate mixers. For more than a year, she dated the thirty-something head of food services at the school. He scooped her up in his Ford Gran Torino for evenings of dinners, movies, and more. But the relationship finally crumbled, as did many others Scruggs would have.

After graduation, Scruggs grabbed an entry-level journalism job with the *Independent-Mail*, a small newspaper in Anderson, South Carolina. The former mill town was numbingly sleepy. The characters on her favorite soap opera, *All My Children*, were having far more fun. Professionally, her talent soon emerged, and Scruggs flashed an ability to find and source stories. Within a year on the education beat, she earned a regional award for a profile of a program that offered pathways for the unemployed to return to school.

Scruggs chafed at Anderson's uneventfulness. The men there who longed for her, especially a fellow reporter named Tony Kiss, soon realized they weren't in her league, instead settling for "close friend" status. On nights filled with Stolichnaya Bloody Marys in quiet bars or one of their homes, Scruggs groused to Kiss about the lack of a decent live-music venue. She missed the energy-filled clubs back in her hometown of Athens that had incubated R.E.M. and the B-52s.

In March 1984, just shy of her two-year anniversary at the paper, the twenty-five-year-old Scruggs craved a true night of fun.

She and Kiss drove to the college town of Clemson, some twenty miles away. After several drinks, Scruggs got into a verbal scrape with the bar owner. He ordered her to leave. She barked in her gravelly Southern drawl, "I work for the paper in Anderson." To the man behind the bar, her words were a threat that she would write something negative. The next day, he called the paper to complain, and the *Independent-Mail*'s editors ordered Scruggs to apologize to him. The headstrong young reporter quit instead.

Scruggs gathered her best newspaper clips and found another reporting job, this time at a paper twice the size in western North Carolina. But the *Asheville Citizen-Times* would be only a pit stop; Kathy Scruggs had grander ambitions. In late autumn 1986, she got the call she had dreamed of: the *Atlanta Journal-Constitution* wanted to bring her to the capital of the South. With a circulation of seven hundred thousand on Sundays, her new employer was not only twenty times larger than her current publication but widely read in her hometown of Athens. She was thrilled to be joining a paper with a storied Southern past. Scruggs arrived at the *AJC* ready for her shot.

THE *ATLANTA CONSTITUTION* LAUNCHED in 1868 in the shadow of the Civil War. Over the following decades, the morning publication grew to regional prominence, featuring not only Henry Grady and his eloquent support for the

New South, but also fellow editor Joel Chandler Harris and his Uncle Remus chronicles of African American folktales. Three-quarters of a century later, during the civil rights movement, another crusading editor named Ralph McGill earned the 1959 Pulitzer Prize for his forceful arguments against intolerance and segregation.

The afternoon competitor, the *Atlanta Journal*, was founded in 1883, and featured the front-page motto "Covers Dixie Like the Dew." It boasted its own celebrated Southern past. In 1922, the paper hired an outgoing, petite Atlanta native named Peggy Mitchell to write for its Sunday Magazine. The following decade, Mitchell wrote her first and only novel, *Gone with the Wind*, which won the Pulitzer Prize and put Atlanta on the literary map forever.

In 1939, James Cox acquired the *Journal*, expanding his media company that would later be called Cox Enterprises. The deal included Atlanta's oldest radio station (whose call letters WSB slyly stood for Welcome South, Brother), and the company soon introduced Atlanta's first TV station. Cox added the *Atlanta Constitution* to his holdings in 1950, and for decades profits soared at both papers. But as the 1970s arrived, news quality failed to keep pace. The *Journal* had focused much of its energy on its well-regarded sports page and on columnists like Southern humorist Lewis Grizzard, the author of such popular books as *Shoot Low Boys, They're Ridin' Shetland Ponies*. Hard news was increasingly becoming an afterthought, and the *Journal* and the *Constitution* saw their reputations lag. The papers would soon combine their newsrooms, with the *Atlanta Journal-Constitution* sharing resources for its morning and afternoon publications.

Then, in 1980, CNN launched its twenty-four-hour TV news channel not far from the *AJC*. The cable network offered an unceasing stream of the day's stories into homes, offices, and later airports. While CNN's numbers were small initially, the network had an outsized societal impact: Consumers began demanding more immediacy, even if the news was less well-reported and at times inaccurate.

Newspapers took notice. In September 1982, editors at the Gannett Corporation debuted a national paper patterned after Americans' TV viewing habits. *USA Today* featured short articles, pie charts, bright colors, and news abbreviated to "chunklets," all designed for readability and speed. Almost no stories "jumped" from the front page to an inside page. "Upbeat" was the buzzword. In the first issue, an airline crash in Spain was headlined, "Miracle: 327 survive, 55 die." Many journalists decried the rise of the media equivalent of fast food, dubbing the publication "McPaper." Legendary *Washington Post* editor Ben Bradlee snarled, "If *USA Today* is a good newspaper, then I'm in the wrong business."

Four years later, when Kathy Scruggs joined the *AJC*, she had a singular goal to work her way into the police beat. But those slots already were taken, so for over a year, she worked as a general assignment reporter downtown, stepping into whatever role the Metro editor needed. Then in mid-1988, editors reassigned her to the Gwinnett County "Extra" section, part of their effort to appeal to highly coveted suburban readers. Scruggs was crushed, confiding to a friend that she had been put on "punishment detail." Like the rest of the team, she worked hard to meet the heavy story quotas the section required. But the job felt like a slog.

One night, Scruggs climbed into the passenger seat of the car of her friend and editor, David Pendered, for a ride home. As the sun was setting, Scruggs lamented her place outside the *AJC*'s mainstream. She badly wanted to cover crime. Pendered had heard all this before from her. "You can quit, you know," he suggested. "No," Scruggs shot back. "This is all I've ever wanted to do."

Scruggs worked to make the most of her time in the suburban bureau, focusing on crime stories whenever she could. She wrote about the slaying of a Gwinnett preschool teacher, the sexual-molestation charges against a youth baseball coach, and the strangulation of an eight-year-old boy. Bill Rankin, who sat with his back to Scruggs, noticed that the cops shared far more information with her than with him. "Who'd want to talk to me when they had Kathy?" he would laugh.

Downtown, the *AJC* brass debated the papers' future, eventually deciding to follow the *USA Today* model. It reached for a veteran of the controversial paper, Executive Editor Ron Martin.

The soft-spoken midwesterner arrived at the *AJC* in 1989 with a clear agenda: Journalists needed to stop writing for other newspeople, as some thought was the case under his erudite predecessor. The *AJC* had to change its relationship with readers, Martin asserted, and focus on what they *wanted* instead of what editors felt they *needed*. Martin brought on board another *USA Today* veteran, John Walter, to become the managing editor and help execute this new vision. Ron/John, as they were known in the newsroom, had come to shake things up.

Ron/John argued that while they believed in aggressive coverage and important stories, those pieces should be handled with more reader friendliness, including graphics. One major edict was a *USA Today*–style "no jump" rule, restricting even the complex news of the day to seventeen column inches. Walter assigned four reporters to focus on TV shows and the television industry. He oversaw the creation of a gossipy around-town column called "Peach Buzz" and a daily traffic piece called "The Lane Ranger." TVs were installed around the newsroom so that reporters could keep track of both local news and CNN.

Reaction inside the newsroom ranged from annoyance to bemusement. Many elite reporters hired by Ron/John's predecessor bolted. But Walter refused to bend to criticism, contending that the paper retained a strong commitment to news, just packaged better. Walter also kept three stacks of defunct newspapers on the shelf behind his desk. Whenever *AJC* staffers complained about the no-jump rule or the traffic and weather stories, Walter would reach back to his "dead papers" pile and wave an edition or two at the protester. He had plenty of choices: the *Washington Star*, *Los Angeles Herald-Examiner*, *Miami News*, *Chicago Daily News*, *Baltimore News-American*, *Kansas City Times*, *St. Louis Globe-Democrat*, *Pittsburgh Press*, *Philadelphia Journal*, *Houston Post*. They were all gone.

In the months after Atlanta was awarded the Olympics following the momentous 1990 Tokyo vote, Walter knew the *AJC* had a unique opportunity to build its brand. He wanted to own the story, to be the go-to media outlet for Atlanta-area readers and, in turn, visitors from around the world in 1996. To do that, the Games would need to be viewed through a very broad prism. This wouldn't just be a seventeen-day sports event. Instead, the *AJC* would cover the $1.6 billion Olympic effort through such varied lenses as security, traffic, economic development, sponsorships, ticketing, transportation, construction, media. That's what readers would care about. And with two million visitors expected to come to town, the blanket coverage would in turn attract advertisers. True to form, Ron/John went an unconventional route, sidestepping the *AJC*'s sports staff and instead naming the business editor, Thomas Oliver, to run the paper's Games' coverage.

CHAPTER 4

Oliver was an unlikely pick to have much of anything to do with sports. A bespectacled part-time musician who once considered the ministry, Oliver had covered the hometown Coca-Cola Company for several years. In 1991, when he was tapped to coordinate the paper's 1996 Games coverage, Oliver literally struggled to spell the word "Olympics." In a pre-spellcheck era, he would stare at the letters, wondering if he had ordered them correctly, repeatedly reaching for his dictionary to look up the word.

BY 1991, A JOB covering the Atlanta Police Department opened up downtown, and Scruggs finally got her wish. She had begun building a reputation as a who-what-and-how journalist, expertly narrating mayhem but rarely pausing for analysis of broader meaning.

Scruggs innately knew that gruesome played best in crime reporting: a woman mauled by pit bulls, two children dying in their family's toy chest, the murder of a fifteen-year-old girl whose alleged killers had connections to Satanism. She wrote extensively about a triple homicide at a budget car-rental company called McFrugal. Quirky worked too: crimes committed by fake police officers, an escape artist sneaking back into a Georgia prison, and a thirteen-year-old bank robber who was arrested when he got hungry and spent some of his newly acquired funds on cheeseburgers at a nearby McDonald's.

Her personal style in sourcing stories was playful and at times outrageous. Scruggs became a regular at Manuel's Tavern, a sprawling bar popular with journalists, the political class, and, most importantly, the police. On Thursdays, known as "cop night," she pulled her car into the lot, reached into her purse past the handgun, and grabbed a bottle of perfume, dabbing on a few drops. Then she marched into Manuel's. The wood-paneled décor was garage-sale eclectic. Neon signs for Budweiser and Lite beers glowed into the central bar area, a portrait of President Kennedy staring down from the wall above the shelves of liquor.

Scruggs slid through the packed bar to the corner where the homicide detectives ended their days. Her outfits never failed to capture their attention, the short skirts, leather boots, and low-cut blouses revealing a bit more of her cleavage than socially acceptable. She tossed back her shoulder-length permed hair and lit a cigarette, its smoke mixing with the scent of decades of spilled beer and grilled burgers. After ordering a Johnnie Walker Red, or two or three, Scruggs pressed the cops for details on the latest murder, refusing to take "no comment" for an answer. "Give me something I can fuckin' use in the paper," she cajoled, adding a sweet smile to soften the demand. The police loved her.

Out on the street, her style was much the same. One night, Scruggs arrived at a murder scene at the same time as the Atlanta cops and stealthily climbed into the back bedroom through a window. Inside, she used what she called the "homicide high step," lifting her feet much farther off the ground than normal to avoid the bugs and spatters of blood. Then she waited for the police to make their way through the house. When they entered the room, they found Scruggs standing next to the dead man. "Hey, where y'all been?" she asked.

Her personal flair often captured more attention than her news stories. She thought nothing of asking a friend to shift her black Mazda Miata convertible while she held the steering wheel and a cigarette in her left hand and a Budweiser tallboy in her right. She starched and ironed her tight jeans. She wore leather miniskirts to the office.

Inside the sprawling *AJC* newsroom, Scruggs was the most colorful and divisive player among the rows and rows of desks. Many saw her as a delightful throwback to the 1930s newspaper wars. She was loud, she was profane. She would burst into the paper's downtown offices in a rush, slightly disheveled, hair pulling from its tie. Her future colleague on the Olympics security team, Ron Martz, marveled that "Kathy never quietly entered into a room. She kind of exploded into it." She lived in Technicolor while much of the newsroom was in black and white. Over time Scruggs accumulated often-conflicting descriptors among her colleagues: tenacious, bombastic, rude, unsparing, wild, authentic.

Scruggs adored newsroom banter, often dishing out an off-color barb about male colleagues' body parts. One morning, her *AJC* colleague Doug Monroe read aloud a news brief Scruggs had written about a man arrested with a shotgun stuffed down his pants.

"Hey Kathy," Monroe yelled across the sea of cluttered desks, "this isn't news. I often carry a shotgun in my pants."

"Yeah, sawed-off," she replied.

Many at the paper were amused. But others, especially women, fumed that she was setting back newsroom equality through her revealing outfits. Did she *have* to wear fishnet tights with those high heels? Her attire did little to dispel a growing "sleeps with her sources" reputation. Regardless, no one questioned Scruggs's extraordinary drive and ability to work sources. One of her editors, Glenn Hannigan, summed up his view of a strong reporter's skills: "Either you're curious as hell—you want to know everything that happened, every single detail—or you're so competitive you can't sleep at night." Scruggs, he concluded, was both.

Scruggs's confidence at the *AJC* grew, and she became comfortable in the belief that she in fact could become Atlanta's leading police reporter. She worked harder and sourced better. But she never could relax in a newsroom featuring televisions by the dozens and an industry rapidly accelerating. News was becoming an unceasingly competitive business, one that required constant, almost obsessive, attention. Crime reporting was its front lines. In her reflective moments, Scruggs knew that those elements would only get worse, that the pace would accelerate. She would simply have to work more resourcefully.

Scruggs had proved early in her days on the police beat that she was up to the task. Just before arriving downtown, she was assigned to cover the fast-moving stories of the related deaths of a federal judge and a Savannah attorney.

As Scruggs reported, U.S. Appeals Court Judge Robert Vance entered his Birmingham, Alabama, home to find a package on the kitchen table. As he opened it, a detonator triggered. Explosives flashed, with chunks of metal and finishing nails flying out of the device and tearing into Vance's chest and stomach. The judge crumpled into the corner of the room, instantly dead.

Two days later, in Savannah, a similar package was delivered to Robert E. Robinson, an African American alderman. The blast ripped off his right arm below the elbow. His face was riddled with metal pockmarks. As he lay bloody on the floor, his shoes appeared to have blown off his feet. Prosecutors later said that Robinson lived for another three-and-a-half excruciating hours.

The *AJC* initially turned to its senior police reporters to cover the investigation. But when a forty-six-year-old junk-store owner named Robert Wayne O'Ferrell emerged as the FBI's lead suspect in late January 1990, editors dispatched Scruggs to get his story. She raced down Interstate 85 to the southeast Alabama city of Enterprise.

The FBI was focused on several key pieces of evidence. Years earlier, O'Ferrell had sent an angry missive to Judge Vance's appeals court after losing a lawsuit against a former employer. The complaint letter's typeface and odd spacing appeared to exactly match the reconstructed address labels on the Vance and Robinson packages. The typeface was also identical to separate letters, clearly from the bomber, claiming credit and threatening more attacks. Nearly one hundred federal agents swarmed O'Ferrell's home and his New and Old Surplus Salvage Store in search of the manual typewriter and other evidence.

Scruggs reached the suspect directly after the searches, reporting to *AJC* readers that "O'Ferrell said the FBI cleaned out the septic tanks at his Enterprise warehouse and New Brockton home and searched the lake near his property, looking for evidence, including a typewriter." She added, "The quiet life of a farmboy who had never been on an airplane was turned upside down." In his defense, O'Ferrell told agents that he no longer owned the typewriter—but hadn't kept any records of that sale or any others in his business.

As many reporters as agents were covering the case, and Scruggs searched for a new angle. On a Sunday morning, she slipped into O'Ferrell's Baptist church and watched him tearfully proclaim his innocence from the pulpit. "From what the Bible tells me, Hell ain't no funny place," Scruggs reported him telling fellow congregants. "It's fire. It's brimstone. And from what the Bible tells me, I ain't going there." After the service, Scruggs grabbed an interview with O'Ferrell, who made his position plain: "Jesus and me knows I ain't guilty."

Days later, the FBI began to shift away from O'Ferrell after having administered two lie detector tests, taken hair and saliva samples, and continuously tailed him. There appeared to be some truth to his claims of innocence, though he also could still be complicit.

Ultimately, the investigation turned to Walter Leroy Moody Jr., who had been convicted in 1972 of sending a nail-filled pipe bomb to his wife in Macon, Georgia, badly injuring but not killing her. The federal appeals court in Atlanta, on which Judge Vance served, had refused to overturn Moody's conviction. The case fell into place.

With the murders squarely in the national spotlight, Attorney General Dick Thornburgh designated a forty-year-old Assistant U.S. Attorney from the Southern District of New York named Louie Freeh to handle the prosecution. Freeh was a rising star in legal circles, having recently won convictions of the leaders of an international heroin-smuggling ring in a celebrated sting known as the Pizza Connection. In November 1990, a grand jury indicted Moody on seventy counts, and Scruggs revisited the O'Ferrell story. The junk store owner told Scruggs, "I hope that when these folks get through, they'll simply apologize for what they've done. I'm not guilty." No apology came.

At trial, Freeh made sure jurors saw Moody as the rational, calculated murderer he was. The evidence showed he had sent the bomb that killed Alderman Robinson in Savannah simply to throw the FBI off his trail. He wanted the bombing to appear racially motivated. The jury deliberated for thirteen hours, then voted guilty on every count. Moody was sentenced in federal court to serve seven life terms plus four hundred years.

AS SCRUGGS FOCUSED ON full-time police reporting, she developed sources all the way to the top of the Atlanta Police Department. Her relationship with Police Chief Eldrin Bell grew so comfortable that one day she took him to lunch at the swanky Capital Grille. There, over shrimp and grits, Bell told Scruggs he couldn't remember a detail she wanted from an investigation. The unfiltered reporter fired back, "You lying cocksucker!" The police chief paused for a second and just started to laugh. Scruggs was always Scruggs.

In 1994, Scruggs welcomed a new head of the Atlanta Police Department, Beverly Harvard, who held the distinction as the nation's first big-city African American female police chief. Harvard was profiled on *NBC Nightly News* and *60 Minutes*. Scruggs wrote a glowing piece about Harvard's promotion. Then she worked to get closer to the chief, calling or swinging by Harvard's office several times a week. Scruggs told the chief they could chat like buddies. Harvard just chuckled, declining to accept the terms. "No, we're not friends at all. You're a reporter. I'm a police chief. That's why we're even talking."

But for Harvard, like most cops, Scruggs's persistence and charm often proved irresistible. During one interview, Scruggs told Harvard, "My mother just loves you." Harvard tried to recall if she had ever met the elder Mrs. Scruggs, finally deciding she hadn't. Scruggs pushed ahead: "She sees you on television, and she just LOVES you." Harvard laughed, adding, "OK, well, tell your mother I love her too."

That same year, having now established herself as the *AJC*'s top police reporter, Scruggs was keen to expand her reach. So, teaming with the FBI's violent crimes "7 Squad" (unrelated to the Secret Seven), Scruggs created a regular column on the region's most wanted fugitives. Over the coming years, Scruggs's column would help the Bureau and other agencies apprehend nearly one hundred alleged criminals.

FBI Special Agent Mike Greene often drew the assignment of delivering the photos, each with a short description on the back, to the *AJC*'s headquarters at 72 Marietta Street. He had grown to deeply respect Scruggs, especially her intensity and drive to help solve crimes. She seemed to have sources at every law enforcement department in metro Atlanta.

One day he drove up with a brand-new agent in the passenger seat. As always, the contrasts between the setting and the reporter could hardly have been more stark: the beige concrete and glass *AJC* building, with its unadorned black-and-white sign; and Scruggs standing next to a bench outside the building, all flash and color, sporting a lime-green miniskirt and go-go boots. *AJC* credentials dangled over a frilly white blouse, makeup heavy, sunglasses perched atop blonde hair. The new colleague ogled and asked, "Who is *that*?"

Greene smiled. "That's the best reporter the *AJC*'s got. She can get a story from anybody." Greene stopped and rolled down the window to hand over the photos. The greetings were quick. Scruggs was always on deadline and in a hurry. But she paused to lean on Greene for more than the pictures. "Come on, you've got to give me a story."

CHAPTER 5

On the damp windy morning of April 16, 1996, a brazen group of Islamic terrorists attacked the crew of a Delta Air Lines jet as it landed at Atlanta's Hartsfield airport. The heavily-armed Algerian hijackers held 225 passengers aboard the Lockheed L-1011, among them seven French athletes, an Indian ambassador, and a U.S. State Department escort. The rebels identified themselves as Martyrs of Allah.

The FBI quickly learned through intel that Martyrs of Allah was a radical fringe group expert in the use of deadly sarin gas. American officials had become well schooled in the dangers of the colorless, odorless nerve agent after an attack in Tokyo a year earlier by the religious cult Aum Shinrikyo. The Japanese group had released sarin into three subway cars, killing twelve. Now, in Atlanta, federal public health officials immediately began alerting medical personnel to have antidotes at the ready.

The hijackers said they were "paying back" Israel, France, and the United States and demanded access to a news team. They wanted food as well. Events quickly turned even more perilous when two of the terrorists identifying themselves only as Mohammed and Mashat threatened to begin killing passengers. Uniformed Delta personnel quickly delivered meals to the base of the aircraft's stairway, including a microphone the FBI had hidden in the packaging. At the same time, the Bureau's Hostage Rescue Team formulated a counterassault plan involving sixteen men. From there, the crisis deepened further. U.S. officials in a makeshift command post at the unfinished Terminal T of the airport learned of a Martyrs terror cell in Atlanta. Its members were reportedly in the process of transporting biological and chemical agents in a van through the city.

It was all a mock crisis. Dubbed "Olympic Charlie," the events were part of security training for the Olympics. It lasted three days and extended beyond Atlanta into North Georgia, where a hostage-taking scenario was played out at the future site of the rowing events. The exercise had been so realistic that Woody Johnson, the FBI's special agent in charge in Atlanta, called a press conference. "We are practicing for situations we hope will never occur," Johnson explained, his tone assuring and even. "We have no reason to think these Games will be anything but safe and secure."

For more than a year, security teams in Atlanta had worked through exercises based on domestic and international threats. Law enforcement dealt with fictional white supremacists, bombers, snipers, and arsonists. There was a mock attack on the MARTA subway system that involved kidnappers murdering passengers one at a time while demanding the release of convicted terrorists. The FBI led practice runs at every Olympic venue. In one, an athlete was taken hostage at the newly constructed tennis center in suburban Stone Mountain where American star Andre Agassi would soon be leading the U.S. team. A decisive helicopter-led response from a fifty-person SWAT team resolved the staged crisis.

After each venue exercise, law enforcement experts, often hot and sweaty from their work, sat in the stands to debrief. What could they have done better? How should they have communicated more clearly? What would happen if real terrorists used a slightly different strategy? After Olympic Charlie, the final field exercise before the Games, senior Justice Department official Merrick Garland created a full after-action report for Louie Freeh, who had assumed the role of FBI Director in September 1993. The document led to additional tweaks in law enforcement's strategies, designed to hone protection to as close to perfect as practical.

But American officials knew that the Games would be filled with challenges. Georgia U.S. Senator Sam Nunn told CNN that law enforcement anticipated as many as twenty bomb threats each day, each requiring investigation. "Hopefully all of them will be hoaxes. Strange people do strange things," Nunn said.

ON APRIL 19, THE day after Olympic Charlie ended, the FBI was on high alert. It was the third anniversary of Waco, and the first one had been disastrous. In 1995, Timothy McVeigh detonated a massive truck bomb outside the Alfred P. Murrah Federal Building in Oklahoma City. The explosion killed 168 people, including nineteen children, mostly from the preschool on the first floor. Eight law enforcement officers were among those murdered. Oklahoma City was then the single worst mass murder ever on American soil. Fortunately, the 1996 anniversary came and went with no tragedy.

But in Atlanta, as the Olympics approached, some local politicians heightened fears instead of calming them. That same spring, Georgia Attorney General and gubernatorial candidate Mike Bowers used a crime conference speech to declare, "I'm willing to bet it's safer to walk the streets of Sarajevo than the streets of Atlanta." The comparison to the war-torn Bosnian capital made national news, and drew swift and angry rebukes. In the *AJC*, Kathy Scruggs framed it as a "cheap shot below the belt" and quoted Mayor Bill Campbell deriding Bowers' "shameless pandering." Her frequent source at the Atlanta Police Department, Chief Beverly Harvard, simply dismissed the Sarajevo parallel as "ridiculous."

The news attracted the attention of the White House too. Vice President Al Gore already had called for an all-hands Olympic security meeting for later that week. Key law enforcement, military, and intelligence leaders from Washington and Georgia were summoned to FBI headquarters. Bowers's comments added a sense of urgency, as did the coming 1996 presidential election, which would determine if Clinton and Gore would serve a second term.

At the meeting, Gore focused on understanding the chain of command among the wide range of entities involved. Presentation after presentation focused on a coordinated approach to securing the Games. Gore cut to the chase: "Who's in charge?" Woody Johnson spoke up, explaining the formation of the Secret Seven and its role on the ground. Should there be a "critical incident," the Bureau's term for a crisis, that group would be central in addressing it.

Gore persisted, asking again, "Who's in charge?"

By the end of the meeting, the chain of command was clear: The FBI would be in charge if there was a critical incident; SAC Woody Johnson was the Bureau's point person in Atlanta.

ON APRIL 27, 1996, eighty-four days before the Opening Ceremony, the Olympic torch was lit in Olympia, Greece. With pomp befitting an early Hollywood musical, a high priestess wearing a gray ceremonial tunic dropped to bended knee to ignite the torch. Billy Payne and ACOG officials then accompanied the flame on a flight to Los Angeles International Airport. As Payne carried the Olympic light down the plane's exterior staircase, the USC band played John Williams's newly composed theme "Summon the Heroes." The song would become a staple at Olympic Games for decades.

For the next twelve weeks, the Olympic Torch Relay crisscrossed the United States like a misguided tourist. The flame, always followed by a backup torch in case the original was extinguished, visited the Santa Monica Pier, meandered along Route 66, and cruised the Las Vegas Strip, which had been intentionally darkened by casino owners. It traveled on horseback over a Pony Express path and was shipped by barge on the Erie Canal. Weeks rolled into months along the torch route, and the flame eventually arrived on the East Coast. In New York, *Today* show host Katie Couric ran a leg. Over the next few weeks, runners brought it to the White House and Thomas Jefferson's Monticello. The torch was carried by descendants of legendary sprinter Jesse Owens. In Selma, Alabama, ACOG Co-Chair Andy Young ran it across the Edmund Pettus Bridge. Finally, in July 1996, the flame crossed the Florida-Georgia border on a serpentine route to Atlanta. In all, ten thousand torchbearers ran part of the relay, touching forty-two states and covering more than sixteen thousand miles.

But law enforcement barely gave it a thought. With all their major exercises completed, the FBI and others were busily moving beefed-up security teams—now thirty thousand strong—into place. Safety, not sport or spectacle, was law enforcement's focus. On CNN, reporter Art Harris told viewers, "While the Games are here this summer, Atlanta will likely be the best protected city on Earth." Then he added, "Even so, for terrorists out to send a message, it's still a tempting target, a stage the whole world will be watching."

CHAPTER 6

Officer Richard Jewell cruised down a straightaway on State Route 17 in full uniform and aviator sunglasses, his foot heavy on the accelerator of his chocolate brown Ford LTD patrol car. He was on the hunt for a wayward herd of cattle.

Dispatch had given Jewell the last known location, just north of Clarkesville. Within a few minutes under the late-day sun, he found the fenced-in pasture and the open gate just off the two-lane road. But scanning the pavement to the east and west, he saw no cows. Across the road ran a vacant grassy embankment bordered by open woods until they disappeared into the rolling North Georgia mountains.

Fellow officers monitoring the radio traffic chuckled over the inability of the new Atlanta-raised road deputy to find a bunch of cud-chewing cows. A frustrated Jewell radioed in yet again: "Dispatch, I've been up and down three times. I haven't seen any. . . . Upp, stand by. OK, I see 'em now." His voice crackled over the airwaves in a rising staccato, "Upp, upp, upp, upp." Then a loud *thump*. Jewell moaned, "Aw sheeeeit."

Over a dozen cows had rushed out of the woods heading back to their pasture just as Jewell was driving by. A young 400-pounder ran headlong into the side of his car. Jewell skidded to a stop, surrounded by cows scurrying across the road, and stepped out of his vehicle to survey the damage. He cursed as he saw the hefty dent in the passenger panels. Sheriff Nix surely would be more than a little unhappy.

It wasn't Jewell's first bovine fender bender. On a service call just days after being handed the keys to his cruiser, he had parked in a farmer's driveway on Sand Belt Road when a cow bumped into a heavy metal gate. Jewell watched in horror as the gate slowly swung and then, gathering speed, clanked into his car's quarter panel. As expected, the sheriff took Jewell to task. But Nix clarified for Jewell and others that he didn't care about dents, per se. He just needed a "body," as he called arrests, to show for them. Livestock didn't count.

Jewell chalked up both incidents to what he began to call "Jewell luck," those moments in which unseen forces in the universe seemed to conspire against his success. Still, he knew blaming karma wasn't going to help him with the sheriff. So, the twenty-nine-year-old deputy focused instead on further honing his credentials and skills as an officer. Beyond his 240 hours of Basic Law Enforcement certification—which finally earned him arrest authority—Jewell enrolled in every course the department would subsidize: Field Sobriety Testing, Radar, First Responder, Tactical Baton, Tactical Rifle, Bomb Response, Haz Mat Awareness. During his time in Habersham County, he would compile 558 hours of accredited training.

Jewell's real education, though, came during his six P.M. to six A.M. shifts. Night after night, he stopped speeders, worked car wrecks, served warrants, and hauled miscreants to jail. Jewell developed into a by-the-book cop with a particular passion for road duty. If a driver's tail light was out, he made a stop. Expired license plate, a stop. Over the speed limit, a stop. Drivers would find themselves staring into Jewell's rotund face, illuminated by flashing blue police lights. The stops were often an excuse for the deputy to put drivers through field sobriety tests. A near teetotaler himself, Jewell had no stomach for intoxicated drivers, viewing himself as a bulwark against highway injuries and deaths.

Beyond his hours on the Habersham roads, Jewell signed up for the Governor's Drug Task Force, throwing on a bandana and a Georgia Police Academy T-shirt, grabbing a machete, and hacking down marijuana plants. He also volunteered as a member of the local High Angle Rescue Team on weekends, donning a climbing harness and a yellow safety helmet. He helped rescue stranded hikers from nearby Tallulah Gorge, where in 1970 Karl Wallenda had famously "skywalked" across a cable stretched one thousand feet above the ravine. Jewell's girth made him a perfect "mule" on the team, using rope to pull heavy objects and people. On one especially grim weekend, Jewell helped hoist a dead body up the steep switchbacks to the trailhead.

Jewell worked to heed the advice of fellow officers who pressed him early on to "lose the city accent" and learn the flow of rural life. One evening, he was called to handle a North Georgia road incident: A driver of a chicken truck had taken a turn too fast and tossed fifty poultry crates onto Highway 197. The birds raced up and down the road and along the embankment.

Jewell ran helter-skelter after them as he futilely tried to grab and re-crate them. Finally, another officer gave him some sage country advice: Just throw some seed on the ground, and let the chickens come to you.

Jewell took every lesson seriously. He wore his uniform and badge #113 proudly and with a deep sense of purpose. At 1:30 one morning, he arrested a father who had been sharing drugs and alcohol with his fifteen-year-old daughter as other younger children ran about the house. The man, incensed over Jewell's decision to protect the children, promised to "hunt you down" and "kick your ass, or worse." Another evening, he was first on the scene, siren blaring and blue lights flashing, after a ne'er-do-well in the tiny town of Demorest exploded a phone booth with a pipe bomb.

For cases requiring backup, Jewell regularly teamed with fellow deputy Brian McNair. A slightly balding officer with wire rim glasses and a knack for storytelling, McNair enjoyed Jewell's quirky style and humor. The two would become close.

During one shift, Jewell and McNair were dispatched to handle a domestic dispute at the home of a suspected drug dealer off Route 441, the main highway through Habersham. As they approached the property, the officers were greeted by a pair of pit bull pups, about eight or nine months old. The call didn't take long, no arrests were made, but on the way out McNair told Jewell, "That guy is bad news." Both deputies sensed they would be back.

Not surprisingly, about six months later, a judge issued a warrant for the same man's arrest on charges of dealing crack cocaine. McNair warned Jewell that this time the assignment would be much more dangerous. Aside from the customary risks of any drug bust, McNair explained that he had driven by the property several times since their earlier visit. The pit bulls had grown larger and been trained to attack. Entry to the house would be perilous.

But to McNair's puzzlement, Jewell seemed unfazed, almost nonchalant. "Don't worry about that," Jewell said. That night, McNair, Jewell, and two others on the High Risk Warrant Team met down the road from the property to formulate a takedown plan. They would approach by foot and surround the house. Jewell surprised McNair again. "Let me be first," he said. No one was going to object, but Jewell's bravado seemed odd.

The team crept toward the fenced-in yard. As the other three waited by the street, Jewell climbed over and vanished from sight. Minutes later he reappeared, waving his colleagues forward. They arrived to the implausible sight of both pit bulls licking Jewell's fingers. He was feeding them bits of hot dog.

Dumbfounded, McNair asked, "Do they just take food from everyone?"

"Oh no," Jewell replied. "I've been feeding them ever since we were out here the last time. I come back every week or two and throw 'em some scraps or somethin'." He had been preparing for this takedown for half a year. As Jewell continued petting and feeding the animals, the other three deputies hauled the crack dealer out of the house.

The pit bull story became Jewell lore at the department, a moment in the limelight that he cherished. Jewell also developed a reputation for outfitting himself and his car well beyond the usual trappings of law enforcement. He bought a personal .357 Magnum, a 9mm, a .35 caliber, and a .36 caliber to add to his growing firearms collection. He shopped for camo, backpacks, and other equipment at Army–Navy surplus stores. Jewell loaded his belt with so many law enforcement tools—guns, ammo, flashlight, handcuffs, keys—that his pants sagged. It didn't stop there; he tricked out his cruiser with additional wig-wag lights on the front grill, a second radio, an extra strobe attached with Velcro to the dashboard. He even added a VHS video camera for filming traffic stops, decades before dash cams became the norm. Jewell did the electrical work himself, sometimes misconnecting the wires. During one install, an electric jolt sent him reeling, leaving his hands blackened for days.

In addition to his overloaded circuit, Jewell stuffed the car with supplies. The back seat held crowbars, battery-powered lights, and a 130-pound battering ram for breaking down doors. He crammed his trunk with plastic tubs containing tape, gauze, condoms, shampoo, soap, painkillers, Band-Aids, water bottles, ointments, and Beanie Babies for children. Extra weapons, huge amounts of ammo, and coiled rope of varied length and thickness all were wedged in too. Jewell wanted to be prepared for anything.

At one accident reconstruction, a fellow deputy told Jewell he was out of spray paint to mark the site. "What color do you need?" Jewell queried. "Orange is good," the officer replied. Jewell shoved his arms through the jumble of his trunk. "Orange?" he asked over his shoulder. "Yeah," the deputy said. Moments later, Jewell plucked out a can of Day-Glo orange paint.

Fellow deputies nicknamed Jewell's cruiser the "Deathmobile." His trunk was now so damaged from his many accidents that he had to use bungee cords to keep it closed. Colleagues feared that if he were ever in a major wreck, he would be crushed by his car's contents even before he hit the windshield. Unless, of course, all the ammo he carried blew first.

JEWELL MOVED RESIDENCES SEVERAL times in Habersham. Ultimately, he rented a small creekside house near the Soque River, living alone with Angel, a Doberman given to him by his West Virginia friend, Dave Dutchess. He bought a used Toyota pickup truck after slamming into a deer with the old Chevy Cavalier he had gotten from his mother. Jewell nicknamed his new wheels "Old Blue."

Money was painfully tight, with Jewell taking home only $272 a week. He needed additional means to cover his rent and utilities, as well as his growing gun collection and the gifts he still loved to bestow on his friends. During his daytime off hours he supplemented his income mowing lawns. He also took a part-time job as a crossing guard at Clarkesville Elementary School, bringing his own flair to the duties. As the kids arrived on the morning buses, Jewell made himself the center of attention. He waved, whistled, and danced as the lights on his cruiser nearby flashed blue. The children laughed and returned his greetings. One week, the school honored him with a special post on its outdoor signboard, even as they made the common mistake of misspelling his name: "Richard Jewel. You're so cool—You get us safely to & from school. The best traffic cop! Thanks!"

A couple of years into Jewell's time at Habersham, Rob Russell joined the Sheriff's Office as a deputy too. Despite their frequent brotherly flare-ups, Jewell was happy to reunite with his old friend from Richway and The Pump. Russell took one look at Jewell's Deathmobile and gibed, "Don't even wash that fucking car; something will fall off that piece of shit." Even so, Russell found himself in the car's passenger seat at least once.

Late one afternoon, just before Jewell started his shift, he and Russell were eating an early dinner at their favorite Mexican restaurant, El Sombrero. Just as they were paying their bill, a call came in over the radio about a high-speed pursuit of two burglary suspects some forty miles away. Other deputies were already giving chase, and Russell suggested they take it easy. But Jewell couldn't resist. He convinced Russell to hop in the Deathmobile, and they raced north. Russell was confident their sprint would amount to nothing, especially when their colleagues lost sight of the car. But Jewell exited onto Highway 197, then immediately looked to his left. There, in a driveway, sat the burglary suspects. Jewell and Russell jumped out, pumping their shotguns. The arrest went down smoothly.

After they brought the pair to the station house, Russell told his buddy, "You have a horseshoe up your ass." If only Jewell's stretch of good fortune could continue.

BY JULY 1995, JEWELL had worked for the Habersham County Sheriff's Office nearly five and a half years. During that time, he had added some twenty dents to his cruisers. Sheriff Nix knew about only a handful of those. Jewell had stuffed a mallet in his car, and after each accident, he would pound out the damage on the spot. Still, the sheriff could easily see that Jewell's car looked like a survivor of the Demolition Derby. So, after Nix got a new vehicle for himself, he assigned his 1994 Crown Vic to Jewell with a caution, "Don't you wreck this thing."

On the first Friday of that same July, Jewell was driving his new cruiser along the darkened Dick's Hill Parkway. The hour was late, in the middle of his graveyard shift, and the road was empty. But Jewell spotted the tail lights of a Mount Airy police car on the long straightaway ahead. He decided to have some fun.

Jewell loved the movie *Top Gun*, including the scene in which Tom Cruise's character, Maverick, buzzed the air control tower. Jewell decided to flick off his lights and step on the gas to "buzz" the Mount Airy car. But Jewell didn't realize that Officer Travis Jarrell was preparing to take a left onto the Grandview Connector. The road ahead and behind appeared deserted to Jarrell, so he had no reason to signal. The officer began his turn just as the speeding Jewell was zipping by him.

Their cars collided, Jewell's right side smacking the front left end of Jarrell's. Jewell strained desperately to control his cruiser, skidding off the road nearly one hundred feet and smashing first into a utility pole and then pinballing off one guy wire and into another. The accident knocked out power for a half-mile in Mount Airy. Jewell's car, as one deputy recalled, looked like it was "hung up on a fishing line." Remarkably, neither officer was seriously injured. Jewell glumly watched as a wrecker towed away the sheriff's badly damaged former vehicle.

When Sheriff Nix heard the news, he was furious. No body, no arrest, no excuse. He demoted Jewell back to the fetid jail. Humiliated, Jewell realized he had squandered his dream of being a road deputy. Now he needed to decide on his next steps. McNair and other friends at the department urged him to take the jailer's job, to let some time lapse for the furor to dissipate. Maybe in a year, or even less, the sheriff would liberate him from the stink and boredom of the lockup.

But the idea of returning to the bottom rung of jailer was too demoralizing for Jewell to even consider. Within a day, he acquiesced to what the sheriff wanted anyway and quit.

With bills overdue and no savings, Jewell desperately needed work. Adding to the misery, he would no longer be able to serve as the Clarkesville Elementary crossing guard when school resumed in August. As much as the teachers and kids liked him, no blue lights meant no job. That modest income, and the joy of daily interactions with the children, were gone.

He worked his North Georgia law enforcement network, checking for other openings. Jewell knew he was qualified. He now had over three years of road experience and hundreds of hours of training. He had even been elevated to firearms instructor by Habersham, his proudest credential, reflecting a skillset his West Virginia friend Dave Dutchess had noticed on day one. Surely there had to be value in all of that. But he knew joining another sheriff's department would be difficult. Word got around quickly when you lost your job. Nevertheless, Jewell caught a break.

Three months before his resignation from Habersham, Jewell and his buddy Brian McNair had begun moonlighting part-time as security officers at Piedmont College, a sleepy Baptist school in Demorest. Around the same time, the campus police chief, Dick Martin, had converted the school's tiny security force into a certified police department. The chief needed more hours from officers who had been through the state's credentialing process. When Martin learned that Jewell was available, he extended the former deputy's schedule substantially and eventually moved him into a full-time slot.

Piedmont College was nestled in the mountains on an idyllic magnolia-dotted campus. Known as a haven for pastors' kids, the nearly-century-old institution had seen its student body double in size over the prior four years. Ambitious Piedmont College trustees had prepared for another big step, hiring Ray Cleere, the former commissioner of higher education for the University of Mississippi.

When Habersham Sheriff Nix received a call from Piedmont as part of a routine background check on Jewell, he tiptoed around the "Would you hire him again?" question. Nix replied that as a practice he didn't rehire employees who had quit. The Piedmont interviewer's written summary concluded, "Nothing really derogatory given on Richard. Sheriff Nix just stated that Richard needed to grow up."

Jewell now earned only $7.50 per hour. Despite the low pay, he was grateful to have a job in law enforcement, even if being a campus cop represented a significant step down. Eventually, he planned to work his way back up, hopeful someday to join the Georgia State Patrol where he could be on the road full-time making arrests and working accident scenes.

At Piedmont, Jewell adjusted to spending far more hours in an undemanding job. He patrolled the campus, handled a smattering of car break-ins, broke up arguments at college sporting events, and investigated the occasional Peeping Tom. But underage drinking soon put him at odds with many in the student body. Habersham was a dry county, and the school had a no-alcohol policy. When Jewell started aggressively enforcing the ban, even recruiting undergrad "informants," students began to complain to the administration about the prying, overzealous officer. Some took to taunting him, referring to Jewell as a wannabe cop or a rent-a-cop.

To overcome the friction, Jewell committed to building relationships within the Piedmont community. He began telling students, "I know y'all are going to drink. Don't do it on campus." Jewell invited undergrads interested in law enforcement for ride-alongs in his campus police car. He ate pizza and played Spades with graduate students in a dorm director's apartment. Jewell even got a boost from the school paper, *The Lion's Roar*, which wrote about him and McNair sharing a Habersham County Citizens of the Year award as part of the High Angle Rescue Team.

One day, Jewell spotted another opportunity to build his campus connections. The campus radio station, WRFP, was looking for deejays, so Jewell volunteered for a slot during his off hours. In his house by the river, Jewell packed up his collection of '80s and '90s rock CDs before each show, adding in a few '70s R&B albums for variety. At the station, the self-proclaimed "DJ Radar" interspersed his favorite songs with advertising messages. It was small-time radio, with the broadcast hardwired into the campus buildings and unavailable outside of Piedmont. But for Jewell, it fused his love for music and his ongoing desire to fit in.

All the while, the campus police officer continued to dream of working his way back into the ranks of "real" law enforcement. He convinced Piedmont to send him to additional training on firearms, high risk warrant service, and rescue techniques. Meanwhile, he began to use the nascent World Wide Web to improve his policing skills. In the school library, Jewell learned how to operate the Macintosh computer with its dial-up phone access. The array of free online law enforcement information was mind-boggling. As an added bonus, Jewell also discovered "chat rooms" that seemed to be filled with women. Unfortunately, his luck with developing an online love life matched that in the physical world. He had gone on plenty of first dates, though few progressed to a second.

Off campus, he kept in touch with his buddies from Habersham County, at times leaving boxes of Dunkin' Donuts on their doorsteps. During the O.J. Simpson trial, Jewell and law enforcement colleagues would meet out on the roads and review the day's events, including how badly the LAPD had messed up the evidence and the case.

Chief Martin regularly offered Jewell feedback. He liked his campus officer but had begun to wonder if Jewell could ever relax. This was just a college campus, Martin reminded him six months into the job. There was no need to write up reports "longer than some death summaries" for minor incidents. The chief told Jewell, "You love your job more, I think, than any other policeman I've ever worked with." Martin advised Jewell to add balance to his life.

But Jewell didn't let up, and his tendency for self-destruction emerged again. In late 1995, Jewell hurtled his Piedmont College–issued Ford Taurus patrol car through the nearby town of Cornelia. A local police officer clocked him going seventy-one miles per hour in a thirty-five zone. After the cop flicked on his blue lights, Jewell pulled into a convenience store and explained, "I was trying to get here before I ran out of gas." Despite the eye-rolling excuse, the officer decided not to issue Jewell a ticket. But he did file an incident report, which found its way to Chief Martin.

Other issues also had begun to raise the chief's blood pressure. Jewell, pining for his days as a road deputy, developed a troublesome habit of expanding his jurisdiction beyond the campus. Despite repeated cautions from Martin, Jewell routinely pulled over drivers on the streets of Demorest for what he termed "courtesy stops," issuing warnings or citations. He also monitored police radio traffic for opportunities to assist. The Demorest police wanted none of it and urged Martin to keep Jewell under control.

After Jewell pulled over one driver for a burned-out tail light, the man lodged a complaint with Demorest City Hall. This time, Martin summoned Jewell for a formal warning, reminding the campus officer what he already well knew: Anything outside campus remained the purview of the local police. Despite the chief's words, in May 1996, Jewell decided to set up another traffic stop in Demorest. Showing off to a student in his patrol car for a ride-along, Jewell pulled over three drivers, two for minor violations and one for a suspected DUI. The officer had finally gone too far. The Demorest police chief called Martin, who drafted a probation letter, then told Jewell he could accept the penalty or resign. He chose to quit. For the second time in less than a year, Richard Jewell lost his law enforcement job.

HIS LIFE IN TURMOIL, Jewell found his professional opportunities in North Georgia bleak after two forced resignations. He thought about trying to sign on with a department back in Atlanta, but after just a few calls to metro area squads, Jewell learned that no one was hiring until after the Olympics, now just two months away. Instead, they were focused on deploying their existing teams for Olympic security.

With law enforcement avenues closed and his mother, Bobi, about to have foot surgery, Jewell set his sights on the Olympics. The Centennial Games surely would bring a surge of temporary hiring, and the credential would look good on his résumé. He made plans to move to Atlanta.

Eleven days after Jewell's resignation from the college, he packed up his rental house. Brian McNair drove over to help, and wasn't surprised to see how much Jewell's house looked like the old Deathmobile. Random items were everywhere: hunting gear, bows and arrows, fly-fishing rods, waders, kitchen gadgets, whatever Jewell thought might come in handy. Clothing was haphazardly strewn about the rooms. The old broken-down Chevy Cavalier sat in the front yard, covered so thoroughly with leaves and moss that McNair had nicknamed it the Chia Pet.

The two men transferred some of Jewell's belongings to a storage bin in Cornelia, and others to McNair's house. The rest went with Jewell down to Bobi's apartment on Buford Highway. On June 1, unemployed and now thirty-three years old, Jewell moved back in with his mother.

JEWELL LOST NO TIME scouring the *Atlanta Journal-Constitution* classified ads for Olympics opportunities. Sitting in the depressingly familiar confines of his mother's Monaco Station apartment, he spent every day for over a week looking for the right job. After initially still holding out hope for an actual law enforcement position, Jewell found himself drawn to a Borg-Warner ad for temporary Elite Security officers. The corporate security firm was an Olympic sponsor. More importantly, at $8 an hour, it offered the highest pay, plus time and a half for overtime. If he could do this job through August, that would bridge him until police forces were ready to hire again.

Jewell sat down to fill out the Borg-Warner application. Immediately, the document highlighted the shortcomings that had come to define this juncture of his life. The "Address" line made him painfully aware he again was living with his mother. For weight, the metric that had so long plagued him, Jewell charitably scribbled his usual weight of 240 pounds. In truth, he knew he always added heft when depressed, which he certainly was. For height, Jewell ticked himself up to 5′9″, adding an inch to help even out his proportions. Under work history, when asked to provide reasons he had left jobs in the last five years, Jewell fudged. For his departure from the sheriff's department, he wrote, "Better Pay." For his latest resignation from the college, he simply entered, "Moved to Atlanta."

Jewell interviewed with a Captain Dawson, who was impressed enough to offer him a job on the spot. The captain asked if Jewell minded working Downtown. No, Jewell replied, though he often referred to Atlanta's high-crime urban core as "The Badlands." Could he work nights? Of course.

He would take any shift, including the graveyard hours he had been covering for six years. Finally, did he know where Centennial Park was? "Well no," Jewell replied, "but I can find it."

Before starting the job, Jewell needed to pass a final knowledge and skills assessment. He studied the 137-page ACOG-created handbook, *Securing the Safest Games Ever*. Most of the contents were straightforward, playing to Jewell's experience. Handling disorderly conduct, managing crowds, completing incident reports. One section, Observation Skills, fit Jewell's strengths as well. The advice, though, was almost Zen-like. "Study your surroundings. . . . Make mental notes. . . . When new or relocated things, sounds or items appear, you will know it."

On June 18, Jewell was well prepared for his assessment. He took the bag-check inspection test and found the glass container secreted inside. The tester reported that Jewell remained calm and showed courtesy throughout the process. On the personal inspection test, Jewell was asked to check a man's pants pocket. Jewell properly asked permission to wand him, then used the metal detector correctly and found a hidden coin. Jewell aced the multiple-choice written exam, scoring a ninety-seven.

Three days later, Richard Jewell began work as a security guard at Centennial Olympic Park. Construction was still under way at what would become the Olympics' most popular attraction. The Opening Ceremony, scheduled for July 19, 1996, was less than a month off.

CHAPTER 7

The *Atlanta Journal-Constitution* newsroom swelled in the weeks leading up to the Games. Writers, editors, and photographers from across the Cox nineteen-newspaper chain rushed into Atlanta in an all-hands effort for blanket Olympics coverage. The *Austin American-Statesman*, *Dayton Daily News*, *Palm Beach Post*, and *Waco Tribune-Herald* each sent journalists. Interns poured in for the summer. In all, the *AJC*'s team working on the Games now totaled a staggering 325.

The paper's Marietta Street offices, reconfigured to accommodate the expansion, buzzed with anticipation. The world was coming. One *AJC* piece noted that "on some days, the population density of the central city will far exceed that of Manhattan Island. Peachtree Street will become a swarming tree-lined promenade." Coverage slipped into breathlessness at times. One Metro section story pushed readers to stock up on coffee because Atlanta's "biggest party season ever" had arrived. "The *Gone with the Wind* premiere in 1939? The Democratic Convention in 1988? The Super Bowl in 1994? They'll all seem like a cul-de-sac Tupperware party in comparison."

Sixty-six staffers had been assigned to specialize in individual sports, then had spent more than a year learning the major players and strategies. For track and field, one huge story centered around Michael Johnson. The superstar sprinter had asked the International Olympic Committee if it would split the scheduling of the 200- and 400-meter races, putting them on different days so that he could avoid overlapping heats and compete in both. No man in the history of the World Championships or the Olympics ever had won both races. The IOC at first rejected his request, but later reversed itself. This would make for appointment television.

Thomas Oliver, now five years into his role as the *AJC*'s Olympics editor, had focused on putting his massive team of journalists into the right places. By mid-1996, months before the start of the Games, thick black binders called budget books held more than a hundred pre-written pieces on sports and athletes. Profiles of superstar swimmer Janet Evans and her upstart rival, a teddy-bear-hugging fourteen-year-old named Amanda Beard, waited in the books. The men's basketball team, featuring Shaquille O'Neal, Charles Barkley, and David Robinson, merited several "walk-ups," canned features that led readers up to the Games.

The *AJC* leaned on its veteran sports reporters for the marquee Olympic events—swimming, gymnastics, and track and field. They had been making themselves regulars at big amateur meets, writing about significant story lines. The paper's readers may not have cared much, but Oliver knew that the *AJC* needed to show each sport's governing body that it was the paper of record for the Games. Coverage of the newly recognized Olympic sports of beach volleyball, women's soccer, and mountain biking became as valued as articles on the Atlanta Hawks, Braves, or Falcons professional sports teams. Oliver even made sure that what he called "the weird sports" were covered. Legal affairs reporter Bill Rankin would cover table tennis. Investigative reporter Carrie Teegardin became an equestrian expert, while Kathy Scruggs's friend David Pendered learned the ins and outs of yachting. Each would be expected to write daily during the Games.

A year before the Olympics, the paper had begun running red graphic ribbons at the top of page 1 counting down to the Opening Ceremony. In its "365 Days to Go" issue, the *AJC* wrote, "For better or worse, all systems are go. Well, most of them, anyway. Any motorist who has tried navigating the city's obstacle course of traffic cones and bulldozers can tell you the construction of Olympic venues is going full throttle." A month out, the *AJC* launched a daily Olympic City special section. The news pages expanded. So did advertising, as local companies embraced Atlanta's excitement, even if the average resident was too distracted to think about shopping for a new car or bedroom suite.

ONE REPORTING TEAM REMAINED well outside the paper's center of energy. They called themselves the SNOT Pod, named after their distinctly nonsports coverage areas of Security, Neighborhoods, and Olympic Transportation.

Kathy Scruggs had been assigned to share the security beat in the SNOT Pod with Ron Martz. Editors intentionally set up what they called a "Lennon–McCartney pairing," creating a team with vastly different reporting styles and strengths. Scruggs covered local cops in her trademark frenetic way, working her sources late at night in bars and digging up copious amounts of inside information. She was so eager to run with what trusted sources disclosed to her that editors often had to slow her down until she got more corroborating details. Martz, on the federal security beat, was far more deliberate. He largely worked from the newsroom, earnestly calling sources on the phone. Then, he would cautiously prepare his articles.

A forty-nine-year-old native of Lancaster, Pennsylvania, the red-headed bespectacled Martz had enlisted in the Marines after high school. While the war raged in Vietnam, Martz was assigned to Marine Corps headquarters in Arlington, Virginia. He worked in the Casualty Section, writing letters to wives and mothers about the deaths of their soldiers in Southeast Asia. Often, he navigated through intensely painful phone conversations. After he was honorably discharged in 1968, Martz signed on with a newspaper in Fort Pierce, Florida, where he wrote obituaries, covered police activities, and crafted headlines. It was small-town journalism, but Martz loved the work.

By the time he and Scruggs connected at the *AJC*, Martz had been a reporter at the Atlanta paper for more than a decade, first in the sports department, then in news. Unlike the typical newspaper reporter, Martz was politically and socially conservative, quiet and studious. He had a passion for history, and spent his social time relaxing with his wife and three children at their suburban home.

In the eighth-floor newsroom, the two security reporters had adjacent cubicles. But during those infrequent hours Scruggs was in the newsroom, Martz often found her so distractingly loud that he picked up his reporters' notebooks and wandered to a vacant desk near the windows and away from her. With the Games nearing, Martz eyed Scruggs as a curiosity, always struck by her big hair, short skirts, and outsized personality. She was so unlike anyone else he knew.

SCRUGGS'S FLOW OF STORIES slowed somewhat before the Games. Thousands of extra security and military personnel were already in town, and violent crime had dropped. Her top-brass Atlanta Police Department sources were preoccupied with deploying their officers for the Olympics. Scruggs had rare time on her hands. Like many Atlantans eager for easy cash, she decided to rent out her two-bedroom condo in the Cross Creek complex in the northwest part of the city to visitors from China. She packed up her belongings and moved to suburban Dunwoody, settling in with her best friend and cousin, Bentley, and her family. The house was still close enough to downtown for Scruggs to frequent the epic parties that would be coming to Atlanta.

On July 4, in the "15 Days to Go" issue, Scruggs and colleague Melissa Turner wrote about a twenty-nine-year-old accountant charged with embezzling $60,000 in ACOG funds. He allegedly used the money to buy a used Mercedes-Benz and a certificate of deposit. Editors relegated the story to page E-7, the back of the paper. In a "13 Days to Go" piece, Martz reported on a stray bullet from an assault rifle that someone had fired into the air near the Olympic Village. As the shot returned to earth, it grazed a National Guardsman stationed at the Georgia Tech campus.

In the "9 Days to Go" edition, Martz noted for readers the repeated mantra of "Atlanta will be the safest place in the world this summer." ACOG security head Rathburn, APD Chief Harvard, and Atlanta Mayor Campbell all had begun using the phrase. "It sounds, at times, like a challenge to every terrorist group seeking an international stage for murder and mayhem," Martz wrote.

RICHARD JEWELL STOOD IN the center of Centennial Olympic Park on a blazing late afternoon in July, watching the flurry of workers racing to finish before crowds arrived in a few days. Music stages were slowly being constructed, sod rolled out, light posts anchored. Construction crews still needed to paint logos and install lighting.

Jewell had hit the jackpot with his assignment to AT&T's light and sound tower adjacent to the main stage. A week before the Opening Ceremony, nightly light shows already had begun. Concerts featuring Ray Charles and Tim McGraw were slated for the coming weeks. "This is the place to be," he told friends. It didn't hurt that the nearby Bud World beer pavilion had begun staffing up with attractive young women.

The details of the park fascinated Jewell. He once had told a friend he was "naturally nosy," and now he asked about many facets of the construction, even at times snapping photos. Pedestrian promenades ribboned through those formerly squalid city blocks Billy Payne had viewed from his balcony in 1993. One of Jewell's favorite elements was the Tribute to Olympia, a seventeen-foot-high and twenty-four-foot-wide fan-shaped bronze sculpture commissioned for the Games by an American Hellenic association. The design depicted three Olympians from distinct time periods in bas-relief. A runner from the eighth century BCE strode forward, giving way to an athlete from the first Modern Games in 1896 and, in turn, morphing into a female competitor in Atlanta.

As he walked the park, Jewell could see that the playful Fountain of Rings would become the most popular permanent feature. The 251 water jets in the shape of the five interlocking Olympic rings shot skyward randomly as high as thirty-five feet, sure to soak squealing children. The water would be illuminated by hundreds of red, white, and amber lights in sync with rotated songs: Yanni's "Santorini," Tchaikovsky's *1812 Overture*, Mannheim Steam-roller's "Fresh Aire Toccata," and Vangelis's "Chariots of Fire."

The day before the park opened, Jewell spotted an old colleague from Habersham County walking toward him. Tim Attaway was a special agent for the GBI, a thin man with a dark, slightly old-fashioned bouffant hairstyle. Several years earlier, Jewell had met Attaway at a murder scene that the agent was handling. They struck up a conversation that day and continued to run into each other every so often, once when they were both cutting marijuana plants as part of the area's Drug Task Force. Rural North Georgia was the kind of place where public safety officers got to know each other.

Jewell was thrilled that Attaway had been assigned to the park detail. Not only was Attaway a warm and welcoming face, but Jewell hoped the GBI agent would help him grow his law enforcement network. Already, Jewell had a plan to foster those relationships. Crews had scattered dark green benches through the park, including near the tower. So, Jewell slid one of the seven-slat benches to the quietest part of the tower's perimeter. Then he pulled over a cooler, dumped in some ice, and stuffed in cans of Coke and bottles of water and orange juice. He declared the space reserved for law enforcement to relax in the heavy humidity that seemingly always filled the park air.

Word began to spread that Jewell was a former law enforcement officer now working as a security guard—and that he had built a small sanctuary for a rest and a cold drink. Jewell's plan was working: As law enforcement settled in, he explained his readiness for his next policing job.

At one point, Attaway was walking the park with Tom Davis, his colleague and park supervisor from the GBI. They were discussing the positioning of security personnel when they saw Jewell waving. Attaway introduced Davis to Jewell as an old colleague from North Georgia, and the men sat down on the bench to chat. Davis was struck by Jewell's humble, friendly nature, even his candor. He decided he liked the portly guard.

Finally, the park opened on July 13. Jewell's hours filled with a combination of guarding the tower, directing visitors toward the restrooms, and reserving the space he had set aside for law enforcement. Dozens of times a night, he told someone, "I'm sorry that bench is reserved for police officers that walk around all day. We let them come and sit for a minute and drink a free Coke." By morning, his voice felt raspy.

Sound and light technicians had begun moving into the tower. Jewell noticed that they would sign their names on the stairs, then add the date and humorous messages. Many were roadies for bands and explained that the practice was designed for one crew to say hello to the team for the next show. When one of the men handed him a marker and pointed to an empty step, Jewell was thrilled. Spontaneously, he scrawled a quote from John Wayne, his favorite actor. The roadies laughed at his selection: "Life is tough, tougher if you are stupid." Jewell was delighted that his signature appeared on the steps leading into the tower, because if someone wanted to get in, "they had to get by me."

Television crews from NBC affiliates across the country arrived next, credentials dangling on lanyards. The guys from Los Angeles seemed particularly friendly. They, in turn, thought Jewell to be gregarious and helpful, except for the occasional visitor, or even tower employee, who left credentials behind. The guard was a stickler for security, routinely refusing to let in those without the proper Olympics ID. Color-coded wristbands changed daily for visitors without permanent badges, and he carefully kept track of those too.

Just before the Games started, Jewell's employer, Borg-Warner, was fired and Anthony Davis & Associates took over the security-guard responsibility for the park. The new company reassigned Jewell to guard a gate along the street. Jewell knew what that would mean: No more law enforcement rest stop, no more prime angles for concerts, no more Bud girls. Jewell fought hard against the move, telling Anthony Davis, the head of the Los Angeles-based company, "That's the only area in the whole place that's running smoothly." Jewell explained that he knew each tower employee by face and ID card. "If the rest of the people around here were doing that, you wouldn't have any problems at all." Jewell won the battle to stay at what he began to call "my tower."

Three days before the Opening Ceremony, the park hosted its first major event. Country music superstar Kenny Rogers headlined a free concert for sixty-five thousand people, and Jewell decided to use a perk of his job. He knew that Rogers was one of his mother's favorites, so he saved a spot for her to spread a blanket on the grass near the tower. Although he needed to work, he paused to bring Bobi water and take a photo with her. Mother and son alike could not have been happier as Rogers and his band cranked up their opening number, "Back in the High Life Again."

ON THE EVENING OF Wednesday, July 17, two days before the Opening Ceremony, TWA Flight 800 lifted off from New York's Kennedy Airport bound for Paris and then Rome. Excited families were heading to their European summer vacations.

For twelve minutes, the plane rose gradually over the Atlantic Ocean, reaching fifteen thousand feet. Then, as the aircraft settled into its course off the coast of Long Island, air-traffic control received an urgent call from the pilot of another midair plane: "We just saw an explosion up ahead of us here . . . about sixteen thousand feet or something like that. It just went down—to the water." As the captain would soon learn, he had just witnessed the fiery death of 230 passengers and crew aboard the 747.

The *AJC*'s headline the next morning bluntly asked the question the FBI was already investigating: "Was it a bomb?" Security at all Olympic venues and the Atlanta airport was on high alert. Ron Martz headed for the Olympic Village, where athletes were preparing for their festive march into Olympic Stadium the next day. He found competitors fully aware of the now almost-stifling level of protection. "It's really sad that sick, coward terrorists are forcing what is really the biggest and best sporting event in the world to have tighter security than some wars we've heard of," American beach volleyball player Karch Kiraly told Martz.

On that same morning, law enforcement officials gathered in Washington and Atlanta for what had become regular nine A.M. and five P.M.

check-in calls. FBI Director Louie Freeh, other key Bureau leaders, and Justice Department senior officials Jamie Gorelick and Merrick Garland were among those dialing in through SIOC, the strategic information and operations center on the fifth floor of the FBI's headquarters. Six hundred miles south, in the FBI's mirrored-glass Atlanta field office, Atlanta Bureau leaders gathered around a secure speakerphone in the conference room of the Olympics operation center. Just outside the eighth-floor room, the FBI Command Center sat darkened, to be used only for a critical incident officials hoped would never come.

TWA 800 was the lead topic for the morning's review. Several senior officials speculated that an act of terrorism had caused the horrific loss of life. It was America's second mass-casualty tragedy in three weeks. On June 25, a group of Hezbollah attackers in Dhahran, Saudi Arabia, had driven a truck filled with thousands of pounds of plastic explosives into the Khobar military complex. They parked in a lot adjacent to an eight-story apartment building that housed American service families, and detonated the mixture of petrol and explosive powder. The blast killed nineteen Air Force personnel, along with a Saudi local; more than four hundred coalition forces were injured. In response, the FBI hurriedly worked with Atlanta officials to secure an expressway off-ramp that emptied out directly adjacent to the Olympic Village.

With the Opening Ceremony scheduled for the next night, it became clearer than ever to law enforcement that no amount of preparation and drills could inoculate the seventeen-day event from danger.

AS JOLTING AS THE TWA 800 news had been, the tragedy was not top of mind for most fans. Kerri Strug and Dominique Dawes would anchor the American gymnastics squad. Mia Hamm and Brandi Chastain would take the field in women's soccer. Canadian sprinter Donovan Bailey aimed for a gold medal to embellish his standing, earned in time trials, as the world's fastest man. Long jumper Carl Lewis would be fighting to become only the third Olympian to win an event four times.

The *AJC* previewed those stories and offered esoterica about the athletes too. Readers learned that "beach volleyball player Holly McPeak did 1,200 to 1,500 stomach crunches a day." At the other end of the scale, "Chris

Humbert of the water polo team consumed 8,000 calories a day, usually starting out with a chocolate-doughnut breakfast and winding up at Taco Bell." Well-known non-athletes began to check into town, all chronicled in the paper's Peach Buzz column. Archbishop Desmond Tutu married a couple at All Saints' Episcopal Church. Actors John Goodman and Dan Aykroyd rode Harleys through the city. Hollywood darlings Demi Moore and Bruce Willis rented a house at the Country Club of the South. Peach Buzz reported that the family of a Georgia native and her New York real estate developer husband had dropped into town. "Marla Maples Trump and her daughter, Tiffany, 2, came home to Georgia." Donald Trump joined them in Atlanta a couple of days later, and the paper reported that he had dropped his heavy black wallet on the floor at the Cheesecake Factory. Walter Moseley, a fifteen-year-old from Florida, found and returned it. "The thanks he got? Donald (who was dining with wife, Marla) signed Moseley's own $20 bill."

ON THE EVE OF the Opening Ceremony, the Olympic Torch Relay finally reached the city of Atlanta. Massive crowds clogged streets in a round-the-clock celebration that included a pajama party hosted by one local bar. Another lounge owner saluted the torch with a flame of his own, igniting 151-proof rum in a shot glass. The crowds were so dense, often ten people deep and spilling into the street, that the torch's progress was delayed by hours.

The flame was scheduled to enter Olympic Stadium around midnight, at the end of the Opening Ceremony. But no one seemed to know the answer to the question posed so often by the media: Who would have the extraordinary honor of lighting "the Big Candle"? as one *AJC* writer called the Olympic Cauldron. Hometown favorites boxer Evander Holyfield and home-run king Hank Aaron were mentioned, as were former President Jimmy Carter and media mogul Ted Turner. The speculation would be settled soon. The 1996 Centennial Olympic Games were poised to begin.

CHAPTER 8

Just before ten A.M. on a steamy Opening Ceremony Day, a man carrying an empty briefcase stepped into a Wachovia Bank branch in Atlanta's northwest suburbs. Thirty-seven-year-old William Waye announced there was a bomb hidden somewhere in the bank and demanded access to the vault.

The teller nervously responded that the heavily fortified door was on a time lock and would require fifteen minutes to open. "I'll wait," replied the robber.

Slipping out of sight, the teller notified authorities. Almost immediately, over a dozen officers swarmed the bank and arrested Waye as he tried to escape out the back. Police then checked for an explosive device. There was none.

Waye had chosen precisely the wrong time and place to rob a bank. Atlanta was fortified with thousands of extra police. And many of them were stationed close to the Wachovia branch, which sat directly on the route of President Bill Clinton's motorcade from nearby Dobbins Air Force Base. The officers who grabbed him scarcely had to move.

BILL AND HILLARY CLINTON, along with their sixteen-year-old daughter, Chelsea, rode in the presidential limo to the seven-building Olympic Village complex now packed with more than ten thousand athletes and coaches.

The two new four-story dorms in the Village held the distinction of being the first in Olympic housing history with air-conditioning in every room. A massive dining hall served athletes from nearly two hundred countries a range of food from macaroni and cheese to kimchee. For entertainment, the Village boasted a video game center, laser tag, an aromatherapy spa, and live concerts by Ziggy Marley and Hootie & the Blowfish. Chapels were available for prayer by Christians, Hindus, Muslims, Buddhists, and Jews. By the day of the Opening Ceremony, the hair salon already had coiffed 1,600 heads, including at least twenty requests for fades with the Olympic rings styled in.

President Clinton wore a U.S. Olympics jacket on stage in the Village amphitheater, standing against a backdrop of dozens of former American gold medalists on risers. He spoke of the Olympic spirit, singling out athletes from both Koreas dining together in the Village. "I've been trying to get the North and South Koreans to talk together for four years, and I haven't done it," Clinton quipped. He closed his remarks with the hopes that the Opening Ceremony and the Games would be the greatest time of their lives.

JUST WEST OF CENTENNIAL Olympic Park stood the Georgia World Congress Center, three huge concrete and glass structures that served as one of the nation's largest convention centers. Now transformed into a major sporting venue, the facility was preparing to host judo, table tennis, fencing, handball, wrestling, and weightlifting.

Hours before the Opening Ceremony, personnel at the World Congress Center's UPS checkpoint did a routine scan of a box. They didn't like what they saw. The X-ray showed all the markings of an improvised explosive device, an IED. Every sports venue had an on-site diagnostics team. This one quickly sent the image to the Bureau's Bomb Management Center at Dobbins Air Force Base for a closer look.

At Dobbins, FBI Bomb Coordinator Don Haldimann studied the X-ray. Law enforcement had been through forty bomb threats and suspicious packages already, even before the Games started. This time, the elements were there—wire, power source, unidentified mass. The package likely contained a bomb. The FBI urgently moved to its "Render Safe Procedure," dispatching a response team for the twenty-minute drive downtown. There, they would decide whether to detonate the device in a containment box, send in a robot, or use another means to defuse the explosive.

Officials quickly shut down that part of the sprawling World Congress Center. The Dobbins team arrived and shot the box with a high-powered water gun. Their aim was true: Water traveling 2,900 feet per second—three times the speed of a .45 caliber bullet—turned the package into a safe mush. When the team examined the collapsed remains, it became clear that the weapon was a dummy device sent by Olympic-sponsor United Parcel Service to test its own security procedures. Haldimann called the UPS head of security to chastise the delivery company. The red-faced executive humbly apologized, explaining that the parcel had been misdirected. A brown UPS truck soon arrived at Dobbins filled with the company's Olympic swag for Haldimann and his team.

At seven P.M., an hour and a half before the Opening Ceremony, law enforcement confronted yet another issue. A man dressed as a security guard breezed past metal detectors at Olympic Stadium. He packed a .45 caliber gun loaded with eleven bullets. The imposter then took a seat in the arena where President Clinton and other world leaders would soon gather. He was discovered when the rightful ticketholder tried to sit. Police arrested the man, who quickly explained that he hadn't meant any harm. He just wanted to see the show. But for law enforcement, the breach was a deeply unsettling way to begin the Games.

THAT NIGHT, 3.5 BILLION people around the globe watched the Opening Ceremony. At the 85,000-seat open-air Olympic Stadium, a raucous crowd cheered on performances by Celine Dion and Gladys Knight, just two of the highlights of a five-hour spectacle. The show was both dazzling, with shadow versions of ancient Olympian athletes, and at times cringe-worthy, with clichéd silver pickup trucks and giant multicolored catfish. A choir during the Welcome to the South portion of the program sang "Hallelujah" and "When the Saints Come Marching In." Composer John Williams conducted an abridged version of his new piece, "Summon the Heroes."

In Centennial Olympic Park, tens of thousands sprawled across the lawns on blankets, newspapers, and cardboard boxes. With Richard Jewell viewing it all from his post at the tower, they took in the Opening Ceremony beamed live to the seventy-foot screen perched above the AT&T stage.

Just over an hour into the ceremony, as twilight dimmed to darkness, the parade of nations began, featuring three hours of brightly dressed athletes. From the stands, former mayor Andy Young felt a swell of emotion when the teams from Iran, Iraq, and Israel marched in together, precisely the hostility-free congeniality he had dreamed of nine years earlier when Billy Payne had arrived in his office.

Finally, the torch arrived, on the last leg of the ceremonial flame's three-month journey to Olympic Stadium. But who had been chosen to light the Olympic cauldron?

The drama built as hometown heavyweight boxing champion Evander Holyfield climbed a hidden staircase from a tunnel under the track. The flame made its first appearance at Olympic Stadium. Like every torchbearer that evening, Holyfield wore stark white track shorts and a T-shirt with a colorful vertical stripe of the Olympic quilt design. He ran part of the track alongside Greek sprinter Voula Patoulidou. The boxer then passed the flame to four-time swimming gold medalist Janet Evans, who ran a loop of the track before a standing, exuberant crowd. As Evans ran up a long ramp at the north end of the stadium, the anticipation rose.

On a platform near the top of the stadium, out of the shadows, stepped 1960 gold medalist and boxing legend Muhammad Ali. The crowd roared as the steady-handed Evans touched the Parkinson's-stricken Ali's quivering torch with her own. The fire slipped across. Ali stood for thirty-four seconds, holding the symbolic flame aloft as the audience cheered wildly, many choking back tears. Then, Ali, shaking visibly, turned to his right, leaned down, and laid the flame onto a thick wick attached to a cable. The fire slowly rose skyward, finally reaching the peak of the 116-foot-high cauldron.

In the stadium infield, athletes gawked and celebrated. Many hugged. Sprinter Michael Johnson high-fived with American basketball stars Charles Barkley and Shaquille O'Neal. The Games were under way.

ON SATURDAY MORNING, SPORTING events seized the spotlight. The U.S. baseball team took on Nicaragua at Atlanta–Fulton County Stadium. Preliminary rounds of gymnastics, fencing, women's volleyball, swimming, wrestling, and a half-dozen other sports filled venues across the city and state. As predicted, Centennial Park emerged as the communal centerpiece of the Games. More than a quarter-million visitors wandered in every day to drink Budweisers, swap collectible pins, sway to international bands, and learn about Dixie heritage at the Southern Exhibition.

Jewell showed up for each of his shifts at least thirty minutes before his six P.M. start time. Hour after hour, as he guarded the AT&T tower, Jewell was asked by tourists, "Where's the bathroom?" or "Where are the bricks?" He patiently answered visitors' questions, his replies always punctuated by the ma'am and sir that Bobi had long ago drilled into him. When a child cut his finger, Jewell summoned medical personnel. An *AJC* reporter followed

Jewell's friend, GBI Agent Tim Attaway, on a patrol through the park. Attaway handled no major incidents. "All in all, this is a good detail," Attaway told the reporter. "It's not life-threatening."

When he wasn't patrolling, Jewell sat in the white plastic chair near the tower entrance, his orange-colored cooler with a white top still overflowing with drinks for officers. He kept a watchful eye on the nightly parade of passersby, all manner of painted faces, drunks, pin-traders, souvenir-hunters. Jewell also took in headliners who played throughout the week: Faith Hill and Tim McGraw, Travis Tritt, the Brian Setzer Orchestra, even a couple of Elvis impersonators. Jewell regularly reached into his backpack for his camera, as he pulled aside any celebrity he could find. His photo collection began to grow. Singers Bonnie Raitt, Queen Latifah, and Emily Saliers of the Indigo Girls all paused to pose with him.

While Jewell was generally warm to parkgoers' needs, some visitors found him oddly protective of his turf. One night late in the week, a woman from the Atlanta suburb of Duluth felt ill. She and her companions looked for a place to sit and spotted a vacant bench behind the light and sound tower. As they approached, Jewell cut in front of them and sat on the bench himself. Looking up, he said, "I'm sorry, you cannot sit here." He explained that the bench was reserved for officers and directed them to other benches at the front of the tower. The group shook their heads and moved on.

Other security guards came by every couple of hours to give Jewell a relief break. Jewell always declined. He prided himself on an iron bladder trained during his years of overnight shifts in Habersham. Jewell's supervisor, Bob Ahring, an assistant police chief in a Kansas City, Missouri, suburb, thought it strange that Jewell never took a break. Instead, he encouraged Ahring to sit down and swap law enforcement war stories.

KATHY SCRUGGS TRIED TO engage in news coverage during the first week of the Games, but her work didn't much interest the editors. Homicides or other serious offenses in Atlanta had continued to drop with the unprecedented police presence. And crime simply couldn't compete with the energy of the largest sporting event in the history of the world.

A few days after the UPS bomb scare, Scruggs filed a short piece describing the incident, adding that the company's officials had called Governor Zell Miller and Billy Payne to apologize. Editors yawned and dropped it on page twenty-six of the Olympics Special section. In another piece, she wrote about an injured judo competitor's ambulance breaking down, turning the story into a question of whether there should be a backup medical transport. She penned another article about Atlanta's subway system hitting records for ridership. As Scruggs was fond of saying, "Boring."

ON TUESDAY EVENING, JULY 23, the Georgia Dome was electric. The women's gymnastics competition featured the Americans battling against the Russians. The USA was gunning for its first-ever team gold. Russia had dominated the sport for nearly five decades.

The Russians had come into the team competition with a slim lead. But the U.S. squad charged ahead late on the final day. With one apparatus left, the Americans had a seemingly commanding lead of 0.89 points and looked to be a lock for the top step of the podium. They almost could hear "The Star-Spangled Banner" playing. But then superstar vaulter Dominque Moceanu uncharacteristically fell once and, shockingly, a second time. Suddenly the Russians appeared to be on the cusp of a comeback victory.

Kerri Strug, considered to be the fourth-best vaulter on the American team, knew the U.S. hopes lay on her shoulders. Standing only 4'9", the eighteen-year-old Arizonan desperately tried to gather herself at the end of the runway. "My heart was beating like crazy, knowing that it was now up to me," she would later recall. But then she thought, *This is it, Kerri. You've done this vault a thousand times, so just go out and do it.*

The crowd stood, the drama rising. Strug readied herself, the diagonal American flag on her leotard rising and falling with her deep breath. She sprinted down the seventy-five-foot runway, flinging herself into a vault that included a handspring and a twisting dismount. She slipped on the landing, fell backward and sat down, both hands on the mat. Something in her left ankle had snapped. When her score was announced, a collective groan consumed the crowd. The gold medal appeared to be headed back to Russia.

Strug had one more vault to go, if she could handle the shooting pain in her ankle. Doctors would later diagnose two torn ligaments. She sat on the sideline with an ice pack, desperately trying to reduce the swelling. Coach Béla Károlyi screamed for her to fight through the pain: "We need it, we need it! Shake it out!" Strug gamely rose for her final attempt.

The crowd at the Dome appeared to inhale collectively as Strug approached the start of the runway again. Ace bandages encircled her ankle. Under her bowl-cut hairstyle, she took a cleansing intake of oxygen. From the floor exercise area, the Russian team stopped to watch. Strug raced down the runway, propelled off the springboard in a back handspring, then soared off the vault into two full midair rotations. She emerged from the spins with tremendous force, then somehow stuck the landing. Almost immediately, Strug held her left ankle upward like a flamingo. She held the pose for a beat and spun ninety degrees to her left to face the judges. Then she spun again and collapsed to her knees.

The crowd exploded. Strug clearly had won the competition for the Americans. Her score of 9.712 appeared almost to be a formality. The USA captured its first women's gymnastics team gold. The scene of Coach Károlyi carrying his injured star to the medal stand instantly became an iconic image of the Centennial Games.

In venues across the city, fans devoured a string of powerful sports moments. Another diminutive phenom, Turkey's 4'11" Naim Süleymanoğlu, won gold in the weightlifting competition, setting a record by clean and jerk lifting 419 pounds, nearly three times his body weight. He was nicknamed the Pocket Hercules. Russian wrestler Aleksandr Karelin, known for lifting his opponents in the air and throwing them, continued his undefeated streak in international matches, capturing the gold in the super heavyweight class for the third straight Olympics.

The U.S. men's basketball team sprinted through its first few games against Argentina, Angola, and Lithuania barely contested. The next competition, versus China, was expected to be much closer, featuring a battle between 7'1" Shaquille O'Neal and 6'11" teen sensation Wang Zhizhi. But the game was never close. With the score 89–41 midway through the second half, the arena staff tried to pump up the crowd with a piped-in Village People hit. Standing near the USA bench, forward Charles Barkley knew the game was so lopsided that he danced along with the crowd, twisting his arms into the letters Y-M-C-A.

AS THE FIRST WEEK drew toward a close, veteran Olympics journalists tucked away their swimming folders and yanked out new ones for track and field. At the *AJC*, editors moved through the black budget books, rolling out profiles on schedule. All was going as planned.

Inside the law enforcement operation, teams from Washington and Atlanta held their nine A.M. and five P.M. SIOC daily check-in calls. The first week brought no shortage of low-level crime. Some bubbas in central Georgia had gone "fishing" with dynamite. A boxer from Uganda had passed counterfeit bills at Wal-Mart, triggering a debate of "Do we jail him or send him home?" Five Armenian athletes had been arrested on charges of kicking down a prostitute's door after paying for services not rendered, while a Spanish athlete was booked for indecent exposure.

At ACOG, personnel had quietly turned down the magnetometers at the sports venues to lighter settings, trying to move the crushing crowds through more quickly. Law enforcement officials were stunned by the lax use of the equipment, with one fuming, "We wanted it to at least detect an AK-47." As had been anticipated, the Bomb Management Center was logging nearly a dozen bomb threats and suspicious packages warranting investigation each day. Fortunately, none was a real explosive.

More-troubling reports emerged as well, ratcheting up the pressure for law enforcement already suspicious that the TWA 800 tragedy involved a bomb. Most worrisome was a Sikh extremist based in Canada who appeared to be headed to Atlanta via tractor-trailer with plans to violently attack the Games. An extensive Justice Department Olympic threat assessment report underscored the reasons for concern. "Sikh cells have carried out bombings, assassinations, and kidnappings" outside India, the document warned. The extremist's most likely target, according to intel, was the India-Pakistan field hockey game on July 27, Day 8 of the Games. India and Pakistan were perennially hostile rivals in both sport and politics. Exacerbating matters, Vice President Al Gore would be in town, attending sporting events at nearby venues.

Throughout the week, top law enforcement officials closely monitored the Sikh threat. The FBI arranged to dramatically bulk up the number of security personnel at the venue. The day before the match, foreign language "ID teams" strolled the area listening for suspicious conversations. On match day, SWAT teams were put in place. But by the Friday SIOC call at five P.M., intel had changed. The Sikh extremist was heading to Seattle, not Atlanta. The SIOC call was unusually brief, finishing up before the 5:30 P.M. start of the India–Pakistan field hockey match, which would end in a 0–0 tie and with no major incidents. As quickly as the terrorism storm cloud had gathered, it dissipated completely.

In Atlanta, after the call ended, Woody Johnson went around the table in the eighth-floor conference room. Did anyone have anything more to report or add? Nope. No, boss. Nothing. Johnson said he would see everyone on Saturday morning. He closed the meeting with a few words of encouragement, harkening back to his days serving in the military and leading the Hostage Rescue Team: "Keep charging. Keep moving forward."

NEARLY EIGHT HOURS LATER, in Centennial Olympic Park, Richard Jewell stood near the gated entrance to his tower. He tensely watched a phalanx of state troopers strain to push back the drunk, dancing crowd to a twenty-five-foot perimeter. The olive-green knapsack, examined just minutes earlier by the bomb assessment team, leaned against a leg of one of the three benches facing the stage.

Almost a half hour had passed since Jewell had spotted the pack and he and Davis had unsuccessfully tried to find the owner. Jewell had cleared the tower. To his dismay, a couple of the tower staffers were perched on the benches waiting to get back in. Jewell barked at them, "No, I want y'all away until we find out what's going on. This is serious. Y'all get away."

Jewell had no doubt that a bomb was in the pack.

The bomb truck from Dobbins was still at least ten minutes away. The squad would pick up the bag with a robot, then place it into a "total containment vessel." The device could be either taken out of the park or destroyed on the spot.

Tens of thousands of revelers remained in the park, oblivious to the danger. Close to the tower, Alice Hawthorne posed as her daughter Fallon prepared to snap a photo. Up on the AT&T stage, the lead singer for Jack Mack and the Heart Attack prepared to roll into another song. "Are you still there?" he teased concertgoers. "Now we have a special treat for you." It was 1:20 A.M.

The explosion was deafening, like a cannon blast at close range. The concussive force flung full-sized men through the air. The ground and nearby buildings shook. Swimmer Janet Evans, answering a German TV interviewer's question across the park, felt the building rattle before she even heard a sound. The California-born swimmer grabbed the journalist's arm in a panic, thinking they were experiencing a major earthquake.

The flash was fiery orange. Whitish-gray smoke billowed skyward, the smell of gunpowder acrid and intense. Many in the park at first thought it was fireworks, part of the concert. Law enforcement knew otherwise. A bomb had detonated.

At first, complete silence surrounded the tower. Hundreds of people lay strewn about the park, while a confetti of wood, screws, and nails began to filter down through the thick smoke. Then, the lack of sound was replaced by screams, wails, and moans. Pandemonium broke out. Many people still able to move raced for the park exits. Others sprinted toward the injured. Everyone, it seemed, was yelling something. Sirens pierced the air as emergency units raced to the park.

One man collapsed with a sucking open chest wound. Another held his left hand aloft, his forefinger severed. A woman clutched her bloodied face, a buckle from the bomb's backpack having blasted into her jaw. A parkgoer standing fifty feet from the stage raced to aid a severely injured man lying prostrate, pieces of his skull spilled on the ground. His left ear appeared to be shorn off and he was clearly going into shock. The Samaritan removed his own shirt to stanch the man's bleeding and cried out desperately for help.

More than two dozen of the injured were law enforcement who had created the perimeter to protect the public. One young trooper gripped his own hand, the bomb having ripped a silver-dollar-size hole straight through it. Another had suffered a broken wrist, which hung limp below his upper arm pocked by metal fragments. GBI Agent Steve Blackwell had been blown ten feet through the air, likening the experience to a kid falling off a bicycle in slow motion. Shrapnel had grazed his neck, just missing his carotid artery, and two chunks of metal embedded in his leg, rendering him immobile.

Tom Davis had been blown to the ground by the blast too. Galvanized metal jutted out of his hip pocket, having flown directly into his badge and credentials. Holes from shrapnel dotted the sides of his loose-fitting mesh vest. But Davis quickly regained his composure, realizing he wasn't badly hurt. The agent waded into the chaos and checked quickly on a few of the injured. Then he spotted a black woman lying in pooling blood. Two bricks next to her were inscribed "Glory to God" and "Goodwill to all people." She appeared to be about 5'2" and was wearing a white T-shirt that read ALBANY STATE. Her body was riddled with shrapnel. Knee, hand, abdomen, chest, upper right eyelid. Davis bent down, placing three fingers to her neck. Feeling no pulse, he moved on. Alice Hawthorne was gone.

After checking another victim, Davis spotted Jewell on the west side of the tower outside the path of the blast's shrapnel, and went to him. Jewell had also been thrown to the ground, but he was unscathed. Davis, with the calm honed by sixteen years of homicide experience, instructed the security guard to write down descriptions of all the people he had seen in front of the tower before the blast. Jewell walked over to the Swatch pavilion, sat down, and recorded what he knew.

Dozens of ambulances lined up on the adjacent Techwood Drive. EMTs hurtled into the park, tending to the wounded. A paramedic yelled out, "If you are able to walk, please follow me. If you are able to walk, please follow me." The uninjured and most of the victims marched toward emergency care outside the park.

Forty-year-old Turkish television cameraman Melih Uzunyol raced toward the scene, his equipment in hand. Suddenly, his heart gave out, a massive coronary seizing his body. The husband and father of two collapsed to the ground and was pronounced dead soon after.

First responders were forced to evacuate the injured more quickly than medical protocol dictated because law enforcement feared there might be another hidden device. The park would be completely cleared of both the healthy and the 111 injured in only thirty-two minutes.

ON SATURDAY MORNING AROUND 1:15, ACOG Chief Operating Officer A.D. Frazier had just undressed, removed his horn-rimmed glasses, and slipped into his office sofa bed. He was working twenty-hour days, and the eleventh floor of the Inforum across the street from the park had become home. Frazier dozed off but soon felt a violent shake of the building's windows.

He leapt from bed, quickly slipping on his khakis and green Olympics golf shirt. He ran to his balcony barefoot and stared at the chaos and the emergency lights below. Bodies were strewn across the bricks of the park. His mind flashed to World War II movies with their vivid, brutal scenes of battle. Rattled, Frazier spun and hurried back inside his darkened office. He switched on the desk lamp and dialed Payne. "Billy, we've got a problem."

Frazier made several more calls. The Games would continue, he knew. Payne would make sure of that. But Frazier had worked six long years planning these Olympics. "Six fucking years," he would repeat long into the future. The '96 Games, and Atlanta, would forever be tarred by this act of terror.

Frazier took off his glasses, put his head in his hands, and wept.

PART 2

A HERO'S TURN

CHAPTER 9

At 1:35 A.M. on Saturday, July 27, 1996, NBC sportscaster Jim Lampley interrupted a taped feature. "We bring you back live to the International Broadcast Center in Atlanta right now—and the mood of our program changes dramatically at this moment because, quite apparently, the kind of incident which you hope will never take place at an Olympic Games has, in fact, taken place." Lampley and co-host Hannah Storm reported what little they knew about a blast in the park and casualties. For the moment, they declined to use the word "bomb," waiting for law enforcement to confirm.

Three journalists on loan to the *AJC* from other Cox publications had finished their work and were relaxing near the park, sipping beer and people watching. When they heard the explosion, they darted toward the scene. Ron Rollins, a copy editor from the *Dayton Daily News*, eventually shoved his way into the park, yelling, "Press, Press." Having nothing to take notes on, he picked up a small piece of paper from the ground. He turned it over and realized it was an empty medical gauze wrapper, stained with a drop of blood. He borrowed a pen from a nearby paramedic.

This was deadline journalism, driven by an adrenaline rush that turns reporters into news-gathering first responders. Rollins dispatched Perry Patrick, on loan from the *Daily Sentinel* of Grand Junction, Colorado. "Perry, run back to the paper now. Run! Run!" Rollins screamed. "This is your stop-the-press moment." Struggling with the humidity and a couple of beers in his gut, Patrick labored the five blocks to Marietta Street, where he arrived at the newsroom and blurted, "There's a bomb in the park." The skeleton team of journalists looked at him like he was crazy. Within a few minutes, a staffer telephoned Managing Editor John Walter at home. Walter ordered the print run stopped, then headed downtown. For the next fifteen minutes in the park, Rollins and another Dayton staffer, Patrick Rini, gleaned what they could from witnesses, now hiding their press badges from law enforcement so that they wouldn't be thrown out of the crime scene.

THE SECRET SEVEN GATHERED on Baker Street, two blocks from the park. More than a year of practice exercises had taught them that this initial meeting to manage the crisis had to be in person. A conference call wouldn't do. When Woody Johnson pulled up, several members had already arrived, including APD Chief Beverly Harvard and GBI Director Buddy Nix. The agency heads, now longtime teammates, quickly agreed on divisions of labor. APD patrolled the streets. Correctional officers ringed the crime scene. GBI agents continued to interview witnesses. The Secret Seven would work together on the investigation, but as earlier agreed, Woody Johnson and the FBI would lead it.

Johnson drew on an unflappability he'd developed spearheading emergency deployments of the Hostage Rescue Team during "oh shit moments," as he sometimes called them. On this night, after being awoken by a duty agent with news of the bombing, his first thought had been family and friends. The Johnsons were hosting thirteen houseguests for the Olympics, sprawled across beds, sofas, and sleeping bags. Many of them, including two of his sons and a daughter-in-law, had been out listening to music at the park. His wife, Kathy, went room to room to do a head count. All were accounted for.

Now, Johnson assumed his role as the Bureau's on-scene commander. Some of the steps were almost rote, after all the planning and field exercises. Set up a forward command post by the park. Call in the Evidence Response Team. Start paperwork for FBI-HQ to designate the case as a major investigation, a "Special" as they were called, to unlock virtually unlimited resources.

Other decisions were made on the fly. Johnson received a call from FBI Bomb Coordinator Don Haldimann, who was supervising the forensics probe inside the park. Haldimann reported that an overeager first responder with the Fulton County Fire Department had pulled a ladder truck too close to the scene. The vehicle's tires crunched over evidence, with nails, metal fragments, and other material embedding in the rubber. Haldimann ordered the truck impounded until the tires could later be rolled and the evidence removed. Soon after, Haldimann decided to postpone the search until daylight, wary of spoiling the crime scene in the middle of the night. More importantly, he shared others' fears that another explosive device lurked in the dark nooks of the park. "Secondary devices," as they were called, were rare in the United States, but caution dictated waiting.

CHAPTER 9

Special Agent in Charge Johnson soon learned there had been an anonymous 911 call just minutes before the blast, from a pay phone just up Baker Street outside the Days Inn. The caller had warned there was a bomb in the park.

TWENTY-FIVE MILES NORTHEAST OF the park, FBI Special Agent Don Johnson, no relation to the SAC, awoke to a call from the FBI Command Center. An agent briefly explained the bombing and the 911 call, and instructed Johnson to report to Atlanta headquarters. The agent dressed quickly and sped to the office.

Before the bombing, the fifty-year-old Johnson had been one of the few Atlanta FBI agents without a specific Olympic assignment, instead designated to a small team manning the office on regular duty. But this time, he was quickly sent back out to secure the area around the 911 phone booth. He jumped back in his car and headed for Baker Street. When he arrived, Atlanta police already had secured the area. So, Agent Johnson joined other officers in search of witnesses and potential suspects.

Law enforcement in and around the park began to collect early leads. A cluster of "Pakistani-looking" men were reportedly seen high-fiving outside the park. A drunken white male in a baseball cap had been looking through debris near a transformer and had given one witness an odd thumbs-up. Four males had suspiciously asked for directions to Interstate 85 in "foreign accents, possibly Russian," while a man in the back seat seemed to be hiding his face.

Agent Johnson interviewed an Atlanta police officer who had arrested a black male in his late twenties for making terroristic threats against the city's hotels. He also took the statement of an eyewitness who said he had watched another African American man in an overly formal business suit talking to a vendor, smoking cigarettes, and appearing "very nervous."

JEWELL READILY AGREED TO be interviewed four times during the early morning hours. He walked investigators through his routine of diligently checking security wristbands, the color of which changed each day. He explained how he had been at the tower the entire time, with the exception of a restroom break around 10:30, a few hours before the bomb exploded. He repeatedly related the story of spotting the backpack and pointing it out to Tom Davis.

Interviewers soon realized Jewell's memory for specifics was well honed. He drew an extensive map of the explosion scene, including an arrow highlighting "me at blast time." He recalled with great specificity the seven twenty-somethings from the Speedo tent who just after midnight had been shotgunning Budweisers from a green bag and throwing their empty cans over his fence. Jewell explained how the behavior of the young men had triggered his call to Tom Davis and, in turn, led to Jewell spotting the pack he thought they may have left behind. Jewell described one of the Speedo Boys as "well tanned and very muscular for his size and you could see the muscles in his abdomen." Another was 5'8", with a white sleeveless T-shirt, brown pants, sandals, dark complexion, dark hair. He detailed the others as well. "If I ever see them again in ten years—they're set in my mind."

Finally, Jewell described how he had watched the bomb techs examine the bag, moved back parkgoers, and cleared the tower. The explosion had knocked him to the grass, wood and metal debris falling around him, he explained. When he got up, Jewell told the investigators, he couldn't believe that several sound and light technicians were trying to reenter the tower to retrieve their keys and belongings. He had screamed at them, "Get out, get out, there might be another explosion."

THROUGH THE EARLY MORNING hours, the *AJC* team grew to nearly three dozen. The presses had been idle since just after the blast. Bert Roughton, Thomas Oliver, and John Walter all had arrived downtown to help manage the coverage. They needed to triage the latest editions of the Saturday morning and afternoon papers, which would soon be sold on newsstands and delivered to *AJC* subscribers. But they focused equally on the earliest Sunday edition, called the Bulldog, that was printed well before normal deadlines and trucked to distant parts of the state. Two days of papers needed to be significantly revised.

The pressure of having fifteen thousand journalists in the *AJC*'s backyard weighed like the moisture in Atlanta's summer air. Reporters from nearly every country on the planet were perfectly positioned next door to the park, at the International Broadcast Center in the Georgia World Congress Center. The German TV reporter who had been interviewing swimmer

Janet Evans had shared his tape with NBC, giving the host channel a jarring piece of on-the-spot footage. *AJC* editors watched the loop over and over on the newsroom screens. CNN, meanwhile, secured the camcorder video of a visitor from California who was serendipitously filming the concert when the blast happened.

Within an hour of the bombing, CNN.com, MSNBC.com, and USA-Today.com all had begun updating their sites on the budding World Wide Web. First came news and photos, then audio and video clips. The internet, once used largely as a chat room destination, was becoming a valued news purveyor.

Despite the immediacy of television and the internet, *AJC* editors believed they had significant advantages. Atlanta was their hometown. Years of establishing their relationships and bona fides with ACOG and local law enforcement should pay off. Editors ripped up the front page of what had been labeled the Final Edition. Rollins and Rini gathered their scribbled notes from the scrounged slips of paper and wrappers and cobbled together a fourteen-paragraph story on the carnage, noting that the explosion came from a backpack, and offering the perspectives of several victims. The headline read simply, PARK EXPLOSION.

AJC presses began to roll again at 3:30 A.M. It was raw journalism, fast, competitive, and sometimes flawed. The subhead read: 4 KILLED AS BLAST RIPS THROUGH OLYMPIC CROWD. They had no photo of the park, and left the earlier image of an unrelated traffic snarl. About an hour later, when editors realized that only Alice Hawthorne and Melih Uzunyol had died, they corrected the next edition. Soon after, the traffic jam photo was replaced with a color picture showing police and EMTs working the bomb site.

Editors also began removing anything in the paper now deemed to be inappropriate. Political cartoonist Mike Luckovich, who had pre-drawn his work for the weekend, had played off the Games' unpopular mascot, Izzy, for the Saturday paper. In one of his panels, kids pointed at O.J. Simpson, exclaiming, "It's the Olympic mascot—Killzy." Another critiqued the commercialism of the Games, featuring a woman in a cast holding a sign, SPRAINED MY ANKLE AT OLYMPIC PARK—AM AVAILABLE FOR ENDORSEMENTS. Luckovich asked for both to be pulled. Instead, he created an alternate, this time depicting gymnast Kerri Strug standing valiantly on the gold medal podium with her damaged leg in a cast labeled "Terrorism." In the caption, she said, "I couldn't let an injury stop me."

From the SNOT Pod, Ron Martz drew on his expertise for a piece explaining that the security team had long known that the park was vulnerable. "State law enforcement officials . . . knew that without metal detectors or X-ray machines at the entrances they could do little more than beef up patrols, cross their fingers and hope for the best," Martz wrote. And he reminded readers of the suddenly unfortunate earlier quote from ACOG Security Chief Bill Rathburn, "The Olympics are a sporting event, not a security event."

JUST FORTY MINUTES AFTER the blast, at two A.M. on that July 27 morning, members of the FBI's Behavioral Science Unit (BSU) were awakened to join the investigation. Who could have placed the bomb? What were the possible motives? The team raced to their underground offices in the FBI Academy at Quantico, meeting up at 3:15 A.M. to begin gathering information. The behavioralists pored over select investigative reports and listened to the 911 tape: "There is a bomb in Centennial Park. You have thirty minutes." The profilers were hard at work.

The BSU had emerged as a valuable arm of the FBI following a series of New York City bombings spanning the 1940s and the first half of the next decade. The "Mad Bomber," as the media called the unknown terrorist, had targeted Grand Central Terminal, the New York Public Library, and Radio City Music Hall. In 1956, desperate local detectives consulted a state Department of Mental Hygiene psychiatrist named James A. Brussel for assistance. Brussel studied the blast scene photos and jeering letters the bomber had sent to newspapers. He then devised a detailed "profile" describing the bomber's marital status, age, religion, Slavic heritage, and even manner of dress. "When you catch him, and I have no doubt you will, he'll be wearing a double-breasted suit," Brussel confidently told them. The jacket would be buttoned. Using the profile as a guide, authorities soon narrowed their search, then arrested George Metesky in his Connecticut home. When Metesky asked to change clothes before leaving for the station, he emerged from his bedroom wearing a double-breasted suit, with the jacket buttoned.

Brussel had essentially reversed the standard psychiatric practice of examining a patient to determine the basis of his or her conduct. Instead, he studied the conduct to determine an individual's identity.

Years later, Brussel tutored FBI Special Agent Howard Teten on his approach, and in the early 1970s, Teten established the Behavioral Science Unit. He and others had come to realize that each crime scene offered markers that helped to identify characteristics and, as importantly, the mindset of the perpetrator. The BSU members weren't psychiatrists or psychologists, but agents who focused on the why and how of criminal behavior. Central to the work was the BSU's national focus: While a local detective might see one multiple killing in a career, the Bureau's unit analyzed them all, year after year. Over time, the BSU amassed an impressive history of successes: Ted Bundy, Jeffrey Dahmer, Atlanta's Wayne Williams. BSU profiler Robert Ressler was credited with coining the term "serial killer."

By the 1996 Olympics, the BSU had fully entered pop culture. The profilers weren't shy about their successes, and the public was intrigued. Ressler wrote a book titled *Whoever Fights Monsters: My Twenty Years Tracking Serial Killers for the FBI*. Several years later, former FBI profiler John Douglas released *Mindhunter*, a bestseller that would later become a hit television series. Jodie Foster starred as Clarice Starling in the 1991 film *The Silence of the Lambs*, in which she played an FBI trainee assigned to interview the cannibalistic serial killer Hannibal Lecter by the chief of the BSU.

Some inside the Bureau questioned the value of behavioral analysis, writing it off as pop psychology. But in 1996 the unit had one very important backer: Director Louie Freeh. Still, there was little the BSU could do with the Olympic bombing 911 call in the early morning hours of the blast. The man on the line had simply threatened to detonate a bomb in thirty minutes, when in fact it exploded in twenty-two. There had been no credible call or message after the bombing taking credit for the act.

AS THE SUN ROSE behind dull gray clouds, the physical investigation cranked up at the twenty-one-acre crime scene. Rain fell throughout the morning. Agents sectioned the park and placed hundreds of small pink flags on wire stands over pieces of shrapnel, creating a scene that felt like a macabre putt-putt course. Next to the tower, a crater sat where the bomber had put the backpack. Clothing and bags lay scattered about, abandoned by visitors fleeing the park or left behind by the injured. Pieces of the bomb were found on the rooftop of the ten-story Inforum building just above A.D. Frazier's office and at an on-ramp to Interstate 75 at the opposite end of the park, some five hundred yards away.

On Baker Street, investigators pored over the phone booth that had been used for the 911 call. Agents crafted plaster casts of footprints around the base. They tented the phone bank and used a fume of super glue to hunt for fingerprints. They bagged a cup that sat atop the booth with a half-inch of beer, and catalogued Winston, Kool, and Newport cigarette butts scattered on the ground. Then, when evidence experts were satisfied, they packed up the phone booth itself, as well as one on each side, and flew them to the FBI's crime lab at Quantico.

Evidence collection in the park would continue until nightfall. Within two days, the ATF would craft a detailed first-take diagram of the explosive device. Agents estimated the IED had weighed forty pounds. Inside the FBI's command post, a team of officers from nearly a dozen agencies soon got confirmation that the bomb had been stuffed into a military-style ALICE pack, as Jewell had said. The components so far: metal pipes, large volt battery, 8d masonry nails, half-inch Allen screws, red and black copper wire, lots of duct tape, timing device. ATF and FBI ordnance experts determined that the pipe bomb was the largest of its kind in either agency's history.

All those present shared one overriding concern: Would there be another attack on the Olympics? They had to find the bomber.

CHAPTER 10

Kathy Scruggs had missed everything.

On Friday night, she had stayed up late partying with Bentley in the den of her cousin's home. The buddies smoked cigarettes, drank wine, and laughed about how their family put the "dys in dysfunctional." Scruggs left her pager in another room, then headed off to bed. She slept through her *AJC* bosses' repeated attempts to reach her.

Just after six A.M. on Saturday, Bentley's husband, Chuck, walked into the kitchen and flipped on the television. He bolted off to wake the two women. "There's been a bombing at Olympic Park."

Scruggs sprung from bed, grabbed her pager, and saw the multiple missed attempts by the paper to reach her. She sprinted out of the house, spewing profanities. By the time she steered her convertible onto the highway, she was five hours behind the story.

INSIDE LAW ENFORCEMENT, THE 911 call drew intense scrutiny. The call center was a source of pride for the Atlanta Police Department, a $38 million state-of-the-art system that already had logged 1.2 million incoming messages in the first seven months of the year.

At 12:46 A.M. on July 27, a female operator had received a call from a bank of thirty pay phones outside the north end of the park.

"Atlanta—nine—one—one," she said.

"Can you understand me?" the caller asked.

"Yah."

"We defy the order of the militia . . ." *Click.* The line went dead. The 911 operator had disconnected him.

Twelve minutes later, at 12:58 A.M., another call came into the emergency center, from a different set of pay phones outside a Days Inn two blocks away. This time, the man got directly to the point: "There is a bomb in Centennial Park. You have thirty minutes." He hung up. The call lasted thirteen seconds.

The 911 operator looked for the street address of the park to send a unit to investigate. Without the address, her computer would not relay a message to a dispatcher's computer. But the park was a state-controlled property and had required no city permitting, so the mapping software had no listing for Centennial Park. The street address was a mystery.

The operator called the Atlanta Command Center (ACC) run by the police department. Her call rolled to voicemail. She tried again, but this time the two parties could barely hear one another. On the third attempt, she reached an APD staffer, who replied, "I ain't got no address to Centennial Park. What y'all think I am?"

At 1:01 A.M., the operator called the Atlanta police Zone 5 dispatcher directly.

Dispatcher: Zone 5.
911 Operator: You know the address to Centennial Park?
Dispatcher: Girl, don't ask me to lie to you.
911 Operator: I tried to call ACC, but ain't nobody answering the phone . . . but I just got this man called talking about there's a bomb set to go off in thirty minutes in Centennial Park.
Dispatcher: Oh Lord, child. Uh, OK, wait a minute. Centennial Park, you put it in and it won't go in?
911 Operator: No, unless I'm spelling Centennial wrong. How are we spelling Centennial?
Dispatcher: C-E-N-T-E-N-N-I—how do you spell Centennial?
911 Operator: I'm spelling it right, it ain't taking.

The dogged 911 operator hung up and called the Atlanta Command Center again. Still no street address—"Ooh, it's going to be gone off by the time we find the address"—but they had a phone listing for Centennial Park. The operator persisted. She called the number and reached a sergeant on duty. "Sergeant Montgomery, do you know the address of Centennial Park? . . . 'cause, I mean I don't mean to upset nobody, but we got a bomb threat over there." He did know it: 145 International Boulevard. The operator plugged the address into her system, finally completing the first step required for APD dispatch.

CHAPTER 10

At 1:11 A.M., thirteen minutes after the 911 call came in, a dispatcher alerted area units to the bomb threat. One of the APD officers radioing back noted that state authorities control the park. Atlanta police units arrived at the Baker Street phone to investigate. At 1:19 A.M., Unit 1593 radioed in with a reminder to let state authorities know of the threat. Dispatch acknowledged, *I'm doing that now 1593.*

At 1:20 A.M., all units heard a more discomfiting message: "Be advised that something just blew up at Olympic Park."

When FBI leadership saw the transcript of the 911 exchanges, they could only shake their heads in disbelief. So many years of planning and practice. So much investment of time and money. Law enforcement was off to a poor start.

THE PARK REMAINED CLOSED to the public on Saturday as law enforcement searched the crime scene. The Fountain of Rings was turned off, flags were lowered to half-staff. With Atlanta's central square now shuttered, visitors downtown were unsure what to do. "The sidewalks teemed with deflated, pin-covered folks who looked as if they'd gotten lost on the way to a party," the *AJC* reported.

Meanwhile, the city nervously looked over its collective shoulder. Threats and suspicious packages seemed to be everywhere. Early Saturday, bomb squads swept all sixty Olympic venues and the Olympic Village. Officials discovered a suspicious device in the Olympic Stadium, where track and field events were scheduled to resume at 9:15 Saturday morning. They found another at the Georgia Dome, site of Olympic gymnastics and basketball. Neither turned out to be an explosive. Striking close to home for reporters, the Main Press Center at the Inforum received multiple bomb threats.

That afternoon, at Underground Atlanta, four blocks from the park, a vigilant visitor spotted an unattended duffel bag behind some shrubs. Inside was a heavy metal object. Police closed off both the mall and an adjacent MARTA station. Woody Johnson notified FBI headquarters. A Render Safe team rushed in to blast the bag with a water cannon. It turned out to be a clothing iron and some garments.

By day's end, Render Safe teams had been sent to over thirty-five locations.

The Bomb Management Center had long grown accustomed to a high volume of threats during the Games, with the Render Safe team deployed more than one hundred times. If the public had known the actual numbers, which would double over the next week, some may never have ventured back into an Olympic event. Most, though, remained undaunted after the blast. Ninety percent of ticketholders showed up on Saturday, barely flinching at stricter bag checks and tighter metal-detector settings.

Sporting events held to their usual schedule that morning, with delays only for periods of drenching rains. Still, the Games felt less festive. Just before the first track and field event at Olympic Stadium, an announcer requested that the crowd stand for a moment of silence "out of respect and sympathy for those who lost their lives in the tragic incident in Centennial Olympic Park." The diving competition, beach volleyball match, baseball game, and every other event that day held similar somber remembrances.

U.S. tennis team captain Andre Agassi offered blunt advice for law enforcement in its search for the bomber: "I think they should hang the guy by the nuts and execute him publicly if they catch him."

SCRUGGS HAD A SINGLE plan of action: Make up for her late start by working her law enforcement sources even harder than usual. Info came quickly. The medical examiner provided details that Alice Hawthorne died from "multiple penetrating injuries" and that Melih Uzunyol's fatal coronary was "precipitated by the explosion," resulting in his death being categorized as a homicide. Even before news about the 911 call was released, Atlanta police connections helped Scruggs learn that authorities had received the bomber's warning before the bomb exploded, but too close to the time of the blast for the area to be evacuated. The voice on the emergency line sounded "like that of a white male." The caller did not identify himself as a member of any terrorist group. Scruggs and six other *AJC* reporters joined forces for a piece that anchored the afternoon front page of the July 27 Olympics Edition.

Scruggs then helped generate a second story. Together with Martz, she hastily cobbled together an article about the possible perpetrator: "The hunt for the Centennial Olympic Park bomber is likely to focus initially on home-grown terrorists or what police officials and security experts refer to as a 'random nut case.'" Current and former law enforcement officials believed the bomber might have militia connections, the reporters wrote.

After filing the pieces, Scruggs jumped back on the phone to dig for more, her roughened Southern drawl instantly recognizable to the police on the other end.

AT TWO P.M., THE FBI opened a hotline for tips from the public. "We would appeal to anyone who might have been taking pictures in the park from ten P.M. until such time as the device went off," Woody Johnson requested at his third press briefing in the twelve hours since the blast. "If you would call in, we would greatly appreciate it."

Almost instantly, the Bureau was swamped with hundreds of tips. Some seemed ludicrous. One caller voiced concern about cross-dressing Ivan the Aryan, who frequented a kinky Atlanta nightspot with women in cages and men on leashes. Other reports had more potential. An Iranian man who had been fired by AT&T was livid about his dismissal, and there was suspicion he could be tied to Islamic revolutionaries. A stage hand with Jack Mack and the Heart Attack allegedly learned of the bomb five minutes before the lead singer had announced "a special treat" for the crowd. A white male in a diner had repeated "It's over, it's over," shortly before the explosion. A former teacher of one of the Speedo Boys called from Maryland to say the young man "had a history of causing trouble."

Dozens of agents continued to collect physical evidence at the shuttered park. Others headed for local hospitals to bag shrapnel extracted from patients' bodies. The FBI insisted that many patients go home in hospital gowns so the Bureau could keep their clothes as additional evidence.

Special Agent Pete McFarlane drew the darkest assignment—observing the autopsy of forty-four-year-old Alice Hawthorne. He photographed and documented her wounds in excruciating detail for later use at trial. He collected the chunks of metal removed from her body, placing them in separate plastic cups: a section of threaded pipe that had entered Hawthorne's chest; a masonry nail that had pierced her brain; another nail that had lodged into her pelvis, with a bit of duct tape attached.

Saturday afternoon, the FBI continued looking into the Speedo Boys who Jewell had described in detail, including them on a mounting list of potential suspects. But the Bureau already had narrowed its focus to one leading contender: a man named Derrick Overstreet.

Witnesses at Centennial Park had described seeing a black Nissan Maxima fleeing the scene. One caught a glimpse of an Alabama license plate. FBI agents in Birmingham quickly learned that a man identifying himself as Overstreet recently had rented the same make and model. They connected the information with a call to the Bureau the week before from a teacher. She had said that a student's boyfriend named Derrick Overstreet had reportedly threatened to blow up the Olympics. The first name in the car-rental records was Trent, not Derrick, but criminals often used partial aliases.

Intelligence indicated that Overstreet had solid militia ties, formerly with the Gadsden Minutemen and currently with the Eastern Diamondback Militia. In addition, law enforcement had developed composite sketches of two suspicious men seen near the tower before the blast. One looked a lot like Derrick Overstreet. Agents fanned out to investigate Overstreet's possible involvement in the Olympic bombing. In one promising development, Georgia militia leaders announced they would be holding a news conference late the next morning in Macon, eighty-four miles southeast of Atlanta. Special Agent Don Johnson was sent to Macon to surveil the event and collect photos and records.

Mid-Sunday morning, Johnson climbed into his Bureau car. The twenty-one-year FBI veteran hadn't come to Atlanta by choice. His career, once quite promising, had not gone as planned. But now Johnson was working on the nation's highest-profile investigation. He had a chance to become part of law enforcement history.

AS A KID IN Gloversville, New York, Don Johnson had moxie. He had swagger, charisma, athleticism. People could tell the boy was going places. Every afternoon, Butch, as his family called him, delivered the *Leader-Herald* newspaper in the idyllic Upstate New York town of twenty-three thousand. Gloversville, nestled in the rolling hills of the Adirondacks, for decades had dominated the tanning industry, producing 90 percent of the gloves made in the United States. It was the late 1950s, and the *Leader-Herald* swelled with ads.

Johnson would roll 130 papers tightly and tote them four blocks east from his Pearl Street home to affluent Kingsboro Avenue. He had angled for that route, aware that wealthy customers routinely rounded up the weekly subscription price of forty-two cents, handing him two quarters. The route also allowed him to walk along and gawk at their spacious homes, dreaming of his own future.

Born on Valentine's Day in 1946, Donald H. Johnson was the second of five children in a strict Catholic family. In grade school, Johnson was chosen as football quarterback, class president, and head of the safety patrol. By high school, he was popular with girls and a lithe dancer at the weekend sock hops. He was named co-captain of the varsity basketball team. Johnson's social set was in the grade ahead, and he soon learned to enjoy cigarettes and Blatz beer. In the evenings, when he went to pick up dates, he schmoozed their dads by saying that his father was Howard Johnson, wryly adding, "Not *that* Howard Johnson," of hotel fame. The line always got a laugh. In fact, the elder Johnson was a blue-collar worker at the nearby General Electric plant.

Johnson's first try at college derailed despite his good head for numbers. Access to unlimited parties and free-flowing beer proved too seductive at the Rochester Institute of Technology. So, in 1966, Johnson was sent to the Army by his World War II vet father. At twenty years old, Don Johnson found himself in Vietnam for noncombat duty as an accounting specialist.

During his two and a half years in Southeast Asia, Johnson stayed particularly close with his sister, Patti. He wrote often, usually trying to keep his letters light, offering news about skin diving and spearing blowfish. Before leave in Bangkok, he teased her with a barely cloaked reference to his fondness for women: "Three guesses what I plan on doing first, your first two guesses don't count." Then, late in his tour of duty, Johnson met a local girl named Sweet and fell in love. He bought her a diamond ring, and they were engaged. But when Johnson returned to Upstate New York following an honorable discharge, his mother, Marion, would have no part of the marriage. Johnson broke it off. Sweet mailed back the ring.

Stateside, Johnson turned to building his life. He got a job in the finance department of the Mohasco carpet plant in nearby Amsterdam, New York. One day he eyed a pretty young secretary of Italian American descent named Cynthia Gerardi, and after a short courtship, he proposed. Don and Cynthia married in 1970 and soon began a family with the birth of their son, Don II.

The ambitious Johnson changed companies and took a heavy load of college night classes while still working full-time. In 1974, on the cusp of graduation from Siena College and with Cynthia again pregnant, he longed for more stability and opportunity. Serendipity struck in the form of the Federal Bureau of Investigation.

J. Edgar Hoover was looking to upgrade the Bureau by hiring former military officers with undergraduate degrees in banking or finance. Johnson fit the bill. At the end of June 1975, Johnson left Cynthia at home with Don II and their newborn son, Greg, for the eighteen-week basic agent FBI training academy at Quantico. His first assignment was in the New Haven office, where he worked standard general crimes, including bank robberies, stolen vehicles, and theft of government property. Like every rookie, he also performed mind-numbing hours of federal-applicant background checks.

Johnson's career soon took off, first with the organized crime section infiltrating the Teamsters Union in Newark, New Jersey, then as a full-time white-collar crime agent in the epicenter of the world's financial markets, Manhattan. He and Cynthia moved the family to the bedroom community of Wappinger Falls, New York, ninety minutes north of the City. At work, Johnson took particular pride tracking down leads in some of the biggest investigations of the day, the "Specials." He assisted in the probes of President Carter's chief of staff, Hamilton Jordan; President Reagan's national security advisor, Richard V. Allen; and the Manhattan targets of ABSCAM, the wide-ranging sting operation that ultimately netted convictions of seven members of Congress.

Supervisors recognized Johnson's knack not only for achieving results but for "bullshitting." Most considered the designation a compliment. They reassigned him to the New Rochelle office to work undercover. Assuming a criminal's persona is among the most challenging and prized in law enforcement, demanding intelligence, wit, and split-second decision making. The 5'10", 185-pound Johnson excelled, working multiple cases to conviction. In one 1983 trial, involving over $450,000 of stolen securities, the jury convicted the defendant on eleven counts of wire fraud, conspiracy, and interstate transport. When the man appealed, U.S. Attorney Rudolph Giuliani filed a forty-page response defending the conviction. The document named Johnson so many times that a colleague sent him the brief with a note calling it "the Donald Johnson undercover agent's story."

During Johnson's extensive travel and nights away, he would frequent bars. At times, he also strayed from his marital vows. But Johnson remained committed to his boys and married to Cynthia. The Johnsons regularly hosted barbecues for neighbors, and the agent fancied himself as a grill master and chef. He spent those evenings lighting up Old Gold cigarettes, drinking beers, and shooting the breeze with friends on the patio.

A Scout leader for his sons, he took their troops camping, often delivering earnest counsel: "Don't be the jerk in the bar"; "Be an optimizer, not a maximizer"; "Be more Lou Gehrig than Babe Ruth." In other words, emulate the humbler Yankee star instead of his flashier teammate. At one football game, Don II ran for a touchdown, then yanked off his helmet and peacocked in the end zone while opposing players looked on. Fans cheered, but Johnson seethed. After the game, he laced into his son: "What is wrong with you? You don't have to show off." Then he added a single word of advice: "Sportsmanship."

Johnson's life came crashing down in 1984.

On the Thursday after July 4, the thirty-seven-year-old left the house around eight A.M., driving his Bureau car toward an interview for a case. He stopped for coffee, then climbed back in the gray Ford LTD, leaving his seat belt unbuckled. Johnson headed west on Interstate 84.

Doris McCallum was driving her red 1977 Mercury Comet in the opposite direction on I-84 when she suffered a stroke, slumping forward onto the steering wheel. The seventy-three-year-old's car careened across the fifty-foot-wide median, then went airborne as it crossed the divider and smashed into Johnson's car head-on.

McCallum and her dog both were pronounced dead at the scene. Johnson was thrown from his vehicle. His left hand, nose, ribs, and sternum were broken. He was briefly knocked unconscious. Blood ran from his face, body, and limbs. After he was rushed to a nearby hospital, he complained of severe chest pains, headaches, and dizziness. His peripheral vision was gone.

Johnson's recovery was slow. His face remained partially paralyzed, a condition that would leave him with a permanent and slightly Cagneyesque snarl to his speech. Financial problems layered onto the physical ones. The FBI allotted only forty-five days of "traumatic pay," then the family went without his income for three months. Neighbors brought food, but the Johnsons soon ran out of money. Desperate, Johnson cashed in his and Cynthia's life insurance policies to cover bills and living expenses. Workers' compensation payments arrived in October but soon expired again.

Six months after the accident, Johnson returned to work on limited-duty status, declining an opportunity to leave the FBI with full disability. He had lost 33 percent of the use of his left hand, 28 percent of his left eye, and 16 percent of his right eye. He could no longer shoot a gun left-handed, nor run well or move easily. As a result, the Bureau had to restrict his role. When asked how work was going, Johnson tartly replied, "My assignments are relegated to crap." At home, sports and Scouting with his sons were out. He tried a camping trip, but his chest seized in the cold and he returned home after just one night.

But there was at least one upside. Shortly after returning to work, Johnson put in a request for his OP, or office of preference. He was granted a transfer to Albany, New York, the closest major city to his hometown of Gloversville and near Cynthia's family. On the surface, life in Albany was good, thanks in part to settlement money from the accident. He bought a red Porsche 911 hardtop, although the flashy vehicle raised eyebrows at his government office. On summer weekends, he took the family to Lake George and loaded them into his new twenty-six-foot Larson inboard motorboat. He loved the boat, complete with galley, two bunks, and maroon trim.

Yet, Johnson had changed. For many, a near-death experience brings a gentler perspective on life. But Johnson's appeared to make him more cantankerous. In the Albany FBI office, as secondhand smoke was being recognized as a public health issue, supervisors instituted a cigarette ban until five P.M. Johnson would wait until the clock struck five, then reach into his drawer for his ashtray. As he puffed away, nonsmoking agents glared.

Johnson anchored himself to the Albany office by aligning with the No. 2, Assistant Special Agent in Charge Bill McDermott. Johnson became the public corruption coordinator, reporting to McDermott, and in September 1986 he stepped into the office's highest-profile case.

Albany Mayor Thomas Whalen III had insisted on maintaining his law firm partnership while serving the city. But an informant working in Whelan's firm told the FBI that the mayor was receiving kickbacks from the firm and city contractors. Johnson and the Albany office leadership launched a major investigation, subpoenaing waves of documents and interviewing well over a hundred witnesses. The media pounced. An *Albany Times Union* political cartoonist published a series of frames depicting Whalen, his firm, and the city's ethics commission as corrupt. Johnson kept three of them at his desk.

The investigation continued for nearly a year, with the local U.S. Attorney, Frederick Scullin, and his senior team following the evidence closely. But the prosecutors grew skeptical there was a provable crime, and appeared to be on the verge of declining the case. Many in the Albany FBI office disagreed with the assessment, chief among them an incensed Don Johnson. The agent prepared a blistering report that not only laid out the evidence he believed proved the case but also accused the prosecutors of having a cozy relationship with the mayor. Johnson singled out U.S. Attorney Scullin.

Scullin fired back in a letter to the Albany SAC, and attached a dense refutation prepared by his office rejecting each of Johnson's suggestions of prosecutorial misconduct. In turn, Johnson churned out an even lengthier document defending what he had written. ASAC McDermott chimed in with a memo in support of his agent.

Several months later, Scullin officially declined to prosecute Whalen. Johnson became persona non grata with the Albany U.S. Attorney's Office.

For a couple of years, McDermott assigned Johnson to matters that didn't involve working directly with the Albany U.S. Attorney's Office. He found Johnson skillful, especially in the nightmarish case of Aliza May Bush, a cherubic girl seventeen days shy of her second birthday. On February 2, 1990, at eight A.M., her mother, Christine Lane, called the Tompkins County Sheriff's Department in a panic to report that Aliza was missing. The front door of their apartment in the town of Lansing, outside Ithaca, had been ajar. Lane had found a single pink mitten at the edge of the driveway.

The sheriff's department suspected kidnapping. As a precaution, authorities administered a lie detector test to Lane, her current boyfriend, and Aliza's father. All three passed. For four days, police and hundreds of community volunteers scoured the nearby woods and fields. "Missing" posters with images of Aliza popped up everywhere. As snow fell, the searchers found nothing. Lane pleaded for the return of her baby.

On the fifth day, the mother received Aliza's other mitten in the mail. Maddeningly, there was no return address, no ransom note. By now, the story had become national news, and ten days after Lane's first call to the sheriff's office, the FBI joined the investigation. One hundred seventy miles south, ASAC McDermott gathered five top Albany agents and headed for Lansing. Don Johnson was among them. They reviewed leads from across the country, but the FBI soon began to refocus on Lane, the mother. A clerk in the general store had seen her drop a package in a mailbox the day before she received the mitten in the mail. Small inconsistencies in her account of the events emerged.

Lane had no car, so the Bureau examined bus and cab records. There was one taxi match in the area. Johnson went off to question the driver at the company office. In front of his boss, the man told Johnson that he hadn't taken a fare at Lane's apartment that night. Johnson left empty-handed, but the interview nagged at him. The cabbie had lied, he theorized to McDermott, adding, "I think we made a mistake by going into the office and having him called in." Johnson explained he thought the driver may have picked up Lane as an off-meter fare, pocketing the money. If Johnson's hunch was right, he wouldn't want the taxi company to know. The man needed to be reinterviewed alone.

Johnson circled back to the driver that night. This time, the cabbie came clean. He had picked up a woman at 11:30 P.M. on February 1 with his meter off. She was carrying a green laundry bag and explained that she was heading to her mother's house to wash clothes. Johnson showed him Lane's photo. The driver was "70/30" sure she was his rider. He gave Johnson the street address of the house.

Johnson's report cemented McDermott's belief that Lane had been lying all along. Using a ruse, McDermott invited her to meet at a local hotel for a "public relations" meeting. Instead, a Bureau polygrapher administered a second test to Lane. This time she failed. Then she buckled. Lane said she had found the girl dead in her crib, suffocated by her blankets. She had panicked, choosing not to call an ambulance. Lane agreed to take the agents to Aliza's body.

Lane directed the caravan to a house less than a mile from her apartment, the exact address the cabbie had provided. Johnson was smoldering. Lane led the officers a quarter mile into a field behind the home on the bitterly cold night, their feet crunching through the snow. Finally, she stopped and pointed to a pile of branches and other debris. Agents foraged through the mound and discovered a green plastic garbage bag, which the cabbie had mistaken for a laundry bag. They opened it. Inside lay Aliza's frozen body, dressed in a pink winter coat and resembling a porcelain doll.

Johnson thought of his own children and snapped. "What the fuck is the matter with you, lady?" he screamed. "Give the kid away! Give the kid away!" McDermott feared Johnson was about to hit the woman. "Don, go," he ordered. "Get back in the car."

Prosecutors didn't believe Lane's story about the child dying on her own. The jury convicted her of manslaughter, and she began a lengthy prison term.

In 1991, McDermott took a job at FBI headquarters. A new ASAC stepped in, with a face all too familiar to Johnson. Bill Imfeld had been Johnson's roommate at the Academy in Quantico twenty years earlier. One night they drove to the Globe and Laurel bar, a favorite Bureau haunt. They would come away with very different recollections of the evening. Johnson later claimed he left Imfeld at the bar because the fellow recruit was involved in what ultimately turned out to be "an unsuccessful indiscretion." Imfeld claimed it was Johnson who was engaged in impropriety. Whatever happened that night, Imfeld ended up walking five and a half miles back to the Academy. Their relationship never recovered.

Prior to Imfeld's arrival as ASAC, Johnson already had seen his workload lessen considerably in the wake of the Whalen investigation. But McDermott always found avenues for Johnson's talents. By contrast, Johnson soon felt that Imfeld wanted him out of Albany. Work became untenable for an agent who had always prided himself on being aggressive. Johnson couldn't take it anymore.

In the fall of 1993, Johnson gathered his family and announced they had the option to move to Atlanta. Cynthia pushed back, hoping to stay close to family in Upstate New York. But Johnson pressed. He explained to the only son still living at home, his high school junior, Brian, that there were opportunities in Atlanta, which would be hosting the Super Bowl in 1994 and the Olympics in 1996. The forty-seven-year-old Johnson never mentioned how unusual it was for an experienced agent to leave his office of preference so late in a career.

WHEN HE MOVED SOUTH, Johnson was assigned to the 7 Squad. The FBI violent crimes unit was filled with what a female instructor at Quantico dubbed "the Atlanta hunks." From the start, Johnson recognized he was an outlier on the team responsible for handling fugitives and bank robberies. Nicknamed "Dapper Don," he continued to dress in dark suits, pressed shirts, and tasteful ties while most others on the squad favored chinos and open-collar shirts. Johnson smoked more than a pack of cigarettes a day and bypassed the early morning weightlifting sessions in the FBI's gym.

Johnson was well aware he had taken a professional step backward. But the transfer had allowed the Johnson family to move to a suburb outside Atlanta called Duluth. He and Cynthia bought a much larger house than they had in Albany. Johnson also had the good fortune to be assigned a fellow Upstate New Yorker, Harry Grogan, as his partner. They had much in common, including having played basketball against one another in high school.

The fifty-two-year-old soft-spoken Grogan was happy to play the support role, and the partners' well-orchestrated tactics bore success. After they arrested a bank robbery suspect, Grogan would drive silently while Johnson sat beside the alleged perpetrator in the back. Johnson would begin the conversation with small talk, searching for common ground—"Do you like the Atlanta Hawks?" or "You got a girlfriend?"—then deftly pivot to the crime. At one point, Johnson and Grogan proudly tallied their streak at twenty confessions in twenty-one interviews.

But one Atlanta case more than any other demonstrated that Johnson was back in form. Three days before Christmas 1994, prison guard D'Antonio Washington was found on the floor of Cell Block C of the Atlanta Federal Penitentiary with his skull smashed in. Anthony Battle, an inmate serving a life sentence for sexually assaulting and murdering his wife, stood nearby in a blood-spattered prison uniform. The guard was rushed to the hospital, but there was nothing doctors could do.

Johnson was among the agents assigned to investigate the attack. He was well aware of the dangerous reputation of the Atlanta Pen, which had once housed mobsters Al Capone and Whitey Bulger. In 1987, the hulking McKinley-era facility had been home to the longest siege in U.S. prison history, a tense eleven-day standoff after a riot by Cuban Marielito refugees who feared being repatriated. Since then, the Pen had remained a violent place. Guards who monitored the 2,800 prisoners were three times more likely than their peers nationwide to be attacked by an inmate.

The FBI's investigative strategy in the death of D'Antonio Washington was straightforward: Gather information from any witnesses among the 180 prisoners in Cell Block C, then interview Battle, the suspected murderer. Johnson was assigned interviews with imprisoned bank robbers, a kidnapper, and a drug "mule." Each claimed to have been sleeping at 8:30 A.M., when the attack occurred.

Finally, Johnson was picked to lead the Battle interview, partnering with GBI Agent Michael McGinniss. The stakes were high. The death penalty would be in order, but without a confession, a conviction was far from certain. And other inmates would feel more empowered to handle their own grievances more violently.

The thirty-five-year-old Battle was escorted in to meet Johnson and McGinniss wearing leg irons, a waist restraint, and handcuffs. The room was windowless, with only a desk and chairs. Johnson asked the half-dozen guards who had delivered the inmate to leave, saying the interview was "strictly between us and Mr. Battle."

Johnson opened by presenting Battle with an FBI form FD-395 to sign. The document included the Miranda rights and a waiver. In 1966, the U.S. Supreme Court had made the rights the law of the land when it threw out the rape and kidnapping conviction of day laborer Ernesto Miranda. Arizona detectives had interrogated Miranda without a lawyer present while he was in custody. The court effectively defined custody as not being free to leave. Under the Sixth Amendment, if a citizen is in custody, that person has the right to counsel unless he or she waives the right.

There was no question that Battle, a federal inmate, was in custody. So, at the outset of the interview, Johnson recited the FD-395 Miranda text and asked the inmate if he understood. Battle stared blankly the whole time, but Johnson and McGinniss saw him blink and also nod. Johnson took those movements as a yes, and handwrote Battle's waiver on the form.

Then the agents asked questions, but Battle remained silent, eyes fixed on a wall, never acknowledging his interrogators. Finally, after thirty minutes, Battle responded to a question about his family. Then his story emerged, angry and in short choppy sentences. A court would later rely on Johnson's written account. "Officer Washington always talked a lot of shit, I didn't like him. He fucked with me," Battle told the agents. "I saw him talking on the phone, I walked up behind and hit him." Battle then described the bloodied ball peen hammer that investigators found behind a vending machine close to the guard's crumpled body.

Johnson took notes on a pad as Battle confessed, stopping at times to give the inmate water and cigarettes. Johnson then rearranged the notes into a cleaner narrative. Following FBI protocol, he got Battle to initial every page.

The guard, D'Antonio Washington, was taken off life support by his family the next day. The confession would be introduced at Battle's murder trial. Battle was convicted and sentenced to death.

THE DAY AFTER THE Centennial Olympic Park bombing, Don Johnson arrived in Macon for the press conference held by a militia leader and an attorney. He got there late—the event had been moved up—but quickly learned that the militia hadn't claimed credit for the Atlanta attack. Nor had there been any mention of Derrick Overstreet. So, Johnson went to the office of the U.S. Marshals Service and collected seven photos of a militia rally two months earlier.

When Johnson returned to Atlanta, he discovered that the Bureau had a second serious suspect. That morning, investigators had learned that a San Antonio woman had alerted the FBI in Texas to the activities of her estranged husband, Khalil Abboud. She believed he was involved in the attack at Centennial Park. The woman shared that Abboud's brother had rented a car three days before and that the pair had driven from Texas to Georgia. He said there was going to be a bombing. Bureau agents traced the brother's Visa card to a Travel Lodge in Dalton, Georgia, about an hour north of Atlanta. They learned that both men had checked in at 2:09 A.M. on the morning of the explosion, forty-nine minutes after the blast. They checked out before noon.

On the Sunday five P.M. SIOC call, law enforcement leaders focused heavily on Overstreet and Abboud. Each seemed promising.

CHAPTER 11

At 1:30 on the Saturday afternoon of the blast, Richard Jewell slid his blue pickup truck into the parking lot of his mother's Buford Highway apartment and wearily trudged up the steps. Since leaving for work at Centennial Olympic Park the day before, he had been awake for over twenty-one hours.

Bobi was visibly shaken at the sight of her only child as he stood in the entryway emotionally and physically drained. He had called in the early morning hours to reassure her he was OK. But she had been awake ever since, watching CNN and other networks, hoping to catch a glimpse of her son. Jewell calmed her down, telling her as much as he could about what had happened at the park. Then, famished and exhausted, he ate quickly and walked down the hallway to his bedroom and closed the door.

Jewell badly needed sleep, but he grabbed the phone on his nightstand and dialed his West Virginia "brother," Dave Dutchess.

"Dave, you'll never guess what happened. I found the bag that had the bomb in it."

"You're shittin' me, Richard."

"No, I found the bomb."

"Wow, Richard. You're a freakin' hero, man. That's awesome."

Jewell described the scene, then grew somber as he focused on Alice Hawthorne's death. Dutchess tried to buck up his friend. "It's sad, Richard, but look at all the people you saved." Still subdued, Jewell could muster only, "Yeah, I guess you're right." They hung up.

Not long after, Brian McNair, Jewell's close friend from Habersham County, called. The two fell into a familiar pattern of talking law enforcement.

"It was just like in the academy, you know?" Jewell said. "I saw something, and I asked 'Is this yours? Is this yours?' Nobody owned it. So, I like, I just backed the hell away from it and I started calling for help."

"Sounds like you did a really good job, man," McNair told him. They talked for twenty minutes or so. Then McNair said, "Man, well, go to bed because you gotta go to work tonight, don't you?" Night shifts, both men knew, were brutal without good rest during the day.

Jewell tried to heed McNair's advice, but he didn't sleep for long. So much had happened, so much busied his mind. Jewell clambered back out of bed and tried to reinject some normalcy into his life. He showered, and walked his Doberman, Lacy. He settled in with Bobi in the den to view news of the bombing, occasionally dozing off. In the late afternoon, Jewell watched Tom Davis at a televised press conference telling reporters that a security guard had found the package, though he didn't mention Jewell by name. Jewell observed President Clinton, speaking from the White House, thank "the brave security personnel" who prevented a much greater loss of life.

The phone rang at one point with an unexpected request. His boss, Anthony Davis, told Jewell that CNN had learned he spotted the pack and helped clear the crowd. Would he be willing to go back downtown to appear on the network that evening? Davis, a gregarious entrepreneur, had grown to like the guard. He encouraged him to agree. "You deserve your five minutes of fame."

Anxiety seized Jewell. He told Davis he would do the interview if the security-firm founder wanted, but he was worried about the questions. In cases like this, law enforcement often held back information so that "when they catch the suspect or subject, they are able to use that evidence against them," Jewell explained. Then there was the pressure of a televised interview. It was well beyond anything Jewell had ever done. Davis didn't seem worried, urging Jewell to just tell what happened and use his discretion.

Shortly before seven P.M., Jewell set the VCR to record and drove himself and his mother downtown in Bobi's station wagon. CNN wanted him for the top of the eight P.M. show and to arrive thirty minutes early for makeup. But traffic crept agonizingly from the Olympics events under way, the fifteen-minute drive nearly quadrupling in length, each passing minute raising Jewell's stress level. As they reached CNN Center across from the still-shuttered Centennial Olympic Park, parking lot after parking lot displayed a "FULL" sign. They were eight blocks away by the time he found an available lot. He raced for CNN, leaving Bobi trailing behind with her ailing foot. Anthony Davis and an AT&T media coordinator, Bryant Steele, were waiting. So were CNN news producer Henry Schuster and a bald and energetic reporter named Art Harris.

Harris and Schuster rushed Jewell upstairs and into the network's makeup room. After he had a quick touch-up, they explained that anchor Jeanne Meserve would be interviewing him remotely from Washington. As they headed to the interview, Davis flipped Jewell a brand-new black baseball cap with his firm's logo. "I'm a marketing guy," Davis was fond of saying. Steele encouraged the nervous Jewell to just be himself.

At 8:18 P.M., Jewell perched alone in the corner of the CNN newsroom set. Unaware of typical media norms, he was now dressed in black from the waist up. Through his earpiece, he could hear Meserve introduce him to the world as the first person to catch sight of the suspicious knapsack. He stared into the glass lens of a large Sony studio camera. Jewell could feel himself sweating, the earpiece stuffed in awkwardly.

For three minutes and twenty seconds, Jewell twisted through her questions, wary of giving away too much. He described the scene with the pack and clearing a perimeter. As the bomb went off, Jewell explained, "I wasn't really thinking of myself 'cause as I was getting up I saw several law enforcement officers who have come to be my friends in the park . . . still flying through the air and landing on benches."

Meserve asked if he had been adequately prepared for his security work. Jewell appeared to relax slightly: "Yes, ma'am. I was in law enforcement before I got this job. Uh. Been in law enforcement for six years in Georgia. And I just came down to Atlanta to do the Games, and then I'm gonna try to get on with an agency here in Atlanta."

Meserve closed the interview and thanked Jewell. He climbed out of the chair and pulled out the earpiece. A CNN staffer unclipped his microphone. He knew he had said "uh" too many times, but Bobi came out of the green room and told him she was proud of him. As Schuster and Harris guided Jewell through the newsroom and toward the exit, people congratulated him for his work in the park. They ran into U.S. Senator Sam Nunn and House Speaker Newt Gingrich, who both shook his hand and thanked him. The CNN producer and reporter made sure they booked Jewell for a second interview the next afternoon.

Jewell and his mother drove home, another grueling, traffic-slammed commute. They finally arrived around 10:30. Bobi made him a grilled cheese sandwich and they sat down to watch the CNN interview Jewell had recorded, not realizing the conversation would replay repeatedly through the hourly news cycles. The Jewells were spent. Sometime around midnight, the security guard dozed off, only to be jolted awake by a phone call from California at two A.M. It was a literary agent encouraging him to write a book. He hung up, at first angry that his brief window of rest had been disrupted. Now he was up, thinking about the possibility of a book. *Could that really happen?* Jewell clicked on the news. Fortunately, CNN and a new network called MSNBC were on 24/7, and NBC's sports coverage offered a diversion. USA's Gail Devers had won a record second straight 100-meter gold medal, bounding into the arms of her coach and husband, Bob Kersee, at the race's end. Canadian track star Donovan Bailey blew away the field in the men's 100, posting a world record of 9.84 seconds. But the lead Olympics story remained the bombing, and those news loops, including Jewell's interview, continued through dawn.

By Sunday morning, it seemed that everyone wanted a piece of Jewell. Just before eight A.M., a pair of GBI agents stopped by the apartment to show him two sketches drawn from witness accounts of unidentified men near the tower before the blast. Jewell immediately recognized one as a ponytailed Speedo Boy. The agents asked Jewell to review the night's events again, and left.

At noon, Jewell had a follow-up interview scheduled with the FBI at an office on the outskirts of Atlanta. The Bureau agents zeroed in on the Speedo Boys. Jewell provided every detail he could recall, but he just didn't see them as viable suspects. As Jewell would tell one agent who questioned him, if the young men knew there was a bomb in the pack, why would they be sitting on the bench right on top of it? He said if it were him, he certainly wouldn't do that, much less be "cutting up" and drawing attention to himself.

Between the two law enforcement interviews, Jewell took time out to page his North Georgia GBI friend from the park, Tim Attaway. The Olympics were ending in just seven days, and his job hunt would begin in earnest. Maintaining good law enforcement relations was important. On this call, he wondered if Attaway might join him for the CNN interview that afternoon. The agent demurred but told Jewell he was proud of him.

He encouraged Jewell to keep writing down everything he could remember about the bombing—maybe they could get together later.

JEWELL REMAINED SLEEP-DEPRIVED, BUT his second appearance on CNN Sunday afternoon was far less unnerving. This time, a driver provided by AT&T delivered him with time to spare, and the network's Art Harris would interview him in person. They filmed outdoors on the CNN rooftop with a bird's-eye view of the Atlanta skyline. For this interview, Jewell wore Anthony Davis's black hat again and a white AT&T polo shirt, his green and blue lanyards with his credentials looped around his neck. Jewell rehashed much of what he had told Meserve the day before, but added that he had identified one of the potential suspects in the sketches the GBI had shown him that morning. He also expressed his concern for the victims and his anger at the bomber.

Jewell and his AT&T handler, Bryant Steele, left CNN and walked outside. There, Jewell did a brief AT&T-arranged phone interview with the *Boston Globe*, then another in person with *USA Today*. Steele also had called the *Atlanta Journal-Constitution* to set up an interview. Since Atlanta was AT&T's southeast headquarters, Steele figured it made sense to keep good relations with the hometown paper.

AJC editors decided to hand the story to Kent Walker, a summer intern from Hampton University in Virginia. Jewell walked down the street to the paper's offices, where he and Walker settled at a meeting space outside Managing Editor John Walter's office for the interview. Walter watched part of the discussion, cringing at the awkwardness between the inexperienced reporter and the uncomfortable source. After the interview, an *AJC* photographer accompanied Jewell and Steele to the edge of the park for a photo op. That gave Jewell his first chance to reenter the still-closed park, fueling a powerful wave of emotions. Co-workers greeted him with hugs, and Jewell pulled out his camera, turning the lens to the blast site to capture a grim photographic memento.

The stories the interviews produced were glowing. The *Globe* focused in part on Jewell's decision to treat the suspicious package as anything but routine, including when the guard had returned to the tower to save employees. "'I grabbed a couple of them and pushed them down the stairs,' he said.

'They were mad at me, 'til the bomb went off.'" *USA Today* gushed, "The biggest hero of the Atlanta Olympics is a man of modest height and stocky build, with no sport other than occasional pickup basketball. He will get no medal and stand on no award platform."

Kathy Scruggs's focus was elsewhere. She and Ron Martz emphasized how closely law enforcement was looking at domestic radicals. "The FBI is investigating two men with ties to a splinter militia group who may have been in Centennial Olympic Park shortly before Saturday morning's pipe-bombing," they wrote in a piece that ran on the front page of the *AJC*'s Olympics Special. The reporters lobbed in a call to SAC Woody Johnson, who confirmed the suspicions about militia and the likelihood that the terrorism was domestic, not international. "'That's a lot of the reasoning we have been using,' said Johnson, who cautioned that the agency was pursuing other leads as well."

JEWELL CONTINUED TO PONDER the possibility of a book, but he needed some advice. So, he dialed his old SBA video game friend and attorney, Watson Bryant. Although the pair hadn't spoken in almost nine years, Jewell left a message on the lawyer's home answering machine. When Bryant called back, he first asked about the radar detector Jewell had bought from him at the SBA. "Where's my hundred bucks?" But Bryant quickly turned to congratulating Jewell on finding the bomb and listening to what sounded like an unlikely publishing deal. He pledged to help if anything came of the idea.

On Sunday night, Jewell finally got some sleep. On Monday, media continued calling, and he did a few interviews by phone. Mainly, though, Jewell took a break to enjoy himself. AT&T had given him tickets to an Olympic baseball game between Cuba and Nicaragua at Atlanta–Fulton County Stadium. The seats weren't great, but the game was exciting. Cuba hit six solo homers in its 8–7 victory and would later win the gold medal. Still, Bobi's foot hurt, so they left early.

When the Jewells arrived home, there was an "urgent" message on the answering machine for Jewell to call CNN. He dialed Art Harris, who asked if he would come back downtown to appear on a program called *Talkback Live*. Jewell declined, uninterested in fighting traffic again. But he agreed to call into the show, and twenty minutes later, he was live on CNN. The segment under way was focused on terrorism and the issue of how much freedom Americans were willing to give up in exchange for security. Jewell answered audience questions about the blast and aftermath. Embracing the network's international audience, he offered his thanks to "the citizens of the world . . . to show the person or persons that this type of activity will not be tolerated." On that final note, the host, Susan Rook thanked Jewell and cut to commercial.

BY THE END OF the day Monday, Jewell's celebrity star was rising fast. AT&T called to ask if he would be willing to appear on NBC's *Today* show the next morning. It would send a driver at six A.M. to take him to the network's set adjacent to the park. Jewell agreed. Then, knowing that Bobi loved NBC anchor Tom Brokaw, Jewell turned to his mother and joked, "Hey, Mom, maybe I can get you a date."

Just after eight P.M., he reconnected by phone with GBI Agent Attaway. "What's up, man?" Attaway greeted him. Jewell asked how the agent was feeling. Actually a little down, Attaway said, explaining that he had been off-duty the night of the bombing, as many of his colleagues found themselves injured and traumatized by the blast. He felt guilty for not being part of the team, but he had no confidants to discuss it with. Like Jewell, he had come down from North Georgia for the Games.

Jewell offered to grab a beer, then had a better idea: Why don't you come over for some lasagna? I made it myself, Jewell told the GBI agent. Attaway didn't want to impose, but how late could he get back to him? "You call me whenever you need me, buddy. We're mountain boys down here in the city," Jewell reassured him, adding that he'd like to talk too. An hour later, Attaway rang back and offered to be there in thirty minutes. Jewell gave directions to the Monaco Station apartment, then bantered, "You just coming to get something to eat, right? You ain't coming to take me to jail or nothing?" Attaway laughed.

While Jewell waited, the Olympics coverage on the TV remained a constant in the apartment. News of the bombing was still plentiful, but the star that night was Carl Lewis. It was Day 11 of the Games, and the legendary thirty-five-year-old U.S. track phenom had dramatically come back from fifteenth place in the long jump the day before to earn a spot in that night's finals. In his final jump in front of the sellout crowd of eighty-two thousand fans, Lewis bicycled his legs forward in mid-air, arms swooping at the last moment before landing with a distance of 27′10¾″. It was the superstar's ninth track-and-field gold over four Summer Games. For the moment, his feat even overshadowed Michael Johnson who that same evening had won the 400 meters in record time. Sportscasters teased the 200-meter finals coming up on Friday and the unprecedented prospect of Johnson winning both.

Jewell was standing outside when Attaway pulled up fifty minutes later. They went upstairs, and Jewell offered lasagna. Attaway replied that he wasn't hungry and asked for coffee to battle his fatigue. "Let's just put some food in your stomach, that's home cooking, I made that myself," Jewell pressed. "I want you to taste and tell me what you think about it, and I'll get you some coffee here in just a second." They settled into the den.

When Bobi walked in, Attaway rose to greet her. Jewell told his mother about Attaway's background in North Georgia, adding, "He's a very good friend of mine." Bobi chatted a moment, noticing Attaway's drawn demeanor. "You look like you lost your best friend," she said. He explained that he had just worked a seventeen-hour day, that fatigue had taken over.

Bobi headed for her bedroom, telling Attaway, "Come back and see us under better circumstances."

Jewell began a long evening of opinion and observation with Attaway. The guard did three-quarters of the talking, as the GBI agent picked at his lasagna. "There should have been 150 dead on that hill, if we hadn't reacted the way we did," Jewell noted. "Every agent out there, every officer out there, every security person out there did everything they was supposed to do." He went on that he was glad he had taken a four-hour bomb training at the law enforcement academy. Otherwise, "Hell, I'd have reached down there and picked the son of a bitch up and tried to take it to lost and found."

The two turned to their mutual respect for law enforcement. Jewell's reverence clearly ran deep. "Every one of these guys is a bigger fucking hero than I am. I mean, in my fucking view of it, if I'm a hero, there ain't a fucking word to describe these guys right here," he declared. "I mean, it wells me up every time I think about it."

Turning to the subject of the bomber, Attaway mused, "You know, I asked myself, what's his motive?"

"That's where I think everybody has got a problem," Jewell replied. "The guy didn't say well, 'This was a revolution' or, you know, 'Another bomb's gonna go off every day during the Games unless certain people were released.' This is just some sicko sitting back at home going, 'Ha, ha, ha, look at the way they're running around now, ha, ha, ha. I fixed 'em now.'"

The conversation turned toward employment. Jewell offered that he had an application pending with Cobb County's police force, but said he knew he would have to lose some weight. His dream job, though, was to become a state trooper. Attaway replied that he had been with the State Patrol earlier in his career. Maybe he could make a few introductions. Jewell brightened, "I'll tell ya what, whatever you could do I, I mean I'm single, and I mean I could move anywhere in the state."

Just before one A.M., after nearly three hours, a drained Attaway headed out. Minutes later, the FBI removed the wire they had attached to record the entire conversation.

Two nights before the FBI wired up Attaway, an intriguing call had come into the state of Georgia call center. Piedmont College Police Chief Dick Martin had phoned to say the school's president had asked him to give law enforcement a heads-up. Richard Jewell, Martin said, had resigned from the college just two months before and had been "in possession of 'how to make bombs' cookbooks." Despite the reference to explosives, the state call center marked the information as level 3 priority, its lowest possible designation. Still, like all leads, it was passed along to the FBI.

The next morning, Piedmont College President Ray Cleere, Martin's boss, wanted to make absolutely certain that the school's message had reached the FBI. So, at 8:10 A.M., he called the Bureau himself to underscore his concern. He had seen the guard interviewed by Jeanne Meserve the night before and wanted the FBI to know that Jewell hadn't been a good fit at the college and had been allowed to resign. The guard, Cleere added, "always wanted to be a hero."

Around noon, AT&T security investigative manager Robert Roper accompanied Jewell to an FBI interview in an industrial part of Atlanta. As Jewell waited for the Bureau's questioning to begin, Roper stepped out of earshot for a private conversation with an FBI agent. Roper was suspicious that the guard may somehow be involved in the bombing. The security guard had insisted on working at "his" tower seven days a week with no days off and had objected vehemently when told he might be transferred to another location.

On the five P.M. SIOC call on Sunday, Jewell had been mentioned as a possible suspect for the first time, although still not on the level of Overstreet and Abboud. One law enforcement official taking notes wrote: "Richard Jewell—ATT security hero. Need to check out."

Some at the Bureau had already been speculating about Jewell. Dave Maples, the FBI's Olympics security expert, reminded the group about an experience at the 1984 Los Angeles Games. Just after the close of that event, a local police officer discovered a ticking IED hidden in the wheel well of the Turkish athletes' bus at LAX airport. The officer, Jimmy Wade Pearson, grabbed the suspected bomb, ripped out the exposed wires, and sprinted with the device to a safe stretch of tarmac over one hundred feet away. "I've never seen anything more heroic than this," LA Police Chief Daryl Gates had proclaimed to the media afterward.

But FBI and LAPD bomb techs were skeptical from the start. One told Maples they had searched the Turkish bus thoroughly before the athletes departed the Olympic Village, aware of Armenian terrorist threats against them throughout the Games. There had been no IED at that point. The next morning, Pearson submitted to a polygraph and confessed to planting the device. Red-faced LAPD officials placed him under arrest.

Maples and others at the Atlanta FBI office couldn't help but wonder whether a similar scenario might be playing out again with Richard Jewell, the guard who somehow spotted a dark green backpack in the shadows of the green wooden bench.

At 9:50 P.M., the Atlanta Division called SIOC with more on Jewell. They related that the guard had been arrested for impersonating an officer, had problems in prior law enforcement positions, and may have had access to a bomb-making "cookbook." Following the call, SIOC re-contacted the BSU, this time with a more specific request: Could they look at Richard Jewell and offer interview advice?

Arrangements were made to deliver Jewell's two CNN video clips to the profilers. A trio of BSU agents were summoned back to Quantico, where they began studying the seven minutes of tape. At one A.M., the BSU called the Atlanta task force for more information and promised to deliver a written analysis by noon.

ON MONDAY MORNING, JULY 29, Louie Freeh surprised line agents by shifting overall responsibility for the investigation now called CENTBOM away from Woody Johnson to another SAC, Dave Tubbs. A Chicago native with a salt-and-pepper mustache and avuncular manner, the media-savvy Tubbs already had been one of the rotating SACs assigned to the Games. The prior year, as the head of the FBI's Kansas City office, Tubbs had gained wide recognition inside the Bureau when his team tracked down Terry Nichols, the second Oklahoma City bomber.

The decision narrowed Woody Johnson's role to overseeing the FBI's Olympics security efforts for the remaining six days of the Games. Despite having spent the past two years preparing to handle any critical incident, Johnson took the news professionally. But in the Atlanta office, many saw the move as a slap to their esteemed boss. Why replace the permanent SAC with a short timer, even one as respected as Tubbs? Did the move portend an outsized role in the investigation by Washington?

Tubbs took the lead in reporting out from Atlanta on the Monday morning SIOC call. Derrick Overstreet and Khalil Abboud remained promising suspects. More information on Overstreet's militia ties had come to light. Abboud, the Travel Lodge overnighter from San Antonio, was being tailed to Texas and agents would soon interview him.

Participants on the call then turned to a hot-button topic: Do we share the audio from the 911 call with the public? The Atlanta CENTBOM leadership urged Freeh to approve playing the tape at the next international news conference hosted by ACOG. With fifteen thousand journalists in town, the media would radiate the chilling message worldwide. *Someone* might recognize the caller's voice. But everyone also knew the move would divulge a key piece of evidence in the hunt for the bomber. The element of surprise could be useful.

Freeh determined the trade-off wasn't worth it. Instead, he decided only to distribute a transcript of the thirteen-second call. Atlanta officials chafed at Freeh's decision, but in the top-down command structure of the FBI, dissent and job security rarely coexisted.

On the same call, the BSU reported that its agents had revisited the investigation after hearing about Richard Jewell the night before. They had determined that Jewell was indeed a logical hero-bomber candidate. A written analysis was forthcoming.

DON JOHNSON DREW THE assignment to drive an hour north to Piedmont College to interview the police chief and others. At 10:30 A.M., he steered his Bureau car onto the magnolia-adorned campus in the Habersham County town of Demorest. He entered the administration building accompanied by another agent, Don White. They settled into the offices of Chief Martin, and Johnson took the lead. His notes would form the basis of every statement attributed to witnesses in his FBI 302 interview reports. Martin explained that he and his wife had grown concerned from the moment they saw Jewell on CNN two nights earlier. Jewell was, in Martin's words, "an individual who lived for the moment, he was an adrenalin junkie who would thrive in this situation." Yet, on his CNN appearance, he looked just the opposite, "nervous and stressed." Martin and President Cleere wondered about Jewell's stability.

Martin described the circumstances surrounding Jewell's departure, explaining how the campus cop repeatedly exceeded his authority, routinely making traffic stops outside the campus for minor transgressions. Johnson took particular note of the guard's habits on campus, writing, "Martin advised that at work Jewell was 'always reading and talking about cop stuff.' This, according to Martin, included guns, ballistic comparisons, etc. Martin stated that Jewell was 'totally engrossed in his job, he ate, slept, and breathed it . . . he didn't have a girlfriend, just the job.'"

Johnson collected a stack of eighteen documents from Martin, including Jewell's employment records, personal medical information, and resignation letter. One of the documents showed that Jewell had taken a two-hour bomb-response class at the Police Academy. Still, Martin said he hadn't thought Jewell would know anything about bombs, but added that another campus officer named Bill Worrell might disagree.

William Worrell, Johnson learned, was a financial analyst at a local phone company. In his spare hours, he served as a part-time officer at Piedmont College and a reserve deputy for the Habersham County Sheriff's Office. He had known Jewell for five or six years.

The interview started innocently enough, with Worrell offering a recitation of the driving problems that led to Jewell's resignation from the sheriff's department. He praised his fellow deputy, offering that he was honest, very observant, and could do solid work. Then Worrell dropped a hammer. As Johnson would write in the 302, Worrell said the guard was "highly aggressive" and "would have never made it into law enforcement if there was a more thorough psychological profiling system." He had difficulty with interpersonal skills, at times being abrasive or condescending. He was quick to charge obstruction of justice. Johnson knew the type. In the parlance of the Bureau, Jewell was "badge heavy."

Worrell confirmed Martin's account of Jewell's obsession with police work. "Jewell lived and breathed police stories, spy stories, tactics, and SWAT," Johnson wrote. The Olympic guard also owned an olive-green backpack that resembled an ALICE pack. Jewell used the internet often to visit recently created law enforcement sites, including the FBI's. According to Worrell, the guard was familiar with other sites too, like Candyman's Candyland, which contained *The Anarchist Cookbook*. But it was a comment Jewell had made about the Olympics that Johnson would find most alarming. The agent ended his 302 with it: "Worrell advised that everyone in the department had casually discussed the Olympics and the possibility of something happening there." After Jewell announced his plan to work at the Games, he added that he "hoped that he could be right in the middle of it."

Johnson left campus and headed off to meet another former colleague of Jewell's at the sheriff's office, Detective Richard Moore. The deputy had little positive to say about his former fellow officer either, as recorded in the 302. Moore described Jewell as generally a loner who couldn't take criticism or a joke.

Based on the earlier interviews, Johnson and fellow agent Don White posed the question to Deputy Moore: Could Jewell have set off a bomb at the Olympics? Moore allowed that the former deputy might be capable of doing it, but only if he thought no one would have been hurt. The agents memorialized Moore's response in their report: "Mr. Jewell might have believed that this could make him appear heroic and this would enable him to get employed as a police officer again."

Johnson returned to the Atlanta office with a raft of new, incriminating observations pointing to the guard. Arriving just after four P.M., he soon found himself in a conference room sitting across from the assembled CENTBOM top brass, including Dave Tubbs and Woody Johnson. With the next SIOC conference call less than an hour away, the team was eager to hear what the agent had learned.

Don Johnson offered an account of the Martin, Worrell, and Moore interviews. He detailed Jewell's fixation on being a policeman, his interpersonal issues, his overzealousness, his interest in bomb research, his hope to "be right in the middle of it."

When the agent finished, Woody Johnson placed his hand on an untitled, four-page single-spaced report on the table in front of him. Across the top, a fax legend read "Jul-29 1996 12:18 FROM QUANTICO NCAVC," the acronym for National Center for the Analysis of Violent Crime. It was the BSU profile. The SAC slid the report across the table, saying, "You could have written this."

Don Johnson's eyes raced across the profile. The document focused solely on Richard Jewell, with no mention of any other suspect. The analysis began with the requisite "The following is based on opinion" disclaimer and included a smattering of "if guilty" caveats. But the echoes from Johnson's half-day in Habersham County couldn't have been more pronounced. Nor could the BSU's conclusion, citing the two CNN interviews as their primary source. The report clearly laid out Jewell as the Olympic bomber.

Normally, the BSU focused on the crime and spelled out characteristics of the UNSUB, the Unknown Subject. This report identified Jewell and offered advice on how to best interview him. More importantly, it all but indicted him. Agent Johnson read the BSU's scenario to himself in near disbelief as others looked on.

Jewell is a "wanna be cop." He also gives every indication of suffering an inadequate personality and requires the trappings of a law enforcement officer (badge, uniform, etc.) to command respect. (The ranks of security guard companies and, to a lesser extent, law enforcement agencies are full of such people.) Unfortunately, for him, he has lost his jobs in law enforcement and, therefore, is without those things which he needs to feel like a complete man. Fortunately, for him, along comes the Olympics and, because of the massive needs, he has no trouble getting a security guard position. Now he must come up with a way to parlay this into a "real" law enforcement position. He is only one among thousands so he must stand out as someone worthy of notice. What better way than to become a hero. The bigger the threat, the bigger the hero. Discovery of a hoax device would not even be newsworthy. Imagine what a hero he would be if the device was discovered and disarmed. The media would be reporting that the device, as constructed and placed, would have killed and wounded scores had it not been for the heroics of Richard Jewell.

The description fit perfectly with what Johnson had just told the assembled leadership. It was as if the profilers had been in the Habersham interviews alongside him.

By the time the Monday five P.M. SIOC call began, the two earlier lead suspects, Derrick Overstreet and Khalil Abboud, had nearly become afterthoughts.

Overstreet had a solid alibi, and witnesses from the park could not identify him from photo spreads. "Trent" Overstreet, who rented the Nissan Maxima seen leaving the park, was an actual person, unrelated to the militiaman. Abboud wasn't panning out, either. After interviews, surveillance, and document collection, the evidence seemed to point more to a bitter ex-wife with a grudge than a bomber with a vendetta. Instead, in light of the BSU profile and Johnson's findings about the guard's history, the SIOC call triangulated around Richard Jewell.

There was one hiccup in the Jewell-as-hero-bomber thesis, however. Atlanta officials told Washington that the time sequence didn't work for Jewell being the 911 caller. At almost the exact time that the call was being made, the guard was in Centennial Park alerting GBI Agent Tom Davis about the package. Director Freeh jumped in, asking for a comparative voice analysis between the 911 recording and Jewell's CNN interviews. The Director also suggested that CENTBOM release the two GBI sketches of unidentified men seen near the bench just prior to the blast. The idea was to give Jewell a false sense of security, an impression that the Bureau was not looking at him.

It was odd to see an FBI Director take such an active role in determining investigative steps in a case, a move akin to the U.S. Attorney General suddenly telling prosecutors in a field office which motions to file. But the clean-cut Director with the deeply lined forehead was calling the shots, eager to solve the case and to keep the FBI moving forward after the debacles at Ruby Ridge and Waco. The eyes of the world were on the Olympics and the

FBI's handling of the bombing investigation. The person responsible for the attack needed to be brought to justice. Director Freeh, who was a former Bureau agent, federal prosecutor, and judge, was determined to make that happen.

One crucial next step would be to search Bobi Jewell's Monaco Station apartment and Richard Jewell's truck. Several floors down, FBI Chief Division Counsel Mollie Halle was pulling together a probable cause affidavit to support a search warrant. She needed an affiant, a highly respected agent to sign it, and recommended her longtime friend and colleague Diader "Di" Rosario. Five-foot-nine, with a graying mustache and close-cropped brown hair, Rosario was a Puerto Rico native known for being calm under pressure and for his good humor. When asked by people if they should call him Hispanic, he would crack, "Don't call me anything that has panic in it." The bilingual agent, a trained hostage negotiator, had been integral to defusing the 1987 eleven-day Atlanta Pen siege, tirelessly building relationships with the Cuban inmates. Supervisors liked Halle's choice. Not only was Rosario a skilled negotiator, but he also boasted a sterling record as an agent, which would be important down the road if he had to testify.

It became clear who would conduct the first interview with Jewell: Don Johnson. Beyond his keystone work on Jewell's background, he had established an excellent track record of gaining confessions, including in the Atlanta Pen guard's murder. Rosario's role as the affiant positioned him to pair with Johnson. Together, the men fit a suggestion in the BSU profile that the interviewing agents be older than Jewell, part of a strategy to earn the suspect's respect as experienced "brother officers."

ON THE SAME MONDAY morning that the BSU had gathered outside the public eye, Kathy Scruggs awoke earlier than normal and again hurtled out of her cousin's Dunwoody house. She was right where she wanted to be, on the A-Team, editors and readers looking to her for newsbreaks. She took an extra deep draw on her Marlboro Light. It was go time.

When the bomb had exploded two days earlier, Scruggs left it to others to mourn and lament. That wasn't her mentality, or her job. ER docs, cops, journalists—their business was to thrive when the world was crumbling. In the past couple of days, her years of cultivating law enforcement buddies, those hundreds of late bar nights, had begun paying off. Her sources had been forthcoming about the possible militia connections.

She barreled into the office, barely glancing at a story headlined FBI PROBES MILITIA LINKS she'd written hours earlier. The piece was already outdated, as the FBI seemed to be moving on. That was the news game. Investigations changed and a journalist shifted to the new story.

Scruggs knew this wasn't the time for the big "think" piece, not that she was good at that anyway. Nor was she facile with phrasing, once lamenting to a friend that "I write like a brick." Instead, this moment required muscle and speed to fend off the thousands of other journalists competing to break news on the bombing story. Be fast, be first. The pressure was intense.

Scruggs laid her reporter's notebook on her mess of a desk. She knew that others in the newsroom saw her as provocative, edgy. But cops never failed to notice, and she desperately needed their help now. Scruggs grabbed the black phone handset and pressed source after source for tidbits on the bombing probe: Atlanta police, Georgia officers, federal agents. What's going on in the case? Any suspects? What's changed? The urgency in her voice rose. Her profanity level surged too. "C'mon help me out here, asshole." She softened the pitch with seductive laughs.

Scruggs didn't know it, but her editors weren't expecting much. Olympics Editor Thomas Oliver figured all the media would learn the bomber's name at the same time, at some future ACOG press briefing. But Scruggs wasn't wired that way. "We're not in the business of being last," she was fond of saying. Still, after hours of calls, she had little to write. Her back throbbed from a chronic condition. She looked over at Ron Martz, but he didn't have much either. Dammit. Scruggs feared the worst: One of the carpetbagger journalists in for the Olympics would break the news in *her* town and on *her* beat.

Finally, she connected with an APD source: Did Scruggs know the FBI was looking at Richard Jewell? Scruggs perked up immediately. Jewell's name had floated around the media nearly from the start; many journalists knew about the '84 Olympics bomb hoax, and they figured that Jewell would be someone the Bureau would at least look at. Since then, though, the security guard had emerged as a bona fide hero. So what did the source have? How did he know? Who could confirm? The caller was short on specifics. He was just passing on a tip.

With the pressure growing, Scruggs dialed one of her more reliable law enforcement sources, someone she had known over the years. The source was about as plugged in as it got. She got down to business.

Hey, it's Scruggs. What are you hearing about the park bombing investigation?

The answer came back, quietly: There's been a significant change.

"Oh yeah? What's this new direction?" *Could it be Richard Jewell?* Scruggs wondered.

The response was tantalizing. "You need to meet me after work."

Early that evening, Scruggs steered her Miata into an open parking space. She slipped into the bar and picked out a quiet spot to wait. A few minutes later, the source walked into the room and sat down. The meeting was strictly off the record—that was understood. They ordered drinks, made small talk. After a few minutes, Scruggs asked the question.

Are there any new suspects?

Yes, the reply came back. One. "It's Richard Jewell."

Scruggs's heart pounded. *Bingo*. Jewell, the hero. Until now.

The source went on, "Jewell fits the profile of the lone bomber, the hero bomber."

"What profile?" she asked.

There's an actual profile, a document, the officer explained. The pattern neatly fits Jewell.

Why? Scruggs asked, frantically writing in her reporter's pad, straining to control her excitement.

The source outlined the profile in broad strokes: frustrated white male, former police officer or military officer, a "wanna be" cop who wants to be a hero.

Scruggs continued to press for details, scribbling notes. The source wouldn't give her a copy of the profile, but hunched forward, offering a stream of juicy details and leads: Jewell had been too eager to stand out from the start, constantly seeking media attention. The guard had lost two jobs in two years, one at Piedmont College as a campus cop and another at the Habersham County Sheriff's Office. If she did some digging, she'd be surprised by what she learned.

Scruggs's heart was pounding. *The FBI believes Richard Jewell did this. And it's my story.*

But then the source dropped a roadblock: "You can't do anything with this until I say so because . . . it might ruin the investigation."

Scruggs's mind whirred. *What?* She had to change the dynamic, figure out some way not to wait until the rest of the media reported that Jewell had been arrested. Scruggs had no choice but to agree. But she quickly countered with a fallback position: "If I get independent corroboration . . . that changes the rules. I am in a different ball game and can run the story. Deal?"

"OK," the source replied.

Scruggs left the bar after half an hour. Her heart pumping, she dialed the *AJC* newsroom, where she reached editor Bert Roughton. "You're not going to fucking believe this," Scruggs screamed into the phone. "I know who they are looking at."

Roughton adjusted his glasses then leaned in hard at his desk, blocking out the clatter of the newsroom. He needed to get this right, to properly relate the information to other editors and to Ron Martz.

But it's a good news/bad news arrangement, Scruggs said, explaining the source's ground rules. The paper couldn't use the information unless it independently sourced it. The reporters had more work to do. "Great stuff," Roughton told Scruggs. "See you when you get back to the office."

As he hung up the phone, Roughton realized the paper had a problem: Intern Kent Walker's flattering profile of Jewell already was rolling off *AJC* presses under the headline GUARD'S QUICK THINKING SAVED LIVES. Roughton leapt up to tell Oliver what he'd learned.

Oliver called the pressroom: "Let's kill that page."

SCRUGGS ARRIVED BACK IN the newsroom several minutes later, adrenaline coursing, her hair disheveled. Martz walked between the cubicles to meet with her on the north side of the newsroom facing the heart of downtown. In his black polo shirt and khakis, he looked a bit like the security personnel

Richard Jewell as a boy: Christmas 1967, as a five-year-old (top); in youth baseball (bottom, left); and as a member of the Towers High School eighth-grade football team (bottom, right)

TOP: Loyal Atlanta Braves fans, Jewell and his mother, Bobi, take in a game.
MIDDLE, LEFT: Dave Dutchess (left) with his "brother" Richard Jewell on a hunting trip in Lost Creek, West Virginia
MIDDLE, RIGHT: Dana and Richard Jewell
BOTTOM: Jewell shows off his catch, with fishing buddy and talk-show host O'Neill Williams.

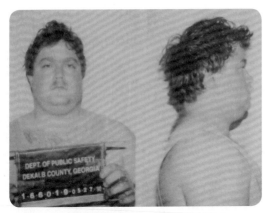

Jewell in his DeKalb County arrest photo

Jewell as a Habersham County Sheriff's deputy

Kathy Scruggs as a young girl (left), and in high school (right), in Athens, Georgia

Scruggs as a young *Atlanta Journal-Constitution* reporter

TOP: Scruggs as a student at Queens College in Charlotte, North Carolina
ABOVE: Scruggs's *AJC* press credentials

Don Johnson (left) with AUSA Jim Harper in the FBI's fourth-floor conference room for a 1997 awards ceremony

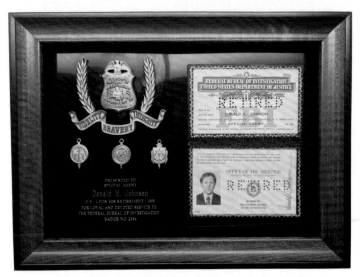

Johnson's retirement plaque with FBI credentials and years-of-service pins

WANTED BY FBI

DON JOHNSON

FOR RETIREMENT   **JANUARY 9, 1997**
5:30 PM - 8:00PM   **MARQUE HOTEL**
PERIMETER CENTER
770 396-6800

**SUBJECT IS DESCRIBED AS A WITTY, SHARP TONGUED,
OPINIONATED WHITE MALE
5' 10" TALL
185 POUNDS
GRAYING HAIR**

CAUTION: ARMED WITH WIT
DANGEROUS: WITH OPINIONS

$ 15.00 BOUNTY

TO PARTICIPATE IN JUST GETTING HIM OUT OF HERE

IF YOU HAVE ANY INFORMATION, PLEASE CONTACT:

FBI - ATLANTA   (404) 679-9000 OR
PAT JOHNSON   (404) 679-6170 OR
HAROLD PHIPPS   (404) 679-3034

The original poster for Johnson's retirement party, with a photo of him shaking hands with FBI Director Freeh. Johnson would insist on it being reprinted without Freeh, and with the year corrected to 1998.

Billy Payne (left) and Andy Young congratulate each other at the New Takanawa Hotel in Tokyo, Japan.

To Kent Alexander with best wishes, Bill Clinton Billy Payne

Opening Ceremony of the Centennial Olympic Games, July 19, 1996

for the Games. SNOT Pod editor Rochelle Bozman joined them as Scruggs recounted what she had learned.

Now, could they confirm the story? This news was too big to run without additional sourcing. Even Scruggs, aggressive as she was, recognized that her insider had set down ground rules they couldn't break. So, she and Martz hit the phones, scrambling to reach someone else with knowledge of the investigation.

But all of their calls ended the same way, with handsets returned to receivers, their notebooks empty. Finally, they had little choice but to wait until morning and try again. Scruggs knew the national media was well sourced in law enforcement, particularly in Washington. With twenty-four-hour news on TV and the internet starting to emerge, she had a restless night ahead.

CHAPTER 13

On Tuesday morning, Jewell jolted upright at 5:30 A.M. The sun wouldn't rise for another hour. He switched on the fluorescent lamp, thankful the beige Princess telephone that had been ringing continuously for the past two days sat silent. Jewell shoved aside the sheets and maneuvered around Lacy.

He had only managed to sneak in a few hours of sleep since last night's dinner with his GBI friend from North Georgia, Tim Attaway. Jewell fondly recalled the conversation, a pair of law enforcement guys just shooting the shit. And this Tuesday was going to be epic, he thought, as he walked downstairs to meet the NBC limo driver. The *Today* show, with Katie Couric.

Early-morning traffic was light, and in no time the limo pulled up to Centennial Olympic Park. Jewell was ushered to the makeup chair. From where Jewell waited, he could see the parade of stars preceding him on the show. Bryant Gumbel interviewed Carl Lewis, who was nearly giddy about winning his record-setting fourth straight gold medal in a Summer Games. After the interview, the track star swung by to shake Jewell's hand, and they posed for a picture.

Jewell's heart leapt when he spotted APD Chief Harvard. He strode over to introduce himself, knowing that a kind word from her could grease a path to hiring in her department. She greeted him awkwardly, seeming to cringe when he put his arm around her for a photo together. *Some people just don't like to be touched,* Jewell thought. For her part, Harvard could only think of the secret she harbored: that the FBI believed Jewell was the Olympic bomber.

Minutes later, Jewell was ushered onto the set, his hair gelled, the face powder diffusing some of his natural sheen and ruddiness. Jewell stood stiffly as the sound technician clipped a microphone to his shirt. His security credentials were left to hang over the white polo, the blue AT&T logo adorning his left breast adjacent to a red Olympic flame insignia.

"Hi, Richard, I'm Katie," he heard. Jewell snapped his usual mental photo as she stood smiling at him. Cream jacket atop an open-necked black blouse. Sparkly blue eyes, her short brown hair closely cropped. "America's Sweetheart," as she was called.

The three and a half minutes on-air were a nervous blur for Jewell. With his demeanor even and his drawl particularly pronounced, Jewell rolled through the story of bombing night yet again: how a pack sitting without an owner looked suspicious, the surprise of the workers in the tower when he ordered their evacuation, the difficulty of moving back the crowd from the prime real estate facing the stage without triggering a panic. "The people would more or less just look at you, they wouldn't want to leave," he told Couric. "So you'd have to ask everybody four or five times to get 'em to move to the middle of the park." The word *times* came out *taaams*. As usual, he was unfailingly polite, sprinkling his replies with "Yes, ma'am."

Finally, three minutes into the conversation, Couric softened her voice, looked directly into his face, and offered: "A lot of people are calling you a hero. Do you feel like one?"

"No, ma'am," he humbly replied, his interlocked fingers resting on the desk. "I feel like I am a person that did the job that I was supposed to do. I was in the right place at the right time and used my training in the way I was taught." Then Jewell redirected Couric's praise. "The real heroes of this are the paramedics, the firemen, all the agents that placed theirselves between the bomb and the people that were refusing to move. 'Cause they took most of the shrapnel and stuff."

Couric offered one final kudo: "You played a big role. You were in the right place at the right time and you did the right thing, Richard. Thanks so much for coming in." With that last phrase, she reached out a hand and tapped Jewell's right forearm with a light touch. Jewell was ebullient. Katie Couric had called him a hero.

Minutes after Jewell stepped off NBC's Centennial Park set, just yards away the gates reopened for the first time since the bombing. Long lines of visitors were greeted with new security measures, law enforcement riffling through their bags and bomb-sniffing dogs eyeing them. But few parkgoers seemed to mind, Jewell could tell. Some first headed toward the AT&T tower where they set up a makeshift memorial to Alice Hawthorne and the other victims, one by one adding flowers. Visitors paused to pray, some on their knees with head in hands as tears flowed.

Tens of thousands began to gather in front of the AT&T stage for a ceremony to reopen the park, featuring Olympic and political officials. Jewell stood removed from the crowd but watched the combined memorial and rally, designed to remember the fallen but also to reassure the public that the worst was behind them.

In a stirring speech, Andy Young channeled his experiences as preacher and politician. "It is unfortunate that our lives are too often defined by the tragedies and suffering that we experience," he told the crowd. But, Young continued, "Martin Luther King Jr. reminded us that unearned suffering is always redemptive." TV cameras quickly panned to King's widow, Coretta. When Young finished, the audience cheered uproariously. The dignitaries, including Young, Billy Payne, and IOC President Juan Antonio Samaranch walked to the front of the stage. They joined for a moment of silence. Then they raised their hands in triumphant defiance, as Payne proclaimed, "Ladies and gentlemen, it is now our pleasure to declare reopened Centennial Olympic Park."

An AT&T representative guided Jewell back to the limo, and the guard hopped in. Jewell liked this driver, and they chatted about deer hunting. As they merged onto Interstate 75, Jewell wasn't focused on the rearview mirror. Had he been, he would have noticed the unmarked FBI cars tailing him.

THREE HOURS EARLIER, AT SIX A.M., Don Johnson had arrived at the FBI office, slipping off his suit jacket in his fifth-floor cubicle. The agent's white shirt was accented by a patterned red tie that draped down over his slight middle-aged paunch. His desk was spotless, not a pen or paper clip out of place.

Johnson needed to prepare for what he knew would be the most pivotal interview of the Olympic bombing investigation—and of his career. Twelve hours had passed since he learned he would lead the interview of Richard Jewell. The interrogation had not yet been scheduled. Johnson figured it might happen toward the end of the week. Still, the agent wanted to be ready. This interview was his shot.

He pulled out the notes from his meetings at Piedmont College and the Habersham County Sheriff's Office. Methodically, so as not to miss a single fact, Johnson pored over every report, as well as Jewell's personnel file. Using military time and shorthanded notations, he jotted down observations on a lined white notepad that would become his personal road map for pursuing Jewell. "0055+/-: RJ advised security looking @ bag under bench."

Johnson read a brief summary of Tim Attaway's dinner with Jewell. The GBI agent had highlighted that the thirty-three-year-old guard lived with his "domineering" mother, took credit for saving lives, needed employment, and had been reveling in the attention. It all fit so neatly with the profile Woody Johnson had slid to him the day before. He pulled the BSU's document from his orderly stack. The profile was easily the most incriminating report in the FBI's growing arsenal. By this point, he had read the characterization of Jewell so often that he had virtually committed it to memory. So, Johnson turned his focus to the other half of the document, the profilers' detailed strategies for how to best interview Jewell.

The BSU had recommended two sequential interviews of the security guard. The first should be "nonconfrontational, nonaccusatory, the second more hard-hitting and accusatory." Johnson and Rosario, the older "brother officer," were assigned to handle the first. They hadn't worked much together, but had spoken often enough during regular smoking breaks outside the building. The behavioralists' report advised the agents to tell Jewell that he was a key witness, honoring his experience of discovering the bomb and possibly even seeing the bomber. The agents should stay friendly and draw the guard out for a detailed accounting of his actions: "Jewell should leave the interview thinking that he is safe and has the respect of the FBI."

Although much of the BSU's remaining advice applied to the second interrogation, Johnson perused it with equal interest for advice relevant to the first, including location. "*If he is taken to the FBI office, he should not observe any chaotic activity. He should only be exposed to a calm environment,*" the report read. Inside, "*Interviewers should not separate themselves from him with a desk or table. A desk or table gives him a psychological barrier between himself and danger.*" Once the interview was underway, the BSU predicted: "*Jewell will probably not ask for an attorney if he is treated as described above. However, if it is found that he lives with or has a close association with an older female (mother, aunt, grandmother, or in the unlikely event, a girlfriend,) that person should not know he is being interviewed by the FBI and that he is a suspect. That older female is probably domineering and controls his life. She will likely inject a lawyer.*"

Johnson noted the BSU's caveats about what *not* to say during the more confrontational second interview: "*Do not ask him if he did it. Asking that question implies you do not know the answer. Tell him he did it and tell him why. He did it at a time in his life when he was out of control and not totally responsible for his behavior.*" The agents should assure Jewell that they recognize that "*he only wants to be a good cop and he has been misunderstood by those he worked for and with.*"

Semantics mattered too, Johnson noticed. "*Avoid using words like 'murder,' 'kill,' 'death penalty,' etc. Try to depersonalize (and decriminalize) the bombing by using terms such as 'the incident,' 'the events of Saturday morning,' etc.*" The interviewing agents should "*make him think they are his friends (something he has never had an abundance of) and want to help him.*" By all means, all interviewers should avoid coming across as judgmental or conveying outrage. "*People have probably judged him all his life and expressed their dismay, disappointment, disagreement, etc. He resents it.*"

Toward the conclusion of the profile, the BSU wrote, "*You have a lot to overcome. If you do not get a confession, you did not fail. . . . It will be hard to confess to such an outrageous and deplorable act.*"

Nonsense, Johnson thought. As Rosario would later say, this was their "shot at the king." Johnson had no intention of there ever being a second interview conducted by a second set of agents. He could break any suspect.

THREE FLOORS BELOW JOHNSON, Rosario also had reported at six A.M. to his desk on the Terrorism Squad. Unlike the 7 Squad agent, Rosario had not been reviewing documents, nor had he been given a copy of the profile. The interview was still days away, he too had been told.

Rosario, dressed in a maroon FBI-logo polo shirt and dark slacks typical of Bureau attire during the Olympics, was on the cusp of fifty. In a month, he would be celebrating his twenty-seventh anniversary with the Bureau. Nearly nine years had passed since his work as the lead hostage negotiator in the Atlanta Pen riot. The agent had been reviewing drafts of a search warrant affidavit for an unspecified location, even before Jewell surfaced as a suspect. FBI attorney Mollie Halle and her staff continued to drop in emerging details of the bombing. Time. Place. Forensics. Witness statements.

Criminal statutes. Legal wanted to have as much done as possible in advance, then add further supporting facts when a prime suspect emerged. Two days later, the search location had been added: Apartment F-3 at Monaco Station, where Richard Jewell lived.

Throughout Tuesday morning, Rosario checked in with legal on the affidavit. Around ten A.M., he and Johnson met with Tim Attaway for a full debrief on the dinner with Jewell, gathering detail that went beyond the short written summary. Then, Rosario went back to another assignment. At about 11:30 A.M., he left the building for lunch.

SCRUGGS AWOKE WITH ONLY one thought: She desperately wanted to nail down the Jewell hero-bomber story, to confirm the leak at the bar. She didn't have to wait long. Just minutes after leaving her temporary Dunwoody residence for the drive downtown, her pager buzzed. The number belonged to a source at the Atlanta Police Department. She rushed to the office and called.

"They're looking at the security guard," the cop on the other end of the line told her.

"How do you know that?" she demanded.

"We are over here talking," the cop said. "Everybody knows it."

Scruggs's excitement mixed with panic. If the Jewell news had already become talk at APD, how long until NBC, the Olympics host network, broke the story? Or hometown CNN with its 24/7 operation? Or even some internet site? In the past, Scruggs had agreed to delay publication of stories she felt might put an investigation at risk. Just the year before, she had kept information out of the paper for months about a corruption probe of the Atlanta police until arrests were made. She never wanted to undermine a law enforcement case. But "Everybody knows it" meant the Jewell story was ready to pop. This was her scoop—and it was in jeopardy.

SNOT Pod editor Rochelle Bozman had worked late the night before, so Martz volunteered for early duty coordinating Tuesday's morning coverage. Scruggs's conversation with the source in the bar was valuable, but he knew the paper needed more. He decided to try Jewell directly.

In Martz's years with the Marines, he often had to talk to families of soldiers killed in service. This call to the suspect would be tricky, but

Martz was unflappable. He hunted down Bobi Jewell's home number, took a deep breath, and punched in the digits, hoping Jewell would pick up. The phone rang far longer than usual, eight or nine times. No one answered, no machine picked up. Martz returned the receiver to the cradle. He would try again later.

Late morning, Bozman arrived at the newsroom, prepared to push the story forward. A twelve-year journalism veteran and single mom attending law school at night, Bozman served as the *AJC*'s legal affairs editor. The thirty-five-year-old had earned a reputation for her unusual wit, once wrapping a neat-freak editor's entire desk in foil, even down to individual paper clips. But professionally, Bozman was serious and held an unshakable commitment to breaking news.

Since Martz hadn't been able to reach Jewell by phone, Bozman decided to send someone to the suspected bomber's apartment, about five miles from the *AJC* offices. She called Christina Headrick, a summer intern from Northwestern University, at home, and asked her to drive to Monaco Station to see what was happening. When the intern arrived at 11:45 A.M., she noticed only a few cars in the parking lot. She couldn't tell if Jewell was home. So, Headrick stayed in her white Volvo and drove to a pay phone across the street on Buford Highway. She dialed Bozman, describing the scene. The editor, thinking far more about the story than any potential danger, instructed the intern to knock on the suspected bomber's door and try to interview him. Headrick was twenty-two and alone.

"What do I say if he answers the door?" the jittery Headrick asked her editor. Bozman thought fast: "Just tell him you want to talk to his mother about the profile Kent Walker had been working on."

Headrick drove back across the road. She climbed the stairs and approached Apartment F-3, then screwed up her courage and knocked on the door of the FBI's lead murder suspect. She waited several tense seconds and knocked again. Despite Bozman's instructions, Headrick still wasn't quite sure what she would say when he answered the door. She wondered if she was in danger.

After more knocking, she heard scuffling behind the door. A man and a dog, it sounded like.

"Who's there?" came the voice from inside. The man sounded groggy.

Headrick didn't know that Jewell had been up past midnight with GBI Agent Attaway and had slept just a few hours before his limo ride at 6:15 A.M. to the *Today* show.

"I'm Christina Headrick, a reporter for the *Atlanta Journal-Constitution*."

"What do you want?" He sounded a little nervous, Headrick thought, his voice trembling.

I would like to speak with your mother, the reporter replied. Is she home?

No, he said. She's at work and won't be home until after five. Clearly, he didn't want to talk. He didn't open the door.

Her disappointment tempered by relief, Headrick retreated down the stairs and climbed back into her car. She drove across the street again to the pay phone, dropped in a quarter, and called Bozman to report the exchange. The call rolled to voicemail. As she headed back to her car, Headrick noticed something odd: Two police cruisers approached the phone where she'd just been. The officers popped out to examine the call box. Headrick found the move so unusual that she waited for them to leave, then returned to call Bozman again. This time the editor answered, and Headrick explained all she had experienced with Jewell and with the officers. Bozman asked if she'd seen other media around. Headrick said no. Bozman instructed her to keep watching. The intern was now on a stakeout.

With the temperature nearing 90 degrees, Headrick settled under the shade of a tree where she could view the apartments. Jewell's 1984 blue Toyota pickup remained parked near the steps. The Buford Highway lanes were busy with cars zipping past at forty miles per hour. Most didn't merit her notice. But then she spotted two unmarked Ford Crown Victorias in the same lot where she sat, each occupied by men in suits. Diagonally across the street, in the parking lot next to the apartments, two more men stared at Jewell's apartment from another unmarked car. *Undercover cops*, Headrick thought, *probably FBI*. She walked back to the phone and called Bozman with another update.

Back in the cover of her own vehicle, she continued to watch the men watch the apartment. Then a short while later, a knock on her driver's-side window startled her. Two men in suits stared in. She rolled down her window. "You are Christina Headrick," one said. "How are you enjoying your summer with the *AJC*?" It was unnerving.

IN THE *AJC* NEWSROOM, the pressure intensified. "Everybody knows it," Scruggs's Atlanta police source had said. The phrase grew in importance with each passing hour. In reality, all the major news outlets were eager to break the story of the bomber's identity. CNN, ABC, and others had begun hearing that the FBI could be looking at Jewell. But none had the level of detail Scruggs did, and none was confident enough to name him as a suspect, much less the lead suspect.

At his desk across the newsroom, editor Bert Roughton worried about naming Jewell at all. The FBI hadn't said anything publicly about the guy, there were no charges, no arrests. "It felt very big to me. Once you go through the looking glass . . ." Roughton later recalled. Full of uncertainty, he walked into the office of Managing Editor John Walter. "John, do we name this guy?"

Walter often used his office as if it were a residence, lying on the couch as he met with *AJC* staffers. He was known as a "nearstander," often to the point of giving colleagues unsolicited neck rubs when they were working. But for all his quirks, Walter was a strong, decisive editor. He knew the media world was at the dawn of a more interactive age, one in which the public insisted on speed.

As Roughton shifted uneasily in the office, Walter sensed the junior editor's nervousness. But on this Tuesday afternoon, Walter was steely. He reasoned that Jewell had put himself out there for his fifteen minutes of fame. Scruggs had learned Jewell was the suspect and her sources were solid. Headrick saw the FBI at Jewell's apartment. For Walter and others, the pattern couldn't be ignored. How can we *not* use what we know? The managing editor made the decision, and Roughton found his confidence infectious. The *AJC* needed to run the story.

SCRUGGS PERCHED EXCITEDLY AT a computer terminal near a glass conference room that had been newly installed for the Olympics. Her notes lay scattered across the desk. Martz stood over her right shoulder. He considered this Scruggs's story, her time to shine. She had found the key source at the bar, and she would get the first byline on one of the biggest scoops in the paper's 128-year history.

Pulling information she'd learned from her source, Scruggs began to type, her long fingernails clicking on the keys. Jewell "fits the profile of the lone bomber," she wrote, later adding in the words "wanna be" and "hero." She was jumpy, full of nervous energy. "Oh shit, where was that?" she blurted, frantically looking through her scattered notes for a detail. She took a deep breath. "God, I need a cigarette," she lamented in the smoke-free newsroom.

For a full hour, each step of the writing process triggered seemingly small but crucial decisions. What do we call Jewell? Is he a "suspect," "prime suspect," "target," or something else? Eventually they settled on "focus of the federal investigation." Bozman, Martz, and Scruggs engaged in far more discussion than with a typical story, debating the phrasing and tone of almost every sentence.

They arrived at a final draft. Now there was one more debate: How should the *AJC* attribute the information when it couldn't publicly identify Scruggs's source, not even by agency? Years earlier, Walter and his boss, Ron Martin, had essentially banned the use of the term "sources" from the paper. Walter disliked the word, believing that it led readers to wonder if the information had been fabricated or fed to a reporter by someone with an agenda. So the paper required any use of "sources" to be blessed by Walter first.

Reporters and editors debated the issue, finally bringing it to Walter. The managing editor declared that the paper should simply lay out the newsbreak without any sourcing, as information the *AJC* knew to be fact. The structure was widely known in the profession as the "voice of God."

The first two paragraphs of Scruggs and Martz's story in final form read:

> The security guard who first alerted police to the pipe bomb that exploded in Centennial Olympic Park is the focus of the federal investigation into the incident that resulted in two deaths and injured more than 100.
>
> Richard Jewell, 33, a former law enforcement officer, fits the profile of the lone bomber. This profile generally includes a frustrated white man who is a former police officer, member of the military or police "wanna be" who seeks to become a hero.

A copy editor, whose job was to read for clarity and grammar, typically would have written a headline for the piece. But Walter took on the task himself, helping to craft the banner: FBI SUSPECTS "HERO" GUARD MAY HAVE PLANTED BOMB.

As a last cautionary step, Martz needed to run the story by the FBI. If the Bureau believed it would undermine the investigation or was inaccurate, the *AJC* may need to hold or revise the article. Shortly after noon, Martz printed out the piece and walked to a quiet bank of desks at the far end of the bustling eighth-floor newsroom. Scruggs and Bozman stood at the SNOT Pod, looking his way while Martz sat at an empty cubicle and dialed agent Jay Spadafore, the FBI's Atlanta part-time public affairs coordinator.

Spadafore had assumed the public affairs role two years earlier, taking on a task previously managed by Di Rosario. Except at the largest FBI offices, the Bureau assigned a line agent to handle media calls on top of their usual assignments. Like Rosario before him, Spadafore had been handed the public affairs job with little training. "You just learn it on the fly," Spadafore liked to explain. "You teach yourself the rules by talking to the media."

In the four days since the bombing, journalists' calls had been constant. Spadafore had offered mainly "no comment." His job was to keep the media at bay and the SACs prepared, even at ease. Prior to the first international press conference, he had humorously assured Woody Johnson, "Boss, don't worry. There won't be more than two billion people watching it on the television." But when the phone rang, and Ron Martz was on the line, Spadafore knew it was time to put aside gallows humor. The reporter was calling about Richard Jewell, the Bureau's top suspect.

Early in the conversation, Spadafore knew he had little to offer Martz. By design, he was largely disconnected from the CENTBOM investigation. He had never seen the profile, nor had he discussed the Habersham interviews with Don Johnson.

Martz explained that the *AJC* planned to run the Jewell story and that the paper wanted to check two things: First, was the piece accurate? Second, would it hurt the investigation? Then, at the instruction of editors, Martz agreed to do something he rarely did: He read the entire story verbatim. Spadafore sat at his cubicle, carefully taking notes on an eight-by-eleven lined pad. When Martz finished, Spadafore offered that most of the article seemed fine, but he couldn't confirm some elements of Jewell's experiences in Habersham County because he simply didn't know. Nor could he comment on the profile. The headline, he cautioned, might be a bit strong.

But Spadafore had misunderstood Martz's intention. Martz was looking for confirmation, which he now had. Spadafore thought Martz was simply calling as a courtesy. Martz then followed up on his second query: Would the *AJC*'s story hinder the investigation? Spadafore shook off any concern, unaware of the interview strategy outlined in the profile. Media had already been calling and mentioning Jewell's name. How much difference could the *AJC* story make?

Spadafore hung up, then headed upstairs to Woody Johnson's fourth-floor office. Notepad in hand, the public affairs coordinator rolled out for his boss what he had learned from Martz. The SAC, with his customary equanimity, took the information in stride, replying with a simple "OK, thank you very much." Despite his stoicism, Johnson knew how significantly a public disclosure of the Jewell information would impact the FBI's process.

Johnson alerted Tubbs and the rest of CENTBOM leadership. Tubbs, far more transparent about his anger than Johnson, was furious about the leak. How did word get out, especially about the profile? Who the hell talked to the *AJC*? The paper's story was about to torpedo the BSU's two-interview strategy. They would need to resort to a hastily crafted, and far inferior, Plan B. There would be one interview of Jewell, and it would have to happen immediately.

At noon, agent Don Johnson received word of the change in direction. He paged Rosario at lunch. The *AJC* was about to break a story that Jewell was the suspect. They needed to get to Jewell's apartment now. Rosario asked where the interview would be conducted. Johnson said that it was being taken care of—just get back to the office ASAP. Rosario did. Johnson had already visited the fourth-floor conference room and had seen the equipment being set up for filming the Jewell interview. That way, the BSU and other agents could later review it.

Johnson and Rosario's drive to Monaco Station took only a few minutes. But when they arrived, they saw a news reporter and a cameraman waiting in the complex's lot. The journalist recognized Rosario from his time as the Atlanta office's media officer. Rosario urged Johnson to drive away.

Johnson motored about a quarter mile down Buford Highway, where the agents called back to headquarters to explain that a few reporters were perched outside Jewell's apartment. They were told to sit tight and wait for instructions. The agents would wait there for nearly three hours.

MID-AFTERNOON, JEWELL'S LOS ANGELES–BASED boss, Anthony Davis, received a phone call from a reporter at the *Atlanta Journal-Constitution*. Her tone at first was sugary sweet. "What do you think about Richard Jewell?" she asked.

"He's a hero," Davis told her. "His efforts saved hundreds of lives. Everyone liked him. He was dutiful to the people in the tower." Her tone turned cold. "What would you say if our newspaper named your hero as a primary suspect?"

As soon as the call ended, Davis phoned Jewell. Bobi answered. She said that Jewell had just left, was headed to work, but had stopped outside to talk to the media. She ran out to get him.

More than two hours had passed since Johnson and Rosario had driven through the complex. More journalists were now clustered in the parking lot. Word of the *AJC*'s impending newsbreak had begun to circulate. At the bottom of the stairs, Jewell had a smattering of cameras pointed at his face. He stood in the shade, yet kept his sunglasses over his eyes.

"How does it feel on one hand to be treated like a hero in the morning and then find out that the FBI considers you a suspect?" one reporter asked. "Do you resent that or do you think that's part of the game?"

"Well, to be honest to you, hearing that from y'all I don't know if that's fact or fiction," he replied, a bit jarred by the question.

"Do you have any way of knowing why they would consider you a suspect?"

"No, I have no idea."

"Did you do it?" the same reporter pressed.

Jewell snorted involuntarily. "No, sir, I didn't do this."

Bobi interrupted to tell him someone was calling from California. Jewell knew that meant Anthony Davis was on the line, and he quickly returned to the apartment. Davis told him about the reporter's call and said to stay home from work.

AT THE *AJC*, COPY editors had already put the final touches on the article that would become a defining moment of the 1996 Olympic Games. They made plans to put the piece on their website.

The paper had been running two Extra editions every day during the Olympics, one in the morning and one each afternoon, aimed at boosting street sales. Now, for the first time during the Games, editors would rip up the afternoon Extra to replate the front page with the Jewell news. By late afternoon, papers began rolling off the press.

By that time, Kathy Scruggs had headed to Buford Highway to see if she could coax an interview out of Jewell himself.

AT 4:30 P.M., AFTER waiting down the road for instructions, Johnson and Rosario headed back toward the Monaco Station apartments. Interview Jewell now, they had finally been told. Time was of the essence.

When they arrived, reporters hollered questions at Johnson and Rosario as they walked toward Building F. "Are you with the FBI?" "Hey, what are you guys doing here?" "Are you coming to arrest this man?" The agents ignored them.

By then, Scruggs had arrived too. She stood in the parking lot in front of her Miata. Wearing stiletto heels and a light-beige summer dress, she drank in the scene. Though she would clearly not get her interview with Jewell, it was for Scruggs a moment of sheer pride.

Walking past Scruggs to the apartment, Johnson and Rosario climbed the steps to Apartment F-3. Johnson knocked. "Go away," Jewell responded from behind the closed door. "Richard, can I speak to you a second? My name is Don Johnson, I'm with the FBI," the agent announced in a nonconfrontational tone. Tentatively, Jewell cracked the door and peeked through. Johnson held open his black leather credentials with his FBI badge, No. 2364. Jewell pulled back the door and the agents walked in, Rosario holding his own photo ID open and above his head so that Jewell could see it as well.

The three men stepped inside the living room, each remarking on the growing media circus outside. Johnson said they wanted to talk to him about what happened at the park. Jewell expressed surprise that agents had not been by earlier to do a more extensive interview. Johnson jumped on Jewell's cue: Well, that's actually why we're here. Will you accompany us to the FBI office?

But Jewell was apprehensive. The media is calling me a suspect, he said. Are y'all here to arrest me? No, both agents assured him, they were not. The guard pressed, Am I a suspect?

Jewell's question hung disquietingly, neither agent immediately answering. Then Johnson replied that Jewell was a key witness. If he came to the office, they even planned to videotape him. The idea surprised Jewell. Videotape? Johnson, sensing his discomfort, quickly manufactured a plausible-sounding rationale: We want to use the footage for a training video for first responders.

Jewell readily agreed to join them at the FBI. *A training video for first responders.* Then, he paused. But what about all the media outside? If he rode with the agents, reporters would think he was under arrest. There was a brief silence. Bobi, whose nerves and patience were frayed, was standing nearby listening. She snapped at the agents, "Can he not drive? I mean, fellas, wake up!" All agreed that Jewell would take his own truck.

Jewell slung his green daypack over his right shoulder, partially obscuring the bold black word SECURITY on the back of his work polo shirt. As he walked out, his Olympics credentials dangled from the lanyard around his neck. Jewell was optimistic. He hoped that once he spoke with the FBI, Anthony Davis would clear him for his evening shift at the park. He could use the money.

As Jewell and the agents walked down the stairs, the media, now in larger numbers, surged forward and barked questions. Johnson and Rosario said nothing as they walked to the right for their car. Jewell angled left toward his pickup, striding purposefully through the mass of reporters. He passed within a few feet of Kathy Scruggs, whose name at that point meant nothing to him.

Another journalist asked, "Sir, what have they told you? Are they letting you go to work?"

"Yeah."

"Did they tell you now not to leave town?"

"No."

"You're free to go wherever you want?"

"Yes. I'm not a suspect."

Jewell mercifully reached his truck, sliding the key into the door lock. He shifted into reverse and backed out of the space, careful not to hit the cameramen beside his truck. He drove off so quickly that he had to wait for

Johnson and Rosario to pass him on Buford Highway and lead the way to the FBI offices.

Johnson radioed in: "We'll be there in six minutes."

AS JEWELL AND THE agents drove, the *AJC* rushed the Extra to street vendors. For once, the internet offered Scruggs opportunity instead of worry, as the *AJC* launched the story onto its own fledging website. To promote the exclusive, editors called the paper's sister TV station, WSB, and the Associated Press to share the news. One of the paper's editors phoned CNN, hoping to maximize attention for the scoop. The network sent a staffer down the street to the *AJC* to grab a copy.

At 5:09 P.M., CNN anchor Bob Cain informed viewers, "We are just getting details on what appears to be a major development in the Atlanta Centennial Olympic Park bombing. *The Atlanta Journal-Constitution*, in a special edition, today identified a security guard named Richard Jewell as the prime suspect in the Atlanta bombing." Cain then held for the camera the copy of the *AJC* he had just received.

The bold headline, FBI SUSPECTS "HERO" GUARD MAY HAVE PLANTED BOMB, filled much of the screen. The bylines of Kathy Scruggs and Ron Martz appeared below.

Just a few blocks away, *AJC* staffers watching CNN on the wall-mounted TVs in the newsroom broke out in applause. Several reporters and editors high-fived as the anchor read Scruggs and Martz's story on Jewell word for word to the world.

Richard Jewell was driving to the FBI, unaware that the article existed.

CHAPTER 14

Inside the CENTBOM task force's eighth-floor conference room on that same Tuesday, the five P.M. SIOC call was already underway as Jewell left his apartment with the interviewing agents. Atlanta Bureau leaders, including SACs Woody Johnson and Dave Tubbs, ringed the oval table. Just outside, dozens of law enforcement personnel from eleven agencies feverishly tracked investigative leads at long rows of workstations.

Five hundred miles north, in the SIOC executive conference room, FBI Director Louie Freeh and his team listened intently on the phone line to the Atlanta update. The conversation soon turned to Miranda. Everyone on the call knew that the warnings were required if a suspect was in custody. But because there were no charges pending, Jewell would be able to leave whenever he chose. After some discussion, a final decision was made: Tell Jewell that he was free to go at any time. But if the guard told the interviewing agents something incriminating that warranted arrest, he should immediately be given Miranda. Johnson's training video ruse did not factor into the conversation. No one on either end of the line was aware of it.

JEWELL STEERED HIS PICKUP truck into a lined space outside the FBI's mirrored-glass Century Boulevard headquarters. He met the waiting agents, Johnson and Rosario, and the three rode the elevator to the fourth floor. They entered the Bureau's offices through a secure door.

In keeping with the BSU's instructions, the agents escorted Jewell away from any chaotic activity, down a quiet, beige-wallpapered corridor adorned with framed photos of President Clinton, Attorney General Reno, and FBI Director Freeh. They entered the SAC's fourth floor conference room, the same space where the Secret Seven had met for over a year planning Olympic security.

In a corner beyond a twenty-foot-long mahogany table, Jewell spotted three chairs arranged in a triangle. To the left was a collection of camera and sound equipment. Straight ahead stood a tall pole with darkened studio lights directed at the corner seat. Jewell had never seen anything like it in a law enforcement setting, but Agent Johnson had told him there would be a taped interview. And this was, after all, the FBI.

Two Bureau supervisors briefly joined them. One welcomed Jewell, thanking him for coming and assuring the guard, "You're free to go any time you want." The other quietly slipped Johnson what appeared to be a handwritten note. Johnson glanced at the text and, betraying no expression, tucked the white sheet into a folder. The two supervisors left the room.

Jewell wedged his bulky frame into the mauve armchair at the corner of the room. His three credentials still hung from his lime-green lanyard, his tortoise-shell sunglasses folded above them. Jewell's American-flag fanny pack bulged from the front of his right hip. His white baseball cap fit snugly on his large head, imprinted with an image of the park's main music stage and the words "AT&T Global Olympic Village." He waited with nervous excitement for the two Bureau agents to begin the questioning. Once they finished, he figured, the agents could tell the media outside that, of course, he had nothing to do with planting the bomb, and he would head for work.

Jan Garvin, a videographer from Quantico, approached Jewell, clipping a lavalier microphone to the guard's lanyard. Jewell pulled off his sunglasses and tossed them aside onto the table. Better to look professional.

As Jewell watched the agents settle into the matching chairs across from him, he captured the details around him: The Union Jack label inside Johnson's suit jacket as the agent pulled it off. The mildly stout gut. The Sig Sauer handgun, model 226, holstered on the back of Johnson's right hip. The mustached Rosario was far less formally dressed, he noticed, in a maroon polo shirt and slacks. The Latino agent sat quietly, notepad in hand. Clearly, Johnson would be taking the lead.

Jewell watched Garvin, now standing behind the agents, adjust his Sony Betacam. The camera angle would capture both Jewell and a podium over his left shoulder bearing the FBI seal and motto—Fidelity, Bravery, Integrity. Jewell knew he needed to push through his exhaustion and stress. But he deeply respected these interviewers, these men he could only dream of being, and wanted to help. He relished the idea that he could be featured in a training video for the highest level of American law enforcement.

It never occurred to the guileless guard that the training video was a ruse. In fact, so much already had escaped Jewell's normally hypervigilant attention.

He had taken the senior official's welcome of being "free to go at any time" as a gesture of friendliness, missing that the FBI was simply creating a record that Jewell wasn't in custody. And it never dawned on an eager-to-please Jewell that the hospitable agent Johnson was his fiercest antagonist.

"What do you prefer being called?" Johnson asked warmly in his Upstate New York accent.

"Richard."

"You can call me Don, let's keep it informal, alright?"

Jewell relaxed a bit.

For Johnson and Rosario's part, they were sitting face-to-face with the man they believed to be the Olympic bomber, responsible for two deaths and more than one hundred injured. Johnson remained confident the interview would lead to a confession, despite the BSU profilers trying to lower his expectations. Still, the pressure was intense, even more so after Johnson glanced down at the handwritten note the supervisor had given him. Titled "Director's Lead," Louie Freeh himself wanted Johnson to ask Jewell if the guard thought the bomb was designed to ambush law enforcement. Johnson was shocked. Never in his two-decade Bureau career had he ever seen or heard of an FBI Director personally engaging in a line agent's interview. Nor for that matter had he or Rosario ever conducted a videotaped interview for the Bureau. So many of the circumstances were odd. He needed to keep his focus.

With Rosario taking notes by hand, Johnson asked the questions. For forty-five minutes, Jewell handled routine queries about his work history, weapons training, extensive gun collection, passion for road duty, and weight struggles. He somberly offered details about being an only child and about his stepfather John Jewell's decision to abruptly walk out on the family. At one point, Rosario brought the guard a red Solo cup of ice water. At another, Jewell's fanny pack made him uncomfortable, so he unclipped it and tossed it near his sunglasses.

As Jewell meticulously filled in the details of his background, he was unaware that FBI lawyer Mollie Halle was sitting in the office next door finishing the search warrant for Jewell's truck and his mother's apartment. Nor did he know that two dozen paces down the hall, FBI supervisors and the U.S. Attorney had gathered. They would soon deliver a message that would change the course of the investigation—and Jewell's life.

BACK IN WASHINGTON, MINUTES before the interview had started, wall monitors directly opposite of Freeh began to air the CNN story on the *AJC*'s newsbreak about Jewell. The Director was livid. He leaned forward, body tensing, hands clenched. How can the newspaper be out in front of us, he fumed to no one in particular, straining to keep a measured tone. "This thing is out of control."

The stakes had been raised, and some around the table—especially senior DOJ attorney Merrick Garland—had been uncomfortable with the original decision not to issue Miranda. Garland, sitting immediately to Freeh's right, had firsthand experience as the Justice Department's lead lawyer on the Oklahoma City bombing case. After Terry Nichols had voluntarily walked into a police station, much like Jewell had just done at the Atlanta field office, the FBI opted not to inform him of his rights. But that decision triggered difficult courtroom wrangling when Nichols's lawyer argued that his client had effectively been in custody, making the statements inadmissible. While the judge finally decided in favor of the government, Garland reminded the others that the process had been arduous.

Freeh conducted a deliberate around-the-table discussion, including gathering the team's perspectives on Miranda, and jotting Yeses or Nos on a notepad. The Director then called down to Atlanta SAC Woody Johnson with a stunning reversal: Interrupt the interview and tell the agents to read Jewell his rights.

Rosario was summoned out of the Jewell interview to the SAC's office, then told of Freeh's decision. The agent was furious. He had never heard of Miranda being administered in the middle of an investigative interview when someone was free to go. Jewell will clam up, Rosario protested. But the Director's decision had been made. U.S. Attorney Kent Alexander,* trying to provide a bit more flexibility, told Rosario he did not have to walk in and

---

* Alexander, of course, is one of the coauthors of this book.

abruptly read the rights. He could wait for the right moment, but not too long. Maybe that would provide some breathing room.

After Rosario left, SAC Johnson worried aloud that the agent could lose his job delaying delivery of Miranda in conflict with Freeh's direct order. So, Alexander called Freeh to explain his thinking. The Director calmly absorbed the news, assuring the U.S. Attorney that Jewell was going to talk with or without Miranda. The overarching concern in Washington, as Atlanta understood it, was to ensure that anything Jewell said could be used against him without a serious court challenge.

Headquarters' view reflected the broader belief that now pervaded the FBI: Richard Jewell was the bomber. They were so convinced, in fact, that a prison cell had been prepared that morning at the Atlanta Federal Penitentiary. If Jewell confessed, he would be transported directly to the maximum-security facility.

Rosario reentered the conference room with a single form on top of his notebook. The agent sat down and pointed to an FD-395, the waiver for Miranda rights. Johnson looked at Rosario, incredulous. His mind wobbled. Miranda? What had happened? Johnson had to think fast. Scrambling but outwardly calm, he settled on a strategy. He would allow Jewell to finish his lengthy explanation about leaving Piedmont College and coming to the Games, ask a follow-up question or two, then shift gears. So, when Jewell finally paused and cleared his throat, Johnson pivoted.

"OK, well, now we get to the part where we're pretty much finished with all the background stuff. We're gonna use it for the purposes I told you before. But in order to do so, I want to go through it just like it's a real official interview, OK?" Johnson told Jewell. "So, what I'm gonna do is I'm gonna go right through it like, uh, walk up and introduce myself to you, basically, tell you who I am, show you my credentials, just like we're doing a professional interview, OK? And then, I'll just ask you a couple of questions like your name and your age, and what I'll do is I'm even gonna go as far as to advise you of your rights. OK? You understand that?"

Jewell nodded slightly, his brow furrowing a bit.

But the videographer, Garvin, who was unaware Jewell was a suspect, needed to swap out his camera's tape. So, Johnson and Rosario took the opportunity to step out of the room. Johnson marched down the hall, where he demanded an explanation from his supervisors on the rights waiver. They repeated the instructions Rosario had heard minutes earlier: You need to issue Miranda warnings. "What the fuck?" Johnson fumed. He felt like his legs had been lopped from under him. Johnson was convinced that Jewell would shut down. But his bosses held firm.

For a brief moment, the agent considered disobeying his supervisors. There was no legal requirement for Miranda, although he surely would be fired for insubordination. Now he had to focus on how he could convince Jewell to keep talking, even with Miranda. Consulting with no one, the agent decided to double down and deliver the warnings within the framework of the ruse.

Johnson stepped back into the room, then signaled to Garvin to turn on the studio lights. He stood before Jewell and flipped open his credentials. "Mr. Jewell, my name is Don Johnson. I'm a special agent with the FBI. And the reason I'm here today is we're doing basically an interview of all individuals who were at Centennial Park when an explosion took off."

He gathered Jewell's name, address, and age, then continued. "Mr. Jewell, as is customary in pretty much all cases of this magnitude, what we do is we advise everyone, you don't have to talk to us. You have certain constitutional rights."

"It's my understanding you graduated from college and you can read and speak the English language, is that correct?" Johnson asked.

"Um, I didn't graduate college," Jewell corrected him.

"High school, rather."

"Yes, sir, I did."

"Do you have any trouble reading?"

"No, sir."

Johnson handed Jewell the FD-395 Miranda form. "I'd like you to kinda read it over, tell me if you understand everything that's on that form."

In the glare of the studio lights, Jewell tipped his pale blue eyes downward, swallowed, and read the text. He sniffled, slipped his tongue upward to moisten his lip and edge of his mustache. As a deputy, he had given the same waiver of rights warnings hundreds of times himself. "You have the right to remain silent. Anything you say can and will . . ." Jewell knew what this meant. This was no training video. *The FBI thinks I'm the bomber.*

The room seemed to shrink. A grayness washed over Jewell, sweat pooling in the crease of his chin. When he spoke, his tone was respectful, querying. "I don't know if I should call an attorney now or not. 'Cause I don't know if this video is for, uh, . . . I don't know if I'm being investigated for this or if this is for what you have told me it is for, after what the newspeople told me."

Johnson strained to appear at ease, but panic gripped him. This was the most important interview of his career. He was staring at the man he was sure was the Olympic bomber, and Jewell was slipping away. Johnson realized that any halfway competent lawyer would end the interview immediately. So, the agent doubled down on Miranda, trying to convince Jewell there was no need for legal help.

"Is there something that, that is bothering you, why you think you need an attorney? It's my understanding you were a hero," Johnson coaxed.

"Well, that's my understanding too. And y'all have told me that," Jewell replied.

"You know what you did. You know what happened there."

"Yes, sir."

"I mean, I don't understand what you're saying. Everything I was led to believe is you were the individual who found this bomb. You're the one that warned them. You're the one that got them out of there. Is that correct?"

"That's what happened, yes, sir."

Johnson spoke evenly, seated with his left leg crossed over his right, his hands clasped as if in silent prayer. The agent shifted to flattery. "You certainly have got a number of years and experience in police work, whether it be private security or public law enforcement. And, uh, we're trusting your judgment at this point in time, your ability to recognize a situation, and you did."

Jewell didn't bite. "Would it be alright for me to call my attorney and see if he can come up here and just sit in? Would he be able to do that?"

Johnson knew he was left with no option but to step out and let Jewell make the call. He was failing, all because of an edict to read rights to a suspect who was not in custody—and in the middle of his interview no less. Who the hell believed Jewell would keep talking with that late switch? *I've lost my guy*, Johnson thought, in a mixture of dejection and anger.

Johnson and Rosario stepped out of the room as Jewell dialed Watson Bryant, his mentor from the Small Business Administration a decade before. He absolutely needed counsel. Yet, Bryant didn't answer at his office or home. Jewell called four times, then tried Bryant's brother and father. All he could do was leave messages.

After he hung up, Jewell paced the room, churning over his predicament. Garvin, the cameraman, tried to make small talk, asking if Jewell played computer games. Jewell was in no mood for chitchat. Then, to Garvin's surprise, Jewell stepped to the conference-room table, picked up a pen, and signed his name to the Miranda form. Next, the guard settled back in his chair and re-clipped the lavalier microphone to his lanyard. "Let's do it," he announced.

In utter disbelief, Garvin stepped into the hallway and signaled for Johnson and Rosario to return. "He signed the form," the videographer told them.

The agents shared the cameraman's incredulity. The guard had apparently reached out to an attorney, *yet still agreed to continue the interview*. Johnson and Rosario returned to the room just eleven minutes after they had left.

The interview resumed. Johnson put on the record Jewell's description of trying to reach legal counsel. He also confirmed the guard was at the FBI voluntarily and had signed the waiver. Then the pair discussed Jewell's responsibilities in the park, finally getting to the night of the bombing. Jewell spoke in long paragraphs, describing in detail his need to take a relief break and his diligence when he returned to the tower to ensure that everyone had proper credentials. Within minutes, Jewell rolled into his familiar story of the Speedo Boys.

Johnson took the opportunity to flatter Jewell. Keep him talking, create a record of his statements. "So, in a very professional or responsible manner, you were double-checking the individual that relieved you?" Jewell replied, "That is correct."

Almost a half hour into the interview restart, Jewell asked if he could call his mother. He knew she was alone in the apartment and would be worried. Indeed, when Bobi answered, she was in near hysterics. The media swarm at Monaco Station had grown to even more oppressive levels. "Mother, calm down. Calm down," Jewell urged. He put his hand over the receiver and asked the agents if they could send someone to her apartment to stay with her. Johnson reassuringly replied, "I think we could send over a couple of mature female agents."

The three men again returned to the interview.

AS JEWELL'S POST-MIRANDA QUESTIONING by Johnson had begun, Watson Bryant and Nadya Light were walking around Centennial Olympic Park. The space had just reopened that morning, and Bryant had closed the office so they could drive downtown to show their support. Light, an attractive Russian immigrant who was both the attorney's paralegal and girlfriend, had told Bryant earlier that she was keen on meeting Jewell. Impressed by the guard's heroism, she hoped to buy him a celebratory meal. Bryant too had wanted to run into his old friend, whom he hadn't seen since their SBA years.

At 6:35 P.M., Bryant spotted the headline with the bombshell news. A woman nearby hawking the *Atlanta Journal* Extra edition cried out, "FBI has suspect. Read all about it." "What the hell?" Bryant yelped to Light. He bought a paper and read the story. He needed to reach Jewell.

Bryant and Light rushed to his SUV, where he had his flip phone. He dialed 411 for the FBI main office number, then called the Bureau. An FBI receptionist told him she didn't know of anyone named Richard Jewell in the building. So, Bryant sped home to check his old messages to pull the number Jewell had left when calling about a possible book deal.

Nearly an hour had passed since Bryant had first seen the newspaper in the park. He and Light arrived home to discover a new message from Jewell on his answering machine. The guard had called to say the FBI was questioning him. The attorney hit *69 to determine where the call had originated. It was the same FBI number he had dialed before.

This time when Bryant reached the Bureau, he demanded to speak with Richard Jewell. "Don't give me any bullshit. I know he's there."

At 7:32 P.M., two and a half hours after Jewell arrived at the FBI office, the interview was interrupted by an "urgent" call for Agent Johnson. Watson Bryant was on the line and wanted to speak to his client. In a brief conversation with Jewell, Bryant shared Scruggs's *AJC* reporting. Then he asked to speak with Johnson.

"What's going on?" Bryant asked the agent, identifying himself as Jewell's attorney. Johnson noted several days had passed since the bombing, and explained, "We're finally doing a formal interview."

Bryant posed the burning question, "Is my client a suspect?"

Johnson scrambled. "I don't know what that term means," he replied, then continued: "Is he a subject? No, he's not a subject. Do we have any intention of arresting him? No, we have no intention of arresting him. And we asked him to voluntarily come here and talk with us. And then we asked him if we could tape the interview. We said that our intention was to use it to train first office agents potentially as to what a first responder does. What an individual must look for. So, I figured we'd knock off two things at once, but somehow this thing is getting out of proportion here."

Bryant asked the agent to put Jewell back on the line. His advice to his new client was succinct: "Shut the hell up and get your fat ass out of there."

Jewell and Bryant agreed to meet at the Monaco Station apartment. "You can't miss it," Jewell told the lawyer. "There are about five hundred press out front." At 7:46 P.M., the interview was terminated. Jewell collected his backpack, sunglasses, and American flag fanny pack.

Johnson made a final effort to preserve a rapport with the guard before he left, referring to the tenor of their exchanges. "Is there anything adversarial about this?" he asked.

"No, sir, there's not, but . . ."

"I think we were making some very positive inroads. We're getting to where we wanted to be. I feel comfortable talking to you and I hope you feel the same way about me."

"Yes, sir."

Finally, Jewell wondered what to do about the media that were now massed outside his mother's home. Johnson clapped Jewell on the shoulder, smiling to evince a sense of law enforcement camaraderie. "I honestly think that with your experience, Richard, you might know more than I would."

Jewell began to leave. "Well, gentlemen, I appreciate your time and concern. I'm going to ease on over that way," he said. "It was very nice to meet you. I am so sorry about this, but I have to do what my attorney says."

Jewell walked to the elevator and through the lobby. With Rosario accompanying him, Jewell waded through dozens of cameramen and reporters in the FBI parking lot as they barked out questions and accusations. In a dizzying twelve hours, Richard Jewell had gone from hero on *Today* to the publicly reviled presumed bomber.

JEWELL DROVE OUT OF the parking lot and stopped into 7-Eleven for a Coke. A surreal processional of Bureau and media cars that was following him paused, then continued the tail back to Monaco Station. There, Jewell navigated through the expanding horde of journalists and climbed the stairs to reunite with his mother. Bobi was still distressed. He tried to calm her, as they worked their way back to the small den.

Bobi sat on the sofa. Jewell settled into a stuffed easy chair. They looked up to see Jewell on TV, the newscaster describing him as the lead suspect in the bombing. They switched channels, to the local Fox affiliate and then finally NBC. Bobi's favorite newsman, Tom Brokaw, came on the screen with Bob Costas. "Mom, there's your man," Jewell pointed. Surely the trusted NBC anchor would give him a fair shake.

But Brokaw's words were crushing: "The speculation is that the FBI is close to 'making the case,' in their language. They probably have enough to arrest him right now, probably enough to prosecute him, but you always want to have enough to convict him as well. There are still some holes in this case."

The Jewells sat back. Bobi was devastated, Richard flabbergasted. His face drained of color, turning from its usual ruddy to ashen. "That low-down son of a bitch," Jewell grumbled.

Bobi's mind, though, had drifted elsewhere. Reluctantly, she had to give voice to the obvious question. "Richard, did you do it?"

"Mama, how could you? No, I didn't do it."

She never asked him again.

LATER THAT EVENING, MAGISTRATE Judge Gerrilyn Brill stepped into the fourth-floor law library at the Bureau's Atlanta offices, where she was met by Special Agent Rosario and U.S. Attorney Alexander.

The no-nonsense judge, a former chief of the fraud section in the U.S. Attorney's Office, settled in at a table in the Bureau's law library. She began to pore over the thirteen-page search warrant application. The document was marked: "Under Seal." Rosario, as the affiant, had certified that the FBI believed that, "on the property or premises of 3649 Buford Highway, Apartment F-3 . . . there is now concealed a person or property . . . that constitutes evidence of the fruits of a crime." The two-page attachment detailed dozens upon dozens of items to be seized: personal files, papers, fingernail clippers, books, pamphlets, eyewear, suitcases, computer disks, as well as wires, nails, batteries, gunpowder, anything that could be used as a component for a bomb.

Brill focused on the affidavit supporting the probable cause to search Bobi Jewell's apartment. The document disclosed up front that Jewell could not have made the 911 call, since he had reported observing the package at the same time the call came in. The judge pondered what the FBI had gathered so far, which was spelled out over nearly nine single-spaced pages, including details of Jewell spotting the backpack and working to move people to safety.

But the incriminating evidence was abundant:

- Witness statements that Jewell had researched IEDs on the internet at Piedmont College prior to the Olympics;
- Records that Jewell took four hours of coursework on bombs, including black powder explosives;
- Witness statements about Jewell's stability, overzealousness, and motivations in Habersham County, where he had lost two police jobs;
- Obsession with law enforcement, including that he "ate, slept, and breathed" the work and was an "adrenaline junkie";
- Jewell's statements that he would be "right in the middle of it in the Olympics" if something happened;
- His statement, just before the blast: "It's a bomb. I've already called law enforcement. Let's get out of here";
- A video the FBI had secured that appeared to show Jewell looking at the scene of the explosion, then running away from the victims;
- A witness account questioning whether Jewell would even have passed a thorough "psychological profiling" to become a deputy.

Much of the most incriminating information in the affidavit came directly or indirectly from the Habersham interviews Don Johnson had conducted the day before.

The final paragraph of the warrant application was a supplement added shortly after the ruse interview fell apart. It noted the media reporting on the case, and that Jewell had terminated his conversation with the FBI earlier in the evening. Then it concluded: "It is likely that Richard Jewell will attempt to destroy and conceal existing evidence as soon as he can."

Judge Brill quizzed Rosario about sections of the document, occasionally requiring more research be done to support probable cause. Ultimately, satisfied with the evidence, Brill signed the warrant for the apartment at 11:42 P.M., and for Jewell's truck a few minutes later. Senior FBI officials debated whether the Bureau should launch a raid on Jewell's apartment that night. But the hour was late. They decided to hold off.

CHAPTER 15

Watson Bryant began Wednesday with a full-throated defense of Richard Jewell.

The night before, he had seen the blanket television coverage triggered by Scruggs and Martz's article, and battled through the media swarm as he approached Jewell's apartment. Once inside, like Bobi, he directly asked his client whether he had committed the crime. Bryant came away convinced Jewell was not the bomber, and told that to reporters gathered outside.

Now, dressed in a white Oxford shirt and an open black North Face windbreaker, the lawyer joined Bryant Gumbel at 7:18 A.M. on the *Today* show set in Centennial Park. Jewell had appeared on the same show just twenty-four hours earlier.

After a perfunctory "good morning," Gumbel opened bluntly, "Your position on this is very clear. Your statement, quote 'He is not a suspect. He is not going to be arrested. He didn't do it. He is a free man. There is no search warrant.' End of quote. If there is no fire, how do you explain all this smoke?"

"I can't," Bryant replied matter of factly. "I have no idea why everybody seems to think that Richard is the prime suspect in this case. I'd like to know, to tell you the truth."

If the lawyer was nervous, as a novice media personality well outside his area of expertise, he didn't show it. With many replies, he added a half-smile, helping him come across as approachable. In turn, Gumbel became more prosecutorial. "Let me ask you a couple of questions," he said, consulting his notes.

"Is it true that your client was arrested in May of 1990 for impersonating a police officer?"

"I have no idea."

"*You have no idea?*" Gumbel asked incredulously.

"No. I don't have his police record."

167

"Is it true that he was at some time ordered to seek psychological counseling?"

"I don't know that either, but I know a lot of people that oughta have psychological counseling."

Later, Gumbel softened a bit, asking about Jewell's emotional state. "Would you characterize him as angry, disappointed, surprised?"

Bryant positioned Jewell as the hero and victim he believed him to be. "He told me that he would do the same thing again no matter what, that he feels like he saved a lot of people's lives by the actions that he took. And that regardless of what happens to him, he would do it again, and that he feels he's being unfairly victimized . . ."

Gumbel interrupted to wrap up with a final question: "Will he be going to work today?"

"I doubt it," Bryant replied, rolling his eyes. "He can't even get out of his apartment there are so many reporters out there. You need a police wedge to make it to the parking lot."

Over on *Good Morning America*, anchor Aaron Brown interviewed a local assistant district attorney about Jewell. Despite having no role in the case, her fireball attitude, pronounced Southern accent, and well-honed flare for drama made the thirty-six-year-old blonde prosecutor a perfect media go-to. She was blunt and accusatory, speculating that Jewell's arrest was imminent. She took issue when another guest on the show referenced Jewell being entitled to a fair hearing. "This is not a jury trial yet, and there is no presumption of innocence as we speak," the lawyer snapped.

The host Brown, sounding a bit bewildered, asked the prosecutor, "If it turns out, Nancy, that he is not the guy, then this leak that started all of this has made life, you'll excuse the expression, hell for this man." Unrelenting, assistant DA Nancy Grace shot back, "Well, I have to agree with you. But you've got to weigh that against the two dead victims."

In Washington, Deputy Attorney General Jamie Gorelick watched the interview on *Good Morning America*. She gasped, horrified at the leap past a presumption of innocence by a local prosecutor. Gorelick grabbed the phone and called U.S. Attorney Alexander in Atlanta. Her message was stiletto sharp: "That woman is the face of justice. Get her off of there." Alexander was equally appalled. He called the Fulton County district attorney, who promised to instruct Grace to stay off the air. That edict was short-lived. By year's end, Grace would resign to become a national legal commentator on Court TV.

Following his television defense of Jewell, Bryant was driving to pick up his daughter at his parents' house. They had tickets for a long-anticipated Olympics equestrian event. But just minutes after he got in the car, Bryant heard a radio report that the FBI had secured a search warrant and was preparing to enter Jewell's apartment. He quickly told his family he would meet them at the horse park later, and drove toward Monaco Station instead. Along the way, Bryant called a lawyer friend to ask about a suspect's rights during a search. As a commercial loan attorney, he was out of his league.

AT 9:02 A.M., FOR the second time in as many days, Don Johnson pulled his Crown Vic into the Buford Highway complex and marched past the growing media herd. He climbed to Apartment F-3. His face was hard, his suit and tie a sharp contrast to the gray FBI T-shirts and navy ATF polos worn by many others on the search team. Johnson knocked, entered, and presented the pair of warrants that Judge Brill had signed the night before.

Jewell was already prepared for the search, having seen the TV news reports beamed from outside his apartment. He had sent Lacy to the vet for boarding. His most loyal and present friend was now gone. Bobi had taken her beagle mix and her cat to a friend's house. Later she would rush past the media carrying the cat's still-full litter box as she ignored a yelled question of "How's Mr. Jewell holding up?" Bobi would spend the day out of the apartment too.

Jewell knew from his own experience conducting searches that he needed to eliminate any possible surprise. So, he had placed much of his gun collection on his bed, then mentioned the weapons to Johnson. He walked the agent back to the bedroom. Jewell offered other advance warning too. His backpack might have bomb residue on it, since it was near the tower gate the night of the explosion. Inside the pack, Jewell offered, the forensics team would find plastic gloves because he was a trained first responder. His old deputy sheriff's badge would be in it too.

Watson Bryant arrived at 9:30, while the apartment was still being secured. He told the agents that he and Jewell wanted to be present for the search. The request was denied. Another attorney advised Bryant to file a

169

motion. Fed up, Bryant told Jewell he was leaving to join his family. He offered Jewell simple instructions: "Say nothing and watch everything."

Jewell would sit for more than six hours on the steps near his front door, dressed in a pair of gym shorts and a hole-pocked basketball T-shirt emblazoned with the message "Just Elevate And Decide in the Air." He forlornly tried to block out the news choppers hovering overhead and the media scrum that had swollen to more than two hundred. Photographers trained their telephoto lenses on the stairwell to capture Jewell as he faced away from them. Kathy Scruggs stood proudly among the media. Her scoop had started an avalanche.

Harry Grogan, Johnson's partner, had tagged along without an assignment. At one point, he found himself standing next to Jewell. "You don't have any storage facilities, do you?" he asked the guard. Jewell replied that he rented a shed for his remaining belongings in Habersham. Grogan asked for a key. Jewell pulled it from his chain and offered the specific location. The FBI would later secure a warrant from Judge Brill for the unit.

Roughly thirty agents prepared to search the Jewells' apartment in stages. A bomb-sniffing dog went in first for an eighteen-minute scan. Next, an FBI photographer and videographer recorded the condition and contents of each room pre-search. Two agents measured walls to prepare an apartment sketch that would help accurately map the location of the Jewells' possessions. Agents began to vacuum every room and flat surface of the apartment, hunting for trace amounts of explosives. They swabbed the toilets, in case Jewell had flushed down evidence. Using a portable explosive detection scanner, FBI forensics experts field-tested the samples. The initial results were negative, but the samples would be flown to the FBI laboratory at Quantico for further analysis.

At 2:47 P.M., thirteen investigators wearing booties and protective gloves swarmed into the apartment. A supervisor read aloud Rosario's affidavit. Each agent was given a copy of the list of items to be seized, and they dispersed to their assigned rooms. Outside in the parking lot, SAC Dave Tubbs stood before the microphones to explain that the FBI was executing a court-authorized search warrant in an "ongoing federal investigative process." No conclusions should be drawn. "Mr. Jewell has not been placed under arrest, and he has not been charged with any crime under our system of justice," Tubbs cautioned. "We emphasize that neither the issuance of search warrant nor the execution of it constitutes evidence of guilt."

Inside, agents continued to comb through the apartment. From Jewell's room, they gathered the guns the guard had pointed out to Johnson, finding additional weapons under his bed and in a dresser drawer. They logged in fourteen firearms in all. Agents seized ammunition and over a half-dozen knives. They boxed up computer disks, undeveloped rolls of film, photos, Olympic pins, and his fanny pack. From the top of his TV credenza, they recovered wood splinters and metal fragments that appeared to be from the park bombing.

Investigators searched Bobi's bedroom, rummaging through her dresser, including what she would later cringe were her "unmentionables." In the bathroom, the agents packed up the floor mat, a bottle of hydrogen peroxide, and *Outrage: The Five Reasons Why O.J. Simpson Got Away with Murder*, a book Jewell was apparently reading. They reached into the hamper to pull out a pair of brown shorts. Investigators snatched the calendar off the kitchen refrigerator. They gathered videotapes from a cabinet, hauling away Disney and John Wayne movies, unmarked VHS cassettes, and cartridges labeled "COPS."

Throughout the search, investigators continued to scour for traces of hair and fibers, eager to match evidence recovered at Centennial Park. They meticulously bagged lint from the dryer and carried off Bobi's vacuum cleaner. They boxed up piece after piece of Bobi's prized thirty-year collection of Tupperware to test later for black gunpowder.

In the late afternoon, word came that Judge Brill had granted the order to allow Jewell into the apartment. Agents required him to slip on booties and gloves. He sat in the living room and watched as the FBI searched, labeled, and boxed his and Bobi's belongings. At one point, he thought he heard a crash in his bedroom, which he presumed was his CD player hitting the floor. "What are you all tearing up?" he asked. Agents said he couldn't go in to check.

At five P.M., agents began to file out from the apartment. Brushing past Jewell, they descended the stairs carrying the boxes and bags filled with the Jewells' belongings to awaiting white vans. They also towed away "Old Blue," his pickup truck. The media eagerly filmed the procession.

At 7:20 P.M., more than ten hours after Don Johnson first knocked on the door, the search was over. The FBI photographer emerged from the apartment after taking "exit photographs." A supervisor invited Jewell to do a ten-minute walk-through. Did the suspect see any damage to property as a result of the search? No. The man then asked Jewell for his gloves and booties, and later logged them in as evidence. Soon after, the FBI handed the guard a receipt for the items seized.

When Bobi returned that night, she took one look at her home and burst into tears.

DESPITE TUBBS'S CAUTIONS, THE media, now cordoned away from the apartment, beamed images of the suspect around the globe. "Richard Jewell sitting by as federal agents put the screws on," one TV reporter intoned over a shot of him on the stairs. Another television journalist summed up the scene: "It is a painstaking process, looking for the smallest piece of evidence and throughout it Jewell remains 'technically free.'"

As the news reports gave way to late-night comics, the barbs sharpened. On the *Tonight Show*, host Jay Leno opened his monologue by remarking that the FBI was questioning "one guy in particular" in the probe of the bombing. "Can we show his picture? Have you seen this guy's picture? Yes, that guy there." They aired a jowly photo of Jewell. "Now, he seems to fit the typical misfit profile, cop wannabe, low self-esteem, and a scary resemblance to the guy who whacked Nancy Kerrigan." Producers switched to a shot of Shawn Eckardt, who had been hired to injure the superstar skater two years earlier.

Leno connected the two: "What is it about the Olympic Games that brings out big, fat, stupid guys?" The audience roared.

That night, the media and law enforcement remained on around-the-clock stakeout at Monaco Station. Inside, the Jewells tried to resettle into their home, but felt violated by the search and smothered by the constant surveillance. They drew the blinds tight. Paranoia washed over them like a toxic wave. Jewell and Bobi quickly became convinced that their phone lines were tapped and the apartment bugged. They were so certain that they began communicating by writing notes to one another. At times, Bobi's cat Bootsie crawled onto the ledge and jostled the blinds. Outside, TV journalists eager for any glimpse of Jewell flipped on their camera lights, illuminating the shuttered windows. To Bobi, it felt like a joyless Fourth of July.

THURSDAY MORNING'S NEWS COVERAGE brought no relief. Media outlets had begun to learn more about Jewell's history. Piedmont College President Ray Cleere offered several interviews, and journalists poked into the guard's love of guns and Dobermans.

Watson Bryant remained Jewell's staunchest public advocate. He appeared on *Good Morning America*, again proclaiming Jewell's innocence, and went on the attack.

"I think whichever rat it was that leaked that Richard Jewell was being considered a suspect in this case ought to be prosecuted for leaking it," Bryant fired. "The fact that this investigation is being conducted under the scrutiny of the media is absolutely ridiculous."

Bryant also raised a concern he thought should be obvious: "I just hope that while the FBI puts a thousand people on Richard Jewell that the real guy doesn't get away or is planning some other act."

Despite Bryant's efforts, many in the media remained relentless. The *New York Post* headlined its front page SAINT OR SAVAGE? Inside, the paper quoted neighbors as calling Jewell "very standoffish, very hard to get to know." He was a quiet loner who acted strangely, the *Post* told readers, citing one man in the complex. One of the paper's columnists, in a piece headlined WHO CHECKED "RAMBO" CROSSING GUARD'S RECORD?, called Jewell "a fat, failed former sheriff's deputy." Only a few publications, including the *New York Times* and the *Wall Street Journal,* remained cautious, carefully stepping around any presumption of guilt.

At the *AJC*, editors threw more than a dozen staffers at the story. POLICE WORK "WAS HIS LIFE," a headline announced above a Maria Elena Fernandez story from Habersham, adding "Some in North Georgia town say Jewell 'was on a power kick.'" Kent Walker, the intern who had penned the flattering profile of Jewell that was yanked, weighed in about Jewell's eagerness for publicity: "For three days, he had shuttled from television station, to newspaper, to wire service to tell of his heroics and to humbly offer, 'I'm no hero.'"

Scruggs led the paper's coverage the day after the search. In a front-page piece headlined NO ARREST MADE YET, she described how Jewell's life was "photographed, categorized and filed" by federal agents during the search.

The paper's most striking piece came from its renowned sports columnist, Dave Kindred. The veteran had joined the media pack outside Jewell's apartment on the morning of the search. Kindred knew he wanted to center his column on the human condition. But how? During the afternoon, a local photographer pointed out to the columnist that there hadn't been a stakeout like this in Atlanta since a series of murders in the early 1980s. Kindred picked up on the idea.

"Once upon a terrible time," he wrote, "federal agents came to this town to deal with another suspect who lived with his mother. Like this one, that suspect was drawn to the blue lights and sirens of police work. Like this one, he became famous in the aftermath of murder. His name was Wayne Williams. This one is Richard Jewell."

Later in the column, Kindred continued with the analogy, quoting the photographer who asked, "Did you see the FBI take those little vacuum cleaners into Jewell's apartment? It's exactly what they did with Wayne Williams." As if the piece weren't pointed enough already, Kindred ended with a final comparison: "Richard Jewell sits in the shadows today. Wayne Williams sits in prison forever."

CHAPTER 16

The men's 200-meter race on Thursday was pushed back to a later timeslot to better accommodate NBC's prime-time schedule. Michael Johnson had turned the competition into even more of a must-see after he captured the 400 three days earlier. Now, the Texan sprinter had a legitimate shot at becoming the first man in Olympic history to win both races in the same Games. In gold shoes, no less.

The city and Olympics fans had moved on from the bombing. The venues had extra layers of security. Patrons had returned to their partying ways, comfortable now that the bomber was cornered. A.D. Frazier cautiously declined to comment on anything relating to the investigation. As the operations chief for the Games, he focused on keeping things moving.

But on the night Johnson had captured the gold in the 400, he mentioned at his press conference that he had been saddened by the bombing in the park, singling out Alice Hawthorne's daughter. An ACOG official seized on the moment and asked Johnson if he would visit the girl, Fallon, in the hospital. Uneasy, Johnson stepped into her room. *What do you say to a fourteen-year-old girl at this time?* he wondered. Johnson didn't stay long, offering words of solace and encouragement. But he hoped his presence and compassion had helped the girl in some small way.

On Thursday night, Johnson's focus returned to what he knew best: running.

His strongest competitor in the 200 would be Namibia's Frankie Fredericks, who had ended Johnson's two-year winning streak in a race a month earlier. At the gun, Johnson, a gold chain dangling from his neck and a gold hoop earring in his left lobe, blasted out to a strong start. But four steps in, he stumbled slightly. Could the muscular sprinter with the unusual stand-up style make up the lag? Johnson rounded the turn and caught Fredericks at 80 meters. Then, with the crowd of eighty thousand overwhelmingly on his side, Johnson seemed to shift into a completely different gear.

As he reached his peak stride, Johnson could tell he was running faster than the 19:66 world record he had set in the Olympic trials several weeks earlier. He ripped through the finish line, chest pressed forward. When he looked up, the clock flashed 19:32, a world and Olympic record. Johnson raised his arms in triumph, then slipped his thumbs inside the straps of his racing singlet and thrust out the USA logo emblazoned across the chest.

Two miles away, more than sixty thousand fans squeezed in front of Centennial Olympic Park's AT&T Stage for a performance by Ray Charles. The audio system was balky, perhaps an issue from the rebuilding of the light and sound tower after the blast six nights earlier. But the crowd erupted as Charles leaned into his microphone and intoned the opening two-syllable word to "Georgia on My Mind." Over at the tower, a new night-shift security guard stood at Richard Jewell's post.

The next night, the fully revived Olympic spirit carried through to the men's basketball team. Now in the finals against Yugoslavia, the Americans went out to a five-point halftime lead. Most in attendance at the Georgia Dome, however, would remember the event more for what came next.

During halftime, IOC President Samaranch walked slowly to center court as the surprised crowd, many of whom had risen for the usual mid-game break, paused and stayed in the arena. Alongside Samaranch was Muhammad Ali, two weeks removed from lighting the Olympic torch.

Ali was there to heal a personal injustice. After he won gold at the Rome 1960 Olympics, the boxer returned to his native Kentucky with the medal proudly draped around his neck. As he would tell the story years later, a waitress at a Louisville restaurant refused to take his order. "We don't serve Negroes," she said. With his characteristic wit, the eighteen-year-old Ali quipped, "I don't want any Negroes. I want some cheeseburgers." The server refused to budge. America's racism cut to Ali's soul. Angry and ashamed, he told friends he flung his cherished gold medal into the Ohio River.

Now, at center court, Samaranch held a re-minted 1960 medal and slipped it around the champ's neck. Ali flashed his world-renowned grin and, despite shaking from Parkinson's, waved to a crowd nearly as boisterous as that at the Opening Ceremony. Then he raised the medal to his lips and kissed it.

THE LEAKS OUT OF Atlanta law enforcement appeared to have stopped.

On Thursday, Assistant U.S. Attorney Sally Yates and her boss, Kent Alexander, had fired off a "6(e)" grand jury secrecy letter to every member of the CENTBOM task force, essentially reminding them that unauthorized disclosures were a crime. Many Bureau rank and file viewed the one-paragraph missive as a stern reminder that Director Freeh and other Bureau leaders were livid over the leak to the *AJC*. Indeed, Freeh launched a formal investigation the same day to make clear to the Atlanta leadership that he fully intended to ferret out the source for reporters Kathy Scruggs and Ron Martz. Going forward, only one response to journalists would be countenanced: "No comment." The prosecutors' letter marked the start of a long public silence by the Atlanta CENTBOM task force.

Meanwhile, the FBI was in full sprint trying to make the case against Jewell. Following the search, the BSU still believed that Jewell was the right guy, with one team member putting the odds at 90 percent. The metal fragments and splinters found in the search caused particular concern. Bombers, murderers, rapists, and others often took trophies from their crimes. Another behavioralist pointed out that Jewell's decision to remain at the FBI even after the Miranda issuance was evidence that the BSU's analysis had been correct: Jewell clearly craved the attention.

But the CENTBOM team knew that far more than speculation would be needed to prosecute Jewell. Forensics were key. The Bureau already had developed a list of components, any of which might connect the bombing to Jewell: 8d masonry nails, No. 7 and No. 9 smokeless powder, duct tape, metal pipes with end caps, and the newly determined timing device, a Westclox Big Ben battery-powered alarm clock. The bomber also had nefariously lodged a steel plate behind the device, designed to direct the blast to inflict more damage.

Agents already had learned that the directional plate had not been nearly as effective as intended. Ironically, part of the credit was owed to Jewell. When the security guard chased off the beer-drinking Speedo Boys, two of them thought about grabbing the large backpack under the bench on their way out. They would take it to the nearby Tabernacle bar where James Brown was singing. The young men kicked it, trying to figure out what was inside. Maybe beer. One of them began to lift the bag, but it was too heavy. In the process, they inadvertently tipped the pack onto its back. The directional plate was then facing up instead of out toward the crowd. One CENTBOM supervisor estimated the death toll in the park would have been in the hundreds had the pack remained untouched and exploded directly into the crowd.

Several categories of forensic evidence emerged as especially promising. Hair and fiber samples had been found stuck to duct tape that the bomber had used to attach the nails to the device's pipe. And a pre-blast fingerprint had been singed into a piece of recovered pipe from the device. Now investigators needed to find a match.

Many of the items seized in the search had been flown directly to Quantico for testing. Agents there examined the evidence in minute detail and compared it to fragments of the bomb and ALICE pack that had been flown up earlier. But the search of the Monaco Station apartment looked like a washout. The vacuumed fibers had tested "not identical," in the FBI's terminology, as did the seized nails. Bobi Jewell's Tupperware had no gunpowder residue. Aside from the unusually large collection of firearms, most of the seized items could be found in any household. The Bureau turned to another possible answer: The device had been constructed elsewhere.

Armed with their forensic information, over a hundred agents fanned out across North Georgia to question owners of stores selling pipe, nails, batteries, wire, and sheet metal. Did Jewell purchase any of those items? When? Were there receipts? They stopped into Army surplus stores to ask if Jewell had bought a military ALICE pack. They probed gun shops for any connection to muzzle loading with black smokeless powder.

Meanwhile, other agents worked round-the-clock shifts to reconstruct Jewell's life. In the wake of the extraordinary media coverage, hundreds of leads were pouring in. Among them: highly troubling, and sometimes dubious, reports of Jewell's connections to bombs and bomb making.

An inmate named Richard Frazier claimed to have firsthand knowledge connecting Jewell with explosives. So, a pair of agents headed for West Central State Prison in Zebulon, Georgia, to interview him about his time served in the Habersham County jail. Three years earlier, Frazier recalled, Deputy Sheriff Jewell was assigned to guard him. At one point, as the pair watched a CNN story about a bombing overseas, Jewell confided that he knew how to manufacture a bomb. A few weeks later, Frazier continued, a group of Habersham inmates were discussing explosives. When Jewell overheard the conversation, he said he would like to set off a bomb in a large crowd. Allegations by inmates were notoriously unreliable, but the prisoner's level of detail made his statement more credible. The agents began the process of scheduling a polygraph.

An inmate at another facility also came forward. In a phone call handled by Special Agent Oliver Halle, Gregory Harkness, incarcerated in Jackson State Prison, described his prior experience with Jewell at the Habersham jail. It was a description Halle found intriguing enough that he drove to the facility an hour south of Atlanta.

Harkness explained that he and Jewell had become friendly in Habersham during the eighteen months that the inmate was locked up there. After the Oklahoma City bombing in April 1995, Jewell spoke repeatedly about the blast and about explosives. He disclosed to Harkness that he had purchased some nitrogen and was eager to experiment with it. Soon after, Harkness and other inmates were allowed out to help officers prepare for a policeman's safety weekend at the local fairground. Harkness and Jewell were paired up for the day, and Harkness claimed that Jewell took the opportunity to show the inmate two bombs he was crafting, each containing black powder. Later in the afternoon, Harkness recounted, Jewell also had asked him if he knew where to buy C-4 explosives. Harkness said he didn't. As the interview wore on, Halle noticed that never once did Harkness ask for any favors in return for the information, which heightened the inmate's credibility. Another polygraph was in order.

Other calls connected Jewell to bombs too. One woman said she had heard Jewell worked at Winston's restaurant south of Atlanta and had threatened to blow up the establishment after being fired. Another man phoned to say that in 1993 Jewell had worked as a cement mixer driver in a Tennessee quarry. He had access to explosives and was "not the most stable person." As with all major investigations with toll-free tip lines, the FBI knew it would need to sort fact from fiction in hundreds of calls. Each required separate investigation. None turned out to be true.

Beyond tracking down prison and phone leads, agents drilled down on Jewell's activities the night of the bombing. They questioned all law enforcement working the area, as well as all seventy security personnel employed by AT&T and every identifiable concertgoer near the tower. They also broadened parameters to see if Jewell's behavior before the bombing had been suspicious.

A construction worker, Tom Willemann, told the Bureau that during the building of another tower, Jewell wandered over to ask what the structure was rated. "What do you mean by 'rated'?" Willemann asked. "That's the tower's capability to withstand a blast," Jewell told him. The construction worker told the FBI he found the question odd.

As the days went on, the FBI obtained subpoenas that allowed agents to go through Jewell's trash and examine his mail. They developed film he had dropped off at a local drugstore. The Bureau built a life history, from his birth to elementary school, church, high school, and technical college. They ferreted out details about his mother, Bobi; his biological father, Robert; his wayward adoptive father, John Jewell. Mindful that bombers often begin building devices in high school, they spoke to friends and neighbors from Jewell's youth. The FBI interviewed his former employers and plenty of co-workers. They reviewed Jewell's error-prone record at the Habersham County Sheriff's Office and Piedmont College, as well as his arrest after the hot-tub incident. Over and over, the same portrait emerged, of a man who was gung-ho and overzealous.

Agents tracked down the MCI call-center employee, who described meeting Jewell at the TCBY yogurt shop and accompanying him to his mother's apartment for his twenty-seventh birthday. She said that at one point, Jewell had told her that he was working undercover at TCBY and he had saved customers during a shift by throwing a bad actor up against the wall. Her stark conclusion: "Jewell could be responsible for the bombing, because he was constantly craving attention and wanted to be a hero."

Agents found Jewell's former roommate at Post Apartments, Todd Welsh, who told the FBI that Jewell always seemed to be in a financial crunch, even to the point that his vehicle had been repossessed. Welsh also found the guard's viewing habits of the TV show *Cops* to be disturbing, including constant rewinding and pausing of episodes to predict or critique officers' action. He said that Jewell's behavior bordered on obsessive.

Beyond Jewell there was the pressing question about the identity of the

Unknown Subject (UNSUB) who had made the 911 call. Jewell was generally a loner, they believed, but he must have had an accomplice. Finding the 911 caller became a top task force priority.

Jewell had listed a "Rob Russell" as an emergency contact in the personnel documents Johnson rounded up at Piedmont College. Russell's name also had surfaced in other agents' interviews as a close associate of Jewell. So, supervisors assigned Johnson to locate and sit down with him. Johnson would be accompanied by Tim Attaway, who knew Russell from the North Georgia law enforcement community.

On Friday, the agents drove to Russell's work, a Marriott hotel in the Atlanta suburb of Duluth. Russell was over six feet tall and looked to weigh more than three hundred pounds. He talked in rapid bursts with a heavy Southern accent. His voice sounded nothing like the slow and deliberate 911 caller.

Russell riffled through story after story about Jewell, at times talking fondly of shared experiences. He told of his decade-long personal and professional friendship, starting with their time at Richway, through their time in the band The Pump. They ate together, then they jogged together to work off the pounds. They both aspired to be cops, the sharper-edged Russell getting the job first, in East Point, then helping Jewell secure his first law enforcement opportunity in Habersham. Russell later joined Jewell there. At one point, Jewell had even lived with Russell and his wife.

But Russell made clear that his relationship with Jewell had soured badly, and the men had neither seen nor spoken to one another for nine months. Jewell, according to Russell, had spread a false rumor that Russell had left the Habersham County Sheriff's Office under investigation for malfeasance. He added that he believed Jewell was simply envious of his promotion.

As Johnson would record in his 302, Russell characterized Jewell as "very aggressive, into everyone's business." Russell encouraged the agents to speak with Jewell's other two close friends, Brian McNair, who had been a colleague at Habersham, and a "cousin" in the mountains of West Virginia who Jewell called his "brother." Johnson eagerly jotted it all down.

That same day, Harry Grogan joined Johnson and Attaway at the Habersham County Sheriff's Office to meet McNair. Johnson pegged McNair at 5'11", 245 pounds. He had close-cropped brown hair and brown eyes, and spoke in an aw-shucks manner that belied his service six years earlier as a Marine, including service in Iraq during Operation Desert Storm.

McNair, whose voice sounded a bit closer to the one on the 911 tape, was unequivocally supportive of Jewell. He praised his former colleague as generous and loyal, and said he couldn't envision Jewell wrapping pipes with nails to inflict maximum damage. "I could see him build a bomb which would blow up in his face, just his luck," McNair bantered. Jewell, McNair told the agents, did have a "brother-cousin" in West Virginia. He had seen the man once briefly. White male, late twenties to early thirties, brown/blond hair. The brother again, Johnson noted. Who was he?

Johnson came away from the interview believing McNair seemed just a little too close to Jewell, had a bit too much in common, acted a little too protective. Russell, conversely, at times seemed suspiciously overeager to distance himself from Jewell, despite being an old friend. And both had mentioned the mysterious man from West Virginia—a third potential 911 caller the FBI now had to find.

BACK IN ATLANTA, FBI agents focused on a single strawberry blond hair that had attached to a recovered shred of the bomb's duct tape. Could it belong to Jewell? They sought another search warrant from Judge Brill, this time to pluck from Jewell's head. The magistrate agreed to the request as long as there was no forced entry into the apartment and the hair was taken in a private setting by medically trained personnel. She rejected an additional request for Jewell's pubic hairs.

On Saturday, August 3, the day before the Closing Ceremony, Watson Bryant called Jewell on the apartment's new phone number, which the guard had changed two days earlier to end the storm of media inquiries. Bryant was hot. "The government wants your hair, palm prints, and a voice exemplar," he barked. "I'm coming over."

At three P.M., four FBI agents and a doctor arrived. Jewell sat stone cold at the dining table, the floor-to-ceiling white drapes closed to keep out the prying eyes of the media. The doctor combed Jewell's auburn hair repeatedly and then, with a small pair of tweezers, plucked a single strand. Then another. And another. And another, until he had bagged the FBI's limit of twenty-five.

He gathered another twenty-five from the comb. Jewell would later tell his mother that the ten-minute ordeal was the most embarrassing experience of his life. Standing nearby, Bryant turned to one of the case agents: "I know you can have this, I know you have a search warrant, but I tell you this: If you were doing this to me, you would have to fight me. You would have to beat the shit out of me."

When they were finished, the agents walked Jewell over to the kitchen table, where they took the finger and palm prints. The agents then turned to the voice exemplar. Jewell was instructed to repeat a dozen times the words on the 911 call: "There is a bomb in Centennial Park. You have thirty minutes." But Bryant stepped in, refusing to let his client speak into the FBI's recording device. "Maybe you can do this, maybe you can't. But you're not going to do it today."

The agents and doctor left. Jewell and Bryant remained in the apartment, alternately stunned and irate.

DESPITE THE THOUSANDS OF journalists in town, few did much original reporting. Many reporters attended ACOG's press briefings, typically comprised of little more than A.D. Frazier explaining that he didn't know anything about the investigation but that the Games were proceeding well. The FBI was no longer participating in the briefings. The journalists in town were largely sportswriters without connections in law enforcement. Hardly any reporters interviewed sources in Atlanta, Habersham, or Washington with direct knowledge of the case.

The *AJC* wasn't breaking more major news on the investigation either. No one on the CENTBOM task force was talking. Instead, the paper speculated on Jewell's status, reported on stepped-up Olympic security measures and new bomb threats, and looked for human-interest angles.

An *AJC* freelancer covered Alice Hawthorne's overflowing funeral at Mount Zion Bethel Baptist Church in Albany, Georgia. Fallon wore a white dress and sunglasses, along with a finger splint and a large bandage covering the shrapnel wounds on her right thigh. Governor Zell Miller, Andy Young, and dignitaries from Washington attended to honor the forty-four-year-old entrepreneur and mother of two who had served in the Air Force.

For her part, Scruggs hunted for sources who could help advance the story, but found few credible ones. She did receive a detailed four-page letter from Gregory Harkness, the Jackson State prison inmate who claimed Jewell showed him two bombs. She shared the information with the FBI, not realizing that Agent Halle was already well aware of the inmate and his claims. But, in the end, there wasn't any confirmation, and she dropped the story.

Scruggs's best sources had gone quiet, including the leaker at the bar, who was upset that the reporter had run with the story. Instead of breaking more news, Scruggs was relegated to covering the hair plucking and fingerprints, a development that Jewell's outraged defense attorney had shared broadly with the media. In a story that ran in the Sunday paper, she made a point of quoting an Atlanta FBI spokeswoman saying that cases built on forensics take a while to complete. Without much fresh information, Scruggs instead wrote about the media circus outside Jewell's apartment. She was no longer out front on the story.

THE FBI EXPANDED ITS exhaustive search to Jewell's previous homes. All the while, the suspect remained largely confined to Bobi's apartment, the dungeon-like space with the blinds still tightly drawn. Watching all of the investigation activity around his client, Bryant knew one thing: Jewell needed a real criminal defense attorney, someone with experience in death-penalty cases. He reached out to Jack Martin.

A criminal defender with over two decades of federal experience, Harvard Law–educated Martin wore horn-rimmed glasses and reminded Bryant of a disheveled professor. But the native Atlantan had a sterling pedigree. Martin had served in Army intelligence during Vietnam and had received the Bronze Star. He had represented hundreds of defendants opposite the local U.S. Attorney's Office and was a former president of the Georgia Association of Criminal Defense Attorneys. Importantly, Martin had experience defending state death-penalty cases and was currently representing the only federal defendant in the district indicted in a capital case: Anthony Battle, the Atlanta Penitentiary inmate from whom agent Don Johnson had extracted a confession for murdering a prison guard.

Martin took Jewell's case, but he worried that the guard soon would be charged and could well be found guilty. Like everyone, he had seen the media coverage. If guilty, death row was a distinct possibility.

Martin agreed to meet Jewell at noon on the Sunday of the Closing Ceremony. As the attorney arrived at Bryant's Buckhead office, the media swarmed his Volkswagen Beetle convertible, the open top offering no cover from the cameras and boom microphones. Martin and Jewell met in a ground-floor conference room. Speaking calmly to try to soothe the shell-shocked guard, Martin opened with his usual advice: "Richard, I'm your attorney, so tell me everything. Our discussions are confidential." Martin took pages of notes on a yellow legal pad. *Jewell seems quirky but credible*, he thought.

Finally, the lawyer stared across the table, took a deep breath, and asked the delicate question he posed to all his clients, especially those suspected of murder.

"Richard, is there anything you haven't told me? Anything at all?"

Jewell squirmed, looked down at his hands. "Well, yes sir, there is one thing."

Shit, here it comes, Martin thought. Guilty or innocent, he'd defended them all.

"Sir," Jewell offered, gathering himself, "I haven't filed my taxes in two years."

Martin stared, barely able to contain his relief and laughter. The lawyer had represented plenty of murderers. Not one had ever mentioned failure to pay taxes. Martin walked out thinking, *This guy didn't do it*.

The conversation was a prelude to what Bryant, and now Martin, hoped would be their master stroke. That same afternoon, Jewell would take a lie detector test. When he passed it, the Jewell team would release the results as a newsbreak right around the Closing Ceremony. They would snare the spotlight with what they knew to be the truth: Richard Jewell was not the Olympic bomber.

Jewell settled in to meet Richard Rackleff, a twenty-seven-year former FBI special agent and polygrapher. Rackleff had performed the lie detector test on Wayne Williams more than a decade earlier, helping to break the case. Now, he ran his own business, administering similar tests and serving as an expert witness. Tall and thick, with owl-like wire-rimmed glasses and a shock of graying hair, Rackleff parked his car several buildings away, then walked through an alley to a back door of Bryant's building, slipping in unnoticed by the reporters out front.

Sitting at a glass-topped wood table in the conference room, Jewell was on edge. Like Martin, Rackleff patiently tried to put Jewell at ease, a critical element for accurate results. Before connecting up the polygraph equipment, Rackleff spent nearly four hours in conversation with Jewell. The guard described himself as a nerd in high school without many friends. He talked about his work experience in auto body, for a veterinarian, at TCBY. They reviewed in detail his time in Habersham, his rises and falls there.

Then, pausing the questioning, Rackleff strapped two sensors around Jewell's chest over the suspect's gray polo shirt. He slipped a cuff on Jewell's arm, then metal clips on his fingers. They talked some more about Jewell's career and his job in Olympic Park, Rackleff calibrating the device along with Jewell's replies as baseline data. Finally, Rackleff began asking about the day of the bombing: Have you ever seen a pipe bomb? Do you know how to make one? Did you have any role in planning the bombing of the Centennial Olympic Park bombing?

At eight P.M., six hours after they had begun, Rackleff had completed the test. He went upstairs to see Bryant, who was waiting in his cramped office for the results.

NINE MILES SOUTH OF Bryant's Buckhead office building, a celebrity-filled Closing Ceremony had just begun at Olympic Stadium. Little Richard belted out "Good Golly, Miss Molly." The Morehouse College Glee Club backed country star Trisha Yearwood. The Pointer Sisters harmonized with Al Green on "Take Me to the River." Stevie Wonder delivered a poignant cover of John Lennon's anthem to peace, "Imagine."

Athletes created a long conga line, joining musicians and huge skeleton puppets. In the ceremonial portion, Atlanta Mayor Bill Campbell handed the Olympic flag to IOC President Juan Antonio Samaranch, who in turn presented it to the mayor of Sydney, Australia, which would host the 2000 Summer Games. Michael Johnson carried the Olympic flag. Meanwhile, the distinction of shouldering the American stars and stripes didn't fall to Carl Lewis, Kerri Strug, or another American gold medal winner. Instead, organizers tapped an unsung hero, silver medal equestrian Michael Matz. Six years earlier, Matz had miraculously survived a plane crash and valiantly led three children to safety, then returned to rescue an eleven-month-old girl. Now, Matz carried the U.S. flag, leading the entire American Olympic squad through the stadium.

As the Games neared a close, Billy Payne and other ACOG officials took stock of the sheer breadth of the Centennial Olympic Games. A record 197 nations had competed, with athletes from seventy-eight of them taking home medals. Three million spectators attended events, buying more than eight million tickets. The television audiences were stunning, with an estimated 3.5 billion people watching around the world.

But, in a moment that incensed many Atlantans, IOC President Samaranch veered from his standard proclamation that the Games were "the greatest ever," a phrase he had repeated at each of the past several Closing Ceremonies. From the start of the 1996 Games, Samaranch had been critical of Atlanta's commercialization of the event. Then there was the bombing. So, this time, the bespectacled Spaniard chose to call the Centennial Olympics "most exceptional." For any TV viewers who might have missed the slight, NBC sports anchor Bob Costas immediately highlighted it at the conclusion of the IOC president's remarks.

Finally, the Olympic flame was extinguished and hundreds of volunteers wearing T-shirts sporting the slogan "Y'all come back" helped usher fans out of the final event of the 1996 Games.

The stadium stands were nearly deserted when, down on the field, A.D. Frazier heard his two-way radio squawk. Could you meet us in the box? Frazier took the elevator up to where Payne and several others of the Atlanta Nine had gathered, having settled into four or five rows of stadium seats. The group stared at the field. For nine years, they had dreamed, traveled, sold, planned, organized, managed, and executed the Olympic Games. Now it was over. Emotions overcame them, a muddle of exhaustion and pride in executing the biggest peacetime event in history. Yet each knew that the reputation of the Games would forever be tarnished by the bombing of Centennial Park. As Frazier would vividly recall later, they sat for nearly an hour in all-consuming silence.

THE SUSPECT

THERE WAS NO ANNOUNCEMENT of the polygraph results from Jewell's attorneys, either before or during the Closing Ceremony. Hours earlier, Rackleff had walked into Watson Bryant's office to deliver the results from the all-afternoon lie detector test. Their client, Rackleff reported, had been a jangle of nerves. The results had been "inconclusive." In other words, Richard Jewell had failed.

PART 3

JUSTICE AT WORK

CHAPTER 17

On Friday night, August 8, five nights after the Closing Ceremony, Richard Jewell waited at his mother's apartment for a delivery from Domino's. Typically, he ordered an extra-large topped with hamburger, pepperoni, and extra cheese. But this time, his "brother" from West Virginia, Dave Dutchess, and his girlfriend Beatty, had come to lend support.

There was little doubt they'd order in. Except for visiting his attorneys, Jewell had continued to close himself off at home. Any movement triggered a flurry of activity by the FBI agents surveilling him from across the street. Then there were the media, who still trained their cameras on the building from any available vantage point. The journalists had set up lawn chairs on the embankment overlooking Building F, and the three traditional networks and CNN had pooled resources to rent an apartment in the neighboring complex for a base of operations—for $1,000 a day.

The Domino's driver pulled into Monaco Station. But before he could bring the pies to Jewell, several media members approached him. Money changed hands, a deal was struck. Seconds later, the deliveryman climbed the stairs, pizza boxes in hand, and knocked on the door. Then he stepped backward, as arranged, so that the photographers and video camera operators could capture prized new images of the Olympic Park suspect.

But Dutchess, who answered the knock, immediately grew wise to the scheme. Using his body to shield the media's sight line into the apartment, he hastily paid the man, grabbed the pizza boxes, and shut the door. There would be no tip.

Bobi had returned to work earlier in the week, but remained frustrated by the media's omnipresence. At one point, after they followed her when she stepped outside to walk Brandy, she rushed back in, screaming, "Richard, get them out of there. I can't even let my dog go to the bathroom." Jewell knew he was even more hamstrung than Bobi. He asked Dutchess to help. The bearded man with a ponytail dutifully marched out the door and tromped downstairs, where he shooed away journalists from the sidewalk directly in front of the building.

The reporters didn't identify Dutchess during the visit. But on Sunday morning, as Dutchess and Beatty pulled away, Jewell spotted an agent jotting something in a notepad. *Probably his license plate*, Jewell thought. As quickly as Jewell's "brother" had arrived, he headed home.

THE CENTBOM TASK FORCE now had six teams working on the bombing, only one with an individual's name attached: Jewell. The additional ones were Investigation, Forensics, Park, Related Activities, and Other Suspects. The Jewell team, which included Don Johnson, clearly was the plum assignment. The FBI had been escalating its effort to solidify the case against the guard. In Habersham, Richard Densmore, a private security operator who had known Jewell from the Northeast Georgia Drug Task Force, told agents that several years back he had seen Jewell with two military-style packs like the one used in the bombing. The drug squad had issued the bags to its members. Over the next several days, the FBI would receive other reports about Jewell owning a green pack. Agents were dispatched to stores across North Georgia that sold Army–Navy surplus and law enforcement supplies. They hunted for any receipts that might tie Jewell to the purchase of an ALICE pack.

There had been more than 1,100 Jewell leads to date, most coming in the wake of the *AJC* story naming him. Jewell supposedly had purchased pipes from specified stores. He allegedly bought "bomb components" at a local pawnshop. He was rumored to have "reloaded" empty shells with bulk gunpowder purchased at area ammo stores. Some callers claimed he belonged to the KKK and militia. One tied him to a radical group called Vampire Killer 2000. Numerous witnesses underscored that Jewell was overzealous and craved the limelight. Several expressly said he was a "wannabe cop." And, continually, callers and interviewees said Jewell wanted to be a "hero." Each lead held its own lure, although agents knew that many likely were either fiction or echoes of media reports.

The Bureau interviewed one potential witness after another, jamming 302s from hundreds of interviews into thick black binders. The reports reflected answers to a largely consistent battery of questions: Did Jewell possess explosives or bomb-making materials? Did he have any electrical or sheet metal training? Did he own written materials about weapons or terrorism? Did he have associates with potential connections to the bombing?

Many on the CENTBOM task force still believed the case would be cracked in Habersham, where Jewell had lived for the prior five and a half years. So, they deepened their investigation in the North Georgia county. They searched Jewell's former residences in Habersham, pulling old carpet out of one to check for explosives residue and hair and fiber evidence. They visited shooting ranges he frequented and explored the Piedmont College toolshed, to which he had a master key. Agents, led by Tim Attaway, even located the Deathmobile, removing wire, carpet, and seat fabric samples.

At Piedmont College, task force agents also reinterviewed Police Chief Dick Martin. He said that a student had reported that Jewell once told him that making pipe bombs was "real easy," and that a part-time campus officer remembered coaching Jewell on how to search the internet, specifically to find bomb information. "Damn, I showed him," the man had lamented.

But some of the most promising leads on Jewell quickly fizzled. Gregory Harkness, the inmate at Jackson State Prison who claimed Jewell had shown him two bombs, took a polygraph test. At the conclusion, the examiner walked out of the room and reported succinctly to Special Agent Oliver Halle, "He flunked the shit out of it." Richard Frazier, the other former Habersham inmate connecting Jewell to bombs, didn't pan out either. The jailed so often harbored antipathy toward their jailers.

Meanwhile, the FBI still needed to find the 911 caller, the co-conspirator. Don Johnson zeroed back in on Jewell's friends. He already had interviewed Russell a second time with little payoff, so he prepared to circle back to Habersham deputy McNair. Sitting in his 7 Squad cubicle, Johnson pored over notes from his first McNair interview and other intel on the deputy. He began listing commonalities between the deputy and his old friend:

1. McNair and Jewell attended police academy together and were roommates at the academy.
2. McNair and Jewell served on a special response team together.
3. McNair and Jewell are known to always back each other up.

Johnson jotted down twenty more points he found of interest. The men worked the same shifts, both had been employed by Piedmont College, attended search warrant school together, and had a one-hour phone conversation on the Sunday night after the bombing. Johnson also focused on McNair's experience in the Marines and the thirty-year-old's penchant for military dress.

Johnson, Harry Grogan, and Tim Attaway went to see McNair again. Moments before they entered the Habersham County Sheriff's Office, Johnson flipped on his tape recorder and offered an intro. "We're about to consensually monitor a conversation between ourselves and Brian McNair," he dictated into the hidden microphone. "This preamble is being put on tape prior to the interview in order to conceal the fact that the interview is being recorded."

The agents and McNair stepped into a private room.

At first, Johnson plumbed for information about Russell, still thinking that McNair, Jewell, and Russell may all be involved in the bombing. "I've heard you guys were known as 'The Three Amigos,'" Johnson claimed. "No," McNair replied. They had all tried to go to dinner together once at a local Mexican joint with their wives and whoever Jewell could bring as a date, but it hadn't worked out.

Johnson shifted gears, his nasal northern twang sharply contrasting with McNair's down-home Southern accent. "Another thing that came out in some of the interviews that we've done is the fact about Richard rewiring some of the patrol cars," Johnson said, probing for evidence of Jewell's technical skills. McNair rolled out a tale of Jewell's fascination with strobe lights. He had wired two double Dash Master light bars in the back of his patrol car and a third in the front. Then he had connected it all into the alternator with plugs mounted on the side with a bracket. "Really?" Johnson pressed, thinking about possible bomb-making skills.

"Yeah. If he had his camera and all the lights going and his CB on and his car radio on, you got in the car and try to talk on the radio and everything would brown out. He had to rev up the engine to give it enough power to talk on the radio." McNair burst out laughing as he finished the story. Not the response Johnson was seeking.

The agent soon grew stern, squelching any further lightheartedness by referring to their first interview. "One of the things you told us was the fact that you thought you knew how to make a bomb, but you couldn't wire the timer."

McNair tried to set the record straight. "Uh, I believe I said then, I said yeah, I could probably read up on it and figure that out. But off the bat I wouldn't know nothing." Soon after, he had to respectfully correct Johnson again, this time when the agent suggested McNair had earlier used the term "overaggressive" to describe Jewell. "I think I said overzealous," McNair interjected. "I don't believe I'd characterize him as overaggressive."

Johnson shifted yet again. "I want you to read something," he said, handing McNair a page with the text of the 911 call. "I just want you to disprove this. I want you to read this for me. . . . I just want to hear your voice."

"There is a bomb in Centennial Park. You have thirty minutes," McNair recited.

"Yeah. Read it slower."

"There is a bomb in Centennial Park. You have thirty minutes." This time, with a nervous laugh, McNair added, "It wasn't me."

"Did you make the phone call?"

"No, sir."

Grogan jumped in at one point, drilling down on potential motive. Jewell had first been bounced from his work at the sheriff's office, then suffered the same fate at the college. He had struggled with money, at one point lacking enough funds to even pay for his car tags. "I mean, everything's going down," Grogan ventured. "He may not have had any choice but to move back with mama. I mean, I just see him sliding down a path that just isn't the way to go and he's looking for a way out some way."

McNair refused to budge from Jewell's side: "That's not the Richard I know." As the interview ended, they drove to McNair's house, where the agents found automotive wire, three boxes of ammunition, and a copy of *The Anarchist Cookbook* that Jewell had given McNair.

Grogan broke off for a separate search, to the junkyard with Jewell's old Chevy, the "Chia Pet Car." In the sweltering heat, Grogan scoured the passenger cabin and trunk. He found an old check register that showed six entries for Pizza Hut and Domino's Pizza, but also payments to Rob Russell, Brian McNair, and a D. Dutchess.

DURING THE SECOND WEEK in August, confidence about Jewell's guilt began to slip inside the CENTBOM task force. Try as they might, agents were unable to move the evidence beyond circumstantial, and new leads had slowed. What if Richard Jewell was not the bomber?

Many of the unmarked videos confiscated in the apartment search were simply more taped episodes of *Cops*. Computer disks held copies of Jewell's mundane Piedmont College police reports, notable only for their excruciating detail and length. Searches of Jewell's storage shed and former North Georgia residences had turned up little of value. Receipts from his purchases didn't align with any distinctive materials used in the Olympic Park bomb. And the pre-blast fingerprint that had been singed chemically onto a recovered piece of pipe did not match Jewell either.

With the case against Jewell in question, on August 13 FBI headquarters assigned a major case number to the CENTBOM investigation, making even more resources available to expand the probe. The task force added several agents to its Other Suspects team and created a new video/photo review group. The FBI gathered every image possible from the park, and created a photographic timeline of the night. ESPN, AT&T, and NBC all had been running nearly twenty-four-hour video in the park.

"Bench A" remained the physical centerpiece of the investigation. Who had been sitting there in the hours before the bomb exploded beneath it? Several people had seen a young white couple resting on the seat, possible important witnesses. Could they be found? The Park team also wanted to reconnect with the Speedo Boys. Back on July 30, one of them told an agent he'd seen a "lone white male with a goatee" on the bench. The man was "wearing a tight-fitting cap cylindrical in shape." But the witness could provide no further description. The FBI decided the lead might warrant a sketch, if they could glean more detail from a reinterview.

EARLY ON, A FEW journalists had offered some skepticism that Jewell was the bomber. Ann Woolner, an editor at the *Fulton County Daily Report*, who had called out the prospect of the guard's innocence the day after the Closing Ceremony, circled back to the Birmingham, Alabama, bombing murder of Judge Robert Vance more than six years earlier. In a column that ran on the legal publication's front page, she linked Jewell to Robert Wayne O'Ferrell, the junk dealer who Scruggs had quoted from the church pulpit. O'Ferrell had been thoroughly investigated by the FBI and identified by the media as the killer only to later be cleared. "I lost my family, I lost my home and everything else I owned," he told Woolner. "I knew I was innocent and they done everything in the world to try to prove I did it."

That same day, the *Arizona Republic* editorialized on the media's behavior even if Jewell ultimately proved to be the actual bomber. "Jewell is the latest victim of media competition running wild in the age of instant information," the newspaper wrote. "Would it be too much to wait for the results of the investigation?"

At the *AJC*, editors quietly assigned Carrie Teegardin, a well-respected veteran of the paper, to delve into how the publication had covered the Jewell story, how decisions were made. The *AJC* would take readers inside one of the biggest and most controversial newsbreaks in its history. Teegardin began a string of interviews with Bert Roughton, John Walter, intern Kent Walker, and others. For more than two weeks, she questioned and even challenged reporters and editors about the *AJC*'s coverage.

The peer-to-peer interview with Scruggs offered unvarnished insights. Scruggs recapped how she got the story from her source at the bar as well as the rest of the timeline. She expressed surprise at the small but growing wave of critics chastising the paper for running a suspect's name without any charges. "When does it not happen? In all the years I've covered law enforcement, there have always been leaks of suspects prior to arrest and we normally write about them," she told Teegardin. "It happens every day. This one just happened to happen in front of the world with all eyes on us." Scruggs focused her criticism on the motivation of other journalists, many of whom had started to whisper about whether the *AJC* had been irresponsible. But they didn't know how solid her sourcing had been. "I think in some part there may be just some jealousy involved and some sour grapes."

Over the next few days, Teegardin drafted a two-thousand-word article. But before she could finish her revisions, her editor informed her that the paper had decided to kill the piece. Jewell's attorneys had grown increasingly vocal, and the paper knew that libel suits could be coming.

Scruggs continued to cajole her sources to take her inside the investigation. But she got little. On August 10, she and Martz wrote about why the 911 system had fallen short on bombing night. The piece ran on C-2 of the Saturday paper.

The far bigger story that day, featured prominently on A-1, was the work of Bill Rankin. The legal affairs reporter had wondered if Jewell could have both made the 911 call and reported the ALICE pack. The timing just seemed too tight.

The lanky, soft-spoken Rankin wandered over to the bank of pay phones outside the Days Inn. Then, he walked to the bomb site. The trip took four minutes and forty-five seconds. Rankin knew the 911 call had come in at 12:58 A.M. Next, he called GBI officer Tom Davis, who told Rankin that he had made his emergency call, with Jewell next to him, at 12:57 A.M. With only one minute separating the two events, Jewell simply could not have been the caller. Rankin wrote the story with Martz.

That Saturday morning, the Jewell camp was thrilled. They finally had a truly positive newsbreak. Bryant wanted to use the article immediately to lambast the FBI, but Jack Martin urged him to slow down. The seasoned defense attorney wanted more facts about Jewell himself. At Martin's insistence, Bryant and his brother Bruce accompanied him to Habersham. They retraced the FBI's steps and interviewed Jewell's friend Brian McNair, as well as a Piedmont College weekend security officer and a student. None of the three could envision Jewell being the bomber. Said McNair, "Richard would look for trouble, but never cause it."

Comforted by the Habersham visit, Martin agreed to use the *AJC* story to create good theater and flip the narrative. On August 13, he summoned the media to the bomb site. Then, in a perfect made-for-TV moment, Martin led the journalists to the bank of pay phones outside the Days Inn while dramatically timing the walk. Once there, he stepped to a bank of microphones and declared the obvious: "You cannot get from that location to that phone booth in less than four minutes, which means that there is no way my client could have made that phone call." News organizations finally had a galvanizing event that portrayed Jewell as a possible victim. Was he innocent? At the least, how could Jewell "fit the profile of a lone bomber" and still have a compatriot?

When reporters called the Atlanta FBI office, agents were still under headquarters' no-comment mandate. They couldn't even disclose that they had earlier told Judge Brill that Jewell could not have made the 911 call. The search warrant affidavit was still under seal. When the Jewell team saw the lack of reaction, they took note and prepared to punch again. They brought back the polygrapher, Richard Rackleff, who rewired Jewell for another round of polygraph questions at Bryant's office: "Did you make the pipe bomb left in the backpack in Centennial Park?" No. "Do you know who put the pipe bomb in Centennial Olympic Park?" No. "When you first reported the back-pack to the GBI, did you know it contained an explosive device?" No. This time, Rackleff's finding was "no deception indicated." In other words, Jewell had passed, easily. A giddy Watson Bryant declared they would announce the results right outside the Atlanta FBI office. But Rackleff, who still had friends in the Bureau, pushed back, and they compromised, holding the media briefing outside the Russell Federal Building in downtown Atlanta.

"Every aspect of that interview supported by the polygraph chart con-cluded that he had no involvement whatsoever," Rackleff told assembled reporters. The results "were unquestionable and conclusive." The media jumped on the story, the *New York Times* quoting Jack Martin saying of Jewell, "The man's a hero, not a villain. He saved lives, he didn't take them." The FBI again said nothing.

In the third week of August, Jewell took a step toward normalcy when he retrieved Lacy from boarding. The media tried to chase him to the vet's office, but he lost them on the highway. He reveled in the small victory.

BRYANT HAD ANOTHER CARD to play. Just before the lie detector test announcement, he had reached out to the firm of Wood & Grant. Wayne Grant, an earnest and even-keeled attorney, had an eye for detail. But it was Grant's partner, Lin Wood, who would be destined to take control of the case.

Wood was a silver-tongued Georgian with notable success in medical malpractice cases and a desire to branch out. If Bryant was the snarky, loyal defender and Martin the cerebral criminal protector, Wood would be the team's pit bull. With deep-set emerald eyes that anchored telegenic good looks, Wood could be charming. But he rarely chose to be so in legal proceedings, usually opting instead for face-ripping confrontation. His personality had been forged at the age of sixteen when he arrived at his Macon home one day to find his father sobbing and his mother splayed out bleeding on the floor. The boy checked her pulse. She was dead. Wood's father claimed she had slipped in the bathtub, but authorities charged him with murder, and he later pled guilty to involuntary manslaughter.

Wood earned a degree from the law school at Mercer University, in his hometown, then began taking on plaintiffs' medical malpractice suits, then product liability cases. In his personal life, lasting relationships did not come easy. Now at the age of forty-three, Wood was on his fourth marriage. In his leisure time, he played baseball—not softball like many in middle age, but hardball.

Wood first met Jewell at the lawyer's office on the twentieth floor of a downtown office building. As they sat at the conference-room table, Jewell could see Centennial Olympic Park over Wood's shoulder. They talked for a couple of hours, reviewing the past few weeks, especially Jewell's experiences with the media. Finally, Jewell asked if Wood would represent him.

"On one condition," Wood replied.

"What's that, Mr. Wood?"

"You're going to have to accept my apology. I believed that you were guilty."

Jewell graciously said he understood.

Wood didn't waste much time before going on the attack. In the *AJC*, he lambasted the media for their "unfair trial and conviction" of Jewell. He told the paper that lawsuits would be coming. "We'll pursue any potential claims Mr. Jewell may have and leave no stone unturned." Wood appeared as a guest on the show of an Atlanta radio call-in host, Sean Hannity. Most of the callers were swaying in Jewell's direction.

Clearly, going on offense was working for the Jewell team. Wood urged his fellow attorneys to think bigger. He wanted to set an event to coincide with the start of the Democratic National Convention, which was opening in Chicago the last week of August. This time they would turn to Bobi Jewell, the brokenhearted mother. Wood and his partner, Grant, hustled to arrange hotel space and get word out to the media. Next, they had to prepare their star. Their concept was that Bobi would speak from the heart, then Grant would edit her words into a six-minute public plea. Bryant and Martin would pitch in too. Wood largely left them alone, but he had one specific request: Save the final lines for me.

Bobi rehearsed for hours, but she couldn't hold it together, her sobbing interrupting the message the media and government officials needed to hear. Grant urged her on, even jotting "low and slow" on the first page to encourage her to keep her emotions in check, but she never once got through the script without breaking down. Finally, the attorneys decided just to hope for the best.

On Monday morning, in a ballroom at a Marriott hotel in northwest Atlanta, Jewell's legal team, now four strong, was present. Wood approached Bobi before her appearance. "This is your chance to save your son's life," he urged. "You have got to get through this. *You've got to.*"

Bobi stood before the media, more than a dozen microphones attached to the wood podium, cameras trained on her from the back of the room. Donning pink-tinted reading glasses, Bobi started strong, her voice full of determination. A tinge of anger punctuated some of the phrases. "The media has portrayed my son as the person who committed this crime. He did not do it. My son is innocent. Richard is *not* the Olympic Park bomber. Richard is *not* a murderer," she said, glancing up frequently from her notes. "Although Richard has never been charged with any crime, he has been convicted in the court of public opinion.

"Four weeks ago, the FBI came into my home and turned it upside down. They took my rugs, they took clothing, they took my books, they took my Walt Disney tapes that I play for the children that I babysit for, they took all of my Tupperware, they went through my personal papers and my personal bills, they took my personal telephone directory, they took my personal calendar, they went through my undergarments. They searched every inch of my home and every single item in my home."

The attorneys looked on, optimistic and nearly incredulous. Bobi was powering through the statement without a single breakdown.

She then directed her remarks to the newspapers and TV networks. "The media has descended upon us like vultures upon prey. They have taken all privacy from us, they have taken all peace. They have rented an apartment which faces my home in order to keep their cameras trained upon us around the clock. They watch our every move. They watch and photograph everything we do. We wake up to photographers, we go to sleep to photographers. We cannot look out the window."

A minute or so later, Bobi related a particularly painful story from their private lives. Jewell had joined her a few days earlier for a rare outing to pay last respects to a close family friend. "When we returned from the funeral home, for the first time, I saw my son sobbing. He said, 'Mama, everybody was looking at me.'" Bobi choked up but forced herself forward. "I don't think any of you can even begin to imagine what our lives are like."

From his seat, Wood watched her struggle, hoping she had the fortitude to make it. A mother's protective genes paired with a personal sense of injustice made for a powerful combination. But he knew that the toughest parts were still to come. Finally, she approached the closing, the one that Wood had personally crafted. The conservative lawyer had long been a fan of Ronald Reagan. And no line in the president's rhetoric had captured Wood's imagination as much as when Reagan proclaimed in Berlin, "Mr. Gorbachev, tear down this wall."

Bobi built up to her version of it. "Please hear me, Mr. President, and please help me. You have the power to end this nightmare. If the FBI does not intend to charge my son, please tell us. Please tell the world." She paused, nearly collapsing in sobs, as she pleaded, "Mr. President, please clear my son's name."

The final words were almost indecipherable. Bobi had kept her composure as long as she could. She continued to weep openly, the month of unbearable strain now overwhelming her. Bryant stepped quickly to her side, encircling her with his left arm. Together, they walked away from the podium.

Within hours, every network featured the plaintive, tearful Bobi on their nightly newscasts. That evening, she appeared on CNN's *Larry King Live*. Overnight, the Jewell narrative had changed.

CHAPTER 18

Public perception may have been shifting, but Richard Jewell wanted his old life back. He desperately longed to be a cop again, to serve a community, to earn a living. He pined for the anonymity to eat at a restaurant or take in a Braves game free from the stares and whispers of strangers. As much as anything, he wanted an end to the oppressive solitude of Apartment F-3, still under surveillance by the FBI and media. His days were filled tediously watching John Wayne movies and playing the video game *Mortal Kombat II*. He and his mother bickered often under the strain.

Bobi was unenthusiastic about Dave Dutchess coming for another visit on Labor Day weekend, arguing that she didn't want to burden others with the family's problems. But, Jewell pressed: "You might not consider Dave your son, but he's my brother." Finally, Bobi demurred.

The FBI recently had identified Dutchess as the mystery man from West Virginia, and now saw him as their most promising remaining lead as the 911 caller. FBI agents had pulled his phone records showing calls to Jewell, including a forty-seven-minute conversation between the men two months before the bombing. On Friday, August 30, Dutchess and his girlfriend, Beatty, again arrived at Jewell's doorstep, riding in on his silver Honda Gold Wing motorcycle emblazoned with paw prints and the moniker "Lone Wolf."

Dutchess immediately sensed the worry that enveloped the apartment. He and Jewell passed notes, as Richard and Bobi had done, all still convinced that the FBI had bugged the home. On Sunday morning, Jewell, Dutchess, and Beatty climbed into Bobi's station wagon. They drove north to Habersham for what Jewell hoped would be a liberating picnic with friends. Three FBI cars followed them to the county line, where two more joined the tail. Jewell decided to make a quick stop at his storage unit. He knew the Bureau had searched it but, stepping inside, his heart sank to see that some items were missing, others had been rearranged. He felt violated yet again.

Less than an hour later, though, the weight lifted. Jewell spent the afternoon at the picnic eating spaghetti and salad, reliving old memories, and playing ball with children. He felt blissfully stress-free, until the ride home.

Jewell, Dutchess, and Beatty said their goodbyes, then loaded back into Bobi's wagon. Dark FBI sedans followed them. Then, a half hour into the trip, two of the Bureau cars unexpectedly sped past them. "Well, that's kind of weird," Jewell remarked to Dutchess. "I wonder why they're getting ahead of us." Jewell decided to pull over to see what the surveillance vehicles would do. Both sedans disappeared over the rolling hills. Puzzled, Jewell pulled back onto the road.

A few miles farther south, however, Jewell looked up and saw a small plane that appeared almost like a kite on a string tied to his car. The aircraft varied from him in direction but not distance. Jewell steered the car onto the off-ramp, crossed the highway, and reversed directions. The plane was still there. It was clear then as they stared in disbelief: The FBI was using aircraft to tail him. Jewell snapped several skyward photos as proof, but his day away from the confinement of Bobi's apartment had been tainted.

The next day in the apartment was once again oppressive, so Dutchess announced, "Let's go for a ride." He pointed to his motorcycle outside. Jewell wasn't eager to venture out again. Plus, he had a bigger concern: "Dave, I can't get on a bike. I've never been on one in my life." Dutchess prodded, and Jewell eventually acquiesced. Climbing onto the bike, he felt awkward and looked almost comical, his head squeezed into Beatty's undersized helmet. But they motored out of the complex, heading up Buford Highway. As always, agents in FBI cars followed. This time, Dutchess had something in mind.

"Watch this, Richard," Dutchess yelled over the wind and road noise. As they reached a red light, Dutchess veered through a parking lot onto another street. In the mirrors, he and Jewell saw the tailing agents hopping over curbs, desperate to keep up. The two brothers laughed.

Down the road, Dutchess navigated his way into a car wash. He and Jewell hopped off and began to rinse the bike as an FBI agent brought his car to a screeching stop along the street. Another went up the road, pulled a U-turn, and parked along the other side of the car wash. Minutes later, Dutchess yelled, "Let's go," and he and Jewell hopped back on the bike and sped off. By then, Jewell was fully into the game. "I know a couple roads," he directed.

"Turn here." Several evasive maneuvers later, Dutchess and Jewell had lost their FBI tail. The pair reveled in the freedom for a few more high-speed minutes, then headed back to Bobi's apartment. The outing had been joyous.

The interactions with the FBI were a warm-up for Dutchess and Beatty's eventful trip north.

The next day, the couple hugged Jewell goodbye and wheeled toward their temporary home with Beatty's parents in Henderson, Tennessee. They were followed the entire route. They stopped home for a few hours, then in the late afternoon rode Dutchess's motorcycle to a nearby McDonald's. A dark sedan pulled behind them, blocking in the bike. A man introduced himself as a local FBI agent assigned to keep an eye on them until backup arrived. A second car sped in. Dutchess and Beatty overheard the agent say he had the "suspect" in hand. Several more FBI and local police arrived, and Dutchess was encircled. They blocked all entrances to the restaurant. Customers inside stared out at the scene.

Through it all, Dutchess was surprised at how polite the agents were. One asked if they could speak with him back at the house. Despite the show of force, the agent explained that the last thing they were looking for was any more attention from the press. "The media has done enough," he remarked.

At the home of Beatty's parents, Bureau agents began interrogating the man they for so long had known only as the cousin or brother from West Virginia. Where was Dutchess on the night of the explosion? In the house where they were sitting. Did he make the 911 call? No. Could Richard Jewell be involved in the bombing? No way. Are you sure? Absolutely. The questioning continued for two and a half hours. Dutchess never wavered, backing Jewell steadfastly throughout. Two days later, agents returned to ask if Dutchess would submit to a polygraph. Will that help clear Jewell, he wanted to know. He got only vague replies. Still, Dutchess agreed to the lie detector test.

They drove to a nearby Holiday Inn, where FBI agents set up Dutchess facing a wall and instructed him to look neither left nor right. Dutchess would long remember the FBI polygrapher's routine of walking away, then coming back and probing some more. Over and over, Dutchess was asked about the bombing, then challenged about his answers.

"You're not telling the truth, Mr. Dutchess."

"Yeah, I am," he retorted with a laugh. "I have nothing to lie about."

The questioner pressed Dutchess repeatedly as he staunchly proclaimed Jewell's innocence and his own. The next day, they met with Dutchess again to inform him that he had passed. The Bureau's best prospect for a 911 caller hadn't panned out.

THE FBI'S QUANTICO FORENSICS lab had completed its full replica of the bomb. The device was massive, weighing at least forty pounds; it was the single largest pipe bomb the Bureau or ATF had even seen. Two of the IED's features were a standard Big Ben alarm clock made by Westclox and a rolled steel directional plate. Agents learned that the clock was one of 250,000 Big Ben models the company had made over the past eighteen years at its Athens, Georgia, plant. They would follow up, but weren't optimistic. The steel, on the other hand, might hold more promise, a flaw in the sheet being a valuable marker. They set out to visit mills in the region.

There was still no apparent link between the device and Richard Jewell, and CENTBOM resources continued to shift to the Other Suspects team. Yet every time the case against Jewell waned, an unexpected chunk of information seemed to drop in. A new witness talked of Jewell studying IEDs on a computer, though the suspect had explained, "I'm trying to learn how to take bombs apart." A North Georgia caller reported hearing a loud explosion behind a house Jewell had rented, then seeing the guard emerge from the woods looking nervous as white smoke billowed over the trees. The CENTBOM task force assigned agents to obtain consents from the area property owners to search their fields and forested areas.

For Don Johnson's part, he believed the case was all there: the timing, profile, motive, and the dozens of interviews about Jewell's past. Plus, Johnson had looked the security guard in the eye. He had no doubt. So, the agent re-centered on Rob Russell. From Johnson's last interview he knew Russell could be prickly and irreverent. When the agent had noted Jewell lived with his mother and then asked how "close" he and Jewell were, Russell had erupted, in a profane, mocking rant: "What the fuck is too close? . . . So now we got gay people over here blowing up motherfuckers?" He asked the agents if they were suggesting that Jewell was a member of a "Gay Bomber's Association"? Or maybe, because the security guard loved to fish, he also belonged to a "Gay Trout Fisherman's Association"?

This time, Johnson would make a case that Jewell *was* the bomber, and let moral outrage fuel Russell's cooperation.

Johnson and GBI Agent Tim Attaway began their interview of Russell with small talk about Russell's five adopted stray dogs. Again, Johnson was carrying a hidden recorder, as in the McNair interview. Johnson soon zoomed in on Jewell. Russell said he had seen the coverage on Jewell's lie detector test. Unexpectedly, Russell interjected, "I actually believe polygraphs are bullshit."

What? Did Russell think Jewell was involved?

Russell cleared his throat and stammered, "I, I, I had to, in, my heart of hearts, there's no way in hell Richard's involved, except . . ."

Except?

Johnson saw an opening. He looked to Attaway to detail Jewell's actions during and after the explosion. The GBI agent drew a diagram of the bomb site showing how close Richard was to the blast victims.

"Police officers down. The Richard Jewell you know would do what?" Attaway asked.

"Go help the police officers," Russell replied. "His butt would be right in there helping the police officers."

Attaway continued to lay it on thick: All those officers down, but Jewell ran in the opposite direction. He wanted to be back at the tower instead of rendering first aid to his brothers in arms. Did that sound like the man Russell knew?

"No fucking way," Russell repeated over and over. For Jewell, helping a downed officer would be his dream scenario. He'd be a hero. "There's no fucking way."

Johnson stepped in to reveal a piece of evidence from the search warrant affidavit. "That's one of the reasons we came back here, is, what Tim described to you is what we actually saw that happened. It's on film."

Though Johnson and Attaway never showed Russell the video snippet, they continued to vividly describe Jewell running in the opposite direction from those who were injured. The FBI agent added one bit of embellishment, saying of Jewell, "He never got knocked to his knees." The clear implication: Jewell knew about the bomb in advance and where to stand to avoid injury. In truth, Jewell had said he was knocked down at the time of detonation.

An hour into the interview, Russell had come around. "I ain't protecting Richard. If he's guilty, I'm kicking his, I'll kill him. You'll have to bar me from the fucking courtroom."

Before wrapping up the interview, there was one last order of business, as Johnson's recorder secretly continued to tape the conversation. As with McNair, Johnson tricked Russell into saying the 911 message aloud.

But the agent soon learned definitively from Bureau experts what he already suspected: Neither man's voice matched the 911 caller.

EVER SO GRADUALLY, JEWELL'S world began to open up. He increasingly ventured out of the apartment. But where to go? He had no job and recognized the futility of applying for law enforcement positions while still under 24/7 FBI surveillance. He visited his lawyers, camping for stretches of the days at the Wood & Grant offices. He tried flirting with a pretty twenty-seven-year-old brunette receptionist working on the same floor, who indulged him in conversation but nothing more. Asked by an attorney if Jewell was harassing her, she replied, "No, he's harmless."

To further help Jewell expand his life beyond the apartment, Watson Bryant's brother, Bruce, offered a lifeline. A man so genial that his friends had nicknamed him Smiley, Bryant coached his son's football team in Atlanta's Northside Youth Organization (NYO). He recruited Jewell to be his assistant coach, and Jewell readily accepted. At NYO, some found Bruce Bryant's choice of an assistant alarming, one mother shrieking, "You're letting *him* coach our boys?" But Bryant remained unflustered. "Look around," he said, pointing to the field's perimeter. "What could be safer than here?" Sure enough, three FBI cars sat idling nearby. At the end of one practice, Jewell felt emboldened enough to usher a group of boys over to meet the agents. The kids asked an agent if they could see his gun; he demurred, offering his badge instead.

Soon Jewell began delivering doughnuts to surveillance agents who were on duty. When he realized they were having difficulty tailing him, he began notifying the drivers in advance where he was going. The agents were grateful and relieved. Earlier, they had suspected him of "evasive driving tactics" with his fast, unpredictable turns. Once they had the addresses, they realized he just had a bad sense of direction and a lead foot.

THE MEDIA TOOK NOTE of the stalled investigation, and the early trickle of skeptical reporting grew to a steady stream. Jack Martin's mid-August walk, combined with Rackleff's polygraph announcement and the FBI's continued silence, offered journalists an opening to push harder for answers. Where were the charges? Where was the evidence? Did we rush to judgment?

ABC News *Nightline* anchor Ted Koppel diverged from his show's regular format for a special report titled "The Bizarre Case of Richard Jewell." The show opened by reviewing the current state of play. "Richard Jewell remains under the watchful eye of the media," Koppel intoned. "The question is whether the media should have passed that information on to you, absent any formal charges."

The changing media environment was only making that kind of coverage more likely, the network's correspondent Jeff Greenfield postulated. "The future, in fact the present, is a world where there's a deadline every minute, where information ten minutes old is yesterday's news, and where the press seems less and less inclined even to ask whether the public's right to know sometimes comes at a very high price."

Koppel turned back to the Jewell matter, introducing Watson Bryant and Jack Martin. Bryant jabbed, saying that the FBI "must be brain-dead by now if they don't know that Richard Jewell is not guilty." But the lawyer saved most of his barbs for the media. Bryant referred to the scene outside Jewell's apartment as a "gang bang." Martin chimed in, "They never examined the story, never asked questions." Koppel pushed back, asking if Jewell's lawyers were suggesting that the media had to wait until someone was on trial. He shared an ABC News–commissioned poll on that very question, asking respondents if it was acceptable for the media to name a suspect before the person was formally charged. Eighty-two percent said no, putting the strong majority at odds with the standard practice of most U.S. newsrooms. The anchor offered his own perspective: "I've said it before on these *Viewpoint* programs, I'll say again, and it's always controversial: We in the media don't deal in truth, we deal in facts." And the fact was, Richard Jewell had been the prime suspect.

Despite Koppel's defense of the Fourth Estate, others in the media continued to shift to Jewell's side. Cartoonists with daggered pens had their say in pointed terms. In one inspired strip, Mike Peters, in the *Dayton Daily News,* created the "FBI Olympics," featuring teams of dark-suited agents competing in events like the "100-meter rush to judgment," "the leak and rumor relay," and "the broad jump to conclusion."

Meanwhile, Bryant had begun taunting the FBI on his home answering machine message: "If this is Louie Freeh, your mother's looking for you." Alternately, he played a separate message for the newspaper, pulling from a cheer used by his daughter's soccer team. "S-T-I-N-K. That's what the *AJC* does all day. You stink. This is Watson Bryant. I'm not here right now."

AT CENTBOM, TASK FORCE leaders reexamined their theories about Jewell. Agents took a second look at the binders full of Jewell-related interviews and began to see a far more balanced picture of the man. Of the one hundred individuals questioned in Habersham County alone, Jewell was broadly perceived as gung-ho and at times even overzealous. But almost no one who knew him well believed he possessed the character of a murderer. Comments like "considered Jewell to be a nice guy," "honest and truthful," and "could not have done the bombing" were sprinkled throughout the 302s.

Among the park witnesses, many key leads couldn't be substantiated. The pen register showed nothing significant as it monitored the phone numbers of incoming and outgoing calls on Bobi's home phone, although not the audio of those calls. Neither did ongoing searches of their mail and trash. The FBI found no militia ties, nor could anyone confirm that Jewell ever owned a stock of gunpowder for reloading his empty shells. And despite a painstaking search of the fields and woods near Jewell's Habersham home, no shrapnel was uncovered.

Inside the Bureau, some questioned whether Jewell was mechanically inclined, or even smart enough, to build a timed IED without injuring himself. Joked one senior FBI supervisor: "He would have been known as 'The Man With No Hands.'"

But nagging questions remained. Where was his green knapsack that resembled the ALICE pack? Why had he been so resistant to being assigned away from the tower? Why did he take his first-ever break the night of the bombing? Why had he been curious whether one of the towers could withstand a blast? Why, according to a new witness, had he told two or three Swatch Pavilion employees just days before the bombing, "You better take a picture of me now because I'm going to be famous"? Only Jewell could answer those questions, but his attorneys were not letting him talk to the FBI.

INSIDE JEWELL'S LEGAL TEAM, clashes erupted over personality and strategy. Wood wanted to win the case in the court of public opinion, then use that momentum in defamation suits against the media that had villainized Jewell. Bryant grew even more prone to lash out at both the press and the FBI. The more cautious Martin pushed Wood and Bryant to muzzle themselves. "Let's allow the process to play out behind the scenes," Martin urged. Bryant swung back, accusing Martin of hypocrisy because he was the one who had taken center stage during the park-to-pay-phone walk. Meanwhile, Wood's relationship with Martin became so frosty that one day Wood snapped at him, "You're just like one of my damn ex-wives. If the suggestion comes out of my mouth, you automatically disagree."

Wood pressed on, hunting for the media outlet whose imprimatur would stamp Jewell as thoroughly innocent in the mind of even harsh skeptics. Already, major TV personalities had been vying for the first one-on-one interview with Jewell, courting the lawyers for what journalists call "the get." Katie Couric personally rang up Jack Martin, singing into his answering machine the Wahoo Wah fight song of the University of Virginia, their shared alma mater. A producer from the *Oprah Winfrey Show* leaned on Bryant, noting that her boss's daily viewership of over twenty million exceeded all three morning networks combined.

But Wood believed that no other news program had the power of *60 Minutes*. As importantly, no television personality had the toughness of Mike Wallace. If Wallace swung to Jewell's side, that could go a long way in convincing America of the guard's innocence. The rest of the legal team agreed. The program's crew first came to Atlanta on September 10 to film the FBI's tail of Jewell. Several days later, Wallace arrived to interview the suspect at the swanky Hotel Nikko in Buckhead. As usual, FBI agents followed Jewell to the hotel.

The show aired Sunday evening, September 22, opening with *60 Minutes*' iconic ticking stopwatch. In the intro, Wallace, in a crisp gray suit and tie, walked alongside Jewell, whose microphone was clipped to the collar of his lightly pinstriped white dress shirt. Theirs would be the lead story.

The segment opened with a seated Wallace gazing into the camera. "Richard Jewell, the man the FBI and the media zeroed in on as the principal suspect in the Atlanta Olympic bombing, says it's all a lie," the correspondent told viewers. "And if it turns out he's right, it could be a very expensive lie. . . . Does Richard Jewell have a case? Was he libeled? That's what we went to Atlanta to find out." Wallace recapped the night of the bombing, up to Agent Forsyth's peek into the ALICE pack. The show cut to Jewell, who recalled a line from his law enforcement training that had long stuck with him: "If you see an ATF agent running, you better be in front of him."

"So, did you start to run too?"

"No, sir."

"You stayed there within ten yards of where the package was?"

"Yes, sir, we were just concerned with getting the people as far away as we could as quickly as we could."

On the show, Wood announced that the Jewell team would soon be suing the *AJC*, as well as NBC for Tom Brokaw's remarks that "they probably have enough to arrest him right now, probably enough to prosecute him, but you always want to have enough to convict him as well." Other suits would follow. At first, *AJC* editors had agreed to be interviewed by Wallace. But then the paper changed course, deciding instead to fax a letter to the *60 Minutes* producer. Wallace summarized the letter for the viewers, as excerpts flashed on the screen. "'Our reporters have done an excellent job of reporting . . . the bombing,' Editor Ron Martin said. 'We stand proudly behind our coverage.'"

Contrary to the *AJC*'s decision, Brokaw made a rare appearance on a competing network to defend his comments: "You know, my job is to report what we're able to find out about what was a crisis in Atlanta, that they were focusing their investigation on this one man." Brokaw was confident, based on high-ranking law enforcement sources, that his reporting had been accurate.

With the FBI still refusing to comment and the *AJC* declining to appear, Wood followed through on his strategy to make his argument directly to the viewing public. He summed up the state of play from the Jewell team's perspective: "The FBI got what it wanted. It got the image of 'We have our man and we have him quickly.' The media got what it wanted. It got a dramatic headline. Everybody got what they wanted. The problem is, they threw over the side an innocent man, Richard Jewell."

After *60 Minutes* aired, little doubt remained where public sentiment stood. Some in the government recognized the FBI needed to either make a case or move on from Jewell.

FOR WEEKS, JACK MARTIN and U.S. Attorney Kent Alexander had been quietly meeting to discuss a resolution. The two had built a rapport working opposite sides of the courtroom for years. Alexander had confided to Martin that his prosecution team had serious doubts about Jewell's complicity in the bombing.

There were still open questions about Jewell's actions, and the two men considered how to best resolve them. They finally settled on a reinterview of Jewell. But there would be detailed ground rules, which would trigger lengthy negotiations with the FBI. Alexander likened it to the clashes ahead of the Bobby Fischer–Boris Spassky chess championship a quarter-century earlier.

Martin wasn't letting his client anywhere near an FBI interrogation room until he had a better idea what information the government had. The criminal defense lawyer worried that Jewell would become entangled in inconsistencies from his prior interviews with the Bureau. So, Martin insisted on seeing in advance the search warrant affidavit and records of every interview Jewell had done since the explosion. In addition, Jewell would receive "queen for the day" status, meaning nothing he said in the reinterview could be used directly against him if there were a later prosecution. Martin also required that all property seized from the apartment be returned prior to the interview.

On the government's end, the Bureau insisted there could be no media presence whatsoever. Agents had tired of the constant pummeling in the press by Jewell's attorneys, especially the unfiltered Bryant and the caustic Wood. If the FBI spotted a single reporter at the interview or the return of Jewell's property, the deal would be off. The questioning would be done on a Sunday at the FBI offices, when area businesses were closed and the risk of a leak the lowest. One FBI agent and one GBI agent would conduct the questioning. Even if statements themselves could not be used, any leads coming out of the interview could be pursued.

Alexander insisted on one more term: The interview could be attended by only one Assistant U.S. Attorney and one Jewell lawyer. The prosecutor counted on the Jewell team selecting Jack Martin, their only criminal defense practitioner. Alexander knew that if either Bryant or Wood participated in the interview, the FBI would walk. CENTBOM agents had grown to despise both men.

The government committed to publicly declare within three weeks of the interview whether Jewell was a target of the investigation. The interview was set for Sunday, October 6.

CHAPTER 19

In a rented trailer deep in the woods outside Murphy, North Carolina, thirty-year-old Eric Rudolph reflected unhappily on his work of three months earlier. The Centennial Olympic Park bomb had not gone as planned.

Size wasn't the issue. He had constructed the bomb with large pipes, each wrapped with masonry nails. It barely fit into his ALICE pack. But despite a directional plate he had inserted, the shrapnel had diffused too widely, and the smokeless gunpowder had been an ineffective explosive.

He vowed that his next device would be much improved. Now the sinewy man with penetrating blue eyes needed to choose a new target.

ERIC ROBERT RUDOLPH WAS born on September 19, 1966, in his parents' home in Merritt Island, Florida, midway up the state's Atlantic Coast. He was the fifth child of six. His father, Bob, worked as a carpenter and airline mechanic at Cape Canaveral, and loved picking his acoustic guitar, sometimes hunching over the kitchen table to jot down notes for new gospel-folk songs. Rudolph's mother, Patricia, had prepared to be a Catholic nun but dropped out, marrying Bob soon after. She raised young Eric and his siblings while pursuing new spiritual paths. She tried a Pentecostal church, then charismatic tent revivals, then Baptist faith communities. The sandy-haired Eric often found himself in interminable living-room prayer meetings filled with song, prophecy, testifying, and speaking in tongues.

Eric was an athletic, outdoorsy kid, roaming the town on his bike with friends after school. At eleven, his father took a job with TWA at Miami's airport and the family moved south to Fort Lauderdale. Eric played Little League baseball. He loved the feeling on the pitcher's mound, the ability to control the pace, the intellectual exercise of trying to stay one step ahead of the batter.

But Eric's life soon grew harsher. Bob Rudolph lost his TWA job, and he began working in construction at the Miami Zoo. The family moved again, sixty miles farther south to Homestead, Florida. The Rudolphs struggled to make ends meet. The schools in Homestead were racial tinderboxes, and Eric resented African American kids for picking on him. His family's spiritual life began to anger him too. While he felt drawn to Scripture, Eric loathed the Rock Church, his family's current faith home. He would later refer to the low-budget house of worship as a "spiritual opium den" led by a minister seeking to get his flock high on the Holy Ghost. As an escape, in his early teens, he increasingly got high smoking pot.

When Eric was fifteen, his father contracted malignant melanoma. The family distrusted modern medicine, so Bob refused chemotherapy. Pat hunted for alternatives, including laetrile, a homeopathic compound made from poisonous apricot pits but unapproved by the FDA. They traveled once to Tijuana for treatments, but Bob soon died.

During Bob's illness, Pat needed to lighten her burden. So, she convinced a family friend to host Eric in the forested western North Carolina community of Nantahala. The ninth grader found the area to be deeply distrustful of outsiders, including the newcomer from two states south. Often Eric would leave school on Friday, spend the weekend in the woods, and return to class on Monday in the same clothes.

After briefly attending Nantahala High School, Rudolph left to be home-schooled. Without a television, he became a voracious reader of history. He pored over the war memoir of William Blackford, a Confederate colonel who rode with General J.E.B. Stuart's cavalry during the "War Between the States." Rudolph marveled how Blackford ran circles around the Union Army while delivering intelligence to Col. Robert E. Lee. He loved soldiers who fought successfully against the elements and long odds: George Washington at Valley Forge; Daniel Boone at Cumberland Gap; Stonewall Jackson at Chancellorsville; George Patton at Normandy. Delving into more-recent events, Rudolph fumed over the American education system, especially teachings that compared giants like Patton and Washington with "pygmies" like Malcolm X, Cesar Chavez, and Betty Friedan.

In western North Carolina, Rudolph was exposed to the Patriots, an extreme libertarian movement centered in part around perceived government threats to guns, property rights, and "Christian America." Many of the theories he heard in the mountains stuck. The "Culture War" that the Patriots

Centennial Olympic Park, with the AT&T tower at bottom right and the Fountain of Rings in the background

Centennial Olympic Park, with Tribute to Olympia statue in foreground

Centennial Olympic Park after midnight on July 27, 1996, the morning of the bombing

Richard Jewell photo from the light and sound tower

ABOVE, RIGHT: Highlighted payphone on Baker Street used for the 911 call
ABOVE, LEFT: 911 tape eventually distributed by the FBI to the media

TOP: FBI mock-up of the Centennial Olympic Park bomb
ABOVE: ALICE pack similar to the one containing the Olympic bomb

Richard Jewell's first media interview, on CNN with Jeanne Meserve

The Tribute to Olympia statue near the blast site where Alice Hawthorne was killed

ABOVE, LEFT: Bomb site the day after the blast
ABOVE, RIGHT: Post-blast temporary memorial in front of the rebuilt light and sound tower

Jewell holding Scruggs and Martz's original story

The media swarms Richard Jewell in the parking lot outside Bobi's Monaco Station apartment.

Don Johnson (left) and Di Rosario approach Jewell's apartment to bring him in for the interview. Kathy Scruggs looks on from the background.

TOP: Miranda form signed by Jewell, Johnson, and Rosario
ABOVE: Previously undisclosed images of Jewell during his videotaped interview with Don Johnson

Jewell performing karaoke in Lahaina, Maui

fixated on was something he'd experienced first-hand in Florida, where the teachers offered what Rudolph termed "guilt and self-hate." The Patriots' talk of a "coming war" also intrigued him, providing a sense of purpose. As a teen at one retreat, Rudolph learned to use firearms, including high-powered AR-15s. He found the experience exhilarating.

In 1984, Eric and his mother, Pat, traveled to rural Missouri for a stay at the Church of Israel in Schell City. The minister was a believer in Christian Identity, a white separatist and anti-government orthodoxy with a deeply anti-Semitic strain. Eric fell in love with an attractive young woman named Joy, but she left for college. Upon her return the next spring, she wanted little to do with Rudolph. He soon returned to North Carolina, bringing with him little from the Church of Israel beyond more anger and disillusionment.

Rudolph enrolled in Western Carolina University. But his argumentative style, forged through his increasingly radicalized perspective, played poorly. In one course, he was assigned a chapter from historian Howard Zinn's *A People's History of the United States*. Zinn argued that American Indians were victims subjugated by colonizing Europeans, a view that set Rudolph off. In an essay, he labeled Zinn's perspective "a pack of lies." The instructor gave him a C and warned him about hate speech.

Rudolph was appalled. He concluded that radicals like the professor and Zinn posed a far greater threat to American values than any forces abroad. "I began to notice Howard Zinns everywhere . . . frustrated communists destroying capitalist society from within," he later wrote. Bit by bit, America was unwinding these basic ethical concepts, throwing away a thousand years of Western mores, he believed.

Rudolph left college after two semesters and began to grow marijuana as a cash crop in the same Nantahala woods where moonshiners once thrived. He studied *High Times* magazine for cultivation tips, traveling to Amsterdam at one point to bring back better seeds. He regularly drove to Nashville to sell his cannabis, and within a few years, was pulling in some $60,000 a year tax-free. But Rudolph began to detest the business and his role in it. He saw himself as "just another greasy cog in the counterculture wheel."

Rudolph's anger toward the federal government continued to grow. He feared its power, lamenting that judicial and legislative decisions had transformed the United States "from being a constitutional republic of rugged individualism into a "nanny state of welfare dependents." The transition, he concluded, amounted to the greatest nonviolent revolution in history.

Rudolph saw only one path for himself: He vowed to become a counterrevolutionary, part of the militant minority eager to confront the liberal regime with force. At the age of twenty, Rudolph dedicated his life to what he called the "national resistance." Violence was a necessary part of the answer.

For training, in August 1987, Rudolph enlisted in the U.S. Army. He entered the ranks at Fort Benning, Georgia, eager to learn all he could and qualify for his Ranger tab. The days were brutal, starting at 4:30 A.M. and packed with intense physical drills, often while carrying a fifty-pound ALICE pack. Rudolph endured the training, the marching, the orders. He mastered his M-16 rifle, then expanded his skill set to other weapons, including the M-60 machine gun.

He learned to evade capture and construct booby traps, Claymore mines, and improvised explosives. Once, he built an IED with an ammunition can stuffed with half-sticks of dynamite and shrapnel. Rudolph was a natural at survivalist activities.

The Army posted Rudolph to the 101st Airborne in Fort Campbell, Kentucky, where he earned his Air Assault badge. Along the way, he made a few friends, who saw him as smart and funny but highly opinionated—often far too opinionated for their comfort. Many were shocked at how quickly Rudolph would trigger about what he considered the absurd amount of power vested in the federal government. He railed against the Army brass, who he complained were forcing him to obey orders from blacks and women. He vented about Jews controlling the banks and media. Bunkmates even heard him praise Adolf Hitler.

He had also come to despise many of the cooks, clerks, mechanics, and others who combat troops derisively referred to as REMFs, for Rear Echelon Motherfuckers. Unlike combatants trained for the front lines, REMFs were career Army, and Rudolph distained their easy paycheck. Middle-aged guys with beer bellies and hemorrhoids, he would sneer later. It didn't help that many were minorities.

By the summer of 1988, after only a year, Rudolph wanted out of the military. In November, he intentionally failed a urinalysis by smoking pot before the test. He was discharged a few months later. Rudolph wrote a friend,

"Surprise, surprise! I'm out of the Army since 25 January. No more slavery, no more nigger standing over me in the morning." He returned to Nantahala, and his first outing was a two-week solo camping trip to a remote area of the national forest, where he stalked wild boar.

For a couple of years, Rudolph remodeled houses with his two older brothers, Joel and Daniel. His passion for national revolution still smoldered, but he was drifting through his mid-twenties. Then, in short order, he was jolted by a string of political events. In June 1992, Bill Clinton, a man Rudolph saw as a purveyor of democratic socialism, became a candidate for president. Later that summer, the FBI and the U.S. Marshals Service fatally shot Randy Weaver's wife and teenaged son at their Idaho cabin at Ruby Ridge. The next spring, after Clinton was elected, the federal government launched its deadly failed siege on David Koresh's Branch Davidian compound in Waco, Texas.

Rudolph heard the rallying cries of Ruby Ridge and Waco. At gun shows, he noticed that the talk had turned more militant. He grew hopeful a violent nationalist-conservative revolution was imminent to fight the federal regime's agenda: an assault-weapon ban; homosexuals in the military; feminism; socialized medicine; globalization. The battle would start with individualized attacks by patriots like himself.

By the spring of 1995, Rudolph had long given up on the American political system. While Democrats now controlled the White House, he felt Republicans were nearly as complicit. "The Republican party is the modern equivalent to the Pharisaical sect in ancient Judea," he wrote, citing Matthew 23:28. "'You are like whited sepulchers, which indeed appear beautiful outward, but are within full of dead men's bones, and all uncleanness.'"

Rudolph became more and more isolated. He took survival trips into the forest. He lived largely off the grid, renting properties under fake names, paying no taxes, holding no credit cards, using only cash and postal money orders. He moved to new lodgings roughly every six months. He knew he had to use his real name on his driver's license and military records, but he assiduously kept those identity-revealing documents to a minimum.

Rudolph's hardened worldview spewed forth when visiting family and friends. As he watched television, which he dubbed the "Electric Jew," Rudolph ranted at the news commentators. When Jewish names appeared in the credits, he would scream at the screen. Sometimes he would fly into Nazi tirades. At a girlfriend's home, he climbed atop a milk crate and announced he wanted to be a preacher. Rudolph proceeded to deliver an improvised sermon, declaring gays were Satan's children and should be killed. Blacks and immigrants fared no better.

By 1996, the revolution still hadn't come. Rudolph decided he would have to spark it himself. In mid-April, he sold the family home in Nantahala for $65,000 and divided the proceeds with his siblings and his mother. He announced that he was moving out west, to strike his fortune, but it was a lie. Instead, he pocketed his share of the money from the sale, burying most of the cash because of a deep distrust of banks. Rudolph then rented a trailer in western North Carolina by Vengeance Creek, some forty miles from his old home, under the assumed name of Bob Randolph. There, he experimented with making explosives, setting them off in hollows on the North Carolina–Tennessee border. Over the next several months, he built five bombs that were ready to go.

He had already selected his first target: the Atlanta Olympics.

Rudolph conjured a plan to detonate one explosive each night of the Games, sowing fear and mayhem. As the blasts shook Atlanta, more than a billion people around the globe would hear his message that leftist values were destroying the real America. Tourists would abandon their plans, taking their money with them. Rudolph doubted he could cause the Games to be cancelled, but he would embarrass and financially damage the powers behind the world event.

In July, Rudolph prepared for his life after the attack, burying an emergency cache of survival provisions in the Nantahala National Forest. He packed a year's supply of wheat, lentils, pinto beans, peanut oil, and rye. Then, he added a Dutch oven, frying pan, tent, tarps, rope, axe, knife, and other necessities. He kept another year's backup supply of food at the trailer.

Shortly before the Opening Ceremony, Rudolph drove toward Atlanta to case his first target. Paranoia rose in him as he neared the city. Gas stations had video cameras, as did restaurants. He had stored fuel in five-gallon containers and brought along food to avoid stopping. Motels, which kept records, weren't an option. Instead, his Nissan truck's camper shell would be his makeshift bed, in a wooded area off Interstate 20, some twenty miles from the city center.

The next day, Rudolph left his truck far enough from downtown to avoid the Olympics security cameras. As he scoped out venues, he soon concluded that a new park in the center of the city was a perfect target for his first bomb. Commercialism was everywhere: Swatch, Budweiser, Coca-Cola. Crowds swarmed the space, especially when live entertainment filled the big stage sponsored by AT&T. *The park reeked of a curious mixture of capitalist greed and socialist idealism*, he thought. The global socialism reminded him of the despicable ideals in that John Lennon song, "Imagine."

As importantly, the park appeared to lack the protection of the official Olympics venues. Rudolph decided to test security there. He hid his eyes behind sunglasses, a hat covering his head. A full beard cloaked his jaw. He changed outfits and hats on each sortie. Security guards might have glanced at him, but never scanned his bag. He had his target.

Rudolph returned to North Carolina and packed the bombs into his truck. He drove them to his wooded spot off Interstate 20 outside Atlanta, then buried the devices in piles of trash.

With the Games already well underway, he needed to get moving to execute his plan of five bombings in five days. For his final dry run, Rudolph approached the park, ornamented with a banner reading GLOBAL OLYMPIC VILLAGE. He carried an ALICE pack, stuffed with food and clothing in case guards searched it. Mindful of video surveillance and omnipresent tourists snapping photos, Rudolph wore a fresh set of clothes, another hat, and clear-lens safety glasses. No one stopped him or asked to look in the knapsack. The test had gone as planned.

On July 26, Rudolph picked out his disguise for the night. He would wear a tan fisherman's cap, along with the clear glasses. As a final touch, he shaved his beard into a goatee. Near midnight, he placed the bomb onto his passenger-side floorboard and drove away from the wooded, vacant lot off Interstate 20. Rudolph parked about a mile away from his target. He hoisted the ALICE pack onto his shoulders, a heavy sweatshirt padding him and cloaking his Smith & Wesson handgun. Despite his having inserted a dowel into the bag to provide more support, the weight was intense. He could feel every ounce of the device inside. The night was humid and soon he was drenched in sweat.

Near the park, Rudolph pulled down his fisherman's cap. No one stopped him as he entered onto the engraved brick pavers. Thousands of people milled about, drinking and celebrating. Music blared from the stage.

He navigated the crowd. At one point, a nearby man snapped a picture of the fountains. Rudolph panicked, certain the photographer had captured him in the foreground. He needed to get his work done and move on.

Rudolph approached three dark green benches on the north side of the light and sound tower facing the stage. He sat down, shoving the pack beneath the seat. Several drunks were wrestling in the grass nearby. A man perched on the other end of the bench glanced often at Rudolph, who in turn tried to evade his gaze. The man finally stood up and left. Rudolph reached down into his pack, set the bomb's alarm clock for 1:20 A.M., and strode out of the park.

Rudolph worked his way through a cluster of pedestrians to a bank of pay phones on Simpson Street. He slipped on a pair of gloves, jammed each nostril with wet toilet tissue, and cupped a small plastic funnel over his mouth. He punched in 911. "Can you understand me?" he asked the operator. "Yes," she replied. "You defy the order of the militia . . ." The operator hung up on him.

Rudolph raced for another bank of pay phones about a block away, outside a Days Inn on Baker Street. He grabbed the handset and dialed 911 again. This time leaving the funnel aside but pinching his nostrils to disguise his voice, he opted to leave out any manifesto. Rudolph concisely told the operator: "There is a bomb in Centennial Park. You have thirty minutes." He hung up. It was 12:58 A.M.

Rudolph then hiked to a rise on Harris Street where he could see the park. To his surprise, a pair of agents already were on their knees in front of the bag, penlights in hand. *Unbelievable*, he thought. *These guys are good*. He had just called and they were already there, presumably trying to disarm the device. Officers had created a perimeter around the pack.

No doubt more law enforcement—agents of the federal government he so despised—would soon arrive too. Rudolph watched the scene unfold until he worried he might be noticed. He walked away, then circled around, eventually returning to the Harris Street spot. He looked at his watch. It was 1:19 A.M.

Seconds later, a loud crack felt like it was puncturing his eardrums. He stared as a ball of fire engulfed the base of the tower. As he recorded later, people near the blast site were "thrown through the air like rag dolls." Those farther away were "dropped to the ground like blades of grass being cut down by an invisible scythe." As a cloud of smoke rose, there was a sudden silence, then pandemonium.

Rudolph hurried back to his truck and headed east on I-20 toward his temporary camping spot. Concern began to turn to panic. Had he been seen? Would he be identified? One witness had clearly seen him on the bench. Another appeared to have captured him on film. Rudolph made a split-second decision to discontinue his daily bombing operation. What should he do with the other devices? They were evidence.

Reaching the vacant lot, Rudolph hunted for the four IEDs amid the garbage piles. In a daze, he had forgotten where he had hidden them. Finally, after an hour of searching, he came upon the other bombs. He set their timers for fifteen minutes and placed them back into the trash piles. He drove to a safe distance, and listened for the explosions. Once he counted four, Rudolph headed back to Nantahala.

Two hours later, he arrived at the Vengeance Creek trailer to load his truck with the additional supplies. Rudolph bolted to his hidden encampment off an old logging trail that followed Lost Creek. He would be well concealed there, deep in the forest of hemlocks, rhododendron, and mountain laurel.

For days, Rudolph lived in his truck, his hips aching from folding himself into the front cab. Every half hour, Rudolph briefly switched on the radio, his ear tuned to any newsbreaks from Atlanta. After a few days, the media reported that the FBI had tagged a security guard named Jewell with the bombing. Still, out of an abundance of caution, Rudolph remained hidden in the forest for three weeks after the bombing. Then he could finally relax. It was time to end his self-exile.

AS SUMMER TURNED TO fall, Rudolph worked in his blacked-out kitchen, experimenting with new materials for his IEDs. Protected by rubber gloves, he toiled over the sink in his trailer's hot, tiny cooking area, a welding mask over his face. Sheets hung from the windows to keep out prying eyes. An exhaust fan sucked out noxious fumes. Meticulously, he mixed explosives and created new devices. Later, he would take the test bombs deep in the dense forest and set them off.

But the new formulas repeatedly failed to produce the desired explosion. Frustrated, he hauled off the pots, baking dishes, and refuse to dumpsters.

Rudolph needed a better answer. He began to venture out to quarries in Georgia, Tennessee, and Alabama looking for a source for dynamite.

All the while, Rudolph pondered those he despised: law enforcement, corporations, sodomites, blacks, Jews. So many opportunities to make another statement.

CHAPTER 20

Don Johnson had begun feuding with the U.S. Attorney's Office.

After the ruse interview, prosecutors had requested a copy of the video. Days later, after waiting for a conversion of the Betamax tape to VHS, they were appalled to see how Johnson had issued Jewell the Miranda rights "just like you are doing a professional interview." Kent Alexander felt sick. He picked up the phone and dialed Merrick Garland in Washington. Borrowing a line from *Apollo 13*, released a year before, Alexander said, "Merrick, we've got a problem." Garland hadn't known about either the ruse or Johnson's twisted delivery of Miranda. In turn, Garland reached out to Deputy AG Gorelick and Attorney General Janet Reno to alert them. They looped in Louie Freeh, and Alexander did the same with SAC Woody Johnson. All then looked to the FBI Atlanta field office and Don Johnson for an explanation.

Agent Johnson already had filed a single-paragraph 302 under his and Rosario's signatures. In it, he wrote that they had advised Jewell of their identities at the apartment and of the "nature of the contact." Johnson added, "Jewell, thereafter, consented to voluntarily follow the contacting agents in his own vehicle to the Atlanta office of the Federal Bureau of Investigation." His implication was clear: There had been no need to read the Miranda warnings. For further information, the agent simply referred readers to the interview transcript, "attached hereto."

Government lawyers rolled their eyes at Johnson's skirting the issue and asked for an expanded 302. They wanted the story behind the story. What had Johnson told Jewell the interview was for? What scenario did he use? What did Johnson and Watson Bryant discuss by phone as the interview ended? Over the next seven weeks, Johnson wrangled with the attorneys until he finally produced a fuller 302 that they could accept. In the report, the agent insisted that Jewell knew the real reason for the interview. Johnson had only mentioned a "potential training film on first responders" to explain away the taping that was about to come.

That was only the start of the agent's problems.

The FBI removed Johnson from the CENTBOM task force. Shortly afterward, the Bureau's Office of Professional Responsibility opened an investigation into all aspects of the Jewell interview. A team of Washington attorneys flew to Atlanta to grill Johnson, Rosario, FBI Atlanta supervisors, the U.S. Attorney, and others involved in the interview. They also questioned SAC Tubbs, who had returned to Salt Lake City after his brief stint running the bombing investigation. In the nation's capital, they sat down with Garland and the behavioral scientists. Johnson hired a personal lawyer and inserted a protest in the preamble of his statement, saying, "I understand I am being compelled as a condition of employment with the FBI to provide this statement." He felt like he'd been set up once before in Albany and had no plans to let it happen again.

On a separate but related track, senior FBI officials kept open their probe into the law enforcement leak to the *AJC*. They intended to find the source of Scruggs's story.

Johnson returned to investigating bank robberies. But his mind remained on Jewell, fully convinced that the guard had been involved in the bombing. The agent began to keep a shadow file on the Jewell case, collecting FBI documents as well as media coverage, some of it personally unflattering to him. In the *Orlando Sentinel*, cartoonist Dana Summers drew a single panel of the FBI men's room. An attendant in a bowtie stood near the sinks, prepared to hand out towels. Another man pointed, "Say, aren't you the agent who was in charge of the Richard Jewell case?" Johnson stuffed the cartoon into his files.

THE CENTBOM TEAM FOCUSED on the return of property seized from Jewell's apartment, in keeping with the agreement with Jack Martin. Prosecutors and agents struggled with how to handle the guard's guns and ammo. There was no legal basis to keep them, as they weren't evidence in the Olympic bombing. But how would law enforcement explain handing over an arsenal to a suspected bomber, even one against whom the case had weakened significantly? Officials decided to return everything but the weapons, which they would return after the interview.

At 9:15 A.M. on the first Saturday in October, Jewell and Bobi went to the FBI building, where they waited in a conference room for the Bureau to bring out the seized belongings. Watson Bryant joined them. Over the next two hours, agents delivered box after box into the room and spread items across a long table. Jewell checked off the FBI's list possession after possession as he and his mother surveyed their life encased in cardboard. His brown shorts from the bathroom hamper, a pair of pliers, a bottle of hydrogen peroxide, his July calendar, a *Mary Poppins* movie cassette, a Black & Decker drill.

Then Bobi stared at her Tupperware. Nearly every piece bore evidence numbers in permanent marker. She burst into tears, bolting from the room to compose herself. Her thirty-year collection had been ruined by the forensics lab.

The Bureau told the Jewells they were prepared to drive a van to Monaco Station with the seized belongings. But they cautioned that if they saw any cameras or reporters at the complex, they would just keep driving and all of it would remain in FBI custody. After the search had been broadcast live by the world's media, the FBI was now insisting on keeping the press in the dark for the return.

The FBI arrived at the complex, where a team hastily marched the boxes up the steps into Apartment F-3 and dropped them in the living room. Bobi directed the agents to unpack the items onto the shelves. The FBI declined. The search two months earlier had taken more than nine hours. The return took less than five minutes.

The following morning, October 6, Martin read through all of Jewell's statements and transcripts of recordings, including Johnson and Rosario's fourth-floor interview. The process took two hours. Jewell already had told him about Johnson's Miranda warnings, but the attorney was flabbergasted by the actual text. Martin was careful to take verbatim notes to share with the other lawyers, and later the media. None of Jewell's five other statements, or the transcript of the Attaway dinner, contained anything surprising. The guard's story had stayed consistent from the start. Martin signaled he was ready to start the final Jewell interview once his client arrived.

Early afternoon, Jewell walked into the FBI's Atlanta headquarters wearing jeans and his Braves baseball cap. Alongside Martin were Watson Bryant, dressed in shorts, and Lin Wood, in a blue blazer and pale blue button-down shirt. Assistant U.S. Attorney John Davis, assigned to sit in on the interview, reminded the Jewell lawyers that they could have only one member of their team present. The ground rules had been hashed out well in advance. Wood pushed back, eager to get in. But the forthright Davis held firm, adding with a finger wag, "You are not a man of your word." Wood spat back. "You are not going to say that to me, you son of a bitch." The combative attorney suggested he and Davis take it outside. In the end, Wood relented. Though both he and Bryant desperately wanted to attend the interview, there was only one slot for each side's attorney. Jack Martin, the Jewell team's criminal lawyer, was the only logical fit.

Martin and Jewell, along with Davis and two interviewing agents, filed into the library. Agents politely asked Jewell if they could get him anything before starting the interview. A Coke? A glass of water? Jewell said he was hungry and recited the phone number of the Pizza Hut on Buford Highway from memory.

Just after 3:30 P.M., Jewell settled in. Martin had told him privately that the prosecutors simply wanted to eliminate him as a suspect. So, he was ready for the interview to get under way, a critical step toward resuming a normal life and returning to law enforcement. The two agents, from their perspective, viewed Jewell as a suspect to be either pursued or cleared. Inside the FBI, those doubting the guard's guilt hoped he would provide critical information about what had happened around the tower between 10:30 P.M. and 1:20 A.M. on the night of the blast.

For nearly six hours, Jewell answered questions in almost savant-like fashion. He quoted full conversations with co-workers, the Speedo Boys, and GBI Agent Tom Davis. He detailed the precise movements of the bomb techs examining the ALICE pack. At times, he grew emotional. When Jewell spoke of the officers forming the perimeter and putting themselves between the pack and the crowd, he began to cry.

Jewell at times was too detailed for Martin's taste. In describing the park, Jewell repeatedly pointed out that his spot at the tower allowed him to see plenty of attractive young women, which was one reason he didn't want to be reassigned. "I mean there were women everywhere," Jewell exclaimed. "I mean, God, it was unreal." On a break, Martin urged, "Richard, cool it on the girls." Jewell pointed out that the press had highlighted his living with his mother so many times that some questioned his sexual preferences. Jewell said he had nothing against homosexuals, but he had enough trouble getting dates without women thinking he was gay.

On the FBI's outstanding evidence pointing to him, Jewell painstakingly set the record straight on each item. He had never looked at bomb designs on the internet, though he did enjoy pulling up diagrams of old World War II planes. He had walked in the woods around Demorest, but never during or after an explosion. He had absolutely no recollection of asking if a tower in the park would withstand a blast or saying he would be famous or a hero.

When agents pressed Jewell on why he took his first-ever break on the night of the bombing, they may have gotten more information than they bargained for. "I had the runs real bad, guys." Pepto Bismol hadn't helped. Other nights, he had no need for bathroom breaks. If he had to go, he'd furtively urinate on the ground behind the back wall of the tower.

The agents plumbed for any sighting of a suspicious white male, other than the Speedos, on the bench. Jewell said he hadn't seen or spoken to anyone else of note fitting that bill. The questioners opted not to show Jewell a sketch that had been done of Goatee Man. To do so would almost certainly mean the Jewell team would alert the media about the sketch's existence to bolster their client's case of innocence.

As the hour approached nine P.M., the marathon interview began drawing to a close. One of the agents asked Jewell if there was anything he'd like to clarify. The guard took the opportunity to vent about what he viewed as the genesis of his troubles. "Just about everything the news media said is half lies, and to me a half truth is the same thing as a lie." As for the leaker, "I'd like to talk to that person face-to-face one day and ask him if his life would stand up to the scrutiny mine has stood up to."

Assistant U.S. Attorney Davis ended the interview with a final question, giving Jewell an opportunity to expressly deny the crime: "Did you do the bombing and do you know anything about who did?"

Jewell didn't hesitate. "Sir, I know nothing about this bombing. I am one hundred percent positive that I know nothing about this bombing. I didn't do it. I didn't set it. I didn't bring it there. I don't know who did, and if I did I'd bring the son of a bitch to y'all tied up like a mummy."

Two days after the meeting, the FBI delivered Jewell's guns. His defense team raced to the media with news of both the return of the search items and the recent interview. The *AJC* ran the story on its front page the next day. "He answered their questions fully and completely," Jack Martin told reporter Bill Rankin. "He couldn't have been more believable. I fully expect, once they've had an opportunity to evaluate all that was said, this will resolve any lingering doubts they have about Richard Jewell." Bryant called a clearance "a matter of common decency." Wood pointedly observed that the FBI had returned more than a dozen weapons, a clear sign that their man was no longer a serious bombing suspect. "Otherwise, why would they have returned all of his guns?"

The FBI remained silent.

KATHY SCRUGGS GRADUALLY AND painfully had begun to recognize that the probe of Jewell was going nowhere. In the first few weeks after she broke the story, she wondered where the government's charges were, whether her source had overstated the case that evening in the bar. As more days passed, competing journalists around town eyed her smugly. Without an arrest of Jewell, had Scruggs simply blustered her way into a false story?

AJC staffers began to carp, quietly at first and then more boldly. Scruggs always had been divisive inside the newsroom for her brashness and sexuality, and now her professional reputation bubbled into the conversations. Did she owe someone a favor? Had she recklessly damaged the paper's reputation? Ron Martz heard the gossip, but dismissed it. He had co-written the first Jewell piece, yet no one was criticizing him. Why the double standard?

With her sources drying up, Scruggs scheduled a mid-October meeting with U.S. Attorney Alexander. She and Martz came to his downtown office overlooking several former Olympic venues. Martz wore a button-down shirt. Scruggs dressed in a short skirt, her press badge dangled atop her low-cut blouse. She still had an FBI Olympic pin stabbed into her plastic *AJC* credentials.

The reporters pressed Alexander for anything he could tell them about Jewell or anyone else the government might be looking at. Alexander declined, saying they knew there was nothing he could say. Scruggs pressed further. He offered only that agents had been traveling around the country collecting additional shrapnel extracted from victims' bodies.

After just ten minutes, the reporters dejectedly stood to leave. But Scruggs paused at the doorway next to a vintage barrister bookcase for her final pitch. "C'mon, Kent, we're the hometown paper. You owe us the story." Then, tossing her blonde curls, Scruggs added, "I won't give you a blow job, but I'll treat you right." Alexander was speechless. It wasn't until years later that he learned "blow job" was a term reporters occasionally used for puff pieces.

That week, Scruggs updated *AJC* readers in an article headlined MONTHS AFTER OLYMPIC BOMBING, INVESTIGATION SHOWS LITTLE PROGRESS. Her lead paragraph stated, "As the FBI turns its attention away from Richard Jewell, clues in the Olympic bombing apparently have taken investigators across the country and back but nowhere near identification of the bomber." Editors ran the piece on page C-4.

FBI LEADERSHIP, SADDLED WITH a former prime suspect in a three-month-long terrorism investigation, decided again to beef up the CENTBOM task force. A flurry of new initiatives followed.

Agents fanned out in a renewed effort to collect outtake video from TV stations. Others investigated sixty "white male" Atlanta bomb threat recordings. In one labor-intensive effort, the Bureau secured 177 boxes of ACOG credential applications and began loading all 500,000 names into a database. Other agents delved into thousands of public records, including traffic violations, gun registrations, and hunting licenses. New arrivals to CENTBOM took over half the second floor, not far from Don Johnson's desk. The agent, still under investigation himself, could only sit and watch. He remained convinced to his core that Richard Jewell was complicit in the bombing.

With hundreds of leads, the FBI desperately needed to narrow its focus, so it decided to develop a new profile. This time, the Bureau would seek the identity of an unidentified subject versus a behavioral analysis of a particular suspect. The BSU was ruled out, having been tainted by its focus on Jewell. So, the task force retained a renowned forensic psychiatrist named Park Dietz. At forty-eight, Dietz already had a history of assisting in the successful prosecutions of very public cases: Jeffrey Dahmer, John Hinkley, and most recently, the Unabomber.

Dietz visited Atlanta to take stock of the evidence and a long list of other suspects. The profile would require far more review and analysis, he said, but one thing was clear: He had little doubt that Goatee Man was the Bureau's guy. In shades of the BSU's original profile, Dietz predicted the man likely lived alone or with his mother and had no close friends. He probably had worked in manual labor, was antisocial even at work, and had been stewing for years about whatever drove him.

ALMOST THREE WEEKS HAD passed since Jewell's October 6 interview. The time had arrived for a final decision on whether to send the non-target letter. The prosecution team drove to the FBI Atlanta office to meet with Woody Johnson and his senior staff, internally calling it the "life after Jewell" meeting. They convened in the fourth-floor conference room, the same place where Don Johnson and Di Rosario had interviewed Jewell twelve weeks before.

The definition of a target, as everyone at the meeting knew, was a person against whom the federal government had "substantial evidence" linking him to a crime. In effect, that made the person a defendant. So, the narrowed question for the FBI became: Did they have substantial evidence that Richard Jewell was responsible for the Centennial Park bombing?

After considerable back and forth, Woody Johnson held the floor. He told the group he knew many agents still harbored suspicions that Jewell was complicit. But clearly, the Bureau did not yet have substantial evidence against the security guard. Nearly three weeks had passed since the interview. "A deal's a deal," Johnson said. He had no objection to the U.S. Attorney sending Jewell a non-target letter. Nor did Louie Freeh.

Alexander already had begun crafting a one-paragraph letter to Jewell's attorneys that would publicly reclassify the guard. He spent days working on it, recasting the five-line text dozens of times. There were so many constituencies to please: FBI, Justice Department, Jewell and his lawyers, media, and public. Finally, he settled on the wording. The U.S. Attorney ran the letter and a separate two-page press release past Merrick Garland, who reported back that Justice had no changes. Headquarters fully supported the U.S. Attorney's Office in Atlanta handling the matter.

Alexander planned to deliver the letter and statement on the day it was approved, Friday, October 25. But President Clinton would be making a campaign stop in Atlanta at noon, with only two weeks left before the election pitting him against Robert Dole. Alexander received instructions from Washington to hold off until the evening news cycle had passed.

The following morning, Alexander and Martin met at a Caribou Coffee shop near Martin's home. For privacy, they crossed the street and sat at a wooden patio table in front of a restaurant closed until lunch. Dispensing with small talk, Alexander pulled out the letter addressed to the criminal defense attorney. Martin read the words carefully:

> This is to advise you that based on the evidence developed to date, your client, Richard Jewell, is not considered a target of the federal criminal investigation into the bombing on July 27, 1996, at Centennial Olympic Park in Atlanta. Barring any newly discovered evidence, this status will not change. I am hopeful that Mr. Jewell will provide further cooperation as a witness in the investigation.

Alexander then handed Martin the two-page release. Not surprisingly, the prosecutor's statement defended the FBI's efforts to find the bomber. But it also expressed regret over the extraordinary intrusions into Jewell's and his mother's lives by both law enforcement and the media. Martin smiled broadly. He anticipated, as did Alexander, that the media would shorthand the letter and statement as a full clearance of Jewell, even though the word never appeared.

Before he left, Martin told the U.S. Attorney that he and the other Jewell lawyers remained angry about the FBI's training video ruse and Miranda. As a courtesy, he wanted the prosecutor to know they planned to reveal both to the media. Alexander nodded ruefully, saying the letter came with no conditions. The two men shook hands and parted company. The news release went out immediately.

As expected, the media universally played the story as a full exoneration of Jewell. Every national network led with the guard's clearance. The front-page headline in the Sunday *New York Times* read, PROSECUTORS DECLARE GUARD ISN'T SUSPECT IN ATLANTA BOMBING. In the Monday *Times*, reporter Kevin Sack filed another front-page story, nearly three thousand words, headlined A MAN'S LIFE TURNED INSIDE OUT BY GOVERNMENT AND THE MEDIA. Having spoken at length in advance with Jewell's lawyers, Sack outlined the training ruse and then quoted Don Johnson's Miranda exchange with Jewell verbatim. Martin said he found the ruse "slimy but legal." The Miranda reading, on the other hand, was indefensible.

Sack also spoke directly with Jewell. The former suspect was particularly critical of the media's handling of his case, saying they "just jumped on it like piranha on a bleeding cow."

In the wake of Jewell's non-target letter, Scruggs teamed with Martz once more, this time to pen a story asking whether profiling had been misused. Scruggs interviewed behavioral science pioneer Robert Ressler, who told her, "A profile is supposed to be a silent tool . . . to shape or direct an investigation for a suspect who is absolutely unknown. Once a person is identified . . . the profile should go away, should disappear." Clearly the FBI and BSU had not hewed to Ressler's caution with Jewell. The profile had served as a key driver of the investigation.

Don Johnson clipped and mounted the Scruggs and Martz piece in disgust, adding it to his expanding Richard Jewell file.

Jewell had a keepsake idea of his own. He copied the clearance letter and the *AJC*'s coverage of it. He collected the original "Hero Bomber" piece, and photos of himself and the lawyers. Then he handwrote personal notes to each member of his legal team, custom-matting and framing the entire assemblage. His notes profusely thanked Wood, Grant, Martin, and the Bryant brothers. He repeated over and over, "I don't know how I will ever repay you."

CHAPTER 21

Two days after the U.S. Attorney's Office released the non-target letter and accompanying statement, Jewell took to the lectern at the same Marriott hotel where Bobi had made her plea two months earlier. Dozens of reporters and microphones awaited him. Jewell wore the same shirt as in his *60 Minutes* interview.

"Thank you for coming here today. This is the first time I have ever asked you to turn your cameras on me. You know my name, but you do not really know who I am. My name is Richard Jewell. As I told you on July 30th, and as the government has admitted to you two days ago, I am not the Olympic Park bomber. I am a man who from July 30th until October 26th lived every waking minute of those 88 days afraid that I would be arrested and charged with a horrible crime, a crime I did not commit. For 88 days I lived a nightmare. For 88 days my mother lived a nightmare, too."

With that, Jewell turned to face Bobi. "Mom, thanks for standing by me and believing in me," Jewell said, his voice quavering, eyes welling. "I love you." Bobi dropped her head into her hands, overcome with emotion.

Jewell added thanks to his lawyers. Then, echoing Bobi from earlier, Jewell succinctly characterized the roles of law enforcement and journalists. "In its rush to show the world how quickly it could get its man, the FBI trampled on my rights as a citizen. In its rush for the headlines that the hero was the bomber, the media cared nothing for my feelings as a human being. In their mad rush to fulfill their own personal agendas, the FBI and the media almost destroyed me and my mother."

The media coverage aligned perfectly with Jewell's sentiments.

Pulitzer Prize–winning political cartoonist Doug Marlette drew a panel showing a "Trial by media" meat grinder with upside-down pants legs and a pair of shoes entering the hopper. A smiling FBI agent leaned over the churned remains on the other end, holding a card with Richard Jewell written on it, and declaring to the shredded mound below ". . . but here's your good name back!" In the *Los Angeles Times*, columnist Mike Downey took the media to task: "This was the year I saw a man lynched, and not with a rope. The man in question is Richard Jewell." A *San Francisco Chronicle* writer offered fellow journalists a terse guideline for when to run a story. "Here it is: Try not to ruin the lives of innocent people."

Jewell may finally have been in a better spot from the public's perspective, but he still struggled on a professional and personal level. He doubted that a police force would bring him aboard after his life had been flayed open with every imperfection fully exposed. He found himself less willing to trust others, his mind circling back often to the lasagna dinner with GBI Agent Tim Attaway. The guard was devastated by the betrayal of a man he considered his friend. How many others had turned on him?

One person Jewell never had doubted was Dave Dutchess. The true-blue West Virginia brother had again returned to Atlanta, this time to show his support for Jewell and Bobi during the clearance. After Jewell's news conference, the media *still* seemed omnipresent. Bobi, in particular, was frustrated, and things boiled over when she returned home from the Marriott only to find an ABC sound truck in the Monaco Station parking lot. The protective Dutchess was fed up. He marched over and pulled a stun gun from his Honda Gold Wing, zapping the device to display its squiggly electric current. Dutchess asked the cameraman if he knew what it was. He did. The West Virginian warned him, "I suggest you get out of here, or I'm going to use it on you." The journalist retreated.

Soon after, Jewell bought a forest green Olympics collector's baseball cap. The front was embroidered in gold with the torch and quilt of leaves, plus the legends "Centennial Olympic Games" and "Atlanta 1996." Jewell used a black permanent marker to inscribe a message on the underside of the tan brim: "Dave, Thanks for being a part of my life. I am sorry for all the trouble being my friend caused you. You are my only brother. Love, Richard A. Jewell."

WITH THE CLEARANCE LETTER in hand and the public now firmly on their side, Jewell's lawyers knew their moment had come to fully attack the most excessive media outlets and seek compensation. The revenge phase would begin in earnest.

On November 6, Lin Wood sent a scathing six-page letter to the *AJC*, putting the paper on notice of Jewell's intent to sue and demanding a prominently placed retraction for the paper's "libelous statements." Under Georgia law, such letters were required before a plaintiff can seek punitive damages. Wood claimed that Scruggs and Martz's original story identifying Jewell as a suspect, and pieces by several other *AJC* reporters, horribly defamed his client. "The *Atlanta Journal-Constitution* ridiculed, accused and vilified an innocent man—and it was all done under the pretense of investigative journalism without any credible evidence to support the writers' statements," Wood wrote. "It is not surprising that the *Atlanta Journal-Constitution*'s articles were wrong—they were based on false statements, rumors, innuendo, inappropriate psychoanalysis and character assassination." The letter named Scruggs, Martz, Walter, columnist Dave Kindred, and former interns Christina Headrick and Kent Walker, among others.

Wood enumerated fourteen offending statements, including two that others in the media had incessantly reprinted and re-broadcast: "Investigators now say Jewell fits the profile of a lone bomber and they believe he placed the 911 call" and "For three days, he had shuttled from television station, to newspaper, to wire service to tell of his heroics and to humbly offer, 'I'm no hero.'"

The attorney took particular exception to Kindred's column comparing his client with Wayne Williams, the alleged serial child murderer. Decency and morality, not just the law, demanded a retraction, Wood claimed. Then, offering the newspaper a taste of what his client had experienced, the lawyer faxed the letter directly to the Associated Press. He sent the original to *AJC* attorney Peter Canfield by far slower courier.

The *AJC* immediately rejected the demand, arguing that its work had been both accurate and responsible. "The apparent basis for Jewell's complaint is that the *Journal-Constitution* was the first to accurately report that he was under suspicion," Canfield said. "That is not the basis for a retraction. Nor is it the basis for a libel suit." Publisher Roger Kintzel added his own statement, expressing frustration over the "endless charges of recklessness and irresponsibility from Mr. Jewell's attorneys," and contending that the paper had reported all sides of the case. The battle between Wood and the *AJC* had just begun.

The next day, Wood set his sights on NBC, giving notice he intended to sue the network. For Jewell, the NBC suit was almost as personal as the *AJC*. Tom Brokaw, once Bobi's favorite, had staggered the Jewells with his on-air confidence about the FBI's case. Jewell's attorneys suspected the direct involvement of the network's marquee anchor would provide considerable leverage to force a settlement. Affirmation of sorts came from an unlikely source.

On October 28, two days after the clearance, NBC's *Tonight Show* host Jay Leno delivered a humorous apology as part of his monologue. He reminded the audience he had called Jewell "the Unadoofus and all this stuff." But the FBI had nothing on Jewell. So, Leno said, "I apologize, Richard. If you are watching, I apologize." Then he continued with mock sincerity, "This has *nothing* to do with the fact that if he wins his lawsuit with NBC, he will be my new boss." After the applause and laughter from the studio audience died down, Leno added: "I think he is suing NBC, isn't he? I was talking to his new chauffeur, Tom Brokaw, today . . . " More laughter.

But the next night, the square-jawed comic was back to more snarky humor. "Well, it's been quite a week. Richard Jewell has been cleared by the FBI. Do you remember Richard Jewell, the Olympic bombing guy? Cleared by the FBI." Then he noted the reports that Gennifer Flowers, a former Bill Clinton paramour, was getting married, and that skater Tonya Harding had saved the life of an elderly woman. Leno moved in for the punch line: "This is like the greatest week in trailer park history, ladies and gentlemen. Oh boy, I tell you. Yes, sir. It is. We celebrate 'White Trash Week' here on the *Tonight Show*."

Wood settled the case with NBC for $595,000. The parties agreed to issue a short statement about the otherwise confidential settlement. For its part, NBC stated that "the protection of confidential sources was a major consideration" in entering into the settlement.

Wood and his partner, Wayne Grant, took aim at others they felt had defamed their client too. The *New York Post*, *Time* magazine, CNN, and Piedmont College all would find themselves in the lawyers' sights.

Jewell's favorite radio station, 96rock, would face off with the Jewell team in a more roundabout way. In mid-August, the program director, Michael Hughes, had written to Watson Bryant, noting that Jewell had displayed its sticker on his truck. Would Jewell be interested in joining 96rock as a security guard and an occasional on-air personality? the station asked. Bryant turned them down. In September, Hughes proposed a billboard ad campaign that would combine Jewell's image with the lyrics of rock songs, pulling the words of the band Drivin' N' Cryin': ". . . Get used to it. The innocent." After some friendly discussion with both Bryant and Jewell, the station continued to develop its outdoor advertising idea.

In October, Hughes proposed that billboards feature Jewell's image alongside a single word: "Freebird." Jewell would be paid $5,000 for his face to be plastered next to a Lynyrd Skynyrd title that he had joyfully performed years earlier with The Pump. Bryant again rejected the deal, explaining that Jewell wanted to be in law enforcement, not to be a radio personality, and that free bird implied a convict who had escaped from jail. But after the clearance, Hughes erected one hundred Jewell-Freebird billboards around Atlanta anyway. Wood's partner, Wayne Grant, sued. 96rock took down the signs and would eventually pay Jewell $50,000.

KATHY SCRUGGS PRESSED AHEAD, trying to find any newsbreaks in the investigation. One strategy: Lean on sources being interviewed by the FBI.

Alex Mendizabal had been working at the park that night. After the *AJC* named Jewell as the primary suspect, Mendizabal told an FBI agent that the guard would introduce himself with, "Hi, I'm Richard, former law enforcement. I'm an ex-cop. Anything I can do for you, feel free to call." Mendizabal told the Bureau that he hadn't seen Jewell at his post just prior to the explosion. But their eyes met as Jewell was standing near the bag. Jewell had motioned to Mendizabal. When they were close, Jewell warned, "It's a bomb. Already called law enforcement. Let's get out of here." The blast came just a few seconds later. The FBI had used Mendizabal's perspective as paragraph 24 of the search warrant affidavit. Scruggs set up a system in which she would call Mendizabal every two weeks to see if he had heard from the FBI. The strategy didn't yield much.

Well after the clearance, she learned of another possible FBI suspect. This one sounded promising. Since September 6, the FBI had been following leads about an employee at a local video company, a self-taught electronics whiz. In the days before the Centennial Park blast, the man talked often about explosives, a colleague told the Bureau. The tipster said the man thought it would be "neat" to see nails go through people. Further investigation revealed potential militia ties. Another witness confirmed the man regularly spoke of bombs. A former roommate disclosed that the man had cleaned his room with uncharacteristic thoroughness shortly after the explosion, then moved out. The FBI discovered that the possible suspect was absent from work on both July 26 and 27.

The Bureau already had spent over two months investigating and tracking down the man. But he was evasive, failing to show up for interviews and, at one point, disappearing for a month. When he finally agreed to a polygraph, he skipped out on that too. Then, in mid-November, out of the blue, he called the FBI and said he would be happy to talk with agents.

The man also reached out to Kathy Scruggs. She probed for details. He told the reporter that he wouldn't take an FBI polygraph because he would fail it. Scruggs in turn immediately called government sources to fish around. Was he a legitimate suspect? Can you help me gather some information about him? But she got nothing. With no confirmation, Scruggs decided not to write about the electronics whiz.

Ultimately, the FBI contacted the man's former fiancée. She disliked his sexual deviance and regular talk of bombs but also provided a solid alibi: They were in bed the night of the bombing. Left with no direct evidence linking him to the Centennial Park bombing, the FBI moved on. Prosecutors monitoring the case marveled at how many crazy people were out in the world.

In December, Scruggs marked her tenth anniversary at the paper. The *AJC* was preparing to shuffle beats. Martz, eager to stay close to home for family reasons, would move to covering juvenile justice. Scruggs would take over the federal law enforcement beat. She could still report on the bombing investigation but obviously not on anything related to Jewell. Still, her trajectory wasn't headed in the direction she wanted. She heard the sniping in the newsroom, and it began to pierce her tough-gal exterior. At lunch with Ron Martz, Scruggs noted how more colleagues at the paper had started to turn against her. It hurt.

AT THE FBI, THE photographic timeline of the bombing night showed a glimmer of promise. Agents unearthed a grainy image of someone they believed to be the actual bomber sitting on a bench by the AT&T tower with what appeared to be a large backpack.

The task force asked NASA to enhance the image. If the agency could distill pictures of the moon or distant planet, maybe it could hone the resolution of the man sitting on the bench. During the scientific presentation, Assistant U.S. Attorney David Nahmias sat in. A Harvard Law grad and former Antonin Scalia clerk, he was renowned on the CENTBOM task force for his sharp mind and endless quizzing of experts. At one point, GBI Agent Charles Stone passed a note to a fellow agent sitting next to him: "If Dave asks one more question, I wonder if that chandelier will hold my weight because I'm fixin' to hang myself."

In the end, NASA couldn't help discern the man's facial features or clothing either. Bomb task force agents began referring to the image of their prime suspect as "Blob Man." Back at the FBI's Atlanta field office, in a moment of dark humor, one agent drew a crude, Rorschach-like sketch in thick marker. It featured an amorphous figure sitting atop a stick-figure bench. He added the headline WANTED BY THE FBI and posted it on the CENTBOM conference-room wall. The Blob Man poster remained there for weeks.

The Bureau continued culling its long list of suspects—or "persons of interest," as the media and law enforcement had increasingly begun calling them in the wake of the Jewell fiasco. The FBI was increasingly confident that Blob Man was indeed the bomber. The timeline was a lock. And the Bureau suspected that Blob Man and Goatee Man were one and the same, although it wasn't yet certain. An NBC cameraman near the scene had a goatee, investigators knew. So did a stagehand for Jack Mack and the Heart Attack. Agents interviewed both. Neither was the bomber.

Task force members reached out to park victims again and again. What had they seen? Could they expand upon their earlier recollections? Special Agent Stu Silver phoned one North Carolina victim who had been riddled with shrapnel in the bombing. The man had little to add to his prior statement. The affable agent asked how seriously he was hurt. The victim listed the injuries: An index finger and part of his thumb had been amputated; he had sciatic-nerve damage; and he had yet to recover feeling in his left foot or much of his leg. His physician predicted his leg wouldn't heal for up to a year. As the call was ending, the injured man asked Silver how the investigation was going. Without missing a beat, Silver replied, "About like your leg."

By December, pressure had been mounting within the Atlanta FBI and U.S. Attorney's Office to make a widespread appeal for the public's help. They needed more leads to determine who and where Blob Man was.

Headquarters was resistant, noting that the timing was hardly ideal. The internal investigations into the leak and Miranda debacle were still under way. An increasingly restive Congress was insisting on answers. The media had been sniping at the FBI constantly since the Jewell investigation unraveled, intensifying the heat. Back in October, rumors had even begun to circulate inside the FBI that Freeh planned to step down. The Director felt compelled to send a memo to all Bureau field offices that he had no plans to resign.

The most troubling aspect of a public appeal, though, was clear: A news conference asking for the public's help would reveal that, after four months of a massive investigation, the FBI still had no idea who committed the Olympic bombing. And what information could they even share? Announcing a search for Blob Man would hardly inspire public confidence or helpful leads. Releasing a drawing of Goatee Man could create an instant alibi for the real bomber once arrested, unless the sketch bore a dead-on resemblance.

But still, Atlanta continued to push. Woody Johnson and others told Washington that calls with new leads had resumed trickling into the Bureau since Jewell's clearance. Several visitors to the park on bombing night reported that they had witnessed suspicious activity but had decided not to inform the FBI after Jewell was identified as the likely bomber. How many callers with new evidence were out there? Johnson asked. Also, proponents of a public appeal noted that memories and interest were fading, creating an urgency to play the 911 tape publicly.

Finally, Director Freeh signed off on the appeal. The FBI put in place a plan to try to replicate the massive news environment of the Olympics. Staffers prepared two hundred audiocassettes for distribution, along with a packet of photos. They readied an 800-number call team. Freeh dispatched his No. 2, Weldon Kennedy, to Atlanta to lead the news conference. On December 9, the Bureau gathered local and national media at the Georgia World Congress Center, the former site of Olympic wrestling, judo, and table tennis competitions.

From the podium, Kennedy offered his appeal for the public's help, dramatically playing and replaying the 911 call for the first time. "There is a bomb in Centennial Park. You have thirty minutes." He read the 800-number aloud four times so that the media and public couldn't miss it. Kennedy didn't show the sketch of Goatee Man—and certainly not Blob Man—but did offer a replica of the ALICE pack. He noted, "As you can see, it is much larger than a book bag." Kennedy asked anyone in the park that night to share with the Bureau any photos, videos, or recollections. As a significant sweetener, the FBI set up a reward of up to $500,000 for information or visual evidence that helped lead to the arrest and conviction of the bomber. To further amplify the request for help, the Bureau agreed for the case to be featured on the popular television program *America's Most Wanted*. Producers arrived two days later.

More than 2,500 calls flooded FBI switchboards, along with 250 photo and video leads. Many were potentially helpful, especially a lead about 13,000 pounds of steel shipped from a North Georgia factory that might match the bomb's plate. Others provided far less of an assist. One Florida man confessed to calling in the bomb threat on the night of the explosion. But when agents interviewed him, he said he couldn't remember the number the bomber had given him. It was three digits: 911. He added that his call went, "There's a bomb in the Park and it's fixin' to go off." The story gave exhausted investigators a hearty laugh.

Five hundred of the calls were written up as new leads, and the CENT-BOM task force felt a new energy in the probe. It ordered a download of all ticket purchasers from ACOG, a huge project but one that could yield names to cross-check. A couple of days after the appeal, the task force separately received an enhanced version of a Canadian video the Bureau had sent to NASA. The two-second clip somewhat more clearly showed a man, likely the bomber, sitting at the end of Bench A at 12:19 A.M. He had a large pack on his back and looked to be wearing a hood or something else on his head. At the FBI's request, NASA took another run at the video snippet. The space agency couldn't come up with facial features but was able to set the height of the person at roughly 6'1" and the size of the bag at 21" tall and 15" wide at its base: the approximate size of an ALICE pack.

The week before Christmas, the FBI also noted an article in the *AJC* by

Scruggs and Martz. In an enterprising piece of journalism, the reporters had interviewed a series of linguistic experts about the newly released audio of the 911 call. The experts shared some observations the FBI found useful. The caller was Caucasian and sober. A clicking sound on the audio was likely the metal pay phone cord tapping against the receiver, an indication the man was fidgeting and looking around.

Most interestingly, a Georgia Tech engineering professor who analyzed the tape through a computer program noted that the voice registered around 15 percent lower than an average male. Based on that, the academic estimated that the caller was likely at least 6'1", Scruggs and Martz wrote. Inside the CENTBOM task force, investigators noted the encouraging match between that prediction and NASA's conclusions about the image of the man in the Canadian video.

DON JOHNSON CONTINUED TO sit on the sidelines working bank robbery and fugitive cases on the 7 Squad. But he remained consumed by the Office of Professional Responsibility investigation. The probe had shifted from the FBI to the Justice Department, and he was irate over being the focus and expected scapegoat. A team of DOJ lawyers had already been down to grill him. The fault, though, he was certain lay not with his own work. It had been inexcusable for Freeh to micromanage and to insist that he and Rosario inject Miranda in the middle of a noncustodial interview. So now, *he* was under the microscope for incompetence instead of the Director.

The first week of December, Johnson learned that Senator Arlen Specter of Pennsylvania would soon be holding a hearing on the Jewell matter. Only Freeh would testify for the government. That "fucking fraud," as Johnson had begun calling him, would undoubtedly hang him out to dry. To make matters worse, he heard Jewell was considering testifying too.

DURING CHRISTMAS WEEK 1996, Eric Rudolph approached the fence of the Austin Powder Company in Asheville, North Carolina. He had found the company—located about one hundred miles east of his trailer—in the Yellow Pages. No security guards, he saw. *They must be on holiday schedule. Perfect.*

He wolfed down a tuna sandwich, slipped a duffel bag over his shoulders, and switched on a police scanner he had hidden under his rain jacket.

A heavy snowfall was predicted. *Infantry weather*, Rudolph thought. *God loves the infantry*.

Rudolph scaled the barbed wire fence then moved toward one of the heavy steel bunkers where the company stored its explosives.

The large locks on the bunker were encased in steel housings to deter bolt cutters. Rudolph pulled out a cordless drill with a titanium bit from the duffel. He removed the cores from both locks, and put in place identical locks he had purchased days before after a scouting run. He climbed back over the fence and walked a distance behind a stand of trees, waiting to see if he had tripped an alarm. For a half hour, Rudolph monitored the scanner and stared through his binoculars. No one came. He entered the property again.

Inside the bunker, Rudolph couldn't believe his good fortune. The walls were lined with boxes of dynamite, cigar-shaped sticks of nitroglycerin in brown wax paper. Each fifty-pound box fit perfectly into his duffel. A wet snow had begun to fall, making his mile-long walk to the truck difficult. He slogged through a cow pasture filled with a mix of mud and manure. But through the night, as the weather worsened into a whiteout, Rudolph lugged his plunder, box by box, back to the truck.

By the time he finished at 1:30 A.M., Rudolph had stolen roughly 340 pounds of dynamite. He drove the payload back toward Murphy, North Carolina, where he steered past his trailer and directly onto an old logging road in the woods. He would resettle the load into laundry tubs, then bury them in separate locations in the forest.

A week later, Rudolph began casing his next target to bomb.

PART 4

ROADS AND ROSES

CHAPTER 22

Richard Jewell awoke on New Year's Day optimistic about 1997. Having celebrated his birthday two weeks earlier, at thirty-four he was ready to find a job and rebuild his life. Meanwhile, his lawyers were eager to prevail in their numerous libel suits and decided to continue building leverage in the court of public opinion. Throughout the past couple of weeks, Jewell had been featured in some of the nation's largest publications.

People magazine named him one of "The 25 Most Intriguing People of the Year" along with Princess Diana and a twenty-year-old Tiger Woods. The magazine wrapped a metaphorical bow around the former security guard's year. "Richard Jewell always wanted to be recognized. To his lasting regret, he got his wish."

Other coverage had been harsher. By contrast, *Time* included him as one of "15 with Their 15 Minutes" of fame. "This time next year, you probably won't remember the names of these 15 humans," the magazine said. Under a photo of Jewell in the park, the caption read: "Richard Jewell. Not a bomber, it turned out—just a bummer for the FBI and NBC." Olympic mascot Izzy, along with Los del Rio's "Macarena," made the list.

To start the new year, the Jewell camp went on what *AJC* reporter Bill Rankin characterized as "a full-court public relations blitz," offering up their client to yet more media outlets. Not surprisingly, the Atlanta paper didn't get one of the interviews. The *Wall Street Journal* ran the first piece on January 3, focusing on Jewell's lawsuits. NBC had agreed to nearly $600,000 in settlement payments, but the story made clear that "the world's most famous security guard" and his legal team were just beginning. Lin Wood told the *WSJ* the litigation wasn't about principle, but about compensating his client for injuries suffered. "You can't spend 60 percent of an apology," the lawyer said, referring to the amount Jewell could expect to collect after attorneys' fees and costs.

Vanity Fair came next. Marie Brenner, an editor at large, had embedded with the Jewell team off and on since October, and in early January the magazine published an expansive human-interest story chronicling the startling turns of events for Jewell. "The Ballad of Richard Jewell," as *Vanity Fair* titled the piece, brought readers the mother and son at their most distressed as they lived like prisoners in their apartment. A striking photo featured the pair staring out from Bobi's couch, forlorn and shocked, uncomforted by their three pets.

The *Vanity Fair* piece became the news hook for a string of television appearances. Jewell and Bobi, along with lawyers Bryant and Grant, sat in with Katie Couric on *Today*. The host noted that she and Jewell had spoken five months before, on July 30, the same day the *AJC* broke its story and the FBI filmed its "training" video. "That morning, you were being called a hero," she began. "I guess we can't say we've come full circle because you don't believe you're back where you were on that morning. Do you think you'll ever regain your good name?"

"No, I don't."

"What do you think people will think of when they hear the name Richard Jewell?"

"What I hear all the time is, 'Well, that's the ex-suspect. That's the one they thought did it.' I don't ever hear, 'That's the one that did his job and, in doing so, possibly saved lives.'"

From there, the group shuttled to *Good Morning America*, where co-host Charlie Gibson trod much of the same ground, focusing on the struggles of the past half-year. A well-coached Jewell reiterated that he longed to restore his "good name" but believed that might be a lost cause. His lawyers had made sure Jewell knew that his loss of reputation formed the crux of his defamation lawsuits, advising him to use "good name" as shorthand.

Was Jewell finding it hard to get his next job?

"I'm still lookin', yes sir. With all the experience that I have in law enforcement, I'm still looking."

"Do you feel there is still an asterisk before your name?"

"There's probably four lines of asterisks before my name." The response brought a laugh from Gibson.

On CNN that night, Larry King unintentionally laid bare the reality of Jewell's notoriety. Coming out of a commercial break, King said in his trademark Brooklyn accent, "We're back with Richard Jewell, the former suspect in the Olympic bombing, and Watson Bryant."

Jewell cut in. "See, you did it yourself, 'the former suspect.'"

"Yeah, you were never a suspect and I am calling you a former suspect and the note says former suspect," King demurred, referring to the producers' intro. "I didn't mean that."

DON JOHNSON STARTED THE new year with a fresh headache. On January 7, he was called to testify at the Richard Russell federal courthouse. The issue: whether the confession he and another agent had secured from Anthony Battle, the inmate charged with murdering the Atlanta Pen guard, had been given freely and voluntarily. In other words, all too familiarly, whether Johnson had violated Miranda. To make matters worse, Jack Martin was handling the cross examination.

On the stand, Martin grilled Johnson over his handling of Miranda with Battle. Wasn't it true that the inmate was in leg irons and handcuffs during the questioning? Yes. Hadn't his client remained silent after Johnson read him the Miranda rights? Yes. So how, Martin asked, did Johnson decide it was appropriate for the agent himself to sign the FD-395 Miranda form on Battle's behalf when no words were uttered? Johnson explained that Battle had nodded when asked about the waiver and offered a "visible blink." Martin seized on the answer. A "blink?" How could a mere blink translate into a waiver of rights? Ultimately, Johnson described the inmate's facial mannerisms and said it was a "double blink." He added, "I don't know how else to describe it. It was obvious to us who saw it, but I don't know how else to say it."

Martin, having made his point that the agent's interpretation was dubious, moved on. He questioned Johnson's professional standing at the FBI following the Jewell debacle. "Agent Johnson, are you currently under investigation by the Office of Professional Responsibility, the Justice Department?" Johnson conceded he was. Martin then tried several tacks to drill down on the actual allegations, but the agent was evasive. He denied knowing precisely what was being alleged beyond "possible misconduct." Frustrated, Martin finally asked, "What is the misconduct, is all I'm asking."

Johnson replied tartly that Martin should know. "You made the allegation, sir."

When Johnson's testimony ended, he walked out of the sixteenth-floor courtroom. The *AJC*'s Bill Rankin, who was covering the testimony, approached the agent to ask for his reaction to the hearing. "You know I have to say no comment," Johnson said. Then pausing, he added, "There are two sides to every story." Rankin ran that quote in the next day's paper in his article under the headline, FBI CREDIBILITY ATTACKED AGAIN.

THE START OF THE year had been slow for Kathy Scruggs. The day before Johnson's testimony about the Battle case, she wrote a short slice-of-life story about the traditional Hispanic festival called Dia de Reyes. Ten days later, she was back on the federal crime beat to hammer out a feature more in line with her passion, an examination of retired FBI profiler John Douglas. The author of *Mindhunter* had just been hired by the family of JonBenét Ramsey, a child beauty queen found murdered in her family's Denver home on Christmas Day, 1996. Ever since the Jewell leak, profiling had become a bit of an obsession for Scruggs. But the *AJC* buried Scruggs's article on Douglas inside the Metro section.

FOR MORE THAN A week in early January, Eric Rudolph cased the Sandy Springs Professional Building in the northern Atlanta suburbs. It was to be his next bombing target.

Spooked by the fear of having been spotted in Centennial Park, he had packed multiple disguises for his reconnaissance. Each day, he parked a mile away and walked by the building three times, swapping out clothes and wigs for every pass. Rudolph thought the three-story white structure with an Italianate façade looked a bit like a wedding cake on steroids. Northside Family Planning Services, an abortion provider, sat inside. A methadone treatment facility was across the hall, and law offices were upstairs. Rudolph hadn't expressed strong anti-abortion views to family and friends in the past. The abortion provider wasn't actually his primary target anyway. Rudolph had a much different plan in mind.

Just after ten P.M. on January 15, Rudolph entered the parking lot of the Sandy Springs building. Rather than approach the building directly, he walked toward some bushes at the edge of the parking lot. He hid a bomb, set the timer for twelve hours later, and left the area. There would be more work to do in the morning.

Rudolph retreated to his pickup but struggled to sleep. He tried to calm himself with Psalm 144: "*Blessed be the Lord my strength, which teacheth my hands to war, and my fingers to fight . . .*" Finally, he was able to rest.

In the morning, Rudolph drove to a Kmart close to the abortion clinic. He slipped on a black wig, knit hat, and calfskin gloves, and slithered around the side of the building. Inside his pack, Rudolph had stuffed an improvised explosive device that included twenty-one half-pound sticks of dynamite in a clear plastic tub, a Westclox Big Ben alarm clock, 4d nails, and a mass of twisted strands of wire. As in the Olympics bomb, he had inserted a steel directional plate cut with an oxyacetylene torch. The device he had hidden the night before was much the same. Rudolph carefully set down the bag at the base of the clinic's ground-floor exterior wall and crept back toward the Kmart lot, pausing to remove his disguise.

The explosion at 9:24 A.M. shook the walls of the office building and shattered all eighteen windows on its south side. It blew a gaping hole in the rebar-enforced concrete, nearly destroying the vacant operating room. Rudolph hopped in his pickup truck and left Atlanta for the mountains. He would listen for news of the next blast on the radio.

Jack Killorin, a veteran ATF agent, had just arrived for his first day as head of the ATF's Atlanta office when an agent greeted him at the elevator. "Mr. Killorin, welcome to Atlanta," she said. "There's just been an abortion clinic bombing." Aware that an attack on a family-planning facility fell under the ATF's purview, Killorin dispatched additional agents to the scene.

In Sandy Springs, law enforcement had cordoned off the back side of the building to collect evidence, and had set up a command post in the front parking lot. Some of the building's lawyers and medical workers waited for loved ones in the front lot too. Several paused to be interviewed by journalists who seemed to materialize almost instantaneously. Fortunately, the clinic wasn't seeing patients that day.

FBI Special Agent Mike Rising pulled up and located the first federal officer at the scene, an ATF agent. Rising offered to summon FBI help, but the fellow agent advised that there was no need. Rising surveyed the bomb site, then decided to call the head of the U.S. Attorney's Criminal Division. He walked toward the front parking lot, away from the clamor of the scene, where he pulled out his bulky phone, leaned against a parked car, and dialed. An hour had passed since the blast, and Rising was put on speaker as he began to describe the scene to several prosecutors.

Suddenly, a second explosion ripped through the row of bushes at the edge of the parking lot, shearing off treetops and jolting news and police helicopters hovering eight hundred feet above. The bomb lifted a car near Rising completely off the ground. The agent writhed on the pavement with nails and wire slashed into the side of his head. "Fuck," he yelled into his phone. "What happened?" a confused lawyer asked. Rising shouted, "Another goddamn bomb went off. I gotta get off the phone." Rising would suffer permanent hearing loss, but the airborne car and another next to it had saved his life.

SAC Killorin and others quickly recognized the purpose of the second device, known as a sucker bomb. The strategy, rare in the United States but more common in European terrorism, surely was aimed at law enforcement and first responders. As Killorin watched the blast on TV from his office, he thought, *That one was for us.*

A pair of *AJC* general assignment reporters cobbled together an initial story on the bombings, making only the final edition of the *Atlanta Journal* with their piece on the known injuries. The paper's headline declared, MORNING OF TERROR LEAVES CITY ON EDGE.

In a follow-up article, Kathy Scruggs detailed for readers the extraordinary luck of Rising and other officers, as well as the media standing nearby during the second blast. Early that morning, a young couple had driven to the building's methadone clinic for treatment. Following the first explosion, they had moved their Nissan to the front of the building, parking near the dumpster where Rudolph had buried his second bomb. In all, six people aside from Rising were hospitalized. Injuries included broken ribs, shrapnel wounds, concussions, and hearing loss.

Investigators worked round-the-clock shifts to identify the bomber, interviewing witnesses and gathering forensic evidence. Several employees in the bombed building highlighted former co-workers who had been fired, including one woman with troubling anger issues. An anonymous source called about a man who lived near the Sandy Springs building and had been overheard talking about a bomb in Centennial Park on July 27. Of particular interest, a methadone patient at the addiction recovery center early that morning had spotted a suspicious character at the edge of the parking lot. He was dressed in a hooded black sweatshirt and carried a duffel and a shovel. The ATF had a sketch drawn, and agents fanned out in the hope of identifying him.

Don Johnson was assigned to the investigative team. First, he retrieved a list of tenants from the building's owner, along with a floor plan. A few days later, he and his partner, Harry Grogan, circled back to the building's owner, who noted disputes with other investors in the property. Meanwhile, Johnson created his own shadow file of other agents' 302s, scanning each for possible connections to Richard Jewell.

An ATF-run task force was soon formed, and dubbed TWINBOM. As roughly a hundred investigators worked to gather clues, one big question loomed: Were they after the same terrorist as in Centennial Park? Clearly, the bomber had used two devices instead of one, and they quickly determined the explosive was dynamite, not black powder. But the timer was a Big Ben clock. Nails had been stuffed into both devices. And the forensics team determined that the TWINBOM IEDs, like the CENTBOM one, contained steel directional plates.

IN JANUARY, JEWELL FINALLY received some form of government recognition for his lifesaving work. The Georgia House of Representatives passed a resolution reading in part: "In a time of too few heroes, Mr. Jewell's actions are an inspiration to all of us, as well as a reminder of the glorious good that remains in our society." Unfortunately, the resolution was not entered into the official record until the next morning, the same day as the Sandy Springs bombing. The media coverage was entirely overshadowed by the new attack.

But the day after, positive media was on its way. Jewell and his mother were flown to Chicago for an appearance on the *Oprah Winfrey Show*. The queen of daytime television led the conversation over familiar ground, with Jewell making many of his well-coached points. Winfrey got more personal too, discussing the stress of being an innocent suspect. Jewell pointed out the fifty pounds he had gained during the past six months. Patting his significantly expanded stomach, he jokingly added, "I'm hoping you can help me. Give me your book or your trainer's number."

Winfrey closed the show with words that Jewell had longed to hear. "I certainly can't speak for the rest of the media or other people," she told Jewell. But "we owe you a big apology for making the judgment in our minds before we heard the facts." Jewell thanked her, adding, "You don't know how much that means to me."

Back home, the defamation cases were continuing to swing Jewell's way. CNN became the second network to settle, writing a $200,000 check for Jewell and another for $50,000 for Bobi. In addition, the network agreed to pay each of them $50,000 for an option to adapt a possible book for television, although few expected either of them to actually write one. Together with the NBC settlement, the Jewells had reached $945,000 in compensation, before lawyers took the usual one-third plus expenses.

But the *AJC* and Piedmont College decided to fight against Jewell's legal team. So, on January 28, Wood, trailed by television cameras, marched into the courthouse to file suits against both organizations, as well as ten individual journalists, including Scruggs and Martz.

Wood submitted the papers, then faced the cameras. Most of his comments focused on the *AJC* case. "The lawsuit, without any question, as many people in the media like to say, it is about money. It's about money and compensation for . . . permanent and significant injuries suffered by Mr. Jewell," he said. "But I don't want there to be any mistake about this lawsuit. It is also a lawsuit about accountability."

The fight against the *AJC* would last far longer than either side imagined. Some of the players wouldn't live to see the result.

CHAPTER 23

As January wound to a close, Jewell rose before sunrise one Saturday. Eager to escape the world of lawsuits, settlements, and media posturing, he flipped on WSB radio. His favorite talk show, *O'Neill Outside*, was on the air. Jewell liked that the folksy host, O'Neill Williams, steered clear of the politics of the day, instead offering hunting and fishing tips. Jewell craved the lifestyle that the host preached each week: Get outdoors with your family or friends for fellowship and human connection.

Late in the show, Jewell picked up his phone and dialed the station. The producer, Williams's wife, Gail, answered, and after a short wait in the queue, Jewell was put through.

"Richard in Atlanta, you're on *O'Neill Outside*," the amiable host drawled in his honey-rich Southern accent.

"I'm interested in possibly purchasing a boat," Jewell told him. Could O'Neill guide him on where to start? For several minutes, O'Neill offered Jewell advice. When the host finished, Jewell gushed, "Mr. Williams, I really appreciate your show." O'Neill thanked him for the compliment, and the call ended.

Still in his bedroom, Jewell thought for a moment, then dialed back. "Ms. Williams, this is Richard again. Would it be possible for me to talk to O'Neill offline?" Sure, she replied. Just hang on and let us finish the show.

Soon, O'Neill was on the line again. They began to exchange broad-brush descriptions of their lives. O'Neill, whose homespun demeanor belied his Emory University economics degree, was observant and sharp. When he heard Richard identify himself as a "shut-in," he probed, thinking he recognized the voice. O'Neill asked for the caller's full name.

"It's Richard Jewell." O'Neill knew his caller's story.

"Well, Richard, it's a pleasure to talk to you."

Sensing a connection, Jewell took a risk: "Would you ever want to go out fishing together?" To his delight, O'Neill agreed.

Several weeks later, on a temperate mid-winter day, the two men met just north of Atlanta. Jewell, dressed in his Atlanta Braves hat and a green windbreaker, climbed into his new friend's pickup truck. O'Neill's twenty-one-foot bass boat was trailered behind them, branded with his show's "O'Neill Outside" logo on the side. As he and Jewell drove toward Lake Lanier, strangers often waved. "Doesn't that make you nervous when they do that?" Jewell asked. O'Neill was puzzled by the question: Do what? Wave, Jewell said. "No, it happens all the time," the radio host said. O'Neill was beginning to see the paranoia that had so infected Jewell's soul.

Out on the lake, O'Neill and Jewell, who was two decades the radio host's junior, fell into the timeworn fishing pattern of tossing lines, waiting, and talking. Conversation flowed easily. By midday on the water, O'Neill and Jewell had slipped into a surrogate father-son rapport reminiscent of Jewell's early days with his stepdad, John Jewell. As Jewell reeled in several striped bass, O'Neill encouraged and complimented him. When the men returned to shore, Jewell proudly held up a striper and O'Neill smiled broadly as someone on the dock snapped a few photos with Jewell's camera. For this day, O'Neill had kept one topic nearly off-limits: The men barely discussed the bombing or its aftermath.

AT THE FBI, THE exhaustive work of the CENTBOM task force appeared poised to pay off. By painstakingly scouring thousands of images of parkgoers on bombing night, the video/photo team had pieced together a detailed timeline of snapshots and video stills. Hundreds of images lined the walls of the photo room. With the tower symbolically in the middle, each wall represented a different direction. The photos then were subdivided minute by minute as people shifted locations through the night.

One image leapt out: A blondish man in his thirties could be seen carrying a military-style pack into the park at 12:11 A.M. Agents circled back to the original video, where they saw him walking through the entrance closest to the AT&T tower. His backpack appeared to be an ALICE pack. When NASA enhanced the tape, it distilled a remarkably clear image of him from the waist up. Despite the party atmosphere in the park, the man looked neither happy nor festive. Instead, he was looking askance, with dark circles under his eyes.

One task force member described him as a "big mean-looking white male." Another commented, "Trying not to be really excited here—but this is really exciting." The blond man soon became known as Pack Man.

The CENTBOM team initially decided not to discuss Pack Man in detail on the daily calls with FBI headquarters. Despite Washington's insistence that Atlanta say nothing to the press without prior approval, headquarters was a sieve in Atlanta's view. In the months after Jewell's name was published in the *AJC*, additional stories had leaked to the *Washington Post*, *Newsweek*, the *New York Times*, and others. The CENTBOM team simply had no interest in another newsbreak dictating the pace and steps of their investigation.

The task force launched an all-out effort to identify Pack Man. The video/photo team worked late into the nights and through weekends trying to determine whether the man left the park without the pack. Meanwhile, a group at the Georgia State Patrol manually hunted for a match among the nearly two million driver's license photos of Georgia men aged twenty-five to forty-five. To speed a search through the five hundred canisters of Kodak microfilm, the Bureau took some two dozen microfilm machines from the dwindling Whitewater investigation into Bill and Hillary Clinton. Other agents analyzed stacks of photos of militia members from surrounding states, police applicants from Georgia, and federal and state felons. They pushed for additional video footage from overseas outlets that had covered the Games.

BY MID-FEBRUARY, AS THE search for Pack Man continued, an already-icy relationship between ATF and the FBI had turned frigid. As the lead agency in abortion clinic–violence cases, ATF was running the TWINBOM investigation. The CENTBOM and TWINBOM task forces were housed in buildings across the street from each other but operated in parallel and rarely communicated. Woody Johnson and Jack Killorin, the two chiefs, tried to set a better tone, as prosecutors urged them to address what had become obvious: The disconnect was impeding the progress in both cases. Eventually, members of each agency agreed to hold informal meetings for updates and information exchanges, gathering at the edge of Century Parkway, the street that separated their buildings. Neither wanted to be seen as ceding investigative control by entering the other task force's space. Finally, the teams drew up a nondisclosure agreement so that they could share photos and samples of steel.

A promising new connection between the CENTBOM device and two TWINBOM IEDs quickly emerged: The steel directional plates showed a match in chemical "fingerprints." Sixty thousand pieces of steel had been categorized by the FBI in past investigations, and the Bureau's metallurgy expert reported he had never heard of a coincidental match. The FBI asked the ATF for more evidence for forensic comparisons to the TWINBOM devices: nails, Tupperware, clock, wire insulation. All of it was slow to come.

Meanwhile, agents on the CENTBOM task force, acutely aware that their focus on Jewell had narrowed the investigation too soon, continued to pore over the hundreds of other potential suspect subfiles. But they mainly concentrated on their UNSUBs, or unknown subjects, with nicknames—Pack Man, Blob Man, Goatee Man, and Hood Man, the name given to the sweatshirt-clad person seen the morning of the Sandy Springs bombing. Now investigators needed their real names.

ON FEBRUARY 21, THE Otherside Lounge was revving up for the weekend. Wedged along a midtown Atlanta stretch of strip clubs, a bowling alley, and fast-food restaurants, the Otherside was fronted by wooden beams and topped with a white stucco roof that gave it an English Tudor look. The diverse club welcomed gays, straights, whites, and blacks. Theme music nights ranged from jazz to hip-hop to live country bands. By ten P.M. on this Friday night, more than fifty people had filed into the Martini Room for piano vocals; two hundred more jammed the main room for dancing as alcohol flowed, a deejay spun tunes, and a disco ball showered the energetic crowd with shimmering light.

Eric Rudolph had discovered the Otherside in the Lifestyles section of the *AJC*. Despite having a brother who was gay, Rudolph abhorred the "radical egalitarians" who, he felt, undermined the traditional institutions of marriage and family.

Rudolph parked his truck close to an expressway on-ramp not far from the club. Ten hours earlier, he had slipped a green polyester East Bay backpack loaded with a thirty-pound IED into the bushes at the front of the Otherside.

That bomb, made up of dynamite, pipes, a steel plate, and 6d wire nails, was set to go off at eleven P.M. Law enforcement again would be the primary target. But first, Rudolph needed to draw them in with a separate device aimed at the "sodomites" in the bar.

On the walk from his truck, Rudolph stopped for fries at a Burger King. Outside, he pulled the container from the bag and carefully inserted an IED one-third the size of the bomb he had planted in the bushes. It was 9:40 P.M. Rudolph set the timer for twenty minutes, and placed the fries on top as camouflage. He walked briskly toward the club, still a distance away. He had to hurry.

As he neared the Otherside, he spotted a police cruiser across the street. Rudolph stepped toward a parked car, carefully set down the bag, and pretended to search for his car keys. It was 9:55 P.M. Only five minutes remained until the bomb would explode. "Leave. Come on, leave," he hissed quietly, but the cop stayed in place. Rudolph would have to call off the mission. Frustrated, he bent down and flipped the kill switch to disarm the device.

But as he stood up, the police cruiser pulled out of the lot and drove away. Rudolph rearmed the device, scooped up the bag, and strode deliberately toward the Otherside. Passing the valet sign crowned with a red STOP emblem, he walked up the side drive to the back. He placed the ticking bomb on a ledge outside the patio and quickly slipped away.

The explosion rocked the patio. Shattered glass and dust filled the air. Car alarms screeched. Most of the nails and pipe shrapnel jetted over the patrons' heads. But inside the bar, one woman fell to the ground as a nail drove through her right arm, puncturing the brachial artery and nearly causing her to bleed to death. Four others also required hospitalization. Guests and staffers ran from the back patio toward the front parking lot.

One uniformed officer, aware of the sucker bomb used in the Sandy Springs bombing a month earlier, combed the bushes. There, he found the green backpack with the second device. Police quickly cordoned off the lot, and called for the Render Safe team, which arrived with a robot. They slowly maneuvered the machine toward the pack, remotely guiding it with a tethered cord. For over half an hour, the operator tried to disarm the bomb, which would allow law enforcement to preserve any hair, fibers, or fingerprints.

Then, as one of the pincers tugged at a strap, the pack fell to the asphalt. Everyone froze, but nothing happened. The Render Safe team decided to take no more chances. They aimed their water cannon at the device, called out "fire in the hole," and hit the pack dead-on. Again, no explosion. Two batteries and a few screws spilled out. The team took aim a second time, called out another warning, and fired. The bomb detonated, its powerful explosion rocketing shrapnel into parked cars, the valet sign, trees, and surrounding buildings. The robot was ruined, but no one was seriously injured.

The next morning, Don Johnson headed up one of the five investigative teams tasked with interviewing local businesses about what they knew or had observed. The owners of a small car-restoration business and a fire-sprinkler maintenance company had seen nothing of use. He tried without success to locate staffers to interview at the nearby offices of PBA-30 and WABE, the Atlanta public TV and radio stations.

Johnson tracked down a taxi company that served the area. Maybe he would have the same luck as when he helped unravel the tragedy of little Aliza May Bush in Albany seven years earlier. The cab firm let Johnson scan through a set of dispatch tickets written by the women on duty the night before. Sure enough, driver #61 had a 10:47 P.M. pickup at the Hot Spot, the strip club across from the Otherside. But this go-round, the lead went nowhere.

AT THE *AJC*, RON Martz spearheaded the first-day coverage, raising the central concern of many in a front-page piece. "The city's third bombing in less than seven months is forcing officials to take a hard look at the terrible possibility that a serial bomber who specializes in hate crimes may be stalking Atlanta," he wrote. The *New York Times* also explored a possible connection to the Sandy Springs bombing, quoting Woody Johnson. "We all recognize that there are similarities here," the SAC said. "We will be searching out the possibility that we have a serial bomber." In fact, he would soon be convinced beyond a doubt.

Three days after the attack, NBC News, Reuters, the *AJC*, and the paper's sister station WSB all received letters that were clearly mailed by the bomber. Each message was written on lined paper, in thick, menacing block letters, with a felt-tipped pen. Either by design or lack of education, the letters were riddled with misspellings and bad grammar.

"The bombing's in Sandy Springs and Midtown were carried-out by units of the Army of God," one of the letters began. The writer then tossed in details of the IEDs he had used in both the Northside Family Planning and Otherside Lounge attacks, noting, "You may confirm with the F.B.I." The author ranted that the clinic had been chosen to protest the murder of unborn children. The second device in that explosion "was aimed at agent of the so-called federal government i.e. A.T.F. F.B.I. Marshall's e.t.c." The attack at the Otherside Lounge "was aimed at the Sodomite bar." Additional bombings would target "all those who push there agenda." The writer closed the letter by saying that he would in the future aim at saving civilians by placing a warning call. It would include a code, 4-1-9-9-3. Then he signed off: "Death to the New World Order."

When the media turned over the letters to the FBI, agents instantly realized the writer was the bomber. He had indeed listed specific bomb components unknown to the public. The Bureau also immediately recognized the five-digit code as a reference to April 19, 1993, the date of the final assault on David Koresh's Waco compound. The Bureau asked the media not to report the contents of the letters, wanting to retain the details of the bomb components to further its investigation. The news organizations complied.

At the *AJC*, Scruggs and Martz tried to help readers discern whether the Army of God was a real organization. They found a loose-knit, fifteen-year-old anti-abortion group that used the name, but few of the experts they interviewed believed the writer's message aligned with a strict right-to-life view. The letter's author appeared to lean closer to an "ultra-fundamentalist, patriot-type person," one expert on extremism told them.

Back in Topton, North Carolina, Rudolph reveled in his certainty at how the mainstream media would perceive the letters he had intentionally seeded with errors. They would blame the "other Georgia," uneducated hicks who did not share the media's ultra-liberal values. Indeed, some of the coverage did precisely that.

THE FBI NAMED THE investigative task force in the Otherside Lounge case OTHERBOM. Like CENTBOM and TWINBOM, this task force also faced an unusually challenging witness scene. In Centennial Olympic Park, agents had an overwhelming pool of tens of thousands of potential witnesses. In

Sandy Springs, they were looking to methadone patients as key witnesses, along with abortion-clinic medical professionals eager to remain anonymous. Now, with the Otherside case, investigators were dealing with a number of gay patrons, especially lesbians, who were skittish about being outed. In the nearby strip clubs and massage parlors, a number of married male customers shared that reticence.

Following up on leads from the Hot Spot, including Don Johnson's, investigators did a series of interviews at the strip club. An exotic dancer nicknamed Silky had seen two men who raised her suspicions. Just after the explosion, they arrived at the club and settled into the VIP area, where the pair ordered only water and juice. During their conversation, they eyed Silky, as if to keep their words private. Then, when police began questioning witnesses outside, she overheard the men saying things like, "Think they're gone yet?" and "They wouldn't know in that time." Silky told agents that the pair left after twenty minutes.

A second dancer remembered a man at "the pervert table," the spot right up front. She described the guy as "a kook," never laughing, talking, or drinking—and, most oddly, never looking at the dancers. At one point, he broke from his aloof manner to slip a bill into the garter of one of the strippers, still refusing to look at her. When the bomb went off across the street, nearly everyone in the club ran outside to see what happened. But the suspicious patron lingered, then walked out slowly. When the crowd herded back into the Hot Spot, he was not among them.

An ATF sketch artist met the dancer to draw the man's likeness, and settled in at a table opposite the woman as she described him. But the dancer soon stopped. The perspective wasn't right. "Can I climb up on the table?" she asked. "I'm used to looking down."

But the leads, like most that the agencies were pursuing, would not pay off.

The Otherside attack heightened the urgency to identify Pack Man. CENTBOM agents created a montage of five images containing a total of nine individuals. Image No. 4 was Pack Man, their primary focus. They also included the Goatee Man sketch as No. 5. Agents quietly began showing the photo spread to state, federal, and military officials outside of the task force. To avoid leaks, they left no copies behind. As an extra precaution, the Bureau had cropped out the backpack from the image of Pack Man. If the man was identified and the media learned he was carrying a military-style pack, the FBI feared another Jewell-like frenzy. No promising leads came from the showings.

Many on the CENTBOM task force had been urging headquarters for weeks to ask the broader public for assistance by sharing the photo montage with the media. Four months had passed since Weldon Kennedy's December public appeal that had elicited a massive response, yet they were no closer to identifying the bomber. The $500,000 reward sat unused, the case stagnated. Finally, they got the OK.

On March 13, Woody Johnson stepped to the microphones in a CENT-BOM news conference. He recapped the exhaustive numbers of the probe so far. "In the Olympic bombing investigation, we have interviewed more than two thousand witnesses, catalogued and reviewed nearly one thousand videotapes and five thousand photographs, and completed more than seven thousand investigative and forensic reports," Johnson said. Now the Bureau was seeking the public's help. The people in the photo spread displayed behind him could have valuable clues.

Johnson asked those in the pictures to identify themselves, and those who knew them to help, adding that the unidentified people were simply witnesses or innocent bystanders. He betrayed nothing of the Bureau's suspicions of the blond man in frame No. 4. He also made yet another appeal for photos and videos, particularly of anyone close to the tower or carrying a military-style backpack. "If you haven't called us before, please call now," Johnson urged, offering a toll-free number. "Don't worry about the quality of your photos and videos of the Park; if you send them in, we can enhance them. . . . Do not worry that it is too late to provide useful information."

The CENTBOM task force eagerly readied for the identification of Pack Man. The SWAT and Evidence Response teams were on alert, as was the Bureau's Special Operations Group of surveillance agents. Miranda, search, and arrest contingencies had been reviewed in advance.

Before the day ended, Pack Man himself called the toll-free number from Sedona, Arizona. Friends had seen his image on TV and let the Atlantan traveling out west know the FBI wanted to speak with him. The Bureau immediately dispatched Arizona-based agents to interview him. Pack Man, it turned out, was a corporate headhunter. The pack, he told the FBI, was sitting in his closet at home. They could swing by the house and his girlfriend would show it to them. Back in Atlanta, agents followed up and, to their chagrin, found the pack unscathed.

The CENTBOM task force was devastated. For seven weeks since the video/photo team had found the Pack Man footage, agents had hoped he was the bomber. Countless hours had been spent trying to identify him. Now, the Bureau's most promising lead had evaporated. The media, including Scruggs and Martz, were oblivious to the drama and simply reported that seven of the nine people in the FBI's pictures had been identified. No one delivered credible information about image No. 5, the drawing of Goatee Man, who resumed his position as the FBI's top suspect.

BY THIS POINT, THE FBI had handed over more selected materials to the independent behavioralist Park Dietz, including the Army of God letters the bomber had sent to the media. Dietz continued to take a more-traditional behavioral science approach than the BSU had eight months earlier. Instead of focusing on a specific individual, he set out to determine the bomber's broad characteristics based on the evidence gathered.

In an April 14 seven-page memo to the FBI, Dietz concurred with the Bureau's belief that the bomber of the Sandy Springs clinic and the Other-side Lounge also had executed the bombing at Centennial Park. He noted the materials used, including the steel plates, and the left-hand twist of the wires. Why hadn't the letter writer claimed credit for the Olympic bomb? he asked rhetorically. Dietz offered four options: "That he does not want to tip his hand about a similar attack he is planning, that he has not found support for the Centennial Park attack even among his ideological compatriots, that he feels ashamed in light of the sympathetic portrayals of the victim who was killed, or that he fears the death penalty."

The bomber, Dietz wrote, looked to be a white male who harbored paranoid sentiments. Those who knew the man would see him as a conspiracy theorist, loner, grudge holder, and critic of anyone trying to limit his rights. When the Bureau arrests him, the behavioral scientist advised, the serial bomber should be interviewed by a county, state, or local officer, not by a federal agent whose authority he wouldn't recognize. Indeed, Dietz speculated, "In each of the three incidents, the bomber was targeting federal agents."

Dietz also wrote: "The bomber will strike again."

THE TYPEWRITTEN LETTER THAT arrived for Jewell in early March was riddled with misspellings and odd syntax. But the author's intent could not have been further from that of the bomber's writings. Kenichi Asano was a longtime correspondent for Kyodo News Service and a journalism professor at Japan's Doshisha University. He was eager to interview Jewell.

Asano's view of media behavior had been cemented nearly three years before. In June 1994, a sarin gas attack on the city of Matsumoto, roughly one hundred miles west of Tokyo, had killed seven residents and hospitalized 144 more. The night of the assault, Yoshiyuki Kouno, a local salesman, stepped outside his home to find his dogs writhing on the ground, frothing at the mouth. A few minutes later, Kouno's wife collapsed and he himself was stricken by the poison gas.

The next day, the police visited Kouno at the hospital. He was in grave condition, and authorities were asked to return when he was stronger. The day after that, unnamed police sources leaked Kouno's name to journalists hungry for a story. Japanese media swarmed the suspect's home as it was searched. One newspaper claimed that Kouno had admitted his "mistake" to a paramedic as he was being rushed to a hospital. A tabloid revealed intimate details of his family's history in a piece headlined THE BIZARRE FAMILY TREE WHERE THE POISONOUS GAS INCIDENT HAD ITS ORIGIN. "Sources" disclosed that Kouno had always been a "strange person."

After his release from the hospital, Kouno was continuously harassed. He argued his innocence but was widely disbelieved. Finally, two years after the attack, prosecutors charged members of the Aum Shinrikyo cult, who admitted their role in both the Matsumoto attack and a similar mass murder using sarin in the Tokyo subway in 1995.

The Kouno incident so outraged observers of the Japanese media that five hundred journalists, professors, and others formed a group called Jimporen, or "Human Rights and Mass Media Conduct." It was time, Jimporen argued, "to instill the element of accountability that hitherto has never existed in Japan, so that the news media becomes as principled as it is free." A particular focus was crime reporting. "The most shameful example of journalistic abuse occurs on a daily basis by reporters on the police beat," one senior Japanese editor argued. Their sources, of course, were law officers, who aggressively leaked against suspects who had limited ability to fight back in the court of public opinion.

Ken Asano, one of the group's founders, wanted to highlight the issues in Japan by paralleling Kouno's case with that of Richard Jewell. In late March 1997, Asano interviewed Jewell in Atlanta. The two men bonded, and Asano urged Jewell to consider visiting Japan. They agreed to stay in touch.

Meanwhile, Jewell longed to rekindle some semblance of a love life. Dating had been out of the question since the bombing, when his presence in public brought stares, whispers, and suspicion. But on the flight to New York earlier in the year for his Larry King interview, Jewell had noticed a pretty woman with long strawberry-blonde hair across the aisle. She looked to be about his age, but seemed visibly nervous. "You don't like takeoffs, do you?" he asked.

To Jewell's delight, the icebreaker worked. They had struck up a conversation, she gave him her card. Back in Atlanta, Jewell called to ask her out, and they met for dinner at a Thai restaurant, a first for Jewell. She noticed that he had impeccable manners, even holding open her car door. After dinner, they went to a nearby pool hall, where Jewell let her "win" two of the eight games as she swept balls into the pockets with her cue. As they were leaving, the hall's other patrons stopped their games to cheer Jewell.

But when Jewell called her for a second date, he learned that Hollis Gillespie was writing a piece for *Atlanta* magazine about their evening together. He was mortified.

Soon after, *New York Times* reporter Kevin Sack reached out to Jewell to write a "Where Is He Now?" story and asked about the Gillespie date and article. Jewell told him the experience had been crushing, another gut punch in his fight to extend trust outside his tight Atlanta circle comprised primarily of his mother and lawyers. "Perhaps more than any other incident," the *Times* reporter wrote, it "seems to have deflated his dreams of normalcy."

When Sack called Gillespie for comment, she seemed befuddled that Jewell could be upset at a piece portraying him as a complete gentleman. "It was a 200-word total French kiss to the guy," the *Times* quoted her.

After the *New York Times* article ran, Gillespie went on offense. "Hey! Richard Jewell, You Owe *Me* an Apology," she declared on the front cover of *Atlanta* magazine. A glam shot of the attractive thirty-six-year-old author took up most of the rest of the page. Two more full-page photos of her appeared inside the magazine. Gillespie's biting article was written as an open letter to Jewell: "Dear Richard, remember me? We had dinner last January? We haven't seen much of each other since." It quoted liberally from pining voicemails Jewell had left on her machine after the first piece ran, including his own apology for questioning her motives in writing the story and the offer of another date: "Maybe we can shoot a game of pool or something, or maybe I can cook you some lasagna or spaghetti or something."

"What?" Gillespie wrote. "You wanted to cook lasagna for a journalistic Mata Hari?"

Jewell's first date in a year had not gone as planned.

CHAPTER 24

The FBI was grasping more than ever. In late spring, two agents traveled to a south Atlanta suburb to follow up with the skinhead who had tipped the FBI to the possible involvement of cross-dressing Ivan the Aryan. The man explained that before the park attack, he had overheard Ivan telling friends that when foreigners came for the Olympics, "I'm going to blow them all to hell." The witness also told the agents that while his own branch of skinheads were "basically trying to make a fashion statement and have fun listening to music," Ivan was rumored to be a member of the Confederate Hammerheads, a bunch of neo-Nazi racists. He had a penchant for wearing Doc Martens boots with red laces and shouldn't be hard to find. Agents soon did locate Ivan, but he wasn't the bomber. It was yet another dead end.

Inside the Bureau's Century Center offices, the Atlanta team found itself with major worries beyond the stalled investigations. Rumors were circulating that the Justice Department's Office of Professional Responsibility had finalized its report on the Jewell interview and that FBI headquarters was preparing to sanction several agents and supervisors involved in the process. The men, especially Don Johnson, might even receive suspensions, known in the Bureau as "time on the bricks."

Colleagues preemptively battled back. In a series of letters striking in their candor and confrontation, Atlanta agents wrote directly to Director Freeh. Harry Grogan, Johnson's partner, asked why OPR didn't start at the top of the FBI in its investigation. The Director, not Atlanta, had made the "wrong decision" by ordering Miranda in the middle of an interview, Grogan contended. Don Haldimann, who had overseen the initial search for explosives in Jewell's apartment, wrote that Johnson was "punished for being a 'good soldier.'" Other agents made similar arguments. All held little sway.

Indeed, Justice's OPR had issued its report internally, and Freeh and headquarters were readying proposed sanction letters to the Atlanta agents. Anticipating blowback from the field, the Director signed off on a lengthy

April 1 memo to the entire Bureau timed to coincide with delivery of the letters. In it, he revealed that OPR had found no intentional violation of Jewell's civil rights and no criminal misconduct. Nor was there an issue with using a ruse, a common investigative technique. But there had been a "major error in judgment," OPR found, in the issuance of Jewell's Miranda warnings "just like it's (a) real official interview." Freeh made it clear that such treatment of the constitutional warnings was unacceptable. He also took umbrage at the criticism that he'd micromanaged the case. The Miranda decision was his prerogative and duty as Director. A summary of the OPR report, Freeh said, would be made public after the FBI's separate disciplinary process had run its course.

Letters were hand-delivered to Agents Johnson and Rosario, as well as to SACs Woody Johnson and David Tubbs, and ASAC A.B. Llewellyn. Headquarters had proposed suspensions for all five. The Freeh memo immediately leaked to the media. The *AJC* splashed a piece by Scruggs and Martz across its front page. In a separate article, the reporters disclosed each Atlanta-based agent by name.

Don Johnson prepared for all-out war, "lawyering up" and insisting in his appeal that he had done nothing wrong. Echoing the letters of support from fellow agents, Johnson argued that Jewell had appeared voluntarily, in a nonconfrontational setting. Plus, the BSU had dictated the approach, creating an untenable dynamic. Most importantly, the Director had changed the interview's ground rules midstream.

In a quirk of timing, as Johnson worked on his response, he received a letter from Washington. "Dear Mr. Johnson," it began, "News of your performance in connection with the 1996 Summer Olympic Games has reached me, and I am pleased to commend you." The letter praised his hard work and professionalism and said a cash award would follow. Johnson knew that similar letters were sent to every agent assigned to the 1996 Games, but it galled him to see the signature: Louie Freeh.

The following month, after appeals by all the agents had been considered, FBI headquarters issued its ultimate findings. Rosario and Llewellyn were both cleared. SACs Johnson and Tubbs received censures, essentially embarrassing wrist slaps. Don Johnson received the only harsh penalty: five days' suspension without pay as well as a censure.

Johnson began serving his five-day brick time, holed up in his white-carpeted home office, the French doors closed. He made it clear to his family that he was unavailable for interruption, as he consulted with his lawyers on how to get the decision reversed and his pay restored. All the while Johnson smoked cigarette after cigarette, stabbing the butts into his burnt-orange glass ashtray on the office desk. Washington had set him up and was ruining his reputation.

At the Atlanta office, agents passed the hat, collecting ten- and twenty-dollar bills from colleagues to cover Johnson's lost pay. The process, relatively common for disciplinary cases, was so successful that there were leftover funds to donate to charity. His colleagues then made a highly unusual plan for the agent's return.

On Thursday, May 29, his suspension completed, Johnson parked at the FBI's office at 7:30 A.M., where he met Harry Grogan. As they walked toward the front door, a gauntlet of more than one hundred current and retired FBI agents and staff stood applauding and cheering. Johnson slowed his walk to take in the moment. From his office above, Woody Johnson peered down through the blinds. One of the gauntlet's organizers had pre-cleared the event with the SAC. As management, he felt he couldn't be down there but let it be known that he wouldn't get in the way. "The troops take care of the troops," the SAC simply said.

The media had been alerted so that Don Johnson's celebrated return would be well covered, even beamed to Washington. CNN was there, as were local TV reporters. Scruggs and Martz were on-scene too, and filed a story for the afternoon paper along with a photo of Johnson wading through the crowd of supporters. They quoted one retired agent on Johnson: "If he had been left to do his job, this whole thing probably would have gotten resolved in a matter of days." Johnson clipped and mounted the article as a keepsake.

While the news coverage wasn't welcome in D.C., it was the Atlanta revolt that took Freeh and headquarters most by surprise. The FBI featured a top-down management structure, almost militaristic in its rigidity, and the gauntlet was unprecedented. Beyond that, didn't Atlanta know Don Johnson's backstory? Personnel records had to be kept private, but there was so much more than the Miranda transgression.

A few months earlier, the *Albany Times Union* had begun to connect the dots of Johnson's career that Atlanta agents seemed to have missed. In a story headlined FBI AGENT LED FAILED INVESTIGATIONS OF WHALEN, JEWELL, the paper summarized Johnson's unsuccessful criminal pursuit of Mayor Thomas Whalen for alleged self-dealing. The article then quoted a city attorney who characterized Johnson's determination to make a case as "an obsession."

But Johnson's history in New York was far worse than what the Albany paper reported. His personnel records reflected a dismaying propensity for severely slanting and even fabricating witness statements in 302s in an effort to convict those he presumed guilty. Witnesses repeatedly came forward to accuse Johnson of twisting their words. His own FBI partner, Agent Thomas Dauenhauer, complained to higher-ups that Johnson rarely, if ever, took out a notepad when interviewing witnesses and suspects, and would then craft his official reports from "memory." Reading through Johnson's 302s, Dauenhauer would fume, "This is bullshit," and refuse to add his initials.

David Homer, the chief of the U.S. Attorney's criminal division in Albany, became so distrustful of Johnson that he told FBI supervisors that prosecutors would no longer accept any 302s Johnson prepared without a co-signature from another agent. Homer reported his decision to U.S. Attorney Frederick Scullin, who replied that Homer should have gone further and barred Johnson from signing search warrant affidavits, or even being a witness for the prosecution.

An Albany OPR investigation followed, and Johnson was threatened with suspension. In response, the agent waged a multi-year battle with the U.S. Attorney's Office, the Albany FBI office, and FBI headquarters. During that time, he ran down leads in cases based in other districts, but was no longer permitted to serve as a case agent in Albany. Finally, in 1993, headquarters imposed a "loss of effectiveness transfer" to Atlanta. In August of that year, Johnson headed south.

ON THE FRIDAY OF Memorial Day weekend, Kathy Scruggs walked into the office of the *AJC*'s law firm for her first deposition with Lin Wood. Scruggs was the centerpiece of the defamation case against the paper. Eleven others joined them in black leather chairs surrounding a white marble conference table streaked with dark veins. Watson Bryant, Wayne Grant, and Jewell were present, eager for Wood's dismantling of the woman who had started the media avalanche. On the opposing side, *AJC* attorney Peter Canfield took the lead in representing Scruggs, while editor John Walter attended to support her.

The reporter had never been sued or even deposed. Beforehand, she spent a full day and a half with Canfield and his team gearing up for the questioning; the lawyers girded her for Wood's ultra-aggressive tactics. As one colleague at the paper put it: "Strap it on and tie it on tight, because he's coming after you."

The deposition began at 9:55 A.M., and Wood delivered as advertised. Wasn't it true she had close ties to the Atlanta Police Department? Yes. Had she ever had a "social relationship" with anyone in the Atlanta Police Department? Yes. How would her reputation fare if she was named as the focus of an investigation as Jewell had been? "I suspect there are quite a number of people that could call in and say quite a few seamy things about you," Wood needled. Scruggs shot back, "I am sure there are."

He drilled hard for the source of the initial Jewell story. She conceded she, not Martz, got the critical tip, but that was as far as she would go. Did someone from APD leak the story? Scruggs wouldn't say. How about the FBI? GBI? ATF? Scruggs remained steadfast. For hours, she repeated the same answer, with little variation: "I am not going tell you that, sir."

Wood returned often to her phrasing that Jewell fit the profile of the bomber, as she had written in her first story. She vehemently defended her reporting and continued to draw a sharp line at revealing the leaker's agency or identity. Finally, at seven P.M., Wood agreed to end the deposition, allowing those in the room to start their holiday weekends on the condition that he could resume the deposition in the near future.

Scruggs had weathered the day reasonably well. But Wood wasn't finished.

JEWELL FLEW TO NEW York for another media appearance, this time with Fox News' Sean Hannity and Alan Colmes. The network had been trying to grab Jewell for an interview since it first went on air seven months earlier. At the time, the producers had written to Jewell that "Fox News Channel will launch, and news as we now know it will never be the same." The twenty-four-hour channel, the invitation said, "will provide Americans with news that is balanced and unbiased." But Jewell and his lawyers had declined the upstart network. Now, Fox News looked to have staying power, and the legal team agreed to have their client appear.

Jewell insisted on bringing Dave Dutchess along for company. They checked into the hotel, then raided the minibar: peanuts, cashews, macadamia nuts, candy, Cokes. Then they had dinner in the hotel restaurant. The two friends were giddy over their good fortune: It was all free.

The next day on the Fox News set, Jewell sat between Colmes and the former Atlanta radio personality, Hannity, for a half hour as the two sympathetically questioned him about his ordeal. They asked what he might tell critics who said, "Oh, maybe he's in this for the money."

"I'd ask them to walk just one minute in my shoes when all this was going on," Jewell replied. "You know, I'm not rich by any means. I'm just a regular working American like anybody else who now can't find a job because of what the press and the FBI did to me."

Colmes followed up. "At least you're not going to walk away empty-handed. You've got some money in your pocket here."

"I'm not going to walk away empty-handed, but I want you to be a realist as well," Jewell explained. "Probably a third of this money is going to my attorneys to fight these people for what they did to me, another third or more of it is going right back to the government. I have to pay taxes on these settlements. I'm paying the government for what they did to me. Now, isn't that hilarious?"

Days later, Jewell found himself in Miami. The American Police Hall of Fame was presenting him with an extraordinary accolade: induction into the Venerable Order of Michael the Archangel, the patron saint of police. For the occasion, Jewell flew down several deputies, including his former partner, Brian McNair. They, along with Bobi, Watson Bryant, Dave Dutchess, and Rob Russell, proudly celebrated Jewell. The evening felt like vindication, with Jewell named a Knight Commander, the highest rank the organization bestowed. Bobi also was recognized for standing by her son.

After the ceremony, Jewell posed with three of his Habersham County Sheriff's Office friends. The deputies wore their summer uniforms, replete with badges, patches, and engraved name tags. Jewell had been invited to wear his own uniform. Having none, he dressed in a blue blazer, gray pleated dress slacks, and a red tie.

Richard Jewell desperately missed being in law enforcement.

CHAPTER 25

As the one-year anniversary of the Centennial Park bombing approached, a somberness fell over the FBI. Despite conducting over thirteen thousand interviews and running down more than fourteen thousand leads, there was no prime suspect, and the serial bomber remained on the loose. In one small victory, the Bureau had prevailed on the powers in Washington to order the consolidation of the CENTBOM, TWINBOM, and OTHERBOM task forces into single multi-agency effort. The FBI would lead the new task force, code-named ATBOM, named for Atlanta.

In mid-June, the Bureau made its fourth public appeal for assistance. For the first time, it released excerpts of the Army of God letters sent to the media following the Otherside Lounge attack. The ATBOM task force was eager to replicate the success of the UNABOM case, in which the FBI published the Unabomber's writings and his brother recognized the disturbing style and context. The tip led to Ted Kaczynski's eventual arrest. The ATBOM leadership reasoned that a member of the public might identify the Atlanta serial bomber through the use of terms and phrases like "sodomites," "ungodly communist regime in New York," and "bureaucratic lackey's in Washington."

The task force also released two sketches from the Sandy Springs bombing. One featured a burly gray-bearded man seen the night before the attack. The other was of Hood Man, spotted around 6:30 on the morning of the clinic explosions, and included a witness's description: white male, dark complexion, thirty to forty-five years old, 180 pounds. The FBI withheld other information, including that the witness had seen Hood Man with a backpack and shovel near the dumpster where the bomber had placed the sucker device.

Law enforcement yet again asked for more photos and videos from the night of the Centennial Park blast, narrowing the time window of the request to between 12:15 and 1:20 A.M. To illustrate what they were looking for, an FBI inspector displayed a blurry image of what appeared to be someone sitting on a tower bench with a backpack an hour before the bombing.

No solid leads emerged, so weeks later, the task force released a clean-shaven version of Goatee Man sketch. Still nothing. Despite attempting to project a public sense of energy, some on the task force now began to think that their best chance of solving the crimes relied on a grim prospect: another attack by the serial bomber.

By mid-summer, with a half-year now passed since the last bombing, Atlantans appeared far more focused on rekindling the Olympics' magic than on another attack or finding the bomber. On July 19, the city marked the one-year anniversary of the Opening Ceremony. Five hundred former Olympics volunteers and a band marched down Peachtree Street in what was billed as the Parade of Memories. Many donned their Centennial Games credentials and volunteer uniforms adorned with Olympics pins. At seven P.M., celebrants gathered at Hank Aaron Drive and Fulton Street for the rededication of the Olympic torch. The structure had been disassembled and moved there to make room for Turner Field, a state-of-the-art Atlanta Braves baseball stadium reconfigured from the Olympic Stadium. Officials re-lit the cauldron one glorious final time.

But the mood shifted on July 27, when even the staunchest Atlanta cheerleaders were reminded of the tragedy a year earlier that would unfortunately always define these Games.

At Centennial Olympic Park, the day brought a solemn remembrance. During the steamy morning, a small crowd gathered near the site of the blast that had killed Alice Hawthorne and Turkish cameraman Melih Uzunyol, and injured 111 others. A ceremony honored the victims, as a wreath adorned with red, heart-shaped flowers provided the backdrop for speakers. One man had flown in from California with $400 worth of candles, simply to pay his respects. John Hawthorne, Alice's widower, spoke haltingly. "Even though it hasn't been easy talking about what happened last year, it was important . . . to remember Alice," he said. "We can't let the world forget."

In an editorial, the *AJC* positioned the park as an "emblem of the resolute and inextinguishable character of Atlanta and the Olympics." On a hopeful note, the paper observed that even as John Hawthorne had spoken at the park, children frolicked in the Fountain of Rings behind him. The scene recalled the lightheartedness of others doing the same before the bombing the year before. And now the unfenced park was still open to all, standing as "the victory of the Olympic ideal of peace over the odious goals of the terrorist."

In Washington, the anniversary brought congressional hearings on the Jewell affair. Just prior to the testimony, the OPR finally released a forty-four-page summary of its final report with each FBI subject's name redacted. Scruggs teamed with Martz for a front-page piece on the findings, which aligned with Freeh's characterization in his April FBI-wide memo. They reported on the fine line that the OPR had walked. There was the "major error of judgment" in issuing Miranda, but no intentional or coordinated violation of Jewell's rights. "It is how Don Johnson incorporated the Miranda warning into the session that is at the crux of the controversy," Scruggs and Martz wrote.

The OPR report also revealed the BSU's involvement in the Jewell pursuit, the *AJC* article continued. "It shows how agents investigating the case in Atlanta, with the help of behavioral scientists at the FBI training academy in Quantico, Va., came to consider Jewell 'as the principal (though not only) suspect in the CENTBOM investigation.'" The report noted that the BSU had offered interview advice and a written analysis prompted by Atlanta's assessment that "Jewell fit the profile of a person who might create an incident so he could emerge a hero." That was the only mention of the word "profile" in the report. Left unsaid: The outsized role the BSU's four-page document had played in driving the case against Jewell, or the profile's quasi-indictment of the guard. The profile was never provided to Congress, the media, or the Jewell team. Nor did Freeh or any other government witness disclose its contents during congressional testimony.

Two days after the bombing anniversary, Jewell testified before the House Judiciary crime subcommittee. The former suspect had spent considerable time preparing, typing notes for his attorneys to consider. Bryant and Wood then massaged Jewell's draft into media-friendly sound bites. "It was as if the FBI and the media had entered into an unholy alliance to blame me for the bombing and did not care about the truth or my rights as an American citizen," Jewell told the subcommittee. He flatly rejected the OPR investigators' conclusion that there had been no intentional violation of his rights. "Apparently, truth to the Justice Department is simply whatever the Justice Department wants the truth to be."

A Democratic congressman from Brooklyn, Chuck Schumer, turned his ire to the untoward nexus of law enforcement and the media: "The most damning thing that happened were the leaks. Mr. Jewell's reputation would not have been besmirched except for leaks. And the dirty little secret is that large parts of the FBI and the U.S. Attorney's Office leak like a sieve." Despite Freeh's public statement a year earlier that the FBI was launching a search for the leaker, the head of the FBI's OPR revealed to the committee that the Bureau had conducted only five interviews. The OPR had concluded early in the probe that the universe of law enforcement people aware of suspicions about Jewell had been far too large to conduct an effective investigation. The OPR had asked Kathy Scruggs to cooperate. She declined.

Woody Johnson testified too, answering detailed questions about the investigation. Johnson's congressional appearance marked his final week as an FBI agent. Earlier that month, the fifty-five-year-old had announced his decision to retire after nearly three decades with the Bureau. Scruggs and Martz covered the news for the *AJC*. The headline read: A YEAR AFTER BOMBING, FBI OFFICE TO GET NEW CHIEF. The subheadline added: REPRIMANDED LEADER WILL RETIRE. This was not how the revered former leader of the Hostage Rescue Team had envisioned his FBI career ending.

Don Johnson secured videotapes of the testimony and clipped every article he could find, further expanding the extensive file he had never stopped keeping on Richard Jewell. Beyond bolstering his own defense, the agent remained convinced the guard was complicit in the park bombing. Someday, he still intended to prove it.

AT THREE A.M. ON August 8, police were summoned to a Buckhead hotel on Peachtree Road. A woman had climbed into the driver's seat of a taxi. The cabbie was ready to drive off, but the woman refused to get out. An officer managed to talk the clearly intoxicated passenger out of the cab and asked if there was someone to pick her up. But she refused to provide a name or number and became verbally abusive. Ultimately, the officer had no choice but to place *AJC* police reporter Kathy Scruggs under arrest for disorderly conduct while under the influence.

The next day, Scruggs discussed the arrest with John Walter, who was scheduled to be deposed by Lin Wood in less than two weeks. Both hoped Jewell's attorney wouldn't have heard about the episode. No such luck. Wood had indeed gotten wind of the arrest and obtained a copy of the APD Incident Report, which he no doubt read with gusto. The officer described the entire sequence of events, beginning with Scruggs's refusal to exit the taxi. Not until the one-sentence fifth paragraph did he write, "Ms. Scruggs did not have any cloths [*sic*] on when she was in the front seat of the cab." In journalism parlance, the officer had buried the lead.

Early in Walter's deposition at Peter Canfield's offices, Wood pounced. What was Walter's reaction when he learned Scruggs was found naked at three A.M. in a cab and arrested?

"My reaction was that I thought you would have a lot of fun with it."

"That was your first reaction?"

"Yes, sir."

"Your first reaction was not to be concerned about Ms. Scruggs's welfare or—"

"That was very much in my concern."

"But your first reaction was to think about me having fun with it, sir?"

"Yes, sir."

Walter's instincts had been dead-on. Not long after the arrest, a local TV reporter spoke with Wood about it. The lawyer remarked, "I've been in a cab, I've been drunk, and I've been naked. But I've never been all three at once."

Despite the stress of the lawsuit, Scruggs was developing a new relationship that summer. One Friday night, she grabbed a cocktail at the Blue Ridge Grill in Buckhead. The bartender slipped a new pour of scotch in front of Scruggs, then pointed out the benefactor, a man seated nearby. Scruggs walked over to thank him. George Hamilton, a professional who specialized in real estate transactions, looked at Scruggs's *AJC* credentials, draped around her neck. "What's that dog tag hanging around your neck? Did your mother put that on you in case you got lost or something?" he asked with an impish smile. Scruggs found the divorced father charming. He found her gorgeous.

A love affair soon developed, and passion with it. One night in her condo, after an especially wild episode in bed, she jumped up, grabbed the snub-nosed .38-caliber Colt from her nightstand, and fired a round into the ceiling.

WOOD KEPT UP THE pressure on other media outlets. He sued Rupert Murdoch's *New York Post* for its references to Jewell as a "Village Rambo" and a "fat, failed former sheriff's deputy." The suit also cited the paper's decision to run a photo of Jewell in camo with an AR-15 rifle above the caption, "DRESSING THE PART: Suspect security guard Richard Jewell clearly fits the profile of the bomber, say federal investigators." The paper would eventually settle, reportedly for nearly a quarter-million dollars.

In early August, Piedmont College considered settling Jewell's defamation case against the school and six employees, including President Ray Cleere and Police Chief Dick Martin. The deposition of an *AJC* reporter just weeks earlier greatly influenced the college's thinking.

Cleere and the school's lawyers decided to sit in on Wood deposing *AJC* reporter Maria Elena Fernandez, interested in her testimony about an interview she had done with the college president three days after the bombing. Wood was formally dressed in suit and tie, as usual, his thick brown hair meticulously parted and combed to the side. He instantly launched into his trademark bulldog style and went after the young reporter. Canfield continually objected. Wood increasingly switched to battling the lawyer instead.

Two hours into the session, tempers boiled over. Canfield insisted on a break and rose to leave. Wood stood and got in the *AJC* lawyer's face. The deposition had devolved into near bedlam. The court reporter went off the record. Wood pointed at Canfield and blurted, "Fuck you, Peter." He then continued down the table, pointing at each of his opponents. "Fuck you. Fuck you. Fuck you."

As Wood stormed from the room, an ashen Ray Cleere turned to his lawyer and asked, "Are all depositions like this?"

Piedmont College and *AJC* lawyers subsequently teamed to ask the judge to require a second video camera to be trained on Wood in addition to the usual one focused on the witness. Beyond the fuck-you incident, they alleged that Wood had made an obscene gesture to Canfield during his deposition of

Ron Martz. Wood responded that he was simply propping up his chin with his fingers. The judge ultimately took the unheard-of step of ordering *three* cameras in the deposition: one on the witness, one on the attorney asking the questions, and one that panned the entire room to include all counsel.

But by the end of August, Cleere and Piedmont College had seen enough. The litigation already had been grueling, and a trial seemed to promise nothing but unpleasantness. The school settled for $325,000.

Jewell was pleased with the money, which Watson Bryant held for him in a trust they had set up. The lawyer had seen Jewell's spending habits as far back as their SBA days and wanted to ensure that his friend didn't burn through the entire nest egg. Already Jewell had begun eyeing Bryant's late-model Nissan Pathfinder SUV, impatient to upgrade his pickup, Old Blue.

In late September, Jewell would have another of his growing list of once-unimaginable experiences. He headed to New York as a guest on the opening night of Season 23 of *Saturday Night Live*, hosted that week by Sylvester Stallone. Jewell had two slots in the show. In the first, he made a brief appearance to stomach-punch Attorney General Janet Reno, played by Will Ferrell. A few minutes later, on "Weekend Update," Norm Macdonald set up an interview with Jewell by reminding viewers that the former security guard had been falsely accused by the FBI and that NBC had settled his defamation case. "Now, Richard," Macdonald deadpanned, "I should point out that it's pretty unusual for Tom Brokaw to make a mistake. I mean, nearly three-quarters of the time—like 60, 70 percent of the time—his stories are accurate."

"I understand that," Jewell replied with a smile, after glancing at the cue card.

"But you're telling us, though, that this just happened to be one of the one-in-three or maybe one-in-2.7 times when he got it wrong? Well, I just gotta believe you."

To close out the skit, Macdonald turned to his final query: "I'll ask you a question that I know everyone in the audience is thinking: Were you, Richard Jewell, in any way involved in the death of Mother Teresa?" Jewell fought back laughter, then responded on cue, "No, Norm, I was not." Macdonald closed with, "Richard Jewell, everyone," and the audience applauded.

Three weeks later, Jewell set out on the trip of his lifetime, along with his lawyer and friend, Watson Bryant. The Japanese journalist and professor, Ken

Asano, had arranged a speaking tour, media interviews, and a conversation with the former suspect in the sarin-gas attack, Yoshiyuki Kouno. Seeing "Konoson," as Jewell called him using the Japanese honorific, "was like looking into a mirror—only the country and names of the innocent were different," Jewell told academics and journalists in a speech. "We bonded as men and as victims because we understood each other's pain as only we could."

Jewell also experienced Japan as a tourist with Bryant, from Kabuki theater to koi. He was mesmerized by the colorful fish, snapping dozens of pictures. The food was far less appealing. Jewell couldn't stomach the bento boxes filled with raw seafood and seaweed that his hosts graciously served. He kept an eye out for burger and pizza restaurants as they were escorted to famous temples and sites around Kyoto and Tokyo.

After their time in Japan, Jewell and Bryant stopped in Hawaii on their way back home. No talks, no public appearances, just two buddies vacationing together. They visited Pearl Harbor and took a helicopter tour of Maui. Finally, the men found themselves in Lahaina on October 31, 1997.

Jewell waded through the costume-festooned crowd of twenty-five thousand revelers on Front Street, the salty scent of the Pacific Ocean a block to his right filling the warm night air. Halloween was in full swing at what had become known as the "Mardi Gras of the Pacific." At Jewell's side strode a long-haired man—Watson Bryant, who for this night had purchased a wig to drop over his thinning hair and emerged as the science-fiction character Xena: Warrior Princess. Jewell had left his own costume back at the hotel, declaring, "I'm going as Richard Jewell." He donned a navy Hawaiian shirt with red and white nautical images stuffed into his khaki shorts.

Front Street was packed with revelers dressed as yellow-caped crusaders, Campbell's soup cans, devils, chefs, soldiers, ghouls. Pretty women flooded past in grass skirts and skimpy bikini tops. Three brunettes dressed as cops in blue uniforms and short-shorts stopped to pose for a photo with Jewell.

A year had passed since Jewell's clearance, almost to the day. The time since had been filled with lawsuits and media appearances, along with job applications, more than twenty of them rejected or unanswered. Through it all, there was a constant ache to rebuild his life. Recently, the *AJC* had scheduled his fourth deposition, which meant that in just a few weeks he would yet again be coached and grilled for hours. But here in Lahaina, no one was instructing him where to be, what to say, or how to say it. Jewell was free to make his own statement.

After sunset, around seven P.M., he and Bryant arrived at the Blue Lagoon, a sprawling watering hole on the ground floor of the open-air Wharf Cinema complex. As it had for over two decades, The Wharf was hosting the island's biggest karaoke costume party. Some of Maui's most talented singers gathered to compete. Bryant, already tipsy, crashed down the steeply angled steps of the bar's entrance. Jewell rushed to his aid. "Watson, you OK?" The attorney was fine, although the divot in his rear would become a lifelong souvenir.

Bryant and Jewell found a spot at the bar and ordered beers. A few minutes later, Jewell spontaneously announced he wanted to sing. Bryant tried to discourage him, painfully aware that his friend and client already had suffered more humiliation in a year than most people do in a lifetime. But Jewell was determined. He wandered over to the deejay, Toddy Liliko'i, and asked to join the contestants' list. Liliko'i, whose name was Hawaiian for passion fruit, explained that he couldn't compete without a costume. Jewell vowed to find one.

"OK. What's your name?" she asked, distractedly working on the list of singers.

"Richard Jewell."

"Is that *really* your name?" Liliko'i snapped her head upward skeptically.

"Yeah, I'm Richard Jewell. I'm the one. From Atlanta." He looked at the deejay, who clearly remained unconvinced. So, he pulled out his Georgia driver's license to show her.

"You sure are," she said, gawking at the photo ID and Jewell's familiar round face. "I'm sorry you had to go through all you went through."

Over the next fifteen minutes, Jewell hunted down a pink lei, which he slipped around his neck, and a straw hat with protruding strands of coconut leaves. "I'm a tourist," he proclaimed to Bryant. The lawyer eyed his friend warily. The competition had begun, and the contestants were surprisingly good. "Richard, you sure you want to do this?" Bryant glanced at the costumed crowd now swelling into the hundreds. "Yep," Jewell replied without hesitation. Bryant backed off.

They drank their beers—Jewell, still not much of a drinker, slowly nursing his—and took in the party. Finally, the men heard Liliko'i announce, "Richard

Jewell." Bryant tensed as his rotund friend walked up. The stage was set with a microphone, speakers, and boxy televisions with lyrics for the singer and the audience. Archways of black balloons created a doomsday backdrop for Jewell. Bryant held his breath.

The opening notes to the classic-rock song Jewell had carefully selected began to trickle through the speakers. He closed his eyes, waited for his cue, and drew the mic to his lips. Jewell knew the lyrics by heart, and he began to sing.

It's all the same, only the names will change

At the bar, Bryant laughed. Damned if Jewell wasn't up there performing Bon Jovi's "Wanted Dead or Alive." And damned if he wasn't killing it on that stage. *Richard can sing!* he thought. Bryant watched stunned as his friend began playing to the crowd, crooning lyrics that echoed his past year's experiences.

Lord I've been everywhere
And still I'm standing tall
I've seen a million faces
And I've rocked them all

For the signature lines of the chorus, Jewell gave it his all:

I'm wanted (wanted) dead or alive
Wanted (wanted) dead or alive

As the closing notes faded, Jewell smiled and bowed to the cheering crowd. Stepping off the stage, the former Olympic bombing suspect jaunted back to the bar. Bryant grinned broadly and congratulated Jewell, whose face beamed. His karaoke experience in Lahaina had been joyful. The momentum was continuing to shift.

FOR A GOOD PART of the fall, in the forests of North Carolina, Eric Rudolph tested improvised remote detonators. He wanted his next ambush to hit the target with a flick of a switch. He bought a paging system with plenty of range, but it lacked enough power to detonate a device. Finally, he tested a remote-control model airplane kit, elated at how well it worked. Now Rudolph had everything he needed: hundreds of pounds of dynamite and a surefire method to strike his targets.

In October, Rudolph and his mother, Pat, took a vacation. He visited Civil War battlefields. They toured the Air and Space Museum and the Museum of American History in Washington, D.C. Ultimately, they reached New York, visiting Times Square and posing for photos there.

After they returned south, Rudolph headed back to his trailer. Thanksgiving passed, and he turned to identifying the location of his next attack. Rudolph knew that Atlanta remained on high alert, so he pulled out a map and slid his finger westward. Birmingham, Alabama. Bingo. Then he went to the local library, where he pulled down that city's Yellow Pages and jotted names and addresses of several women's health clinics.

THE COMBINED HUNDRED-MEMBER ATBOM task force got a new chief in the fall. Woody Enderson arrived from Charlotte, North Carolina, with a strong sense of optimism. "There are some cases that we realistically don't feel like we can solve, but this is not one of them," the twenty-six-year FBI veteran told Martz and Scruggs. "We have extraordinary patience. We just won't give up."

Soon, Enderson and Jack Daulton, newly installed as the FBI's Atlanta SAC after Woody Johnson's retirement, stood before the media for another press conference. Staffers had placed components from each of the three Atlanta bombings on display. From the Olympic Park bomb they showed 11-gauge steel for the directional plate, olive-green foam padding, tape, and a wooden handle. Enderson ran through the items, reminding the public multiple times that they may have seen those items purchased, alone or in some combination. Noting that the bomber used three or four pounds of smokeless powder in his park device, Enderson used the chemical as an example. "Before the Olympics, did you sell a quantity of that type of gunpowder to anyone, either all at once or in several sales within a short time frame?"

Enderson knew how long the odds were. Privately, he joked to colleagues, "The good news is that we have fifty thousand witnesses. The bad news is that we have fifty thousand witnesses." But continued public disclosures were their best chance.

"In their strongest public appeal to date," Scruggs and Martz wrote, investigators rolled out a detailed shopping list of materials that went into construction of the devices. The decision to release the components' list was "nearly unprecedented for federal agencies and appears to indicate that the investigation is bogged down." The offer of a $500,000 reward still stood. For the next two days, Scruggs wrote follow-up stories about how the devices might have triggered, and that more than two hundred calls had come into the task force in response to the public appeal. Many of the leads merited additional work, she reported. Scruggs worked her sources to keep tabs on the most promising of them. No journalist wanted the bomber caught more than she did, and she fully intended to be the first to identify him by name.

IN THE FALL, DON Johnson had sent a fax from his home computer to the OPR team in Washington. He intended it as a simple message, explaining that all future communications should go through his legal counsel. But the OPR focused on the cover sheet, which was topped by the fax legend, "Johnson Investigations LLC." Had the agent opened a private business while still working for the FBI? The OPR informed Johnson that he was again under internal investigation, this time for unauthorized outside employment. Johnson defensively explained that he had taken a private investigator's course in anticipation of starting a business when he retired from the FBI. But he hadn't taken the certification test yet, and had not established any corporate entity. Johnson Investigations LLC was just a name.

In late November, less than two months after the initial contact by the OPR on his latest case, Johnson was cleared of any wrongdoing. Still, the agent was fed up. In December he announced he would retire at month's end. Within weeks, Don Johnson turned in his four Bureau-issued guns, bulletproof vest, pager, and badge #2364.

Colleagues on the 7 Squad planned a goodbye party, creating an invitation designed to look like a fugitive poster. "Wanted By FBI," it declared. Below, it read, "Armed: With Wit. Dangerous: With Opinions." The flyer featured three images of Johnson, one as a boy, another as a young agent, and a third of him standing in the Atlanta office shaking hands with his nemesis, Louie Freeh. Johnson saw no humor in the third photo and demanded that a new invitation be reprinted, without the Director.

The party was a subdued affair. Roughly two dozen colleagues and family members attended. Later, in keeping with FBI tradition, the SAC's executive assistant forwarded goodbye letters sent by Johnson's former colleagues. "Dear Don," her cover note said, "attached are the letters I received for you when you retired. I apologize for holding on to them so long. I was hoping to get more so I could have them bound, but employees rarely do these letters anymore." Only three agents had written.

A FEW WEEKS AFTER Jewell returned from Japan and Hawaii, the phone rang. A friend of Bobi's from church had been talking to the police chief of a small town about forty miles southwest of Atlanta. Luthersville, population 750, had only a single flashing traffic light, and one combination burger/hot dog/convenience store called Bubba-Doo's.

Chief Paige McNeese needed a new officer and wanted Jewell to apply for the job. Jewell's heart leapt. He immediately filled out the application. Under the space for "Date You Can Start," he put down "ASAP."

On the Friday before Thanksgiving, Jewell drove to Luthersville to interview with McNeese, a Marlboro-smoking former Marine with a thin, deeply lined face. The chief liked the thirty-four-year-old Jewell from the moment they met and offered him a job after the first conversation. The pay was low, just $8.50 an hour, well below the $12 an hour Jewell earned during the Olympics. The police department was poorly equipped, McNeese cautioned Jewell, and the town full of retirees. "Go home and think about it over the weekend."

"Chief, I don't have to think about it," Jewell replied. "I want the job." On Tuesday, November 25, 1997, he was sworn in as a police officer for the city of Luthersville, Georgia. For the first time in nearly a year and a half, Richard Jewell donned a police uniform and a badge.

CHAPTER 26

Robert Sanderson was a popular cop in Birmingham, Alabama. A square-jawed thirty-five-year-old with a pug nose and dark bushy eyebrows, he was known to all as "Sande."

In his nine-year career, the officer had stacked up a string of big-and-small policing moments. He once saved the lives of a sheriff's deputy and a drunk as they fought by yanking both out of harm's way an instant before an 18-wheeler was about to hit them. Another time, Sanderson stood beneath a burning building as a woman jumped, injuring himself as he caught her. No one was surprised in 1996 when local officials selected the popular officer and Air Force veteran to run a leg of the Olympic Torch Relay as the flame wound toward Atlanta.

Sanderson's home of Birmingham once was known as the iron and steel capital of the South. In 1903, the city commissioned the world's largest cast iron statue: a fifty-six-foot-tall likeness of Vulcan, the Roman god of fire and forge. It stood atop a 124-foot marble-clad sandstone pedestal in Vulcan Park on the southern edge of town. By the early 1960s, though, after a nearly two-decade-long run of some fifty dynamite attacks by white supremacists, Birmingham had taken on a far darker nickname: Bombingham. Most famous was the shocking murder of four girls at the 16th Street Baptist Church as Sunday school let out on the morning of September 15, 1963. But in more recent years, Birmingham had built a reputation as an increasingly progressive city with a thriving university community anchored by the University of Alabama at Birmingham, or UAB as most called it.

At seven A.M. on January 29, 1998, Sanderson completed his eight-hour graveyard shift. He had been coaching a rookie officer, as he liked to do, and the pair had made a few marijuana busts and chatted about the prior Sunday's Super Bowl. It had been an exciting game, with John Elway's Denver Broncos knocking off Brett Favre's Green Bay Packers.

Sanderson stopped for coffee before driving to the New Woman All Women Health Clinic, where he was subbing on a private security shift for a fellow officer. Protesters were common at the facility, which performed abortions three days a week. Usually they were peaceful, but some had slashed tires and thrown paint on the employees' cars. Sanderson was there to ensure the staff's safety, and welcomed the extra money to support his wife and two stepsons.

The officer pulled his van into the New Woman lot and parked next to the two-story white brick building with its pair of distinctive burgundy fabric awnings. He paused for a brief chat with his wife, Felecia, from his car phone. "Be safe. I love you," she told him. "Alright, baby. I love you too," Sanderson replied before getting out of the vehicle. A lone protester stood beyond the property line, ready to heckle those who approached the clinic. Minutes later, a couple and their teenage daughter drove up. Sanderson told the father that the clinic wouldn't open to the public until eight A.M., but that someone would be around soon to let them in.

As Sanderson conducted a routine patrol of the grounds, clinic nurse Emily Lyons swung into the parking lot in her BMW convertible. The forty-one-year-old mother of two wore pink scrubs and a blue sweatshirt. She had tied her long auburn hair into a ponytail. Lyons was responsible for opening the office that day, stepping in for another nurse out on maternity leave.

ERIC RUDOLPH WAS RUNNING late. Early-morning traffic entering Birmingham had been far worse than planned. He needed to reach his position soon.

A month earlier, Rudolph had cased the New Woman clinic on five consecutive mornings. He knew the opening routine well. A "rent-a-cop," as he called them, showed up first to do a perimeter check. Then a female staffer arrived around 7:30. The cop escorted her to the entrance, where she picked up the *Birmingham News*, pulled out her key to open the door, and then they both disappeared into the building.

Rudolph parked more than a mile south of New Woman. Jumping out of his truck, he rushed down Valley Avenue, turning toward the clinic and passing a McDonald's. Near Vulcan Park, Rudolph stopped briefly to retrieve a blue flannel jacket and a long brown wig from his book bag. He secured the hairpiece with a dark-blue knit hat, then put on a cheap pair of aviator glasses to complete the disguise. As an extra precaution, Rudolph had holstered a Heckler & Koch 9mm inside his waistband. He left the remote control and a change of clothes in his bag, then resumed his quickened pace toward the clinic, falling in with students heading to class.

Rudolph arrived near the parking lot and set up a direct sight line to the awning-covered main entrance. Standing less than one hundred feet away, he quickly surveyed the scene.

The night before, Rudolph had snuck into the lot and placed a tool box on the ground near the entrance. It contained a thirty-pound IED filled with a dozen or so sticks of dynamite, a directional plate, and ten pounds of nails. To maximize the device's effectiveness, he affixed tent stakes to each corner to raise it slightly off the ground. Then Rudolph draped fake foliage over the toolbox, giving the green mass the appearance of an artificial shrub. With his new remote-detonation system, he didn't need a timer or a secondary device.

At 7:33 A.M., from his spot near the clinic lot, Rudolph watched the woman in pink and gray head up the walkway to pick up the daily paper. She had spotted the odd-looking bush ten feet away and was pointing it out to the male rent-a-cop. The man pulled out his retractable baton and bent over the foliage to take a closer look.

He's found it. Gotta do it now! Rudolph thought. He pulled the book bag up to his chest, unzipped the top, and flipped the switch.

The blast threw Sanderson fifteen feet. His face and scalp were peeled back, his right arm detached, his uniform blown off. Only his gun belt was left, draped around his waist. A woman who had witnessed the blast went to Sanderson's aid and knelt next to him. His chest was still laboring, as if he was gasping for breath. By the time first responders arrived, Sanderson would be dead, the first American killed by a bombing at an abortion clinic.

Emily Lyons was alive, but barely. Blood flowed from hundreds of nail and shrapnel wounds all over her face and body. An inch-and-a-half piece of flying metal had pierced her right eye. There was a gaping hole in Lyons's abdomen and her intestines were ripped up. At the hospital, doctors would put her chances of survival under 20 percent.

Rudolph, rocked by the blast, picked himself off the ground and zipped his book bag closed. The bomber's instincts told him to run, but he knew others would be rushing toward the scene. He needed to walk deliberately, unnoticed, and to find a discreet place to change his disguise.

JERMAINE HUGHES, AN EIGHTEEN-YEAR-OLD pre-med student at UAB, had been doing laundry at his dorm a block and a half away when he heard the massive explosion. Racing to the window, he stared at a plume of blue-white smoke. Hughes went outside as people rushed toward the scene. But he noticed someone walking in the opposite direction at a purposeful pace. Hughes made rough mental notes of the man's physical features, especially as he saw him cross the street and then accelerate into a near-run.

The student boldly climbed into his car and followed the man. He drove four blocks, trying to keep a safe distance to avoid notice. The guy ducked into an alley, so Hughes steered around the other side. Seconds later, the man emerged but looking different. His hair was shorter, his jacket and hat now gone. He wore dark sunglasses despite the overcast morning. Hughes feigned having car trouble so that he could get a better look. Seconds later, he lost sight of the man.

For about fifteen minutes, Hughes tried unsuccessfully to both relocate the guy and get help calling the police. Finally, he parked and ran into a nearby McDonald's, where he borrowed the office phone to dial 911. Hughes blurted his description to the operator, trying to recall details as the woman impatiently interjected questions and the two began talking past each other. Soon, Hughes was disconnected. The student called back, trying to improve his description when a remarkable coincidence occurred: The guy walked past the McDonald's.

A local lawyer named Jeff Tickal, who was in the McDonald's eating breakfast, had caught an earful of Hughes's side of the call. When he heard Hughes yell "I got him, I got him," Tickal began barking out a detailed description of the man's features and clothing for Hughes to relay in real time to the 911 operator.

Then, as Hughes waited for police, Tickal jumped into his own car to follow the man. Almost immediately, Tickal saw the suspect loading something into a gray Nissan pickup truck with the North Carolina plate KND1117. He wrote down the information on a McDonald's coffee cup. Tickal then tailed the truck, at one point even pulling alongside it and getting a good look at the driver. Seconds later, Tickal spotted a police cruiser and reported the license plate and descriptions of both the vehicle and its operator. Meanwhile, Hughes had jumped back into his own car and driven off looking for the man. At one point, he briefly caught up with the suspicious character and also jotted down the plate number. Police soon had matching reports of the suspect and vehicle.

ON HIS WAY OUT of town, Rudolph paused to drop two letters in the mail. He then traveled northeast for about a half hour, stopping at a vacant lot in Springville. He set the wig, boots, and clothing on fire with gasoline. Using soap and water, he shaved off his mustache in the sideview mirror. Then Rudolph steered his truck 220 miles back to the wooded mountains of western North Carolina.

At his trailer on Cane Creek Road, Rudolph felt paranoia wash over him. He had seen the skinny black kid staring at him. Did the guy call the police? To find out what investigators might know, Rudolph flipped on the radio for news at the top and bottom of the hour. The clinic guard he had killed was an off-duty cop, Rudolph learned, a fact certain to raise the intensity of the probe. But, to his relief, there was no word of any suspect.

At 5:30 P.M., in an effort to relax, he headed for a video store in Murphy to rent a movie. He chose *City of Industry*, a violent revenge drama with Harvey Keitel and Timothy Hutton. Back at the trailer, he popped it into his combination TV/VCR and hit play. But Rudolph couldn't settle down enough to make it through the movie. He turned off all the lights and darted from window to window, peering out for any sign of law enforcement. Finally, with the film still playing, he rushed down the trailer's three wooden front steps to the Nissan. Through the evening, Rudolph busied himself moving supplies to a secret cache, then spent the night in the woods.

The next day, Rudolph realized his paranoia was misguided. The trailer was just as he left it, and no surveillance agents were in sight. He returned the movie and rented another, *Kull the Conquerer*. Back at the trailer though, he again flipped on the radio. The newscaster reported that a Birmingham witness had seen a man climb into a gray truck after the bombing. Authorities, the broadcast continued, had begun hunting for the vehicle and its owner. Rudolph, jolted by the news, ran to his bedroom in sheer panic. He flung his clothes onto the floor, rolled them into a bundled bedsheet, and tore away from Cane Creek.

Once in the truck, Rudolph learned the news had gotten worse. At six P.M. Eastern Time, Doug Jones, the recently appointed U.S. Attorney for the Northern District of Alabama, announced that a man was spotted leaving the scene in a gray Nissan pickup truck. That truck was registered to Eric Robert Rudolph of Marble, North Carolina. Rudolph froze when he heard his name. The feds knew his identity. The U.S. Attorney's disclaimer offered no solace: "Don't draw any conclusions. Rudolph is only a material witness."

Rudolph hid in the woods until nightfall, then drove back toward Murphy with $800 of cash in his pocket. He swung through Burger King; then he went to the Bi-Lo grocery store, where he bought $109.66 of oatmeal, peanuts, raisins, tuna, batteries, and other nonperishable provisions. The groceries, he figured, would last six months if he was conservative. Rudolph then headed into the Nantahala, where he abandoned his truck. He walked fifteen miles into the forest that was now his home.

AT EIGHT P.M., THE FBI readied an approach on Rudolph's Cane Creek trailer.

In the previous hours, the Bureau had been fortunate that Jack Thompson, the sheriff of Cherokee County, North Carolina, had tracked down the location through local contacts. The address on the truck registration had turned out not to be Rudolph's. And the FBI quickly learned that the man lived largely off the grid: no credit cards, no tax filings, no voting record.

Here at Cane Creek, the truck was gone, and no one appeared home. As a precaution, two SWAT team agents dressed in body armor and carrying semiautomatic rifles entered first. Indeed, Rudolph wasn't there. They had missed him.

Inside the ramshackle trailer, the small kitchen had an open container of Quaker Oats and a nearby pot of water, a sign that the Rudolph may have been readying a meal before leaving hastily. He had left four pistols and three rifles behind. In his bedroom, agents found the dresser drawers open, clothing strewn about. One shirt appeared to match the pattern described by the Birmingham witnesses.

The surveillance team remained on stakeout at Cane Creek for three days on the chance Rudolph would return. He didn't.

Back in Atlanta, FBI agents scrambled to their rosters of assigned leads. *Was Rudolph my guy? Did I miss him?* One by one, with great relief, they saw that his name appeared on none of their lists. Remarkably, in a year and a half of work by three task forces, Eric Rudolph had never been in any database.

KATHY SCRUGGS WAS AT her condo in Atlanta when her pager buzzed just after the explosion at New Woman. She glanced at the device, then turned to her boyfriend, George Hamilton: "There's been a bombing in Alabama."

Other *AJC* reporters covered the news from Birmingham, but Scruggs, feeling the thrill of the breaking story, drove two hours to Murphy to report on the search. "Federal officials are scouring the mountains for Rudolph," she wrote in a front-page piece co-bylined with Ron Martz. "'Nobody's seen him and they don't have any leads. They're working in Cherokee, Macon, and most of western North Carolina,'" Sheriff Thompson said.

But Martz and Scruggs had bigger news to share with *AJC* readers. The Birmingham attack appeared to be linked to the Atlanta bombings. Both Reuters and the *AJC* had received new Army of God letters, they reported. The text was scrawled in the same block-letter handwriting as the prior missives. This five-sentence message mostly spewed hate about abortion, but the signature indicated the author had a broader agenda. "Death to the New World Order," it blared, adding a specific code, as in previous letters. The reporters did not disclose the 4-1-9-9-3 code.

ATBOM task force leader Woody Enderson conceded to Scruggs and Martz that the letters bore "striking similarities" to those received after the Otherside Lounge bombing. He cautioned that a copycat bomber could be involved, although that seemed highly unlikely. As the reporters disclosed in their article, the FBI had not publicly revealed the Waco code from the earlier letters.

Meanwhile, a separate Birmingham task force was soon created and designated SANDBOM in memory of the fallen officer.

MORE THAN A HUNDRED agents swarmed into the mountains of North Carolina in search of Rudolph. The FBI set up a forward command post in Murphy, a town of 1,600 in the state's far southwestern end. Agents battled the brutal terrain of the 531,000-acre Nantahala National Forest, the land pockmarked with hundreds of caves and mine shafts. Dense rhododendron, hemlocks, and mountain laurel hid copperheads, rattlers, wild boar, and bear. Some of the rises were so steep that one observer likened them to black diamond runs at ski resorts. Helicopters swooped in all directions in search of the suspected bomber.

A week into the hunt, a pair of coon hunters stumbled across the gray Nissan truck, license plate KND1117. At 10:30 P.M. on February 7, in a biting sleet, the hunters led agents into the woods and back to the truck, shrouded in rhododendron and spindly trees. The law enforcement team crept up on the vehicle. At least one member hoped, even expected, to find Rudolph dead inside from a suicide. But no one was in the vehicle. Agents searched the truck, uncovering a wide range of Rudolph's possessions: photos, receipts, a swastika medallion, a rosary, rental contracts, condoms, a Johann Sebastian Bach cassette. They also found traces of a key ingredient in nitroglycerin-based dynamite in the truck. After a thorough search and analysis of Rudolph's trailer, they discovered it there too.

Several days later, U.S. Attorney Jones filed a criminal complaint charging Rudolph with the Birmingham bombing. A federal warrant was issued for his arrest.

A reinvigorated Scruggs wrote a series of articles about the search. The bombing and letters were big news in Atlanta, and the *AJC* gave several of her pieces front-page play. In one story, Scruggs walked readers through the use of bloodhounds brought in from around the country. One dog handler drove his animals along a twenty-mile stretch south of Murphy in search of Rudolph's scent. Federal agents and journalists tailed along in what Scruggs called a "stop-and-go-caravan." Each time the handler let the dogs out, a half-dozen TV news crews clambered out of their news vehicles to film every sniff.

Throughout rural North Carolina, agents went door to door searching for leads to find Rudolph. They cautioned residents they might be back to search their homes, if necessary. Other agents, Scruggs wrote, investigated forensics connections, trying to link black and red wire used in the Georgia and Alabama bombings to a Radio Shack store in western North Carolina. The FBI also combed the area for the source of the devices' steel directional plates.

The hunt was complicated by some locals who viewed the FBI's tactics as heavy-handed and a minority of whom saw Rudolph as a folk hero. A local restaurant posted a sign trumpeting "Eric Rudolph Eats Here" even though law enforcement frequented the place. Another introduced FBI curly fries to reflect the Bureau going in circles. T-shirts and bumper stickers went up for sale featuring the slogans "Run, Rudolph, Run" and "Eric Rudolph: 1998 Hide and Seek Champion." Even Scruggs's boyfriend, George, bought a sticker.

February spilled into March with the only reports of Rudolph being "Elvis sightings," as Scruggs termed them. She reported for readers about Rudolph's survivalist background and history of living off the grid. He paid bills in cash or money orders and had no credit cards or bank accounts. Sometimes he used the alias Bob Randolph. "Ever since being discharged from the U.S. Army in 1988, Eric Rudolph apparently set out on a deliberate path to leave no footprints," Scruggs wrote.

So far, he had been remarkably successful.

ON THE SECOND SUNDAY in March, in one of the more bizarre episodes of the case, the fugitive's thirty-seven-year-old brother, Daniel, decided to film a home movie. Apparently exasperated by law enforcement and press scrutiny, Daniel turned on a video camera in the garage of his home near Charleston, South Carolina. Wearing a jacket and tie, he looked straight into the camera: "My name is Daniel Kerney Rudolph, and this is for the FBI and the media." He removed his jacket, sat down, and rolled up a sleeve. Next, he placed his left arm down on a work bench and grabbed the handle of a large compound miter circular saw with his right hand. Daniel Rudolph then cut off his left hand above the wrist, as it flipped in the air and dropped off-camera. Rudolph then drove to the hospital, where he checked himself in. A local deputy sheriff later broke into his garage and retrieved the hand so that an EMS worker could put it on ice and bring it to the hospital. Surgeons would successfully reattach it.

Within days, Scruggs reported the gory episode based on a law enforcement source's account. She later interviewed a couple who had gotten to know the Rudolphs when they bought the family's home in 1996. The husband told her, "Daniel appeared to be the most grounded of all of them."

IN MAY, THE FBI announced that it was adding Rudolph to the Ten Most Wanted Fugitives list. The Bureau doubled the reward for assisting his capture, to \$1 million. In the *AJC*, Scruggs quoted one task force member as cautioning, "We don't anticipate that he'll be quickly apprehended as a result [of the reward]. Some are apprehended within hours and some aren't apprehended for a number of years." A new Wanted poster included the photo Rudolph had taken in Times Square the prior November, his mother cropped out of the picture. As part of Rudolph's new status, the volume of leads increased, but their quality did not.

DESPITE THE INITIAL BOOST from her involvement in the Rudolph coverage, Scruggs still struggled on a personal level. In late April, State Court Judge John Mather sided with Lin Wood and ordered the *AJC* to disclose the leaker's name in the Jewell case. Peter Canfield vowed to appeal. The next day, Scruggs endured her second deposition by Wood. He had a single agenda item: She could either reveal her source or state on the record that she was defying the court's order. If the latter, fines and possibly jail would come into play.

Peering at Scruggs over the top of his reading glasses, Wood asked, "Ms. Scruggs, would you identify for me, please, the individuals who provided you information about Richard Jewell which was published in the *Atlanta Journal* Extra article headlined FBI SUSPECTS HERO GUARD MAY HAVE PLANTED BOMB"? The newspaper's lawyer objected and instructed her not to answer.

Wood erupted at the attorney, noting the judge's explicit mandate to reveal the source. "You are instructing this witness to disobey a direct order of the court entered into this case yesterday afternoon? Is that what you are doing?" He turned to Scruggs: "Are you going to answer the question, ma'am?" "No, sir," she replied. Those were her only two words in the deposition. She looked on as Wood vented, then terminated the proceeding. The entire session had lasted only four minutes.

Scruggs and her writing partner, Martz, now realized that they actually might be facing imprisonment. The *AJC* lawyers assured them otherwise. Canfield and the paper's editors repeatedly encouraged them to stand firm, explaining that truth was the ultimate defense in a libel case; Jewell had indeed been the FBI's lead suspect. Inside the *AJC*'s Marietta Street newsroom, Bill Rankin began urging other journalists to rally behind the accused reporters: "If they are taken to jail, we will all march over there with them," he declared. Everyone hoped it would never come to that.

The third deposition was even worse for her.

Dressed in a royal blue suit jacket and a matching conservative blouse, Scruggs was sworn in. This time, her speech slurred. She looked repeatedly to her lawyers for guidance. Her eyes appeared glassy and, at times, she rolled them up into her sockets so that only the whites were visible. She twisted her torso often, trying in vain to get comfortable. Again, she refused to identify her source. Wood pressed. Had she met the source after work? Objection. At a bar? Objection. Was anyone else present? Objection. At one point, a frustrated Wood snarled, "I am not done with you, Ms. Scruggs. We are not done. You are not going to be able to run and hide."

The lawyers argued while Scruggs sat in abject physical pain. For years, she had conducted newsroom interviews lying on the floor when her back ached badly. She had done what she could medically, even having breast reduction surgery a few years earlier. But her chronic back problems had reached crisis levels. Wood asked about her discomfort. Sensing there was more amiss, he asked what medication she was taking. Desyrel, last night, she replied. The drug was used to treat depression and insomnia. Anything that morning? No, Scruggs answered.

What she didn't disclose was that she also regularly took Percocet for pain and Xanax for anxiety. She layered on other meds for blood pressure and cholesterol, as well as Fen Phen for weight loss. Scruggs was desperately trying to handle the pressures from the case, the Rudolph search, and her physical ailments. For relief she visited several doctors, multiplying her prescriptions. She filled some of them twice at different pharmacies. Her boyfriend, George, knew she was taking too many, and he tried to get her to cut down. For a time, he hid her drugs at his house. When she came over for pills, he would act as her personal pharmacist, dispensing only what he thought she needed.

But Scruggs broke up with Hamilton, and although they remained friends, he began dating someone else. The new girlfriend, soon to be wife, understandably didn't want Scruggs around. So, Hamilton took to hiding the pills around Scruggs's own home. When she called to tell him she had run out, Hamilton would ask how many she needed. To add levity to an otherwise dire situation, he sent Scruggs on scavenger hunts. She eventually found the pills.

Scruggs tried to stay connected to family and friends. Her beloved father, Bubber, lent a sympathetic ear, but he had no magic answers that could help his daughter with the lawsuit, back pain, or growing depression. Her cousin, Bentley, had children and found herself increasingly busy raising them. Scruggs's brother, Lewis, was rearing his family too, as well as running the growing insurance business his father had started. The siblings, nearly a decade apart in age, had never been close anyway.

RUDOLPH HAD SIGNIFICANTLY UNDERESTIMATED the difficulty of living in the wilderness. The fugitive had arrived in the woods weighing 190 pounds and had shed fifty of them in the five months since. His waistline shrank by six inches, a result of too many days consuming only five hundred calories while burning thousands more than he had anticipated. Rudolph decided to hike fifteen miles to the headwaters of Little Snowbird Creek, where he had stashed a one-year supply of food. Through the thick woods, his arduous walk would be double that distance.

When he finally reached the cache, Rudolph was crushed. Bears had ransacked his supplies, and there was not a scrap of food left. He knew he could fish and kill the occasional deer or turkey. But he desperately needed staples like oatmeal and beans as well as foods rich in fats. He still had most of the $800 he had taken into the woods. It was time to put the cash to use. It was time to seek out George Nordmann.

NORDMANN WAS A SEVENTY-ONE-YEAR-OLD Navy veteran with passions for farming, his ultra-Catholic religious faith, and far-right political views. A silver-haired Florida native with an easygoing manner, he had purchased a ten-acre plot in the North Carolina town of Nantahala in the mid-1970s, then opened his Better Way Health Foods store a dozen or so miles away in Andrews.

One of Nordmann's regular customers in the early 1990s was Eric Rudolph. On his weekly visits to the store, Nordmann would regale him with conspiracy theories of the coming apocalypse. The last time Nordmann and Rudolph had spoken, the older man pontificated for an hour about the Waco siege.

Rudolph slowly zigzagged his way several miles through the mountains to reach Nordmann's house, a ramshackle structure with a corrugated metal exterior and a half-dozen rusted cars in the front yard. Once there, the fugitive cased the home. From a hideaway on a nearby bluff, he monitored Nordmann's comings and goings. For the first few days, Rudolph stole eggs from Nordmann's chicken coop. Soon, he grew bolder, breaking in while Nordmann was working at the store. Rudolph began to cook, bathe, and eat Nordmann's vitamins. He even started watching videos from his absent host's collection, among them *The Great Escape* with Steve McQueen. Rudolph found it apropos.

To Rudolph's delight, in the basement, he discovered a massive and varied supply of food stacked six shelves high. He stuffed his backpack full of wheat, beans, tuna, honey, and corned beef. He also loaded up on the health-food proprietor's mineral and protein supplements. As payment, Rudolph left a $100 bill on the counter. Nordmann was baffled by the money and grew concerned when he began noticing items missing from his home. One day, a cast-iron skillet he rarely used mysteriously appeared on the stove. He changed the lock on his door.

On July 7, early in the evening, Nordmann drove up his driveway. Out of nowhere, a scraggly man dressed in green fatigues appeared. He had a two-inch beard and hair pulled into a ponytail. Nordmann recognized Eric Rudolph immediately.

"You have to go," Nordmann sputtered. "They're looking for you."

"I won't hurt you, George," the fugitive replied. "I'm starving. Need food bad."

The men spoke as they stood by the chicken coop, and Nordmann soon relented. He advised Rudolph just to lay low for another eighteen months or so, until Y2K. Everything would collapse after the worldwide computer crash as December 31, 1999, turned to January 1, 2000. Rudolph said he knew about it but would need food to make it that long. Wearing gloves to avoid leaving fingerprints, Rudolph handed over a lengthy grocery list and pledged to pay in cash. He also asked to borrow the Toyota Corolla that Nordmann drove to work each day. The older man said he would pray about it and let him know. In the meantime, he gave Rudolph a sack of groceries. The fugitive thanked him and said he'd return in two nights. Rudolph then retreated back to the woods.

Two nights later, on July 9, Rudolph approached Nordmann's house. The Corolla was gone, the store owner nowhere in sight. Nordmann had left garbage bags in the kitchen filled with supplies. He also left a note: "God says no about the car."

Incensed, Rudolph wrote back: "Sorry you were fearful in helping me. The feds and dogs will never find me. A call will tell you where your car is located." Rudolph left five $100 bills, then tossed the supplies into a badly rusted pale blue Datsun pickup parked among the deteriorating vehicles outside. He hot-wired the truck and drove toward the woods with his new reserve of fifty pounds of rye, three gallons of honey, one hundred gallons of rolled oats, two pounds of cayenne pepper, canned tuna, bags of pinto beans, jars of coconut oil, batteries, peroxide, and a New Testament, among other things.

Nordmann returned home, saw the Datsun was missing, and panicked. He destroyed Rudolph's note, then waited two days before calling the sheriff. By then, Rudolph had again disappeared deep into the Nantahala National Forest.

WITH NORDMANN'S INFORMATION IN hand, the task force relaunched the massive manhunt for Rudolph with new intensity. Scruggs joined in. She reported that the number of agents searching for Rudolph, which had dropped to thirty-five before the Nordmann sighting, immediately doubled. Then it doubled again, and would soon swell to over two hundred. Helicopters and tracking dogs once more descended on the mountains of western North Carolina.

On July 13, authorities discovered the Datsun pickup near a turnoff to a remote campground in the Nantahala forest. A note inside read, "Truck broke down. Call George Nordmann at Better Way Health Foods in Andrews, North Carolina." The fugitive had abandoned the truck more than fifty miles from Nordmann's home.

Scruggs wrote a story nearly every day for two weeks, covering the post-Nordmann search. At first, she optimistically told readers that investigators thought they were fifteen hours behind Rudolph. The *AJC* ran a new drawing of Rudolph that the task force had ordered up based on Nordmann's description. GBI artist Marla Lawson, who had done the original Goatee

Man image from Centennial Park, sketched Rudolph as far more bohemian but handsome. She found him good-looking, as other women did too. The FBI thought the reaction was unfortunate but added the new image to its Wanted poster. Still, Rudolph remained elusive.

AS THE FBI'S SEARCH flagged, so did Scruggs's spirits. In early November, she was arrested for a second time in Buckhead. "The suspect was in the roadway," the officer wrote in his incident report, "barely able to stand on her feet, creating a hazard to herself and to the other vehicles and pedestrians in the area." The officer helped the impaired forty-year-old reporter into his squad car and took her to the Atlanta City Jail.

A week after the arrest, Scruggs took a medical leave from the paper. Her cousin, Bentley, could no longer contain her frustration. She whacked Scruggs across the chest, venting, "You're going to die." Scruggs laughed despondently: "I don't want to live long anyway."

Three months later, in February 1999, Scruggs called Bentley late in the evening. "I've taken twenty-two Xanax," she told her cousin before hanging up. Bentley frantically drove over and tried to unlock the door with her key, but Scruggs had put the chain latch on. Bentley broke in and called 911. By the time emergency responders carted Scruggs to the hospital, she was chatting up the emergency team. Bentley could only look on in awe at the tolerance Scruggs had clearly built up to the powerful drugs. Atlanta police listed the case as an attempted suicide. Scruggs soon extended her medical leave.

RICHARD JEWELL'S LIFE AS Luthersville cop was taking a far brighter turn. On April 10, 1998, an attractive and buxom brunette case agent for the Georgia Department of Family and Child Services (DFACS) stopped by the Luthersville police station asking for help. She needed to remove two kids from a rundown trailer in a poor, rural part of town. The process might be tricky because a known cocaine and marijuana dealer lived in the trailer with the children's mother. "Oh, we've been looking for that guy," Jewell told the caseworker, Dana Story. "We'll drive you out there."

When they arrived, Story watched as Jewell and two other officers knocked and announced themselves. She heard banging and scuffling inside the trailer. The mother came to the door, and the lawmen ordered her to take the kids outside. Story rushed up to escort the mother and children to safety. The police pushed their way into the trailer and soon emerged with a man in handcuffs.

After the arrestee was out of the way, Story told the officers that she had learned from the mother that a bigger dealer was coming soon. Jewell and the others decided to wait. Story handed the children off to their grandmother, then had little choice but to wait too. The officers were her ride back. But she was excited to see a drug bust, even if it was an unusual way to spend her twenty-eighth birthday.

As the hours passed waiting for the dealer to show, Jewell regularly walked by making small talk. "Your hair sure does look pretty," he said on one pass. He complimented her easy smile on another. When Story looked cold, Jewell loaned her his jacket.

Finally, the dealer rolled up and the cops arrested him too. At eight P.M., Story and the officers headed back toward the police station. Jewell asked if she wanted to come in and watch them count the confiscated money. Story said yes, figuring it would be an interesting new experience. After the bills were logged in, the officers spread them and the bagged drugs across a table. They took photos, with Jewell making sure he got a picture of himself behind the contraband. Then, he suggested to Story, "Go sit behind there, Dana, and we'll get your picture." She took a seat, and a fellow officer snapped a shot of her.

Minutes later, Jewell escorted Dana to her Jeep. He waved, and she started it up. He began to walk away, then turned back.

"Your headlight is out," he told her.

"OK, I'll get it fixed."

"You *better* get that fixed," Jewell said with a flirtatious wink. "Don't come back into my town without your headlight working or I'll have to give you a ticket." He offered to install it for her if she returned with the part.

She told him the offer was sweet.

The next week, Story drove back to the small brick Luthersville police station, where she asked for Officer Jewell. "I came by to show you something," she said, turning on her replaced headlight. She had made the repair herself.

Jewell was impressed. They chatted. He learned that Story had grown up in a close-knit but strict Southern Baptist family in the south Atlanta suburbs. She had played softball as a catcher at West Georgia College. Jewell screwed up his courage. "Would you ever want to go out with me sometime?" he asked. She readily agreed.

After Dana gave Jewell her number, she called her mother. "You won't believe who just asked me out. Richard Jewell!"

Everyone in town knew who Jewell was. They soon were reminded again. Just before midnight on Friday, May 8, a panicked mother ran into the Luthersville police station carrying her five-day-old child. The infant was choking and turning blue. Jewell quickly performed CPR, saving the baby's life. The next week, Police Chief McNeese offered a commendation. The local paper, the *Meriwether Free Press*, reported the story as front-page news under the headline, JEWELL SAVES INFANT'S LIFE. The piece included another exciting bit of department news: Jewell had been promoted to sergeant.

After several dates, Jewell took Dana to meet Bobi. The nervous new girlfriend was shocked at the unvarnished, at times vinegary, exchanges between Jewell and his mother. The relationship was quite different from those in the more genteel Story household. The Jewells snapped, carped, and at times even cursed at each other. The tension made Dana anxious, and she often responded to stress by growing nauseous.

The three went to dinner at an Italian restaurant, but Dana ate only a few bites. After dinner, back in the car, Jewell stepped hard on the accelerator. From the back seat, Bobi barked at Jewell to ease off his lead-footed driving. "Richard, *slow down*."

The stress rose, and Dana knew what was coming. But it was too late. She leaned out the window and threw up.

Despite the rocky experience, Jewell and Dana's relationship blossomed. In the evenings they watched John Wayne movies together. He called her College Girl; she nicknamed him Barney, for the Mayberry cop Barney Fife. Jewell liked to cook, especially lasagna or pasta with his "secret recipe" sauce, usually made up of jarred Prego or Ragú with some extra spices and meat mixed in. He began to send her numeric pages of 1-4-3, representing the number of letters in "I love you."

CHAPTER 27

By the end of January 1999, a full year had passed since Rudolph's last bombing. Federal grand juries in Atlanta and Birmingham had indicted him for all four terrorist attacks, but the fugitive was nowhere to be found. The FBI followed reports of phantom spottings, vacation-cabin break-ins, and other leads to no avail.

The *AJC* ran a series of articles marking the anniversary of the Birmingham clinic killing. In one, Ron Martz likened the search for Rudolph to the Vietnam War. He compared the alleged bomber with the resourceful and elusive Viet Cong, who powerful American military forces could not defeat. Also, as in the Southeast Asia conflict, Washington officials would drop in every so often to buck up the law enforcement troops. Louie Freeh had visited North Carolina twice.

Scruggs officially returned from medical leave in April. But with little to report and her physical pain acute, her workload was light. By that point, following an unsuccessful appeal by Canfield, Judge Mather gave Scruggs and Martz sixty days to reveal their sources. At the top of the paper, the publisher, Roger Kintzel, supported the reporters. "We believe in your integrity and your honesty, and we believe that everything you have done has been in the best interest of all of us," he wrote to Martz. "You should know—and I have told Kathy this—that we continue to stand behind you with all the determination we had more than two years ago when the suit was filed."

In early June, with Scruggs and Martz continuing to stand firm, the judge ordered them to jail for contempt. *AJC* lawyers immediately appealed, buying time. Other news organizations—including the *New York Times*, the *Washington Post*, and *ABC News*—rushed in to back the reporters, arguing that First Amendment rights were at stake. Scruggs found the proceedings exhausting.

Her days at the paper were often spent outside Atlanta, and as part of a southeast reporting unit, her infrequent articles often bore the dateline of surrounding states. In August, she wrote a short piece about a meteor passing by eastern Alabama and western Georgia. A few days later, her byline topped a story about a Tennessee arsonist who torched a barn, angry over an early-childhood program for immigrants. In late September, she returned to Alabama for a feature about a man who was murdered when someone placed a bomb on his lawnmower. For the December 31 paper, Scruggs wrote a roundup of terrorism risks at New Year's celebrations across the southeast. Professionally, it was her least productive year since college.

Scruggs had begun to wonder whether she had a future in journalism. She took stock of her credentials for a possible career shift, a fresh start. For some time, she had been consuming anything she could read about behavioral science, layering onto her interviews of Robert Ressler and John Douglas, two of the biggest stars in the field. She was well versed in much of the surveillance, disguise, and wiretap literature. At home, she would watch *CSI*, *Law and Order*, and other crime dramas. From there, it was a short leap to imagining herself as a private investigator. She had begun taking an evening class.

In late January 2000, Scruggs and Martz marked the two-year anniversary of the Birmingham bombing with a catch-up piece. Law enforcement questioned if Rudolph was still alive. "My gut instinct is that he is still there, in a cave, and he's dead. That's only my opinion," they quoted one former ATF director saying. An FBI supervisor who had run the UNABOM task force disagreed, contending that people had said similar things about the Unabomber during long stretches between attacks. "It's not good enough to say he's dead and go home," the FBI supervisor told the reporters.

THAT SAME MONTH, JEWELL and Bobi joined Dana's family for a belated Christmas celebration at her parents' house. Dana, sensing that her relationship with Jewell had reached a decision point, already had cautioned him not to propose to her in public. With her tendency toward anxiety, she worried.

During the celebration Jewell excused himself at one point, slipping out of the room. When he returned, Dana was sitting in a chair. Dressed in jeans and an orange golf shirt, he knelt, and she caught on immediately. "Oh no, you're not," she gasped. "You're not doing that here. No, no."

Undaunted, Jewell continued. "I know you didn't want to do it in front of anybody. But, I feel like your family and my family, we're all in this together and we all love each other. I want to spend the rest of my life with you. Will you marry me?" He presented her with his grandmother's wedding band until they could select an engagement ring together. All three of their parents looked on with joyful tears. Jewell and Dana set the date for September 29 at the Storys' faith home, the New Hope Baptist Church in Fayetteville, just south of Atlanta.

BY SUMMER, THE PROSPECTS of catching Eric Rudolph had continued to dim. There had not been a single sighting in the year since Nordmann had reported the fugitive's appearance. Scruggs wrote a piece for the July 1, 2000, paper that captured the state of play. The headline said, RUDOLPH NOWHERE TO BE FOUND OR TALKED ABOUT.

> As the name of Eric Robert Rudolph fades from the lips and minds of the people in western North Carolina, law enforcement remain convinced the accused bomber still is hiding under their noses, even as federal investigators all but end their presence in the area.
>
> "There is no reason to believe he's not here," said Capt. Bob Scott of the Macon County, N.C., sheriff's department, which polices much of the search area for the elusive Rudolph. "There have been no other bombings and it was the last place he was seen."
>
> By Friday, federal agents had cut their staff to about a dozen and completed their move from a large vacated Andrews, N.C., textile plant to space at the National Guard Armory. The manhunt once had involved upwards of 200 federal agents, Georgia Corrections officers and GBI agents.
>
> "It's forgotten about," said Peggy Ellison, owner of the Lake's End Grill in the Nantahala. "Nobody mentions it anymore, unless tourists come in and see my sign."
>
> The sign—"We Survived the Rudolph Manhunt 1998–1999– 2000?"—is the last reminder in the restaurant that was once the central gathering place for searchers and reporters.

Rudolph slipped into oblivion on Jan. 30, 1998, a day after he was allegedly seen shedding a blond wig and jumping into his pickup truck moments after a bomb exploded at an abortion clinic in Birmingham.

When investigators arrived at the trailer Rudolph was renting in Murphy, N.C., the movie "Kull the Conqueror," a fantasy about barbarians fighting in caves, was still in his VCR. Books about "tunnel rats" in Vietnam and aerial photographs of the area were also found, authorities said.

Mine and cave expert Darren Freed of Hendersonville, N.C., has been looking for Rudolph since September 1998, and the federal government is paying his expenses. Freed has documented more than 1,000 gold, silver, sapphire and ruby mines in the area—most of which remain unsearched.

"I don't think he'll be another D. B. Cooper," Freed said. "I think he will eventually be found, and this will eventually be a movie. I just wish it had closure."

Scruggs shared his wish, but her optimism was fading.

A couple of months later, George Hamilton's phone rang. On the other end of the line, Scruggs's cousin, Bentley, had an edge to her voice: "George, have you heard from Kathy?" "No." That wasn't unusual. They had remained friends, but Scruggs had pushed him away after his marriage and her illness. Now, Bentley hadn't heard from her either. Since Hamilton lived closer to Scruggs's Woodstock home, would he check on her? Full of worry, Hamilton made the drive to the distant northwest suburb where she now lived.

The door to her split-level house was closed but unlocked, so he walked in, calling her name. Sadie, Scruggs's beloved Rottweiler, raced to him. The lights in the house were on, but the mess in the kitchen told him something wasn't right. Milk sat on the counter, food was left out, none of it looking fresh. He climbed up to the master bedroom, again summoning, "Kathy." Her bed was unmade. Then he looked in the garage and saw her car. "Oh shit," he whispered. She must be in the house.

"Kathy!" Hamilton repeated aloud desperately as he went room to room. He finally arrived at the hallway bathroom, and pressed against the door.

Resistance. He knew she was on the other side. *Oh God*, he thought, forcing the door open. Scruggs was lying on her back at an angle, wedged between the bathtub and the toilet. Hamilton reached down to check her pulse. She was alive. He called 911.

The first responders took her to nearby Kennestone Hospital. When the ER doctor came out after three A.M., he explained that Scruggs's kidneys had failed. Authorities later determined that she had probably been wedged into that spot where Hamilton found her for three days. Pain pills had overwhelmed her again.

Scruggs remained in intensive care for two weeks. Martz visited, and he could tell she was trying to be upbeat, asking about the newsroom and the latest in his life. But he could see she was struggling. So much of her trademark vivacity had been siphoned away that she was almost a different person.

After she was released, Scruggs pushed herself to heal. She was losing much of her hallmark blonde hair as a result of renal failure, so Bentley took her wig shopping. The trip seemed to lift Scruggs's spirits. The reporter took time to write personal notes. On May 22, her mother Nancy's birthday, Scruggs penned, "Please have a wonderful birthday. Your love is so special to me." The next month, she sent Bubber a Father's Day card. Inside, she handwrote, "You are still my hero. I love you. Kathy."

On a Spring night in 2001 in suburban Dunwoody, Scruggs sat on Bentley's porch, sipping cocktails. The best friends chatted, as they often did, about their family, wild exploits of old, and *All My Children*, Scruggs's favorite soap. Then Bentley repeated a question she'd asked often over the three and a half years since Scruggs had broken the Jewell story. "So, who was your source?"

Scruggs had always wanted to protect her cousin from the clutches of Lin Wood. If Bentley didn't know, the lawyer couldn't squeeze her. But this time, Scruggs paused. Bentley sensed her hesitation. Was she wavering?

Indeed, this time Scruggs didn't shut Bentley down. Instead, she playfully responded, "You would be able to guess. It's a detective on TV, and you lived in Boca."

Bentley thought hard. What would Boca Raton, Florida, have to do with this? She tried to work through the possibilities. TV? Boca? Scruggs tossed out another clue. "It's the name of a TV character."

Then something clicked for Bentley. Crockett and Tubbs, she guessed, the fictional detectives from *Miami Vice*?

Scruggs urged her cousin to think some more.

"Wait, who was that actor?" Bentley puzzled. "You mean Don Johnson?"

Scruggs grinned, sat back, and sipped her drink. Finally, her best friend was in on her most coveted secret. Special Agent Don Johnson had been her source at the bar.

ON JULY 27, 2001, the fifth anniversary of the Olympic Park bombing, the *AJC* ran a front-page update about the tragedy. The paper chronicled Rudolph's disappearance into the Nantahala National Forest, noting that the FBI's price tag for the so far futile search had surpassed $24 million. The piece checked in briefly with a few of the bombing victims before circling back to Rudolph. It made no mention of Richard Jewell.

That evening, Jewell enacted his own bombing remembrance, with a ritual he had begun four years earlier, on the first anniversary. He and Dana climbed into his SUV and drove the hour northeast to Atlanta, speeding as usual. They sat in near silence, the classic rock station switched off. Jewell dressed in his customary T-shirt, jeans, and baseball cap.

They parked near Centennial Park, in a lot that five years earlier had been lined with vendors hawking Olympic swag. Stepping out of the vehicle, Jewell moved purposefully, eager to avoid attention from visitors in the park. He didn't pause to read any commemorative bricks. Instead, he headed directly for the exact location where Alice Hawthorne had been killed. He knew this spot by heart.

Jewell carried a vase with a single red rose and a scrawled note. Silently and tenderly, he kneeled, setting the offering on the ground. Then Jewell bowed his head to pray for the one person in the park he couldn't save that tragic night.

AS THE WEDDING APPROACHED, Dana wanted a large collection of bridesmaids, eleven in all, including Jewell's goddaughter, Heather Dutchess. Jewell chose Dave as his best man, and then drew heavily from his legal team for his side of the wedding party; Watson Bryant was a groomsman, while Lin Wood and Wayne Grant were asked to be ushers. Rob Russell and O'Neill Williams would be in the wedding party as well.

The invited guests included Mike Wallace from *60 Minutes*, who sent a telegram with his regrets. Jewell's criminal lawyer, Jack Martin, couldn't make the event either, but at Jewell's request gave the couple a gift card to Home Depot. Richard Rackleff accepted the invite, making for a rare transition from polygrapher to wedding guest. Such was Jewell's post-bombing life.

Two and a half weeks before the wedding, America was devastated by the tragedy of September 11, 2001. Jewell drove home to be with Dana, eager to be by her side at such an emotional time. The attack also changed a small element of Jewell's wedding plan. He already had ordered his groom's cake, a Southern tradition, with a hunting and fishing motif. After 9/11, he changed the design to an American flag.

Jewell barred the media from the ceremony, arranging for local sheriff's deputies to guard the front and back entrances of the church. With no news cameras or reporters to worry about, he could thoroughly immerse himself in the big day.

By two P.M. on September 29, 2001, one hundred and fifty guests had filed into New Hope Baptist. The bridesmaids walked down the aisle wearing eggplant-colored dresses. Jewell escorted Bobi, then waited for his future wife. Dana grinned broadly as she walked toward him on her father's arm. She wore a formal gown with a full satin train, her brown hair covered with a white lace veil. Dana took her time in the procession, waving and briefly chatting with well-wishers in the pews. When she finally arrived at the altar, she kissed her father and stepped up. Jewell teased her about her Hollywood-style red-carpet walk.

They stood before Rev. Barry Thompson, a minister at Dana's family's church, who coincidentally had been Jewell's youth minister two decades earlier at Brookhaven Baptist Church. Thompson was in on Jewell's first prank. As the couple turned to face the minister, he said, "Dana, Richard wanted me to let you know that everything's going to be OK." Then he opened his Bible to expose an air-sickness bag. Dana looked at Jewell, who whispered, "We got you covered." He then discreetly opened his tuxedo jacket, revealing a second bag. Dana burst out laughing.

The reception downstairs featured a four-tier wedding cake, along with Jewell's American flag groom's cake, and a celebratory table of MoonPies and RC Cola. Poster boards displayed photos of the bride and groom in their separate lives. At center table sat a framed image from the day the Jewells had met. Jewell had merged their two photos from the Luthersville drug bust into one, showing them sitting side by side. The caption read, "The Famous Drug Bust, where they met."

Southern Baptist weddings don't typically feature dancing, but Jewell had insisted on a traditional first dance. Church officials agreed to allow a single song, and in the social room, the Jewells began swaying to Journey's power-ballad "Faithfully." Thirty seconds in—before the song arrived at the time-honored wedding-reception lyric of "I'm forever yours, faithfully"—Dana heard a loud *riiiiip*. Jewell had stepped on the back of her train tearing it away from the gown's bustle. Dana gathered the fabric in her arms and tried to keep going but couldn't. The couple just laughed and cut the dance short.

Later, the Jewells made their way outside, where they were sprinkled with red rose petals and birdseed. As they stepped into the back of the stretch limo, Bobi and Dana's mother already had planted themselves back there, a final joke for the new couple.

IN THE SUMMER OF 2001, Kathy Scruggs had been living through ups and downs. Mostly downs. The pressure of the lawsuit never strayed far from her psyche. The *AJC* had won a major victory when the judge declared Jewell a temporary public figure, raising Wood's legal burden. Now, in addition to needing to prove that Jewell had been defamed by the paper's reporting, he also had to show actual malice in its decision making. Despite the higher hurdle, Scruggs knew the case was far from over. Judge Mather continued to hold her and Martz in contempt for not disclosing their sources. That decision remained on appeal.

Scruggs cloistered herself at her heavily wooded home. She pushed away most of her friends, rarely going out and almost never inviting anyone but family to visit. At times, her depression hit so hard during her mother's visits that Scruggs would leave the living room, walk into her bedroom, and close the door behind her, shutting Nancy out. Social interactions often were limited to her Rottweiler, Sadie.

But during the last week of August, Scruggs phoned her longtime reporter friend, Tony Kiss, who had remained at the Asheville paper. "I'm feeling a lot better," she told him. "I think I can go back to work pretty soon." Over the next day or so, Scruggs made several other check-in calls to family and longtime friends.

Then, on September 2, 2001, Scruggs turned the thermostat in her house to an unusually cold setting. She grabbed some pills to ease her pain and downed them one by one. Three days later, a friend found her lying unconscious in her home. This time, there was no resuscitating her. After an autopsy, the coroner ruled the cause of death as acute morphine toxicity. He listed the manner of death as "Undetermined."

Scruggs was forty-two years old. She would never know of the 9/11 terrorist attacks that occurred the following week. Nor would she learn the fate of the Olympic Park bomber. Her last published story had been the seven-paragraph piece more than a year earlier that had begun, "As the name of Eric Robert Rudolph fades from the lips and minds of the people in western North Carolina . . ."

On a sweltering September 6 afternoon, Kathy Scruggs was buried in a graveside funeral at Oconee Hill Cemetery, in the shadow of the University of Georgia football stadium. The family's longtime minister spoke of Scruggs as bright, brash, outspoken, and gifted. The service was packed with family, journalists, friends, and members of the Atlanta Police Department.

Her parents endowed the Scruggs Family Writing Center at Athens Academy in her honor. Perhaps a future student would win the prizes that she had dreamed of.

CHAPTER 28

In his early years as a fugitive deep in North Carolina's Nantahala National Forest, Eric Rudolph had neared starvation. He would later write about one of his lowest points.

Weak and desperate for food, he had gathered his energy to forage a creek for salamanders. Finding a few, he hungrily slurped them down like slimy spaghetti noodles. The creatures churned in his stomach, adding acute heartburn to his woes. Rudolph wanted to die. Stumbling back to his camp, he happened upon a doe. But the desperate fugitive couldn't muster the strength to raise his rifle in time for the kill and watched as the deer bounded into the woods. Seconds later, Rudolph noticed flies swarming above ferns some thirty yards away. Weakly walking over for a closer look, he saw a fawn dozing on the ground. Less than a week old, he gauged. The animal's head rested peacefully on its petite hooves. *Bambi*, Rudolph thought. Mustering what little energy he had left, Rudolph unsheathed his knife. Pinning the head with his boot and grabbing the fawn by the hind legs, he stretched its body taut and ran his blade across the throat. He carried the bloodied carcass back to his camp, where he gutted it and made a life-saving stew.

By 2003, Rudolph had learned to adjust to the challenges of survival. He gathered rich-in-fat acorns each fall instead of leaving them on the ground to rot. When he could kill a wild turkey, boar, or deer, he cured meats into jerky for later. To enhance his diet with more calcium, Rudolph crushed cooked turkey bones to a powder. During the summers, he stole fruit and vegetables from the outskirts of Nantahala that he could eat or dry.

Eluding the FBI had been a constant preoccupation, especially after George Nordmann reported him. The searchers and helicopters took on the appearance of a full-on military assault. But Rudolph found no shortage of caves, boulders, and dense foliage for hiding. And, as a general strategy, he avoided pathways used by hunters or hikers, which he called the "lines of drift." He kept a pair of Leupold 10x28mm binoculars looped around his neck, and monitored the FBI's movement from well-hidden mountainside perches.

At one point, he built a bomb and considered blowing up the Bureau Command Center at the Armory in Andrews. As the months became years, he watched the task force's numbers dissipate. He buried the IED across the street from the Armory and kept the three hundred or so pounds of dynamite he still had buried in four separate underground caches.

THE PLAQUE IN DON Johnson's home office reflected his new status. The esteemed FBI credentials, which he had carried in his pocket for more than two decades, now declared "RETIRED" in hole-punched lettering. Badge #2364 was out of the field. He had officially opened Johnson Investigations LLC., the company name that had made him the target of the OPR's final inquiry.

Johnson teamed with his former Bureau partner and fellow retiree, Harry Grogan. Leaning on their bank-robbery bona fides, they won an $80,000 contract to review security readiness at the branches of a large Georgia S&L: camera angles, dye-packs, teller training. Similar engagements followed. Johnson was the rainmaker.

One attorney turned to Johnson to salvage a wrongful death case slated for trial. A teenage girl had been rushed to a hospital after a horrific car crash. She died after emergency room personnel left her languishing for hours following a shift change. The wrongful death trial date was approaching, but the attorney hadn't yet conducted some of the key interviews. Johnson saw an opportunity for leverage. He quoted the lawyer his and Grogan's usual hourly rates, then proposed alternate terms: We'll do the interviews and if you lose the case, you pay us nothing. But if you win, we get triple our normal fee. The attorney agreed. The former agents found the witnesses, and the case settled for nearly a million dollars. Johnson and Grogan garnered hefty paychecks.

In his personal life, Johnson was a regular at the Foghorn Grill, a suburban watering hole he'd found soon after moving south to Atlanta. Johnson rarely spoke about work but was known by the regulars as "FBI Don." He would grab a booth, often with Dick Ottman, a fellow Upstate New Yorker and retired Kraft Foods sales manager. The men drank, smoked, and talked sports and the state of the world. The only FBI topic they ever discussed was the case of Richard Jewell, who the agent referred to as "that little fat fucker." In the years following the bombing, Johnson told Ottman that the case against Jewell was "airtight." Others at the Bureau wouldn't listen, the retired agent lamented. Without elaboration, he blamed the *AJC* for screwing things up. When Eric Rudolph was charged in the Olympic bombing, Johnson blurted to Ottman, "That's bullshit."

Eventually, Cynthia Johnson learned that her husband had also struck up another close relationship at Foghorn's, with a woman named Paula. It was not his first affair. Cynthia was furious. The two separated, and Johnson moved out of the family home and into a nearby townhouse. Paula moved in.

Marriage was not the only bond Johnson broke. He and his investigative partner, Grogan, were asked by a former Assistant U.S. Attorney to meet about a potentially lucrative engagement on a new case. Work had begun to dry up for the two former agents, and tapping into the network of ex-AUSAs in private practice would open a new avenue of possibilities. They discussed the appointment for days. Johnson would leave his townhouse back door unlocked so that they could meet in advance. Then Grogan would drive, as he had when they were FBI partners.

Grogan arrived on the designated morning, uncharacteristically running a bit late. He let himself in, expecting to see his former partner shaved, dressed, and ready to go. But Johnson wasn't downstairs. Grogan yelled up, "Don, we gotta get going." His partner shouted back, "I'm not going." Grogan was shocked. "What do you mean you're not going?" Silence. Grogan considered pushing back, but he knew his former partner's tone and stubbornness well enough to recognize the answer was final. Livid, Grogan returned to his car and sped to the meeting alone. He didn't get the work. It was the last conversation the two men would ever have.

Johnson's health worsened. In late 2001, his breathing became significantly more labored and routine exercise was difficult. Doctors diagnosed him with emphysema and COPD, assigning him a regimen of inhalers and pills along with light treadmill walking. They urged him to quit smoking, but he lasted only weeks before drifting back to what had become a two-pack-a-day habit.

When Christmas arrived in 2002, the usually stoic Johnson took stock of his life, then broke down and openly wept in front of one of his sons. The relationship with his boys had fractured after his permanent separation from Cynthia. His FBI career, once a source of pride, had dissolved in a muddle of internal investigations. The retirement that followed had been a disappointment, in part because of his declining health. In early 2003, Johnson's lungs were so strained that doctors prescribed an oxygen tank. Despite that, Johnson continued to frequent Foghorn's, bringing along his cigarettes but not his oxygen. Ottman, well aware of his friend's medical condition, asked why he was still smoking. Johnson just shrugged and offered a fatalistic, "We all gotta die from something."

On a mid-March evening, his son Don II swung by to say hello. Their relationship had turned icy after Johnson left Cynthia. But as the years passed, the two men gradually reconnected. The father was frail, but animated. He had just visited Home Depot, and enthusiastically displayed a plan to remodel his kitchen with new counters, cabinets, and appliances. He even thought he might do much of the work himself. Don II's mind flashed back to their days together in Upstate New York, when his father would help build Pinewood Derby cars. A few days later, Johnson's youngest son, Brian, stopped by. This time, the elder Johnson was shivering, wrapped in a blanket as they watched Duke play Central Michigan in the NCAA tournament.

The next day, Sunday, March 23, 2003, Don Johnson died of a COPD-related heart attack at the age of fifty-seven. Six and a half years had passed since the Olympic Park bombing, five since his retirement from the Bureau. Johnson was cremated, and there was no service. His three sons gathered at an Atlanta bar to raise a glass to their father—nothing fancy, very short, just as Johnson would have wanted. Later, Johnson's youngest sister had a single brick placed at Bethlehem Veterans Memorial Park outside Albany, New York. It read "Donald Johnson—Vietnam War—Sergeant."

There was no mention of the FBI.

CHAPTER 29

In the pre-dawn hours of Saturday, May 30, 2003, a rookie cop named Jeff Postell was well into his overnight patrol in Murphy, North Carolina. The graveyard shift had been uneventful in the gateway to the Nantahala, a few traffic stops, a few calls. It was a slow start to the weekend.

Postell had been on the job for less than a year, the newest member of the five-person Murphy force. He had been so eager to become an officer that he put himself through the police academy so that he could be sworn in just days after he turned twenty-one, the minimum for the Murphy squad. In the ten months since, he had established a reputation as a hard-working, zealous officer. Postell handled graveyard shifts.

Shortly before 3:30 A.M., the officer pulled behind a Save-A-Lot grocery store for a standard business check. He turned off his lights and would restore them once he rounded the corner. Postell always liked to vary his routine, not set a pattern.

As Postell turned into the alley, he spotted a gaunt dark-haired man crouched down on the pavement. A prowler, Postell figured, or maybe a breaking-and-entering criminal. The man scrambled behind a stack of milk crates near the loading dock. Postell flicked on his patrol car's alley lights and pulled to a stop. When he saw what he thought was a gun, the officer called for backup, then swung open his car door to use as a shield. Crouching behind it, he drew his own weapon and yelled, "Come out. Put your hands where I can see 'em."

The man put up no resistance, obeying Postell's commands first to emerge from behind the crates, then to drop to the ground and put his hands behind him. Postell cuffed him. The arrestee was dressed in a fatigue jacket, black T-shirt, dark pants, and worn Adidas sneakers. The object in his hands wasn't a gun at all, but a long black flashlight. He told the officer his name was Jerry Wilson but soon enough the Murphy Police Department figured out otherwise.

Five years and four months after being identified by law enforcement following the Birmingham bombing, Eric Robert Rudolph was now in custody.

As the world soon would learn, Rudolph, despite a reputation as a vaunted survivalist, had been living as a homeless dumpster-diver, albeit a resourceful one. For the past three summers, his routine had been to set up a small temporary camp in the woods outside Murphy. Then, late at night, he would sneak into town to sort through refuse at places like Save-A-Lot, mainly for fruits, vegetables, and meats. He would dry and cure them for the lean months ahead. Later, agents would find remnants of other items Rudolph had plucked from Murphy's commercial trash, including copies of magazines, *USA Today*, history books, even a Taco Bell uniform.

The national media and satellite trucks descended on Murphy by the score. News stations broke into their regular programming for special reports.

Hours after the arrest, the FBI led a press conference. Nineteen minutes into the briefing, the baby-faced officer, Jeff Postell, returned from his home where he had gone to get some sleep. A reporter yelled out, "Can Officer Postell tell us about this morning?" Dressed in his blue short-sleeved Murphy Police Department summer uniform, Postell stepped to the bank of microphones with a casual "How ya doing? How are ya?" The media horde asked a series of questions as the officer factually and humbly described Rudolph's uneventful arrest. One reporter pressed, asking how it felt to capture one of the nation's most wanted fugitives. Postell offered a reply that echoed another hero from nine years earlier: "I'm just glad I was out there doing my job and was glad I was in the right place at the right time."

The next day's headline in the *AJC* trumpeted FINALLY CAUGHT in bold type. Just above it, the paper ran four photos, one from each of the terrorist attacks Rudolph was accused of committing, starting with Centennial Olympic Park. Kathy Scruggs was no longer around to cover the news, but her former colleagues already were churning the first of dozens of that month's stories about Rudolph.

On June 2, 2003, Rudolph made his first appearance in the Alabama court. The judge appointed Richard Jaffe to lead the defendant's death-penalty defense in Birmingham. The attorney, who was Jewish, had agreed to take the assignment despite Rudolph's visceral anti-Semitic views. Jaffe, who had deep experience in capital cases, strongly opposed the death penalty and was a stalwart defender of the indigent. Later, at Rudolph's Atlanta arraignment, a judge appointed the Federal Defenders Program to represent him. Paul Kish, a tenacious and talented attorney in that office, would assume the lead.

AT THE TIME OF Rudolph's arrest, Jewell was just beginning a new job. He had signed on as a police sergeant with the Pendergrass Police Department, about an hour north of Atlanta. The police chief, Rob Russell, had convinced him to take the position. It would mark their fourth time working together.

Pendergrass was even smaller than Luthersville, with only 450 residents and five police officers. Historically, the city had experienced little violent crime, but it held two claims to fame. On weekends, visitors from around northeast Georgia flocked to the town for its self-proclaimed "world's largest indoor flea market." And the year before, Pendergrass had led the state in per-capita revenue from fines, fees, and forfeitures. In other words, it was a very successful speed trap. But that didn't bother Jewell, who still loved road duty.

When Jewell arrived, Russell handed him the keys to a new police cruiser, a white Ford LTD. Since the town's new bypass road had recently experienced a series of injury crashes, Russell decided to add large yellow lettering to the back of the vehicle: Traffic Crash Reduction Unit. Both men chuckled over the irony that the car would now be driven by Jewell, given the new sergeant's history of wrecks.

Jewell's first year and a half were mostly consumed with the typical crime of a small town: wrecks, a few crack cocaine arrests, an occasional break-in. That all changed on December 29, 2004.

On a crisp Wednesday evening, Jewell's fellow officer on the force, Christopher Ruse, spotted a GMC Sierra pickup with a burned-out headlight going 68 mph in a 55 mph zone. The forty-seven-year-old former Marine flashed on his blue lights, and the driver pulled over. But as Ruse approached, the driver sped off. Ruse ran back to his car, radioed in a "10-80" chase, and took off after the fleeing vehicle. Hearing the report, Jewell turned on his own lights and siren and raced from the opposite direction to intercept the driver. But as the pickup approached, the driver swerved and zoomed by Jewell, as did Ruse. Jewell quickly turned around and joined the high-speed pursuit.

Within minutes, the driver of the pickup hit a slight bend in the road and lost control of the vehicle. The truck flipped upside down off the side of the road. Ruse screeched to a halt. Following protocol, Jewell stopped directly behind him, using his fellow officer's cruiser as cover. Neither policeman had any way of knowing that the truck's passenger, Richard Whitaker, had outstanding arrest warrants in two counties. Nor did they know he routinely carried a .45-caliber semiautomatic pistol and a 9mm semiautomatic handgun.

Jewell approached the driver's side of the overturned vehicle, Ruse the other side. Jewell, with his weapon drawn, barked at the driver, "Let me see your hands." Suddenly, several shots rang out. Jewell glanced to his left to see Ruse fall. He handcuffed the driver as quickly as he could, then raced to check on Ruse. By then the shooter had fled into the nearby woods.

Jewell frantically tried to administer first aid. But there was nothing he could do. Ruse was lying flat on his back, his face and mustache covered in blood, which had begun pooling beneath his head. The shooter had hit the officer dead center, the large-caliber bullet entering through the tip of the officer's nose and coursing through his brain.

Officer Christopher Ruse was rushed to a nearby hospital. He would soon be pronounced dead.

AT THREE A.M., JEWELL sat in Russell's Pendergrass Police car at the end of a subdivision cul-de-sac. Russell cut the motor. The street held the silence of a rural small town, the moon full, the night clear.

For a long while, the two friends sat in pained silence, trying to cope with what Russell called "forever devastation," the kind one never fully gets over. What-ifs filled their minds. Could Jewell somehow have gotten there a few seconds sooner? Should they have spotted the shooter's gun? What if Ruse had run toward the driver's door instead? What will happen now to the slain officer's wife and kids?

When Jewell and Russell eventually began to speak, their talk turned to God and the afterlife, still more full of questions than answers. Why did Chris have to die? How does a soul even get to heaven? How long until Chris would be looking down on them, or was he already?

Finally, in his grief and anger, Jewell reached down and unbuckled his gun belt. He tossed it aside. Then he reached to his chest and removed his badge. He let that fall too. "Fuck this," Jewell spat. "What are we doing this shit for?"

For so long, he had wanted nothing more than to wear the uniform, to be a police officer. Now Richard Jewell questioned why.

BY MARCH 2005, MUCH had changed in the U.S. Attorney's Office in Atlanta. Dave Nahmias, who years before was the most junior prosecutor on the CENTBOM team, had assumed the Atlanta office's top role. Sally Yates had become Nahmias's First Assistant U.S. Attorney and managed the office's Rudolph prosecution. In Birmingham, U.S. Attorney Alice Martin had succeeded Doug Jones as her office prepared for that upcoming trial. The Birmingham case, based on the strength of the eyewitness sightings of Rudolph, would go first. The judge had set the trial for May, just two months away.

The FBI's evidence trove was massive, based on years of investigating Rudolph and his four attacks. In the Birmingham probe and Rudolph hunt, the number of 302s had reached seventeen thousand. The Atlanta bombings had generated more than double that. There were thousands of potential exhibits at trial tying each bombing to Rudolph, including rocket igniters recovered from the defendant's campsite. Also, dozens of witnesses were prepared to testify to the bomber's hatred, motives, specialized military training, and voice—the same voice they recognized from the Centennial Park 911 call.

The forensics work of the Bureau and what had become the consolidated Southeast Task Force was especially powerful. They solidly linked specific components of the various devices to show the bombings were the work of a single man, namely Eric Rudolph: Radio Shack product #278–567 wire; Shuford Company model #PC-618 duct tape; oxyacetylene-torch-cut Gallatin Steel plates from a single production run; Rubbermaid-brand food containers with almond-colored polyethylene lids and clear polypropylene bases; and trace amounts of identically matching nitroglycerin.

But the government knew that the smallest and hardest-to-find pieces of evidence could be most compelling for a jury.

Agents had hand-sorted hundreds of thousands of postal money order receipts, hoping to find one that would link Rudolph to bomb-making. They knew he commonly used that payment form to avoid having his purchases traced. Ultimately, the strategy paid off. Investigators uncovered a money order in Rudolph's own handwriting under the name "Z Randolp." He had used it to order a manual titled *Kitchen Improvised Fertilizer Explosives*. When the government subpoenaed the publisher's records, it learned that the title may never have been sent, but another was: *Ragnar's Homemade Detonators: How to Make 'Em, How to Salvage 'Em, How to Detonate 'Em*. The company had mailed it directly to Rudolph's P.O. Box in Topton, North Carolina.

Rudolph's attorneys, though, planned to mount a vigorous defense after reviewing the seven hundred thousand pages of discovery produced by the prosecutors. While the government's evidence was plentiful, almost all of it was circumstantial, especially in the Olympic bombing case.

Atlanta federal defender Paul Kish settled on a two-pronged defense strategy. First, he would invite the jury to play a variation of the children's game "Where's Waldo?" Could jurors spot Rudolph's face in any of the thousands of still photos and hundreds of hours of video the FBI had gathered from the night of the bombing? Given the Bureau's repeated requests for help, he knew the answer would be no. Second, Kish would argue that there was far more evidence that Richard Jewell was the Olympic bomber than Eric Rudolph. The Bureau had devoted thousands of hours to proving that the security guard was the perpetrator. Indeed, even after the non-target letter was issued, the word had been that some agents remained unwavering in their belief that Jewell was either the bomber or complicit in the attack.

Behind the scenes, there had been discussions between prosecutors and defense attorneys of a plea deal, but no real movement. Once an Attorney General signs off on pursuing the death penalty, as John Ashcroft had done two years before, the current Attorney General would have to personally reverse it. With no mitigating circumstances and an unrepentant defendant, there was little chance that Attorney General Alberto Gonzales would do so.

Until the dynamite.

The government had long suspected Rudolph of stealing the roughly 340 pounds of nitroglycerin dynamite from the Austin Powder Company in December 1996. Experts from Quantico and ATF had concluded that Rudolph had used only thirty pounds of it in his post-Olympics bombings. They also pointed out that nitroglycerin becomes more volatile over time. Atlanta U.S. Attorney Nahmias wanted to know for certain if Rudolph was responsible for the theft and, if so, where he had hidden the remaining explosives.

As soon as Paul Kish learned of the U.S. Attorney's inquiry, he and a fellow federal defender drove two hours west to Birmingham to see Rudolph. They had represented the defendant since his arrest two years earlier, and had never heard of additional dynamite.

The lawyers met with Rudolph in his private prison suite at the Jefferson County jail, with the Birmingham defense attorneys joining in. Their client, now pale from lack of sun and almost pudgy from free-flowing food, sat on one side of the stainless steel table; the Atlanta attorneys sat on the other. Kish was all business.

Did Rudolph steal the hundreds of pounds of dynamite as the government claimed? "Yeah, I stole the dynamite," he replied, as if it were manifestly obvious. He also knew exactly where he'd hidden every stick of it. Rudolph had other news too. He had built a bomb that he once considered detonating at the FBI search headquarters in Andrews, North Carolina. In fact, he had often sat hidden on a nearby bluff watching agents come and go. He specifically mentioned seeing Sally Yates there, who he recognized from news accounts. "I could have killed her too," Rudolph told Kish.

The lawyer realized that he now had a solid bargaining chip for plea negotiations. Kish called Yates with news of the dynamite's existence, though not the unwitting peril she had been in. Yates already knew the risk of the aging explosives, having traveled to Quantico for a full briefing. She and Nahmias both feared that an unsuspecting Boy Scout camping in the Nantahala National Forest could pick the wrong spot to drive in a tent stake and blow up himself. With the Birmingham trial coming up, plea negotiations started in earnest.

Led by Yates, the government struck a tentative plea deal. Rudolph would be required to help them locate all the dynamite, which would then have to be rendered safe. In exchange, prosecutors would seek permission from the Justice Department to drop the death penalty case so that Rudolph would be sentenced to life without the possibility of parole. The government checked in with the victims. All eventually assented, though Emily Lyons, who had gone through seventeen surgeries, was especially reluctant.

Kish returned to Birmingham, bringing topographic maps and a colleague who was an avid hiker. The criminal defense attorney was flabbergasted at Rudolph's ability to recall with absolute precision where he had buried four separate stashes of dynamite. He cited streams, boulders, and tree trunks from memory. Rudolph also pinpointed the spot where he had buried the bomb intended for the FBI. It was fifty yards off a road directly across from the Armory that had housed the search headquarters.

The defense and prosecution were ready to move forward with the deal, but the Justice Department's Capital Crimes Section stood firm, offering the bottom-line reply "We don't negotiate with terrorists." Nahmias called Christopher Wray, the Assistant Attorney General who oversaw the Criminal Division. The two men had forged a friendship as prosecutors in Atlanta, both reporting to Yates after Alexander hired them. Later, Nahmias had served in Washington as Wray's chief deputy. During the call, Nahmias outlined the rationale, specifically the risk of having increasingly unstable dynamite buried throughout the Nantahala. Wray fully appreciated the logic, but suggested that they let the internal DOJ process run its course.

The decision unfolded just as the men hoped. The AG's Capital Review Committee soon agreed that prosecutors should be allowed to withdraw the notice to seek the death penalty. Wray then signed off, passing the recommendation up to Deputy Attorney General Jim Comey, who agreed as well, and forwarded the paperwork to Gonzalez. The Attorney General approved the recommendation. Rudolph would plead guilty and live out his remaining years in prison.

ON APRIL 13, 2005, Eric Rudolph appeared in federal court in Birmingham for his plea dressed in an orange jumpsuit. The week before, officials had located and rendered safe the buried dynamite, with five massive explosions throughout western North Carolina.

Rudolph watched as prosecutors outlined the "factual basis," the evidence they would have presented at trial. At the conclusion, U.S. District Judge Lynwood Smith asked the defendant if the government had proved its case in the bombing of a Birmingham women's clinic. "Just barely, your honor," Rudolph replied.

"But let me just cut to the chase," the judge said. "Did you plant the bomb that exploded at the New Woman All Women clinic?"

"I certainly did, your honor." Observers couldn't miss his smirk. Soon after, Judge Smith declared, "The defendant is now adjudged guilty."

Several hours later, the spotlight moved to Atlanta, where Rudolph was scheduled to plead guilty to the other three bombings. A line formed late that morning at the downtown Richard B. Russell Federal Office Building. It was the same stark white, twenty-three-story structure that housed the SBA, where Richard Jewell and Watson Bryant had worked together two decades earlier. Later, in 1996, Jewell's lawyers had trumpeted his successful polygraph from the building's plaza.

Just after lunch, a crowd swelled in the atrium outside the courtroom. Nearly nine years had passed since the frantic days of the Olympic Park bombing, followed by the Sandy Springs and Otherside Lounge blasts. Agents, prosecutors, media, and victims all wanted a look at Eric Rudolph, finally in shackles. Richard Jewell walked off the elevator, slim and tanned, in pleated khakis and a pale blue button-down shirt. He and Dana were holding hands as they moved into an overflow room to watch the proceedings on a live video feed.

Rudolph entered the courtroom having changed into a gray suit and open-collared shirt. He appeared calm and noncombative. As at that morning's hearing in Birmingham, the proceeding was designed for prosecutors to state the factual basis. Yates had assigned three Assistant U.S. Attorneys to handle the government's showing. Victim statements would come at a sentencing hearing months later.

But the first AUSA, Phyllis Sumner, surprised both the prosecution and the defense with an unusually dramatic presentation of the Centennial Park bombing's harm to the victims. She told the judge of shrapnel spraying in every direction; more than one hundred seriously injured victims requiring hospital treatment; the Turkish journalist dying of a heart attack. In addressing Alice Hawthorne's death, Sumner made a sweeping gesture toward the victim's daughter, Fallon, who was in the courtroom.

At the defense table, Rudolph grew increasingly agitated watching Sumner personalize the case. Sitting next to him, lawyer Paul Kish knew Rudolph's temperament, and he began to worry that the bomber would back out of the plea if the government continued in the same accusatory tone. Kish shot a glance at Yates, who had already grasped the situation. She whispered to AUSA John Horn seated to her right to tone it down during his presentation, and scrawled a note to the youngest AUSA on the team, Joey Burby, who was sitting at the far end of counsel's table. Be "flat and boring," Yates instructed. "No emotion."

In the overflow room down the hall, Jewell was suddenly reliving the Olympic Park bombing as he watched the closed-circuit TV. He gritted his teeth, his face reddening, fists clenched. His body shook. He was nearing hyperventilation. "Richard, you gotta calm down," Dana whispered, fearing a heart attack. "*You gotta calm down.*" The only saving grace, she thought, was that they weren't in the same room as Rudolph. She believed her husband may well have leapt up and charged at him.

Within a few minutes, the drama subsided in both rooms. AUSA Horn offered up a straightforward recitation of the case the government was prepared to make in the Sandy Springs and Otherside Lounge bombings. Then AUSA Burby, in outlining the ties between Rudolph's Birmingham bombing and the Atlanta attacks, delivered what would become renowned as the most boring factual basis in the history of high-profile cases in the Northern District of Georgia.

Rudolph had calmed down, and the hearing proceeded to conclusion. Judge Charles Pannell asked the defendant, "Are you guilty of these charges?" Rudolph replied simply: "I am."

The Jewells rode the elevator down to the lobby, again walking out hand in hand. The media swarmed, splitting the couple apart and giving Dana her first glimpse of the 1996 life Jewell had endured. Grudgingly, he paused to tell the journalists, "Now everybody in the whole world knows that he did do it. He said it in court."

Then the Jewells walked out into the Atlanta sunshine and climbed into his SUV. As he merged onto the interstate, Jewell glanced in the rearview mirror with a paranoia that still lingered. This time, there were no cameras, no unmarked cars following him.

Relieved, he stepped on the gas and busted through the speed limit.

No longer a suspect, Richard Jewell—husband, son, officer, hero—was headed home.

Richard Jewell chose not to attend either of Eric Rudolph's sentencings. He had no desire to ever lay eyes on the man again.

In Atlanta, thirteen victims spoke during the proceeding, while others submitted written statements. They told the terrorist and court of their permanent physical, emotional, and financial injuries: severed nerves, broken bones, hearing loss, amnesia, seizures, depression, lost jobs, and insolvency. When John Hawthorne, Alice's husband, stood, he described the nine years since his wife's murder as "a long, continuous night of weeping." The day of the hearing would have marked their eighteenth wedding anniversary.

The judge sentenced Rudolph to four consecutive life terms plus 120 years with no possibility of parole. In Birmingham, the judge there added two more life sentences. The serial bomber has been imprisoned ever since at the supermax penitentiary in Florence, Colorado, often called the "Alcatraz of the Rockies." Rudolph was assigned to the same prison area as Unabomber Ted Kaczynski.

The 1996 Games fortunately left behind plenty that was positive. The Olympic Village was converted to thousands of college dorm rooms on the Georgia Tech campus. The former Olympic Stadium became the home of the Atlanta Braves for two decades and has since morphed again into the Georgia State University football stadium.

But by far the most striking physical legacy has been Centennial Olympic Park. Renovated several times since the Games, the park has become one of the city's most popular outdoor venues. Events, often free and open to the public, have ranged from a Dalai Lama address on "inner disarmament" to the annual fireworks extravaganzas that light up the Fourth of July skies. The park also has catalyzed a vibrant renewal of the formerly down-and-out sector of the city. The Georgia Aquarium, World of Coke, College Football Hall of Fame, and National Center for Civil and Human Rights all now adjoin the twenty-one-acre site.

Inside the park stands a bronze statue of Billy Payne holding an Olympic torch. The man who first dreamed of bringing the Olympics to Atlanta later was chosen to chair Augusta National Golf Club, host of the Masters. Near Payne's statue, the fan-shape sculpture depicting three eras of Olympians still bears shrapnel marks from the blast. A few blocks from the park, the City of Atlanta erected a statue of Andy Young, the man who in many ways was the linchpin in turning the Olympic dream into a reality.

There is no statue, plaque, or marker for Richard Jewell. Former ACOG official A.D. Frazier speaks of the Jewell episode as "an unfortunate but convenient myth." Convenient for law enforcement that got its suspect. Convenient for the media that got its story. Convenient for Olympics organizers who could move the Games forward with fans and athletes believing the bomber had been safely cornered. Convenient for everyone but Richard Jewell.

In the internet age, the *Atlanta Journal-Constitution* has struggled like most of America's metro newspapers. Its current staff numbers 140 journalists, well shy of half the total number of *AJC* and other Cox reporters assigned to cover the Games in 1996. John Walter, Thomas Oliver, and Bert Roughton all retired from the paper. But each held firm to his belief that the *AJC* made the right decision to print Kathy Scruggs's initial scoop. Scruggs's writing partner, Ron Martz, taught a college ethics course for several years, using the bombing case and decision to publish as a highlight of his curriculum. The former staffers' views on journalistic integrity notwithstanding, to a person they have empathized with the plight of Jewell and his mother. "Of course, I feel bad for his mom," Roughton told us. "There's a part of me that would love to buy her roses every week for the rest of her life."

LIN WOOD, JEWELL'S LEAD libel attorney, continued his client's lawsuit against the *AJC* until 2012, largely at his own expense. In January of that year, the Georgia Supreme Court let stand a lower court decision that the stories by Scruggs, Martz, and others were not libelous. The lower court reasoned: "[B]ecause the articles in their entirety were substantially true at the time they were published—even though the investigators' suspicions were ultimately unfounded—they cannot form the basis of a defamation action." In other words, truth was a defense. Dave Kindred's column connecting Jewell to serial killer Wayne Williams was, the court wrote, "'loose, figurative language'" and could not reasonably be viewed as stating actual facts about Jewell himself.

Along the way, Wood parted ways with his longtime partner, Wayne Grant, and ascended to the ranks of the nation's preeminent defamation attorneys. His clients have included the parents of JonBenét Ramsey, who were wrongfully implicated in the murder of the child beauty queen. Watson Bryant, the earliest defender of Richard Jewell, married Nadya Light and continues to be a sole practitioner. He and Bobi Jewell signed movie deals with Warner Bros. for their life stories. Jack Martin remains a highly respected criminal defense attorney who late in his career has continued to take on death penalty cases.

The Jewell family did achieve one additional legal victory, despite the loss to the *AJC*: Bobi sued the federal government over her ruined Tupperware and other items damaged or missing from the search. She received a check for $2,500. Watson Bryant keeps an enlarged framed copy in his office.

THE KEY LAW ENFORCEMENT players in the Jewell saga all moved on. Former Special Agents Woody Johnson and Dave Maples joined forces to open a small private security firm where they worked for years. For a short time, Di Rosario joined them. Merrick Garland, the Justice Department attorney who fielded the first call from Atlanta about the mishandling of Miranda, was nominated by President Barack Obama to become an associate justice of the U.S. Supreme Court. With a presidential election on the horizon, albeit distantly, his name never reached the Senate floor for a vote.

On January 30, 2017, ten days after Donald Trump was inaugurated as the nation's forty-fifth president, he fired acting Attorney General Sally Yates for insubordination when she refused to enforce a travel ban aimed at predominantly Muslim countries. Yates had served for twenty-seven years as a federal prosecutor, including stints as U.S. Attorney in Atlanta and as Deputy Attorney General. Several months later, the president also fired FBI Director Jim Comey, who more than a decade before had signed off on the Rudolph plea agreement. Trump then appointed as the new Director Chris Wray, who also had approved the plea deal.

AFTER RUDOLPH'S SENTENCING IN 2005, Richard and Dana Jewell bought a 26.6-acre spread in middle Georgia. They named it Black Sheep Farm. The land was cheap, the deer hunting bountiful, and a large pond on the property's edge teemed with catfish and bass. The Jewells kept eight dogs, five cats, and a goat named Billy, who Jewell loved to wrestle.

Jewell remained trim and continued to grow his collections, often to near-hoarder levels. Dozens of fishing rods. More than a hundred guns for hunting and target practice. Nearly two thousand law enforcement and first responder matchbox-size vehicles. Sometimes he splurged on one-off items, like a thirty-pound bronze of Lady Justice, blindfolded and holding a set of scales aloft. For one birthday, Dana gave Jewell a thermometer backed by a large image of Barney Fife. Jewell laughed and nailed it onto a post of his work shed behind their home.

But Jewell continued to lose weight, for the wrong reasons. He was diabetic and had developed a heart condition borne of the disease, genetics, and bad diet, then exacerbated by stress. Doctor visits became frequent, and for a time Jewell took a disability leave from his job at the Meriwether County Sheriff's Office, which he had joined to be closer to home. At one point, he had a toe amputated due to a severe infection. Dana stayed on him about his diet, but Jewell confided to Dave Dutchess during one of their phone calls that he kept Dairy Queen sundaes hidden in the freezer.

On August 29, 2007, Dana called the house from work to make sure her husband was awake for a doctor's appointment. When he didn't answer either the home phone or his cell, she rushed back to the house. Dana arrived to find the dogs howling. One of them, a chocolate Lab named Duke, led her back to the bedroom. There, her husband sat motionless on the floor, leaning against the couple's armoire with a peaceful smile gracing his face. Richard Allensworth Jewell was dead of a heart attack at age forty-four.

Jewell's well-attended funeral was held at the Brookhaven Baptist Church, his childhood congregation that had welcomed him and Bobi back to Atlanta after John Jewell had deserted them. Outside, the media stood vigil under threatening skies. The group was far smaller than nine years before, when Kathy Scruggs stood in the Monaco Station parking lot watching Don Johnson escort Jewell to the FBI's "training video" interview.

In the sanctuary, a single bagpiper played "Amazing Grace" as more than a dozen law enforcement brethren sat in dress uniform at the back of the pulpit. Photos and remembrances of Jewell—his badge, dress gloves, medals—blended with large and colorful floral arrangements sent by well-wishers from as far away as Japan. Jewell's youth minister recalled a young Richard zealously racing through the church aisles to ensure that all congregants held programs for the Sunday worship. Lin Wood and Watson Bryant both delivered eulogies.

As the service neared its close, Dana and Bobi comforted each other on the front pew. A twenty-one-gun salute echoed through the church as seven sheriffs' deputies outside each fired three rounds skyward. A trumpeter played "Taps" to signal Jewell's official "end of watch" as an officer.

Years later, Dana tattooed the numbers 1-4-3 on her ring finger, the numeric message Jewell would page her for "I love you." She quietly continues her husband's annual ritual of visiting Centennial Park on the bombing anniversary. But she now leaves two roses—one for Alice Hawthorne, one for Richard Jewell.

Today, more than two decades have passed since the Centennial Park bombing. Perhaps revisiting the tale of Richard Jewell will encourage the current media to pause longer and presume innocence before rushing to suggest guilt. Perhaps law enforcement will use the Jewell case as a rallying cry to treat leaks of individuals' names as criminal acts, not just inevitabilities. And perhaps all of us in the news-consuming public will reconsider our expectation of immediacy and ponder the benefits of returning to an era when accuracy was prized over speed.

In the end, of course, the presumed guilty could be innocent. A named suspect might even turn out to be a hero.

ACKNOWLEDGMENTS

Posted on a wall in the cottage that has served as our office for five years is a lined yellow sheet with a list of honor: the twenty-three people we interviewed who were so overcome by the emotional pull of the Centennial Park bombing and its aftermath that they openly wept in front of us. They are friends and family of the characters, cynical journalists, hardened law enforcement, and Olympic planners. This list continually helped inspire us to fully tell the true stories in *The Suspect*.

We wanted to acknowledge all who helped make this book possible. We started with an arbitrary cutoff, jotting down names of people who generously spent more than an hour with us. But we stopped after the fourth page. The number was just too big. Many are mentioned in the source notes or the book itself. Most, alas, are not. But to everyone—and you certainly know who you are—thank you for sharing your stories. Each anecdote, every detail factored into *The Suspect*, whether on the written page or not.

That said, we would be remiss not to single out a few people. In the Jewell camp, Lin Wood was incredibly generous from the start, eloquently and passionately walking us through his years with Jewell and freely sharing the massive files from the case. Thanks to Kimmy Bennett Hart for her patience in arranging so many trips to the office and warehouse. Watson Bryant is a natural storyteller, and his unfiltered recall of events from twenty-plus years back was at times jaw-dropping. His files also enhanced our understanding. Jack Martin was on point to protect an innocent man's life; we're grateful the case never got that far, as we are for his assistance and files. Jewell's longtime friends who each still call him "brother"—Dave Dutchess, Brian McNair, and Rob Russell—could not have been more open, entertaining, or heartfelt. Bobi, of course, shared insights as only a mother could, graciously spending hour after hour with us. And we are especially indebted to Dana Jewell, the love of Richard's life. She welcomed us into her and Richard's home, Black Sheep Farm, entrusting us with his life story and many of his earthly possessions. We hope we did not disappoint.

Don Johnson's family members—Don II, Brian, and Patti—were accommodating and open. We owe particular thanks to Don II for the loan of all his Dad's extraordinary files. We have tried to tell your father and brother's story fairly and honestly. And we also want to particularly acknowledge Johnson's Atlanta FBI partner Harry Grogan, who always gave it to us straight. Also from the Bureau, Woody Johnson, Dave Maples, A.B. Llewellyn, Perry Smith, Steve Emmett, Don Haldimann, and so many others answered endless questions, all with chips-fall-where-they-may candor. At the APD, many thanks to Beverly Harvard and Jon Gordon. At the GBI, Tom Davis, Vernon Keenan, Charles Stone, and Brad Parks, among others, were of great help. Thank you also to the unsung heroes at the ATF and so many other agencies who played critical roles in tracking down and convicting Eric Rudolph. Also, we deeply appreciate Dave Nahmias, Sally Yates, and others from the U.S. Attorney's Office for allowing us to call on your prodigious memories so often. And Paul Kish, who offered firsthand insights into Eric Rudolph and the defense.

To help us animate Kathy Scruggs, we offer our gratitude to Ron Martz, Bill Rankin, Lewis Scruggs, George Hamilton, Tony Kiss, Susan Parke, and, especially, Bentley Allen, who gave us revealing insights into the real Kathy beyond what we could have ever hoped. At the *AJC*, Bert Roughton, Thomas Oliver, Peter Canfield, Kevin Riley, and many others offered crucial perspective. They also helped us appreciate that—Richard Jewell aside—no newspaper has ever covered an Olympic Games as thoroughly and as well as the *Atlanta Journal-Constitution*. Indeed, the paper's robust archives became an invaluable research tool for us throughout the book. Elsewhere in the media world, special nods go to Jonathan Ringel at the *Fulton County Daily Report* and Kevin Sack at the *New York Times* not only for their excellent journalism but for their assistance as we gathered information for this book.

Billy Payne, Andy Young, A.D. Frazier, Charlie Battle, Horace Sibley, Susan Watson, and many others from the Atlanta Games patiently offered their invaluable assistance and recollections. At the Atlanta History Center, Donald Rooney, Sarah Dylla, and Sheffield Hale assured that we had access to the Center's troves.

ACKNOWLEDGMENTS

In Hollywood, we first became part of the Richard Jewell project thanks to the inquisitive mind of Ezra Edelman. He and producers Kevin Misher and Andy Berman navigated to bring us aboard. Our book-to-film agent Jerry Kalajian and attorney Andy Velcoff partnered to help achieve remarkable results. Jeff Stepakoff of the Georgia Film Academy was always there for guidance. We were delighted when Warner Bros. acquired the rights to our book. Consulting on the upcoming Clint Eastwood film was a great honor.

At Abrams Press, editor Garrett McGrath first had a passion for this project, championing it with savvy and offering a much-needed path when surreal turns of events shifted deadlines forward, backward, and sideways. We tested the patience of executive editor Jamison Stoltz as often as any authors could, yet his enthusiasm for *The Suspect* never waned. We know many authors say this, but we couldn't have had a better team than Garrett and Jamison. On the Abrams marketing and publicity side, hearty thanks go to Alex Serrano and Kimberly Lew.

Finally, our book agent, Sarah Smith at the David Black Literary Agency combined vision, energy, reassurance, calm, and humor throughout this most unlikely journey that has now become *The Suspect*. Thanks for your unflagging faith in the story and in us.

Our earliest readers offered critical feedback to help us shape this project. We would have a far lesser book if not for Larry Auerbach, Jeff Ball, Andy Brenner, Gregory Colbert, Scott Dorfman, Melissa Fay Greene, Jim Grien, Mark Kantor, and Neal Shapiro.

FROM KENT:

From my heart: To my amazing wife, Diane, I am forever in awe of and in love with you. Thanks for all your book patience and encouragement. Nicki and Kayla, *muchísimas gracias y amor* for living your dreams, which inspire my own. I'm also eternally grateful to my parents, Miles and Elaine, for the values they have instilled in two generations, and now a book. To other family and friends (as well as complete strangers) who have endured years of my talking through book anecdotes and scenes, thank you for your indulgences and keen observations. I also want to acknowledge Richard, Kathy, and Don. All were acquaintances in life, but now seem so much more. And, finally, to my extraordinarily talented coauthor and friend, Kevin Salwen: We did it, partner.

FROM KEVIN:

Kent, you could be maddening as hell, because you *always* wanted a better book. I can't be more grateful. Here's to you, pal, and may the scotch go down smoothly. My personal team of confidants were invaluable in talking through this project. Special thanks to Harry Plant and Amy Rao (yes, Amy, it's done), Anne Kenner and Jim Scopa, the Stanford DCI cohort, and a passel of others too long to name who patiently sat through my stories and excuses. My family heard "Can I call you later, I'm on deadline?" far more often than anyone should have to stomach. Huge hugs to Andi, Val, Steve, their kids, and June, Don, and Bob King for your love, patience, and cheerleading. My young adults, Hannah and Joe, could not have been better wingpeople. And of course, my wife, Joan, who seemingly can do it all, is not only the rock of the family and love of my life but a helluva reader. I am grateful beyond words.

What's it like to be the weakest guy in the room? What happens to a life when every claim, every speculation is beamed to hundreds of millions of impromptu judges, years before social media? Those were among the things we wondered when we teamed up five years ago to research and write *The Suspect*.

In the book, we weaved together the lives of three main characters. Richard Jewell, of course; Kathy Scruggs, the ambitious and colorful reporter; and Don Johnson, the equally driven and sanctimonious agent who made the case that wasn't. The three represent the media, the FBI, and the man caught in the middle. As our initial guide, we relied heavily on Kent's extensive contemporaneous journal that he kept as the U.S. Attorney often working behind closed doors at the FBI. But that soon gave way to even richer original source material.

Thanks to our main characters' families, friends, and colleagues, for several years we have been entrusted with more material than we imagined still existed from so long ago. Fourteen file boxes of Jewell's personal records, including thousands of photos that chronicled his life and many scenes in our book. Ten file boxes of Johnson's densely stuffed folders recording his professional and personal life from Vietnam on. A full library of the 1,200-plus articles Scruggs wrote during her *AJC* career, along with the files of her *AJC* writing partner, Ron Martz, on the Olympics bombing investigation. Her family also provided a wonderful family scrapbook reflecting her life from baptism forward.

The mountain of records from Jewell's fifteen-year court battle with the *AJC* also proved critical in sorting the tale of *The Suspect*. Lin Wood doggedly saw the case through to the end, well after Jewell's death. He generously made available to us tens of thousands of pages of neatly sorted court records and shared dozens of additional boxes loaded with news articles, memos, letters, videos, and Jewell's unedited writings. Watson Bryant and Jack Martin were equally generous with their extremely helpful boxes of files.

To write the story as accurately as possible, we culled through thousands of pages of law enforcement records. Many came from records requests, others from former agents' files. Then we set out to truly know the characters and complete the story, as well as to add as much color as possible. To do that, we conducted 187 original-source interviews in homes, offices, and by phone, many of them with our characters' closest confidants. Those conversations were also immensely helpful in resolving gaps and conflicts in the law enforcement accounts.

One special note on Jewell's own voice: Although he never kept a true diary, we found three particularly prized sources to capture an unvarnished, uncoached vision of who he was. First was the secretly recorded lasagna dinner with Tim Attaway that Jewell believed was a chance to openly share his thoughts on the Centennial Park bombing experience with a friend and potential job connection. Second, after the start of Jewell's virtual imprisonment in his mother's apartment, he began a narrative of his days in an iterative series of bullet-pointed documents he called "From Blast Forward." Third, we couldn't believe our good fortune when Lin Wood offered a few more boxes of "Jewell stuff" he had stored at his home. Inside we discovered that he had kept two and a half hours of videotaped interviews, which he and Wayne Grant had conducted with Jewell just weeks after the bombing. Collectively, those three sources allow our readers to see and hear the real Richard.

Marie Brenner's impressively reported February 1997 article for *Vanity Fair* was the result of her embedding with the Jewell team for several months; her twenty-two-page piece wonderfully captured the atmospherics around Jewell, and much more.

We often turned to the archives of the *Atlanta Journal-Constitution* for rich and thorough reporting on all manner of topics we needed to research. Among the many other news sources that were helpful, time and again the *New York Times* and *Fulton County Daily Report* rose to the top for different aspects of the book.

Eric Rudolph was the subject of two excellent books, both of which we recommend to readers wanting to know more about the actual bomber and the search for him: *Hunting Eric Rudolph* by Henry Schuster with Charles Stone (2005) and *Lone Wolf* by Maryanne Vollers (2007). We drew from both to weave the real Olympic bomber into our story. Eric Rudolph himself later published an autobiography from prison titled *Between the Lines of Drift*. We relied on the 2015 edition, a 150,000-word tome, to add details of the Olympic bombing and three other attacks, as well as the terrorist's life on the run.

A word on dialogue: When we had a tape, a document, or an individual's recall of specific conversation, we put that exchange in quotation marks. In cases where a source's recall was more general, we used dialogue that was true to the characters but left off the quotes.

When we consolidated our twenty-nine chapters plus prologue and epilogue into a single manuscript, we were shocked to realize we had compiled 2,139 footnote entries. Our editor suggested writing these narrative source notes instead. We eagerly agreed.

Prologue

Many of the details about Jewell's day-to-day experiences throughout this book came from our interviews with his mother, wife, friends, lawyers, and co-workers. But Jewell also described them himself in his legal proceedings in the libel cases and in statements to the FBI. The descriptions of Bobi's apartment came from photos and videos. We created the ticktock of bombing night from six interviews of Jewell conducted by law enforcement and AT&T within thirty-six hours of the bombing. Dozens of FBI 302s and GBI reports provided other points of view. We also interviewed GBI Special Agent Tom Davis and reviewed and photographed a thick scrapbook his wife, Jane, had compiled during the Olympics in 1996.

PART 1: STRIVING
Chapter 1

Both Billy Payne and Andy Young patiently walked us through the bid process and strategy from their individual perspectives. The former mayor's recollections about how Payne's audacious Olympics idea triggered memories of his four-year-old self in New Orleans stands out as a truly unforgettable moment in our reporting. Members of the Atlanta Nine and other Olympics organizers sat with us as well to share their own memories. Much of the detail about the bid process was also well chronicled in the media at the time, with a special tip of the hat to Bert Roughton's work in the *Atlanta Journal-Constitution*. Of course, having access to the actual bid materials was helpful. Several excellent profiles were written about Payne, including those by John Huey in *Fortune* and Donald Katz in *Sports Illustrated*.

Chapter 2

The descriptions of Jewell's upbringing and childhood experiences came from a series of interviews we did with his mother and friends from his youth. Bobi Jewell's remembrances of her son were vital to showing his first twenty years. For Jewell's early job experiences and his Habersham years, many of the best details came from his three closest friends, Dave Dutchess, Brian McNair, and Rob Russell, as well as his SBA buddy and later lawyer, Watson Bryant. We also had access to thousands of Jewell's pages of personnel records, depositions, FBI 302s, police reports, commendation and reprimand notes, and Jewell's own memo about the hot-tub incident. The FBI, of course, unearthed nearly every facet of Jewell's life from birth on, and we had access to much of that material.

Chapter 3

Security planning for an event the size of the 1996 Games is a complex business, and several important sources helped us understand all that was behind it. At the FBI, Dave Maples, Don Haldimann, Woody Johnson, and others took us back inside the planning process and detailed the field exercises and deployment of security personnel. Kent participated in the process as U.S. Attorney. Beverly Harvard offered details on the Secret Seven. At ACOG, A.D. Frazier and Bill Rathburn unpacked the organizing committee's approach to security planning and much more. The Kennedy School of Government at Harvard crafted a comprehensive review of security for the 1996 Olympics. John Buntin's work for that case study became a valuable resource, including his direct quotes from Stock Coleman.

The material about the creation of—and debates around—Centennial Olympic Park were gleaned from insights by Billy Payne, as well as the *AJC*'s extensive coverage. Payne's dream of the park was very real, but some local business leaders had already started assembling tracts for a for-profit venture. Law enforcement's perspective on the park came primarily from interviews with the FBI's Dave Maples and Woody Johnson, the GBI's Vernon Keenan, and ACOG's Bill Rathburn.

Chapter 4

The picture of Kathy Scruggs's early years derived largely from interviews with her cousin, Bentley Allen; brother, Lewis; and several friends from her childhood and early career. The family scrapbook that Lewis loaned to us, and their mother, Nancy, compiled, was wonderfully helpful. Tony Kiss and Susan Parke helped fill in details of Scruggs's social and professional life in the Carolinas. In Gwinnett and Atlanta, the descriptions of Scruggs's career emerged from interviews with more than a dozen colleagues, particularly David Pendered, Bill Rankin, Doug Monroe, and Ron Martz.

Chapter 5

After-action reports by the FBI, Justice Department, Defense Department, and Georgia's State Olympic Law Enforcement Command Center, as well as Kent's personal journal, provided a rich trove laying out law enforcement's thinking about its security role. The descriptions of Olympic Charlie came from one of those reviews and interviews of officers who participated. Several journalists also reported extensively about security planning, including Ron Martz at the *AJC* and Henry Schuster and Art Harris at *CNN*. Again, the Kennedy School study was a helpful in-depth report.

Chapter 6

Jewell preserved a robust record of his time at the Habersham County Sheriff's Office of training records, plaques, certificates, interviews, and reports. His wife, Dana, loaned those to us. In addition, Jewell had so many photo albums and loose images that he seemed to have been trying to capture every scene of his life in color prints. There's even a photo of his "Chia Pet" car parked under a tree by the river. Jewell also took many snapshots of himself, long before "selfies" came into vogue.

We relied heavily on detailed recollections by McNair and Russell about Deputy Jewell's time on the roads of North Georgia. For the section about Jewell's tenure at Piedmont College, we used the lengthy statements and testimony of Ray Cleere and Dick Martin, among others, as well as 302s and interviews with students Jewell befriended, particularly Brad Mattear. At times, we found conflicts between Don Johnson's 302s and the later testimony of those he interviewed. For instance, Dick Martin testified that he had told the FBI agent in no uncertain terms that Jewell was not the bomber, but Johnson's 302s clearly suggested otherwise. Attorney Jack Martin provided us with copies of memos from the interviews he conducted at the college and in Habersham, as well as fifteen pages of handwritten notes from his initial meeting with Jewell.

Chapter 7

The transformation of the *AJC* newsroom into a nearly all-Olympics-all-the-time media outlet was quite the feat. Many of the paper's former staffers helped us understand how that worked, including our interviews with Thomas Oliver, Melissa Turner, Bert Roughton, Glenn Hannigan, and John Glenn. Ron Martz took us inside the SNOT Pod. Attorney Peter Canfield offered the legal perspective and beyond. He loaned us a 134-page in-house publication called "Cox Olympians" that included bios of every reporter and boasted of having "the largest army of journalists ever assembled by one newspaper to cover a single event."

Jewell's own observations of his time in the park were particularly useful in this chapter. They come partly from his October 6 pre-clearance interview with the FBI. We combined those insights with those from his depositions in the *AJC* and *New York Post* lawsuits, as well as his interviews by others, including lawyers Wood and Grant. More than one hundred FBI 302s and Rapid Start entries allowed us to understand how people around the AT&T tower thought and felt about him.

Chapter 8

The opening anecdote about the attempted robbery of a Wachovia bank branch was compiled from contemporary news reports and Kent's journal. The Atlanta History Center holds, by far, the largest repository of artifacts, photos, and videos from the 1996 Olympics, including costumes from the Opening Ceremony. Its doors and archives were always open to us. The three-volume "Official Report of the Centennial Olympic Games," edited by one of the Atlanta Nine, Ginger Watkins, provides a detailed chronology of the buildup to the Games and beyond. Sprinter Michael Johnson layered on his recollections of the sights and sounds on the field in an interview with us. From the law enforcement side, FBI Bomb Coordinator Don Haldimann was instrumental in explaining the Bomb Squad's Render Safe Procedure. Kent's journal was our primary road map for the various threats, absurd and more serious, continuously facing the Games.

The explosion and the moments that followed were compiled from videos, photos, the hundred-plus GBI and FBI witness statements, hospital reports, our own interviews (especially with Tom Davis and A.D. Frazier), and FBI photographic records and slides.

PART 2: A HERO'S TURN
Chapter 9

The most compelling accounts of the park as the smoke cleared came from the GBI. Dozens of agents fanned out in the early morning hours with hotel stationery and whatever other paper they could scrounge to record eyewitness accounts of the explosion and immediate aftermath. FBI 302s, of course, soon followed. Also, we found *Sports Illustrated*'s in-depth oral history of the park bombing night, compiled in 2012, to be a valuable source for on-the-record interviews, including victims, witnesses, media, law enforcement, and park employees. To understand law enforcement's immediate response and ultimate analysis of the blast, we interviewed more than two dozen former agents and officers to re-create that night, including Woody Johnson, Don Haldimann, Steve Blackwell, Tom Davis, and Vernon Keenan. Jewell's multiple interviews with law enforcement in the immediate aftermath of the bombing guided our writing about his actions.

We were able to access Don Johnson's thought process partly through his lengthy sworn statement to the Office of Professional Responsibility, and even more fully through the ream of documentation he handwrote, typed, and copied for his personal attorneys. We also benefited from official statements by others, as well as the final OPR summary report. The internal watchdog's findings conflicted significantly with Johnson's own account. For a window into Johnson's life outside of work during this time frame and others, we relied in part on our interviews with two of his sons, Don II and Brian.

The action inside the *AJC* was built on interviews with Thomas Oliver and Bert Roughton, among others, as well as two written pieces, one a case study for Columbia Journalism School by journalist Ronald Ostrow, and another article in the trade publication *Editor & Publisher* by Jack Bass.

Chapter 10

Kathy Scruggs's activities in the early morning came from our interview with Bentley Allen. The 911 call into the Atlanta emergency dispatcher is verbatim from the APD transcript. The *AJC* reported on the call, as well as on the crowds who flocked downtown. We were again guided by Kent's journal about early stages of the investigation, including calls to the hotline. Details came from scores of government reports. Former Emory physician Dr. David Feliciano, who oversaw the Grady Hospital medical response, provided jolting X-rays showing shrapnel embedded in unnamed victims, including the backpack buckle lodged in one patient's jaw. FBI photos of the now-removed bricks next to Alice Hawthorne's body added yet more pathos to the scene. And Special Agent Pete MacFarlane's FBI 302 description of Hawthorne's autopsy was chilling, as was the autopsy.

Don Johnson's background in the "Happy Days" era of Gloversville came from childhood friends who had walked paper routes, attended classes, and played sports with him. Al Fagant and Tom Eagan were especially helpful. His sister Patti shared letters and photos. An internal FBI report and depositions from Johnson's lawsuit after his 1984 car accident provided valuable details on that horrific event. Our account of the agent's experiences with the FBI in Albany was drawn from roughly a dozen interviews we did with former colleagues, as well as from Johnson's extensive files of internal memos on his cases and disputes, and from articles about the Whelan case in the *Albany Times Union*. His sons shared memories of Johnson as a parent. His Upstate New York colleagues offered insights into his work life, as well as his straying from his marital vows. The story of the Aliza May Bush search came to light during an interview with Johnson's former colleague and friend Bill McDermott. To further fill out the facts, we relied on coverage in the *New York Times* and the *Buffalo News*, as well as a 1993 book, *From Blood to*

Verdict, about a murderous year in Tompkins County, New York. Johnson, of course, kept his own file on the case, including the "Missing" posters and photos of two-year-old Aliza.

In Atlanta, Johnson's FBI partner, Harry Grogan, offered detailed descriptions of their interview techniques that led to the pair's run of confessions. The Anthony Battle case, and Johnson's role in cracking it, were supported by the agent's 302 and Johnson's testimony. The suspicions about Overstreet and Abboud, as well as the investigative details about them, came from FBI and GBI documents and were discussed in SIOC calls summarized in Kent's journal. We have fictionalized those names to protect the identity of men who were investigated but cleared.

Chapter 11

The scenes that open the chapter were created partly from depositions of Jewell, Bryant Steele, Anthony Davis, and journalists in the *AJC* newsroom. We supplemented those accounts with interviews of Bobi Jewell, Dave Dutchess, Brian McNair, and CNN producer Henry Schuster. A well-researched article reconstructing key elements of the Jewell media experience appeared in the April 2000 issue of *Brill's Content* magazine. It was titled "Just Doing Our Job." We culled Jewell's perspective largely from his own recollections in the videotaped interviews by Lin Wood and Wayne Grant and his document, "From Blast Forward."

Chapter 12

The Behavioral Science Unit often goes by different names, which were changed in the years before and since the Jewell investigation. We chose to simplify this for readers by using the single name Behavioral Science Unit, or BSU, as most agents still referred to it at the time. Several sources helped with the Unit's history, including *Mindhunter* by John Douglas and Mark Olshaker, *The Bureau: The Secret History of the FBI* by Ronald Kessler, the FBI's website, and a 2007 piece in the *New Yorker* by Malcolm Gladwell.

Jewell's status as an emerging suspect came from Kent's journal, as supported by FBI 302s and subsequent author interviews. The mounting evidence about Jewell was culled from 1996 FBI interviews of individuals at AT&T, Piedmont College, the Habersham County Sheriff's Office, and elsewhere.

Don Johnson's decision to hold on to his work files, including his handwritten notes, allowed us to further piece together the growing case against Jewell. Our own interviews with more than a dozen FBI agents and prosecutors were also useful in reconstructing the Bureau's decision to narrow the case to Jewell as the primary suspect. The descriptions of Louie Freeh's unusual level on involvement was a consistent theme among those agents and others.

Kent had seen the profile when the BSU first faxed it down, but the July 29, 1996, document was held so closely that he was only allowed to read it and then was required to hand it back. So, we were delighted when we stumbled across multiple copies in Don Johnson's folders that matched up to the almost entirely redacted version produced by the Bureau in response to a FOIA request. We finally had our hands on the actual BSU document that was so key in propelling the investigation and became the wellspring of Scruggs's article and the lawsuit that would follow. (We do not believe Scruggs ever saw the actual profile.) Most outside the FBI have long believed that the profile merely described a generic bomber, not Jewell himself. Some have even remained steadfast in their belief that a profile never even existed.

The scenes of the leak at the bar and in the newsroom were drawn primarily from Scruggs's descriptions sprinkled through her 433-page deposition, as well as her interview with fellow reporter Carrie Teegardin. Our conversations with Ron Martz, Bert Roughton, and Thomas Oliver added much to the flavor, as did other Teegardin interviews with Rochelle Bozman and John Walter.

Chapter 13

Jewell's depositions, along with the countless photos he took of his home, the park, and his encounters with celebrities, helped us pull together the scene that opens the chapter. Beverly Harvard described for us her emotions while posing with him for the picture near the *Today* show set.

The lead-up to the ruse interview came from notes, memos, and correspondence written by Don Johnson as well as sworn statements to the OPR by him and other agents. The Atlanta field office also submitted a chronology. Those documents were wonderfully detailed, although sometimes in conflict. When in doubt, we usually opted for the ultimate findings of the OPR.

The unfolding action of Tuesday at the *AJC* came from Scruggs's recollections to Teegardin, as well as detailed descriptions from our interviews with Martz, Christina Headrick, Maria Elena Fernandez, Roughton, Oliver, and others. Their depositions and those of Walter and Bozman were also helpful. Jay Spadafore and Ron Martz each shared with us their perspectives of Martz's call to the FBI about the newsbreak to come. We also studied news footage of the scene at Jewell's apartment. In one remarkable clip in the Monaco Station parking lot, we were able to see Jewell walking within a few feet of Scruggs just after Johnson and Rosario split off toward their Bucar for Jewell to follow them to the FBI. It was the only time, to our knowledge, that all three of our lead characters were in the same place at the same time.

Chapter 14

Our reconstruction of the Jewell interview—and the actions in the FBI's Atlanta and Washington offices—was based heavily on an FBI videotape and transcript of the interrogation. (Our quest to uncover the videotape and transcript could make for a chapter itself.) Di Rosario's log provided the timeline. Our conversations with agents and prosecutors—including A.B. Llewellyn, Woody Johnson, Mollie Halle, and Perry Smith—provided color and perspective from outside the room and in Washington. Kent, who was at Woody Johnson's side, took notes on the conversations for his journal, which he also summarized in his sworn statement to the OPR. FBI videographer Jan Garvin, who remained in the room during the entire process, was invaluable in filling in details when the camera wasn't rolling. Watson Bryant shared with us his half of the phone call with Don Johnson, colorful as usual.

For the scene in the apartment with the Jewells, we relied on our interview with Bobi and on Richard's own accounts to the media, his attorneys, and Dave Dutchess.

Chapter 15

We studied well over a dozen contemporaneous news accounts, both televised and written, to help create the scene outside of Apartment F-3. From the inside, Jewell's and Bobi's own words filled in their points of view. The FBI's extensive search documentation was invaluable in laying out the details of the day: the warrant, affidavit, raid plan (marked "ARMED AND

DANGEROUS"), apartment diagram, Don Johnson's time log, and the Evidence Recovery Log that listed every item seized. FBI 302s, our interviews with Bobi, Watson Bryant, and FBI agents, and news articles provided additional texture. The Jewells' post-search experience of living inside the apartment came from Jewell's own accounts; interviews with Bobi, Bryant, and Dutchess; and Marie Brenner's *Vanity Fair* article. Bobi's phone was never tapped. At the *AJC*, Dave Kindred walked us through the thinking behind his controversial column. The piece also was often a topic in depositions.

Chapter 16

The Muhammad Ali cheeseburger story comes from an *AJC* piece written by sportswriter Mike Tierney. Ali's account of throwing his medal into the river has been widely reported but also widely questioned. Michael Johnson recalled for us the meeting with Fallon Stubbs as well as the thrilling 400-meter race.

FBI 302s led us through the incredible litany of leads, real and imagined, about Jewell, from the Buford Highway yogurt shop to the quarries of Tennessee and beyond. Oliver Halle explained the Harkness accusations and their debunking. We also relied on the handwritten letter the prisoner sent to Scruggs. The other inmate, Frazier, was the subject of several FBI reports. The hair-plucking scene was a combination of our interviews of Watson Bryant, Bobi, and Dave Dutchess, who spoke at length with Jewell about the incident. The FBI documented it too. Marie Brenner in *Vanity Fair* offered an excellent account of that experience that Jewell found so humiliating. Jack Martin offered us the insights from his initial interview with Jewell, including the suspect's "confession" out of left field about taxes. Richard Rackleff helped us understand Jewell's polygraph report and results, as well as the mechanics of how tests are administered.

The Closing Ceremony was of course televised and well covered. But A.D. Frazier took us behind the scenes to relive the organizers' time of silent reflection.

PART 3: JUSTICE AT WORK
Chapter 17

Jewell's own recollections informed the pizza scene, as laid out in his video-taped interview in August 1996 with Wood and Grant. Dave Dutchess gave us additional texture. The CENTBOM task force's investigation is meticulously chronicled through 302s reflecting witness interviews and evidence collection in Atlanta, North Georgia, and around the country. Don Johnson's secret tapings of McNair and Russell, which he preserved on duplicate audio cassettes and retained for his files, generated valuable transcripts of the agent's style and strategy.

The FBI's unfruitful efforts to make a forensic case against Jewell came from Kent's journal and author interviews. Bill Rankin shared with us his thinking behind his four-minute march that inspired Martin's. Also, Martin described his own thinking and experience. There are several very good media reports about Lin Wood, but the lawyer generously met with us multiple times to provide firsthand takes on his background, motivations, and strategies. That included an inside-baseball look at what went into Bobi's powerful "please clear my son's name" press conference that helped shift public opinion.

Chapter 18

The scene of Jewell and Dutchess being tailed by an FBI aircraft first appeared as part of Jewell's videotaped interview with his lawyers. Dutchess corroborated the incident with us and added detail. Jewell, of course, kept the photos of the distant plane. The West Virginian also shared his girlfriend Beatty's contemporaneous single-spaced, three-and-a-half-page memo recounting the motorcycle ride home and the FBI questioning. Dutchess described for us his polygraph. The Bureau's fresh wave of leads after Jewell was fading as a suspect came from Kent's journal, as confirmed in 302s and through our interviews. The Russell interview, like that of McNair, was transcribed as part of the case record. As with his earlier McNair interview, Johnson kept a duplicate cassette which provided a reliable source of tone and innuendo.

Bruce Bryant told us about the parents' reactions to Jewell coaching youth football and the kids visiting the FBI cars. Two Bureau agents tasked with tailing Jewell related to us their initial concerns about his seemingly evasive driving tactics and then laughingly told us the reality. On September 6, 1996, Kent, along with Sally Yates, Dave Nahmias, and John Davis, filed a memorandum with the court (under seal) summarizing the FBI's remaining concerns about Jewell using an enumerated still-remaining-questions format. On page one, the prosecutors wrote that Jewell remained a suspect but added a caveat that reflected the opinion they had held for weeks: "To be sure, it is quite possible that Jewell had no involvement in the bombing, and there is evidence Jewell did not commit the crime." The memorandum included examples.

Chapter 19

Schuster and Stone's *Hunting Eric Rudolph* and Vollers's *Lone Wolf*, coupled with the government's very detailed factual basis used at the Rudolph plea, provided much of the raw material for this chapter. Most major media outlets circled around to profile Rudolph after his capture, notably CNN and the *New York Times*. And, of course, the *AJC* covered the investigation throughout. We layered in detail and color from a number of sources.

We relied in part on Rudolph's writings when they were the only source. His book, *Between the Lines of Drift*, usefully took us inside the Nantahala National Forest, his caches, and his hideouts. On those locations, FBI photos taken after Rudolph's arrest corroborated his accounts. Some of his claims, though, stretch and indeed break credulity. For instance, Rudolph contends he never meant to injure anyone in the Centennial Park bombing, that he only wanted to disrupt the "global collectivist" event. But as the reader knows, he placed his bomb—wrapped with masonry nails no less—in a crowd of fifty thousand. Equally preposterous is Rudolph's after-the-fact assertion that he is a pro-life martyr. Before Rudolph's plea, the government extensively interviewed family members, friends, old girlfriends, and Army associates. There was virtually no evidence of him even opining on abortion.

Finally, Rudolph contends that the Centennial Park bomb weighed nearly one hundred pounds. Earlier, though, the FBI forensic team had built a mock-up that estimated the device at only forty pounds. We wrote to Rudolph to ask about the discrepancy. In his handwritten reply, he explained, "The actual device contained 6 pipes, not 3 as the FBI mockup. Hence the weight difference."

Chapter 20

The dispute between Johnson and prosecutors over the 302s concerning the training-ruse video interview and Miranda came from Kent's personal involvement, as well as follow-ups with Sally Yates and Dave Nahmias. We were able to re-create the events leading up to the October 6 interview through correspondence and memos from that time, including Johnson's twice-revised 302s. Jack Martin was particularly helpful in sharing his detailed recollections and written records. The section on perceptions of Kathy Scruggs in the newsroom came from more than a dozen interviews with reporters and editors at the time who held widely divergent views of her.

We have quoted Jewell's comments during his October 6 FBI interview from the 254-page transcript. We also interviewed participants from the day, including Jack Martin. Park Dietz's memo about the identity of the actual bomber became part of the CENTBOM team's file on the case. Many elements of Dietz's profile of the actual bomber were strikingly accurate. Don Johnson's continued belief that Jewell was involved came from his own documentation, as well as from interviews with his partner Harry Grogan, other former colleagues, and Dick Ottman.

Chapter 21

The Dutchess stun-gun anecdote was first reported in *Vanity Fair*. When we visited Dutchess in West Virginia, he layered on some further detail and showed us the Olympic cap Jewell had inscribed to him. The exchanges between Lin Wood and Peter Canfield about the litigation against the *AJC* were drawn from their actual letters. The *AJC*'s defense in this chapter and throughout the book was crafted from the paper's statements in published accounts, from court records, and from author interviews of Peter Canfield.

The CENTBOM team's reboot on the case was documented in the FBI records and Kent's journal. Don Johnson's description of Louie Freeh as "that fucking fraud" came from a reliable source who would prefer to remain unnamed. (Based on Johnson's pitched battles with FBI HQ, we have no doubt he said that and worse.) Eric Rudolph wrote about the specifics of his break-in at the Austin Powder Company. The CENTBOM task force was aware of the large dynamite theft and had obtained records, though it would not connect it to Rudolph for some time.

PART 4: ROADS AND ROSES
Chapter 22

Jack Martin provided us with the transcript of his examination of Don Johnson, along with side commentary and files. Rudolph's perspective on the Sandy Springs bombing was melded from several sources: his own writings, *Hunting Eric Rudolph*, *Lone Wolf*, and the government's detailed factual basis for Rudolph's plea in 2005. We also interviewed Agent Mike Rising and watched the chilling news footage of the bomb exploding nearby as reporters conducted live interviews. The FBI's photo files provided excellent detail on this bombing and all of the others. Although Don Johnson wasn't a key player in the investigation, his records helped us fill out the blast and aftermath. At the time, he still thought Jewell might be connected and kept an extensive shadow file of the investigative 302s. The Jewell team's media strategy was derived from articles and videos the attorneys and Jewell himself preserved, as well as author interviews with Wood and Bryant.

Chapter 23

O'Neill and Gail Williams took us through their relationship with Jewell, including his early morning call to the radio show and the fishing trip. Not surprisingly, Jewell documented the day with photos. The Pack Man scene and the Bureau's efforts to find him came from investigative records and discussions with then-members of the U.S. Attorney's Office, particularly Dave Nahmias. The Japan anecdotes came in part from letters from Ken Asano to Jewell, TV coverage of the former suspect's trip there, Jewell's photos, Jewell's and Bryant's files, and our interviews with Bryant. The Kouno story, well documented in the international media, was described in the writings of Asano and others. Hollis Gillespie's articles about her date with Jewell appeared in *Atlanta* magazine.

Rudolph's perspective on the Otherside Lounge bombing, as with Sandy Springs, comes from *Between the Lines of Drift*. We drew details for the blast and aftermath from government records and our interviews with agents directly involved, especially Charles Stone of the GBI. Once again, Don Johnson preserved his investigative file, although it was slimmer than the one on Sandy Springs. Apparently, even Johnson didn't suspect Jewell of bombing the

Otherside Lounge. We also drew from the released Army of God letters and other materials at the government's July 24, 1997, news conference. In fact, the Bureau held several media events, and each provided helpful resources for the book. The sketch vignette was drawn from agents' and prosecutors' memories, and was also referenced in *Hunting Eric Rudolph*. Beverly McMahon, the owner of the Otherside, generously spent time describing for us the bar's atmospherics before the blast. She also painfully shared her perspective on lives that were forever altered. One example: A number of teachers in town for a convention were at the club that night. Following the blast, several were outed and lost their jobs.

Chapter 24

Ivan the Aryan was featured in an unusually entertaining FBI 302 and other records. The OPR's actions were well documented in original materials that several of the investigation's subjects provided us. Don Johnson's hundreds of pages of records, including his own writings about the investigations provided enough detail to write a separate book. His files contained the letters several agents wrote to headquarters accusing Washington of scapegoating the Atlanta agents. Johnson's triumphant gauntlet walk, as well as agents' passing the hat, emerged from our interviews with Woody Johnson, Harry Grogan, Don Johnson II, and Oliver and Mollie Halle, among others. Don Johnson's missteps in Albany that led to his "loss of effectiveness" transfer were fully captured in the massive files he kept. For other perspectives, we interviewed several of the agent's former colleagues from Albany who were familiar with the reasons for the transfer.

Scruggs's experiences with Lin Wood were gathered from her depositions. We also interviewed several *AJC* reporters about how it felt to be deposed by the lawyer. Peter Canfield offered additional perspective about Wood's approach to deposing witnesses. Not surprisingly, their views contrasted sharply with the attorney's own, as well as those of the rest of the Jewell legal team. Jewell's trip to New York for the mini-bar raid and his appearance on *Hannity & Colmes* emerged from videos, travel records, and our interview with Dave Dutchess. Brian McNair and Bobi Jewell discussed the trip to Miami for the American Police Hall of Fame.

Chapter 25

The grim observation that the FBI might need another bombing to help solve the case came from an interview with GBI's Charles Stone. The *AJC* featured full coverage of the one-year Olympics and park-bombing anniversaries, allowing us to capture the spirit of Atlantans revisiting the glory of the Games. The hours of congressional testimony we reviewed bore some helpful tidbits, including the OPR's invitation to Kathy Scruggs to testify. Local TV reporter Dale Russell shared with us Lin Wood's quip, "I've been in a cab, I've been drunk, and I've been naked. But I've never been all three at once." Wood confirmed it. Bentley Allen and many others generously shared details of Scruggs's sense of style, favorite cocktails, most-watched soap operas, love life, and more.

Ray Cleere's moment of shock at the Fernandez deposition was first described in the *Fulton County Daily Report* and confirmed to us by Piedmont College attorney Patrick McKee. Yet again, Jewell's photo albums helped walk us through his *Saturday Night Live*, Japan, and Lahaina experiences from his vantage point. Watson Bryant helped considerably with play-by-play commentary on each. Toddy Liliko'i shared with us her surprise at meeting *the* Richard Jewell. Johnson's third scrape with the OPR was yet again well documented in his files. We built the sequence of his retirement decision, poster, and party from the agent's files and interviews with his sons Don II and Brian, Harry Grogan, Mary Jane Caudill, and former AUSA and friend Jim Harper. Jewell's hiring in Luthersville was crafted from several *Atlanta* magazine articles by Scott Freeman and personnel records in Lin Wood's files.

Chapter 26

In this chapter, we drew from many sources to detail the bombing of the New Woman clinic on January 29, 1998, as well as Sande Sanderson's professional history and the heroics of Jermaine Hughes and Jeff Tickal. Maryanne Vollers's *Lone Wolf* and Henry Schuster and Charles Stone's *Hunting Eric Rudolph* were especially well researched on this bombing and the chase. We also pulled from nurse Emily Lyons's memoir, *Life's Been a Blast*, and Rudolph's *Between the Lines of Drift*. The *AJC* and other media covered the incident extensively. Former U.S. Attorney, and now U.S. senator, Doug Jones layered on his observations for us. The website Officer Down Memorial Page (odmp.org) offered touching and insightful remembrances of Officer Sanderson.

Descriptions and photos of the bombing and Rudolph's forest hideaways, as mentioned above, were shared by the FBI, which corroborated key portions of the bomber's own account. Kathy Scruggs wrote often in the first few weeks of the chase, and periodically through 2000. When we could, we let her be the reader's guide to the investigation. Daniel Rudolph's decision to cut off his hand was covered in the media at the time. But we were fortunate, in a way, that former FBI Assistant Director Bob Blitzer was able to recount for us the details of the film, which he had watched in horror with others at Bureau headquarters.

Our descriptions of the pressure that Scruggs faced around her depositions came from her cousin Bentley and brother Lewis, as well as friends George Hamilton, Lisa Griffin, Tony Kiss, and Susan Parke. Hamilton shared his hide-and-seek games with her pills. Lin Wood shared a videotape of Scruggs's May 22, 1998, deposition session, allowing us to see firsthand her personal struggles. Rudolph's encounters with George Nordmann were primarily pieced together from the bomber's own account and the two books about him. Marla Lawson told us about her experience sketching a new image of Rudolph from Nordmann's description, updating her Goatee Man illustration.

Dana recalled for us in colorful detail meeting her future husband at the drug bust and how their life together unfolded. The *Meriwether Free Press* highlighted Jewell saving the baby and his subsequent promotion.

Chapter 27

Martz shared with us Roger Kintzel's memo to him supporting both him and Scruggs. When the reporters were ordered to jail, the Georgia First Amendment Foundation and others in the press wrote earnest pieces in support of the reporters. George Hamilton described driving Scruggs to her private investigation courses. He also related the scene of searching her Woodstock home and finding her unconscious. Bentley Allen walked us through Scruggs's reveal that Don Johnson was the primary source for the original leak. We were able to reliably confirm that fact through two additional sources, thus allowing us to answer a question that the FBI and attorneys for Richard Jewell had not.

Dana Jewell described for us the marriage proposal and Jewell's Alice Hawthorne ritual at the park; Lin Wood also spoke of the guard's annual prayer at Jewell's funeral. We pulled together the wedding sequence from interviews with Dana, Bobi, Dutchess, Watson Bryant, Rev. Barry Thompson, Rob Russell, and O'Neill and Gail Williams, among others. Wedding photos from the day enhanced our descriptions. Scruggs's final weeks were compiled from interviews of multiple friends and family, as well as from the autopsy.

Chapter 28

Rudolph's killing of the doe came from his own writings. At his plea, Rudolph released a nine-page manifesto that, among other things, revealed his detailed plan to bomb FBI's search headquarters in Andrews. The FBI, through Steve Emmett, shared a terrific set of images of the caches buried around the Nantahala National Forest.

Don Johnson's life in retirement was informed by conversations with two of his sons, Don II and Brian; his sister, Patti Moratta; and several former agents, including Harry Grogan, Cliff Cormany, and Brooke Blake. Johnson's drinking buddy Dick Ottman helpfully described the evenings at Foghorn's. The description of Johnson's final days came from his sons and personal medical records. The memorial brick was lovingly placed by his sister, Patti.

Chapter 29

Murphy police officer Jeff Postell was profiled in the *AJC* and on CNN and other media outlets after his unlikely arrest of Rudolph. All three books on the bomber, including Rudolph's own, offer riveting accounts of the capture. The news conference featuring Postell and other law enforcement was carried on C-Span in 2003. We were struck by how closely Postell's comments paralleled those of Richard Jewell on the *Today* show, nearly seven years before. Both were asked if they felt like heroes. Each humbly demurred, saying, "I was at the right place at the right time" and just doing my job.

We first learned of the heartbreaking scene of Chris Ruse's murder in our interview with Rob Russell, whose storytelling brought life to that emotional scene. The current Pendergrass Police Chief, Brant Erickson, layered on more detail, as did articles from the *Athens Banner-Herald*. Special Agent Brad Parks of the GBI ultimately made the entire investigative file on the

Ruse murder available to us through an Open Records Act request. Dave Dutchess, along with Russell, shared with us Jewell's haunting regrets that he could not save the officer's life.

The government's case against Rudolph was drawn from the factual basis delivered at the bomber's guilty plea. We interviewed defense attorney Paul Kish and prosecutors Sally Yates and Dave Nahmias for further detail. Current FBI Director Christopher Wray walked us through the process for reversing the decision to seek the death penalty.

The final scene in the courtroom derived from a combination of Kent's own recollections and those of the defense attorney, prosecutors, Dana Jewell, and reporters.

Epilogue

Much of the opening section about Atlanta's post-Olympics legacy came from the authors' personal observations. The *AJC*'s decline occurred in waves of layoffs and buyouts in the internet era, and mirrored the experience of most American metro papers still in business. The court records are clear that the *AJC* stood by the legitimacy of its decision to break the Jewell story, which we confirmed with the journalists involved. The section about the resolution of the Jewell lawsuit also came from court records. The accounts of John Hawthorne and other victims were drawn from the transcript of Rudolph's Atlanta sentencing.

We reviewed Jewell's medical records detailing his decline. Dave Dutchess spoke with us about his final conversations with his friend. Dana walked us through Jewell's death scene when we visited Black Sheep Farm. Bobi, Lin Wood, Watson Bryant, Bruce Bryant, and Dana all shared their memories of the funeral, along with their hope that one day Richard Jewell would be remembered by all as a hero.

An invitation from the publisher

Join us at www.hodder.co.uk, or follow us
on Twitter @hodderbooks to be a part of
our community of people who love the very
best in books and reading.

Whether you want to discover more about a book
or an author, watch trailers and interviews, have the
chance to win early limited editions, or simply browse
our expert readers' selection of the very best books,
we think you'll find what you're looking for.

And if you don't, that's the place to tell us what's missing.

We love what we do, and we'd love you to be a part of it.

www.hodder.co.uk

@hodderbooks

HodderBooks

HodderBooks